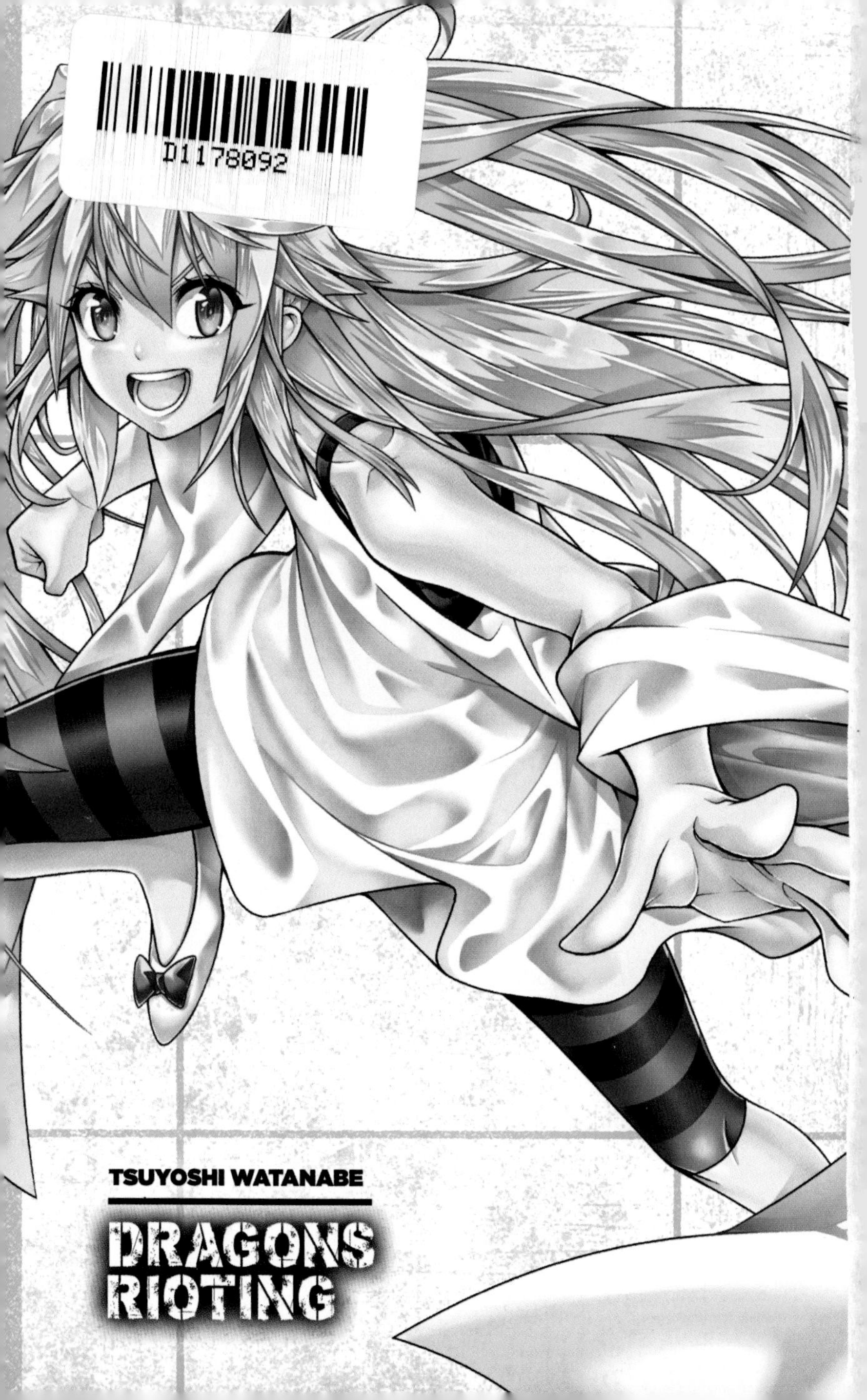

TSUYOSHI WATANABE

DRAGONS RIOTING

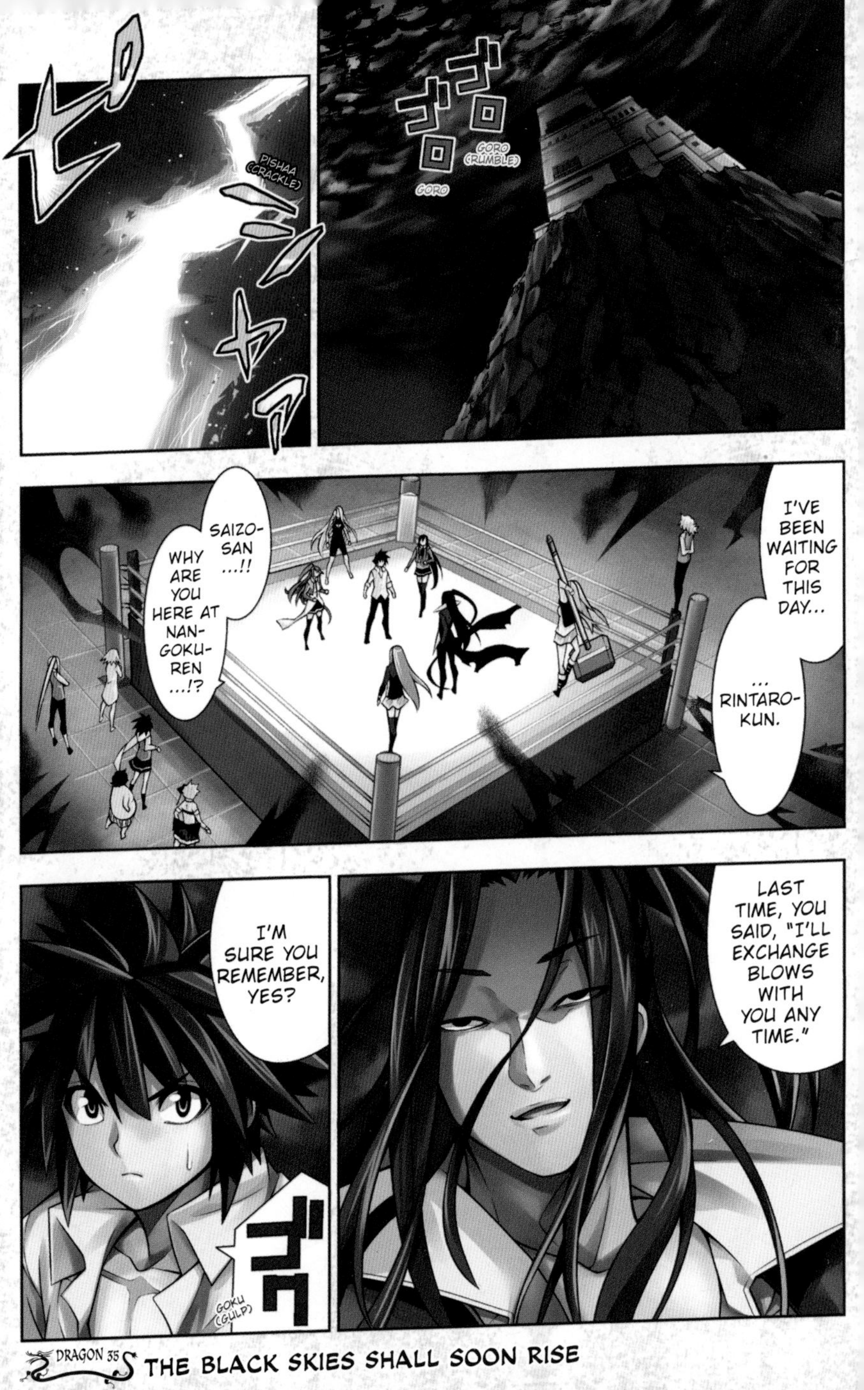
GORO (RUMBLE)
GORO
PISHAA (CRACKLE)
I'VE BEEN WAITING FOR THIS DAY...
... RINTARO-KUN.
SAIZO-SAN ...!!
WHY ARE YOU HERE AT NAN-GOKU-REN ...!?
LAST TIME, YOU SAID, "I'LL EXCHANGE BLOWS WITH YOU ANY TIME."
I'M SURE YOU REMEMBER, YES?
GOKU (GULP)

DRAGON 35 THE BLACK SKIES SHALL SOON RISE

TSUYOSHI WATANABE

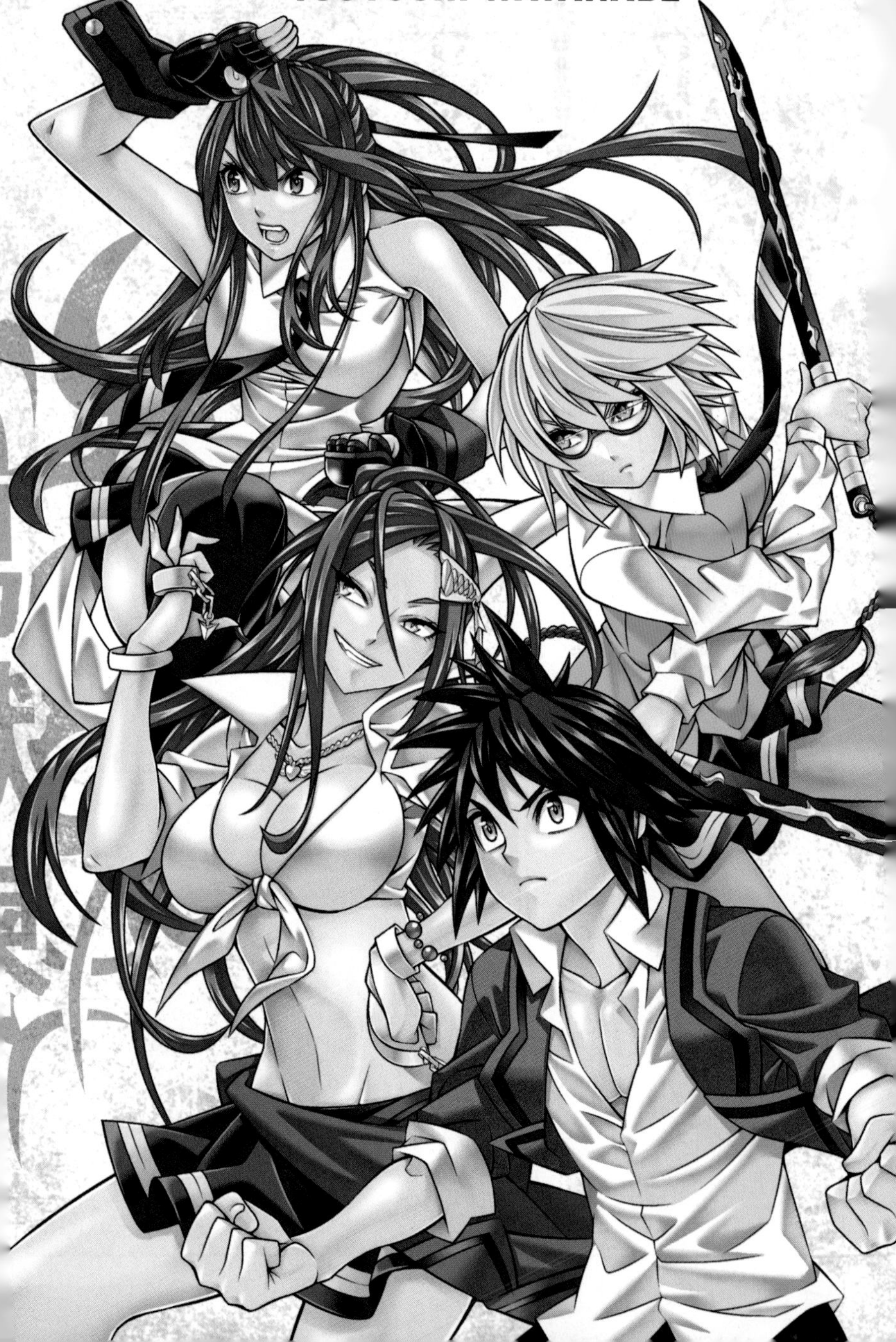

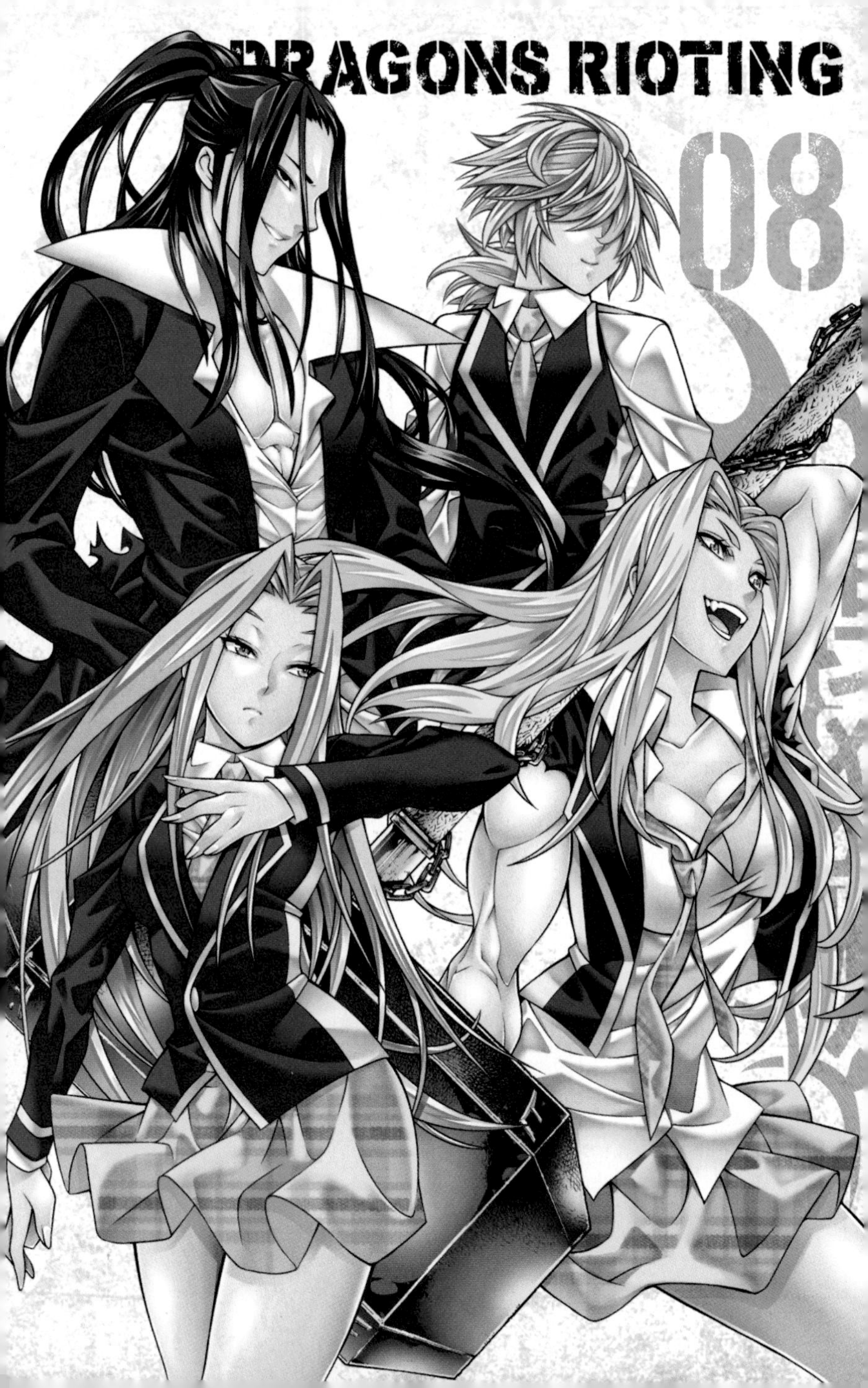
DRAGONS RIOTING
08

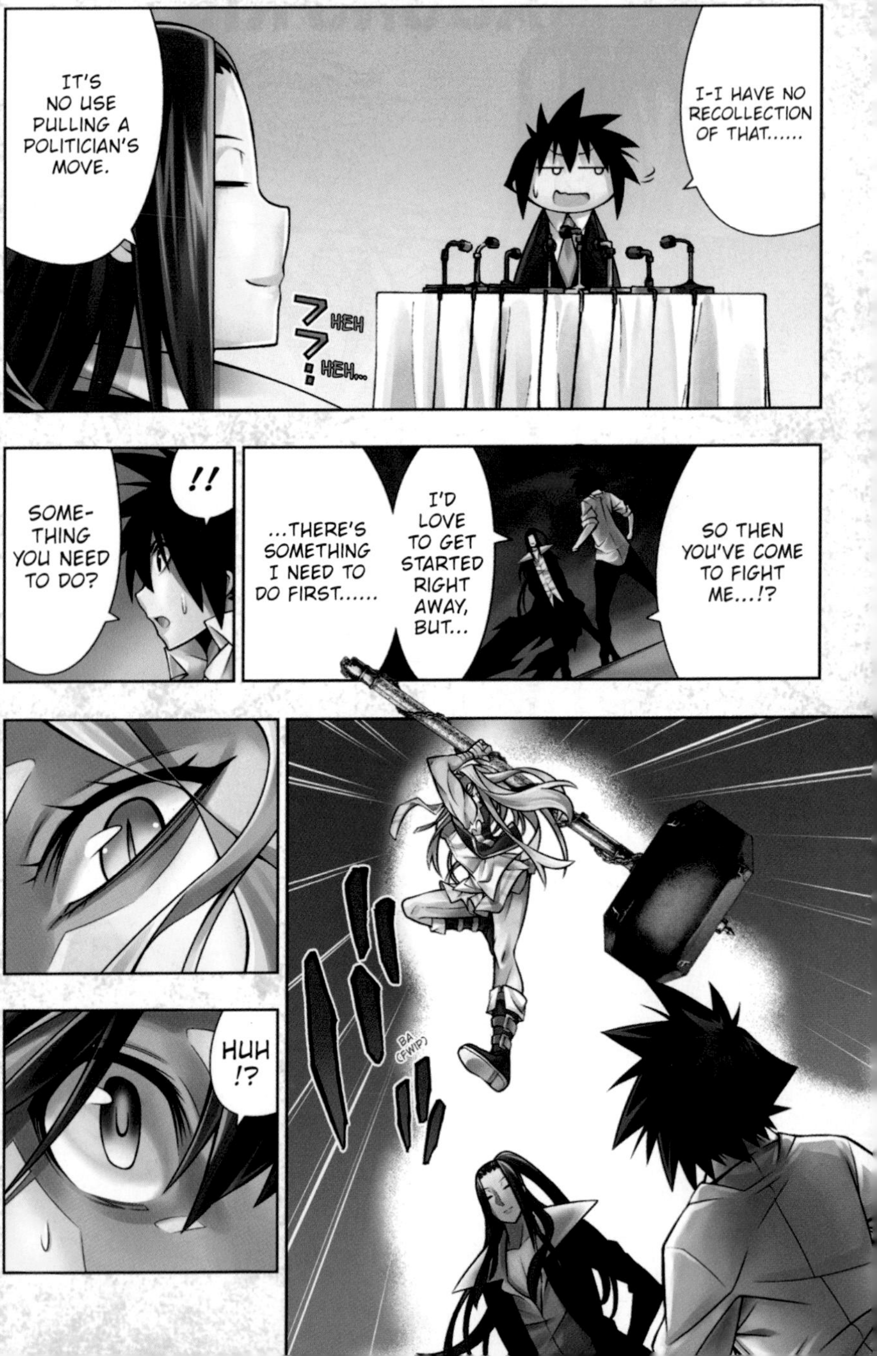
I-I HAVE NO RECOLLECTION OF THAT......
IT'S NO USE PULLING A POLITICIAN'S MOVE.
HEH HEH...
SO THEN YOU'VE COME TO FIGHT ME...!?
I'D LOVE TO GET STARTED RIGHT AWAY, BUT...
...THERE'S SOMETHING I NEED TO DO FIRST......
!!
SOME-THING YOU NEED TO DO?
BA (FWIP)
HUH!?

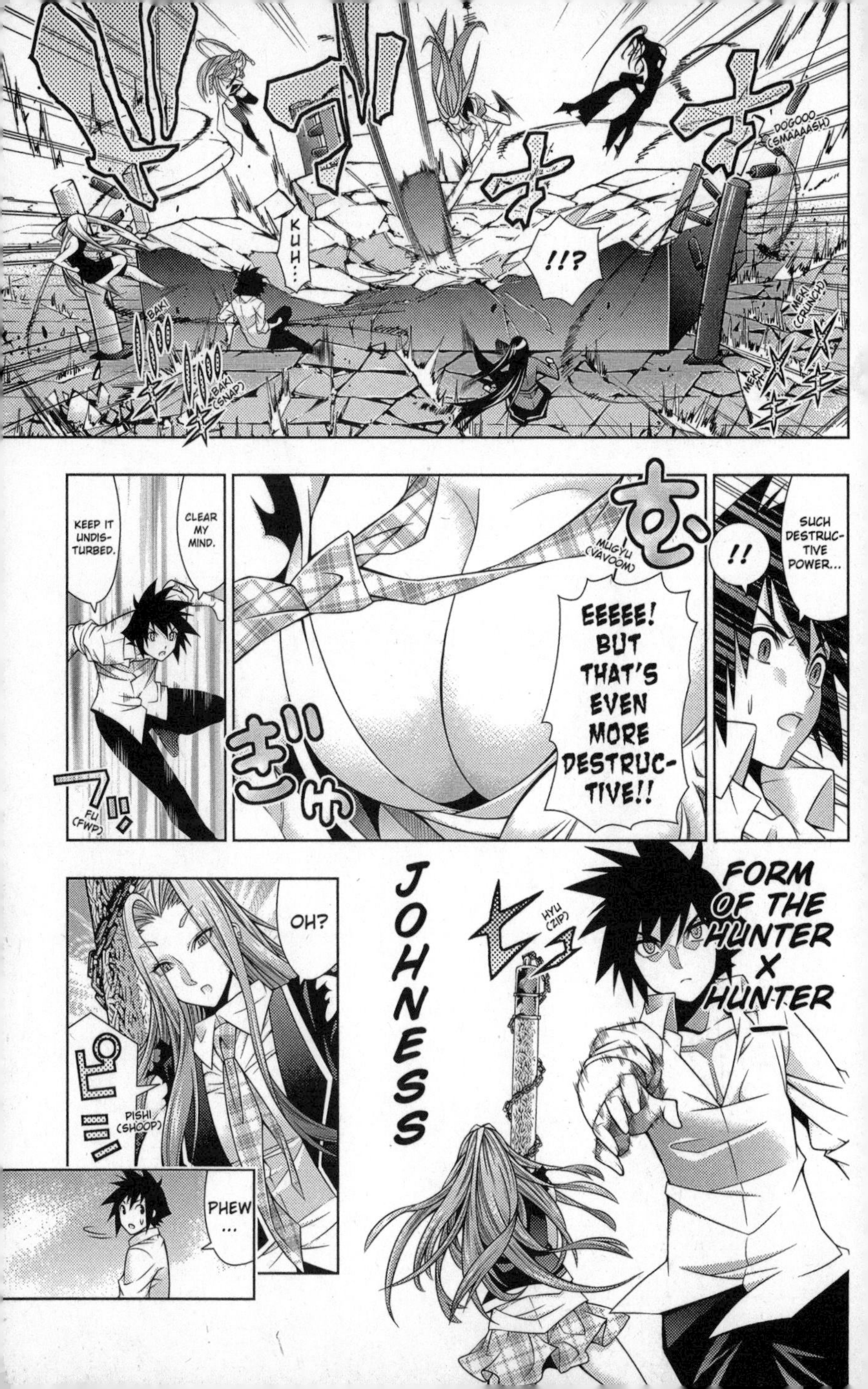
DOGOOO (SMAAAASH)
!!?
KUH...
MEKI (CRUNCH)
MEKI
BAKI (SNAP)
BAKI
SUCH DESTRUC-TIVE POWER...
!!
MUGYU (VAVOOM)
EEEEE! BUT THAT'S EVEN MORE DESTRUC-TIVE!!
CLEAR MY MIND.
KEEP IT UNDIS-TURBED.
FU (FWP)
FORM OF THE HUNTER X HUNTER—
HYU (ZIP)
JOHNESS
OH?
PISHI (SHOOP)
PHEW ...

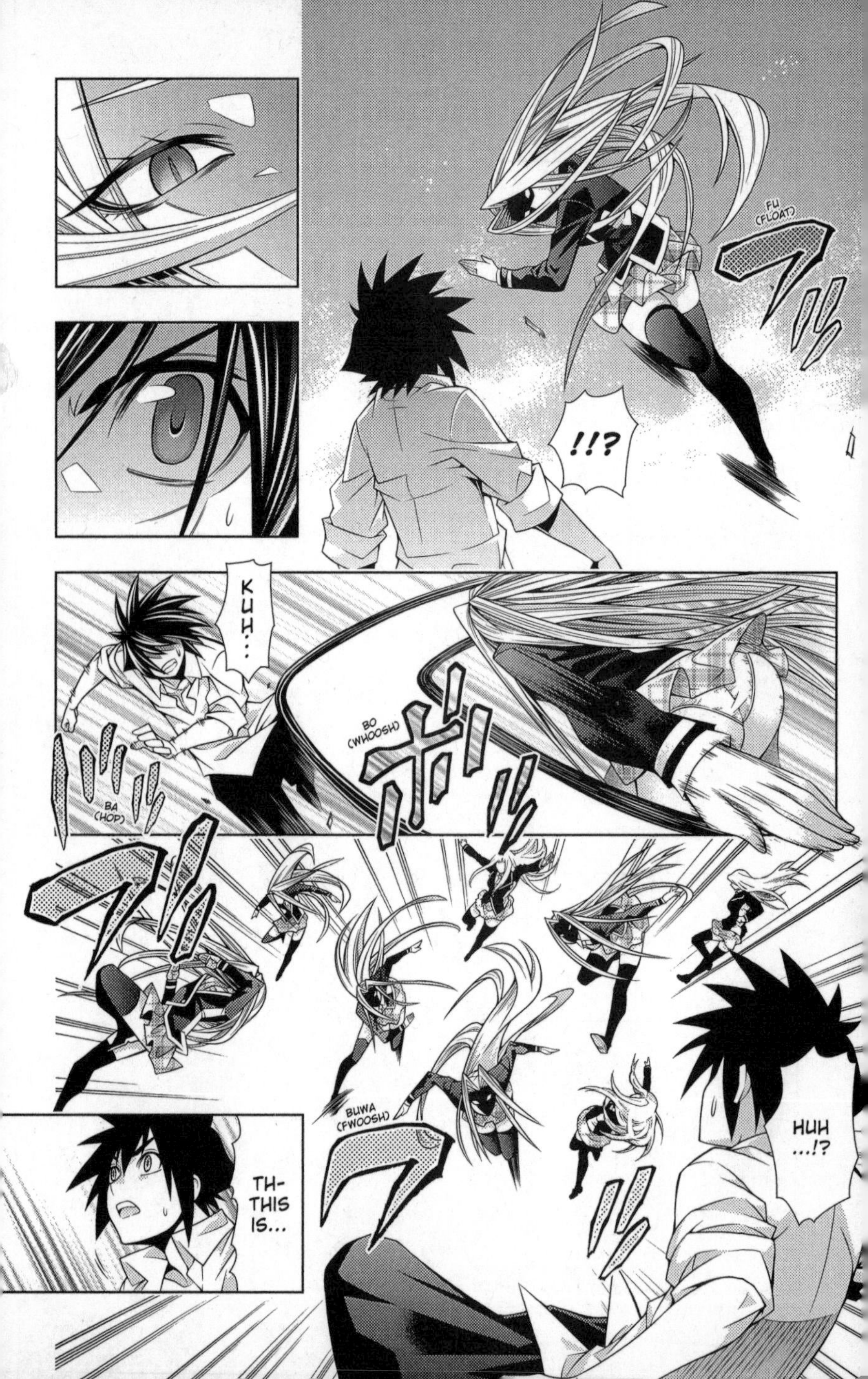
FU (FLOAT)
!!?
KUH...
BO (WHOOSH)
BA (HOP)
HUH ...!?
BUWA (FWOOSH)
TH- THIS IS...

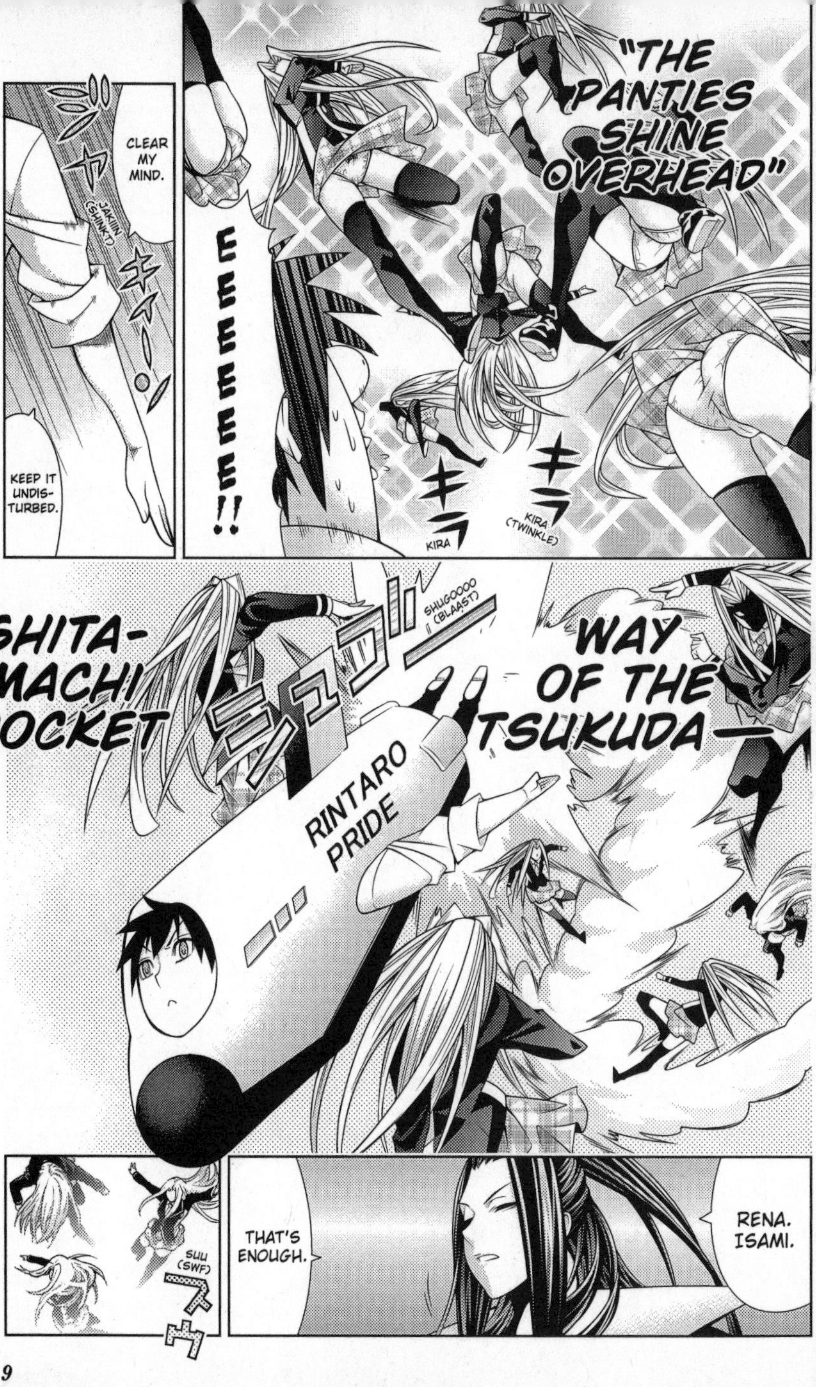
"THE PANTIES SHINE OVERHEAD"
EEEEEEEEE!!
KIRA (TWINKLE)
KIRA
CLEAR MY MIND.
JAKIIN (SHINK!)
KEEP IT UNDIS-TURBED.
WAY OF THE TSUKUDA—
SHUGOOOO (BLAAST)
SHITA-MACHI ROCKET
RINTARO PRIDE
RENA. ISAMI.
THAT'S ENOUGH.
SUU (SWF)

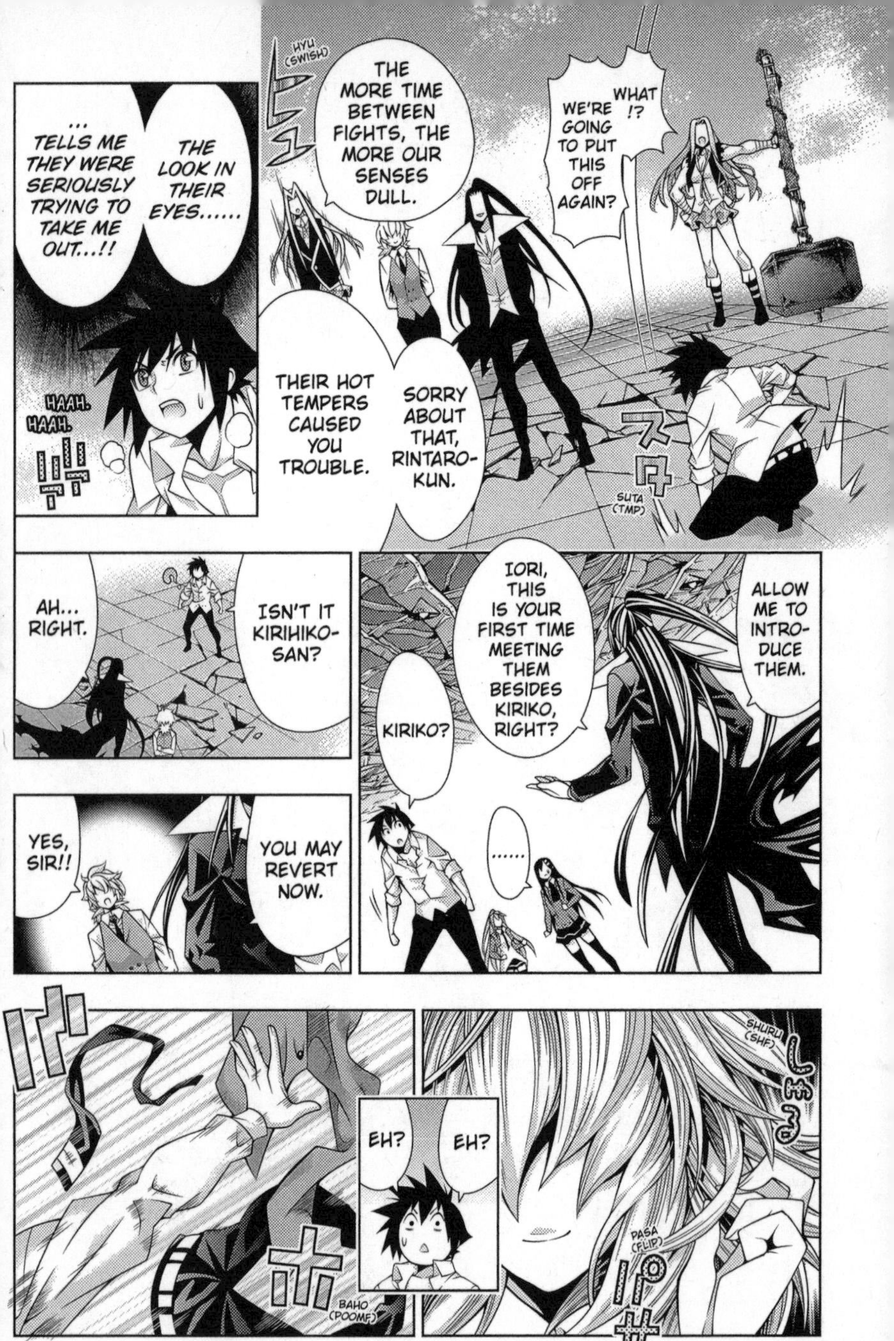
WHAT !?
WE'RE GOING TO PUT THIS OFF AGAIN?
HYU (SWISH)
THE MORE TIME BETWEEN FIGHTS, THE MORE OUR SENSES DULL.
SORRY ABOUT THAT, RINTARO-KUN.
THEIR HOT TEMPERS CAUSED YOU TROUBLE.
SUTA (TMP)
THE LOOK IN THEIR EYES......
... TELLS ME THEY WERE SERIOUSLY TRYING TO TAKE ME OUT...!!
HAAH. HAAH.
ALLOW ME TO INTRODUCE THEM.
IORI, THIS IS YOUR FIRST TIME MEETING THEM BESIDES KIRIKO, RIGHT?
KIRIKO?
......
ISN'T IT KIRIHIKO-SAN?
AH... RIGHT.
YOU MAY REVERT NOW.
YES, SIR!!
SHURU (SHF)
PASA (FLIP)
EH?
EH?
BAHO (POOMF)

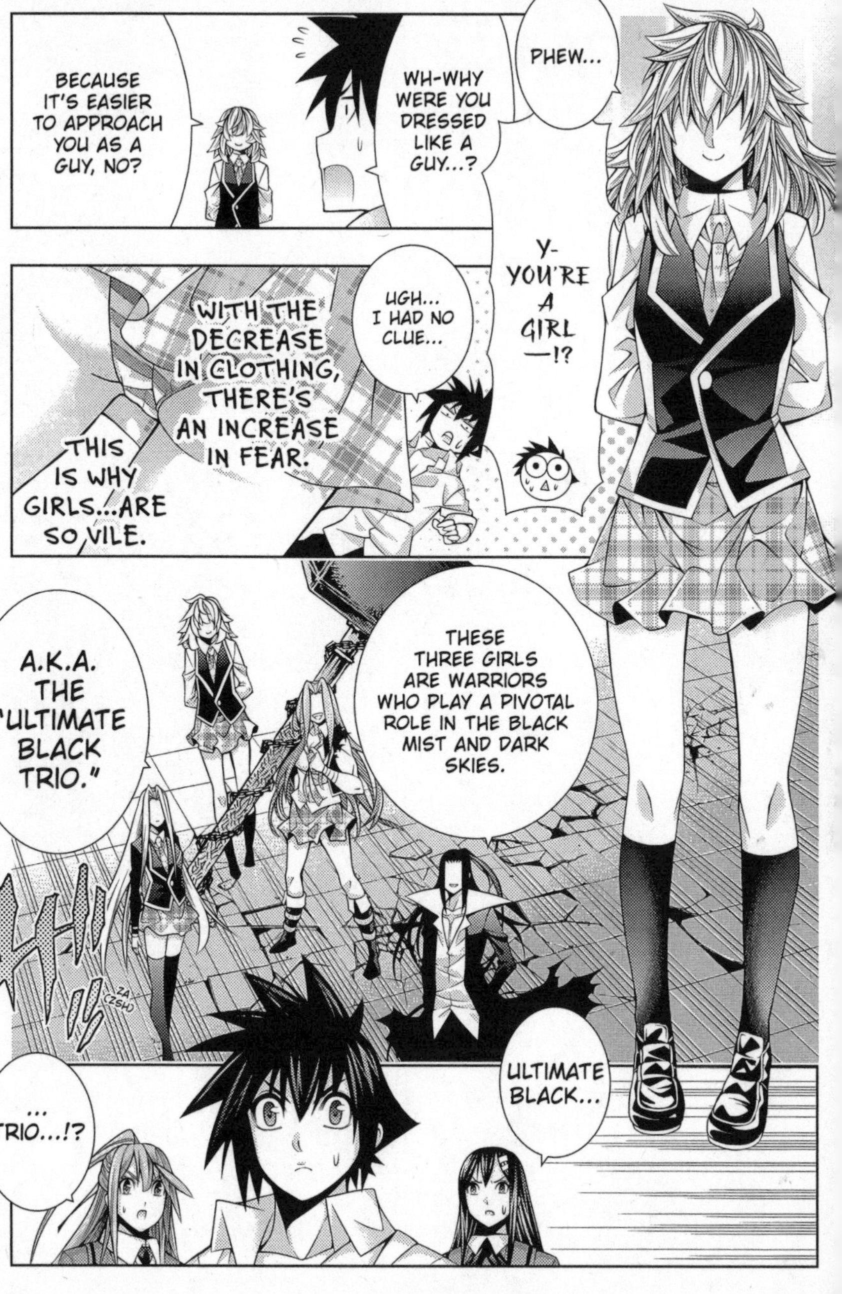
PHEW...
Y-YOU'RE A GIRL—!?
WH-WHY WERE YOU DRESSED LIKE A GUY...?
BECAUSE IT'S EASIER TO APPROACH YOU AS A GUY, NO?
UGH... I HAD NO CLUE...
WITH THE DECREASE IN CLOTHING, THERE'S AN INCREASE IN FEAR.
THIS IS WHY GIRLS...ARE SO VILE.
THESE THREE GIRLS ARE WARRIORS WHO PLAY A PIVOTAL ROLE IN THE BLACK MIST AND DARK SKIES.
A.K.A. THE "ULTIMATE BLACK TRIO."
ZA (ZSH)
ULTIMATE BLACK...
...TRIO...!?

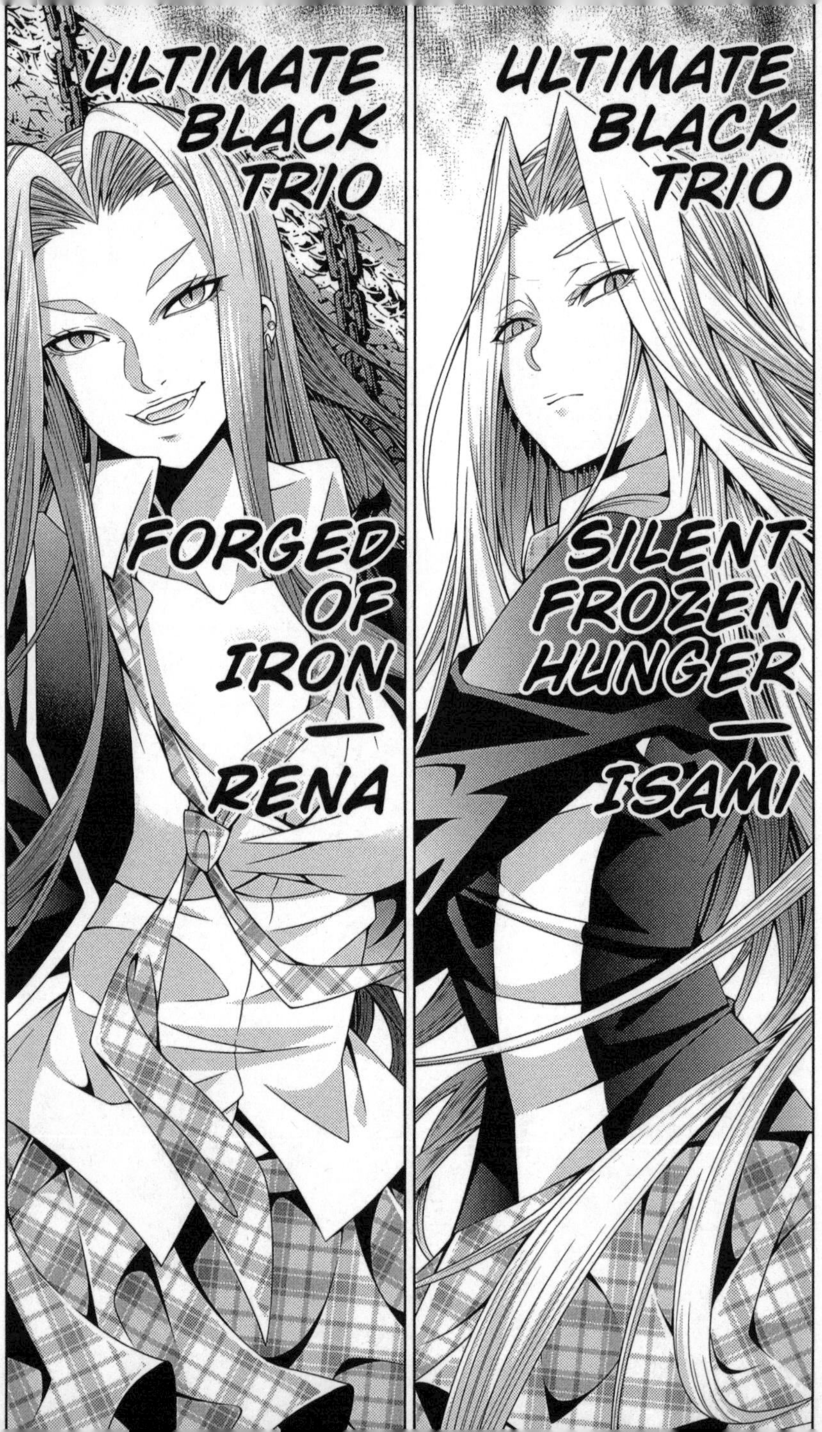
ULTIMATE BLACK TRIO
SILENT FROZEN HUNGER — ISAMI
ULTIMATE BLACK TRIO
FORGED OF IRON — RENA

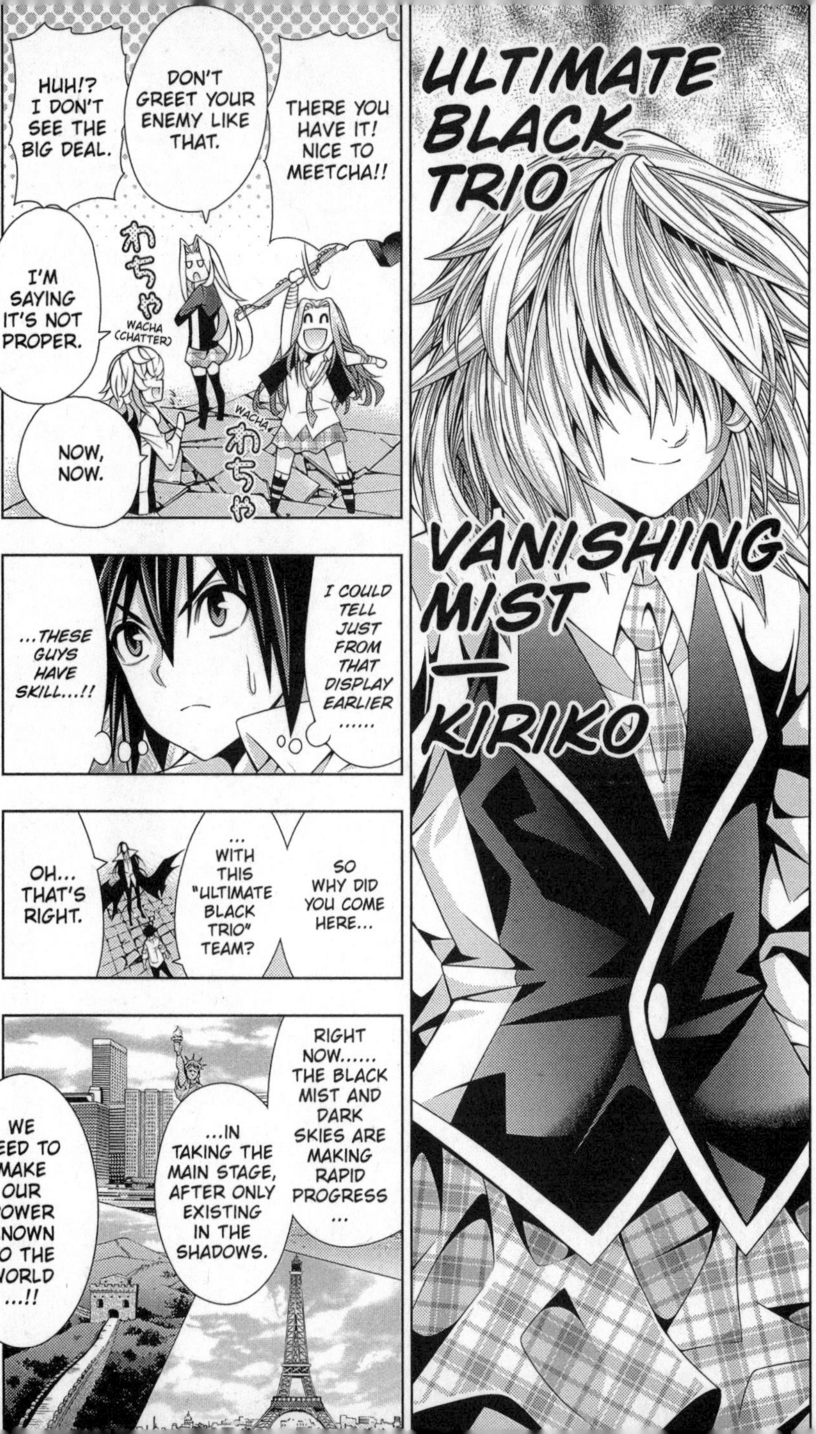
ULTIMATE BLACK TRIO
VANISHING MIST — KIRIKO
THERE YOU HAVE IT! NICE TO MEETCHA!!
DON'T GREET YOUR ENEMY LIKE THAT.
HUH!? I DON'T SEE THE BIG DEAL.
わちゃ
WACHA (CHATTER)
I'M SAYING IT'S NOT PROPER.
WACHA
わちゃ
NOW, NOW.
I COULD TELL JUST FROM THAT DISPLAY EARLIER ......
...THESE GUYS HAVE SKILL...!!
SO WHY DID YOU COME HERE...
...WITH THIS "ULTIMATE BLACK TRIO" TEAM?
OH... THAT'S RIGHT.
RIGHT NOW...... THE BLACK MIST AND DARK SKIES ARE MAKING RAPID PROGRESS ...
...IN TAKING THE MAIN STAGE, AFTER ONLY EXISTING IN THE SHADOWS.
WE NEED TO MAKE OUR POWER KNOWN TO THE WORLD ...!!

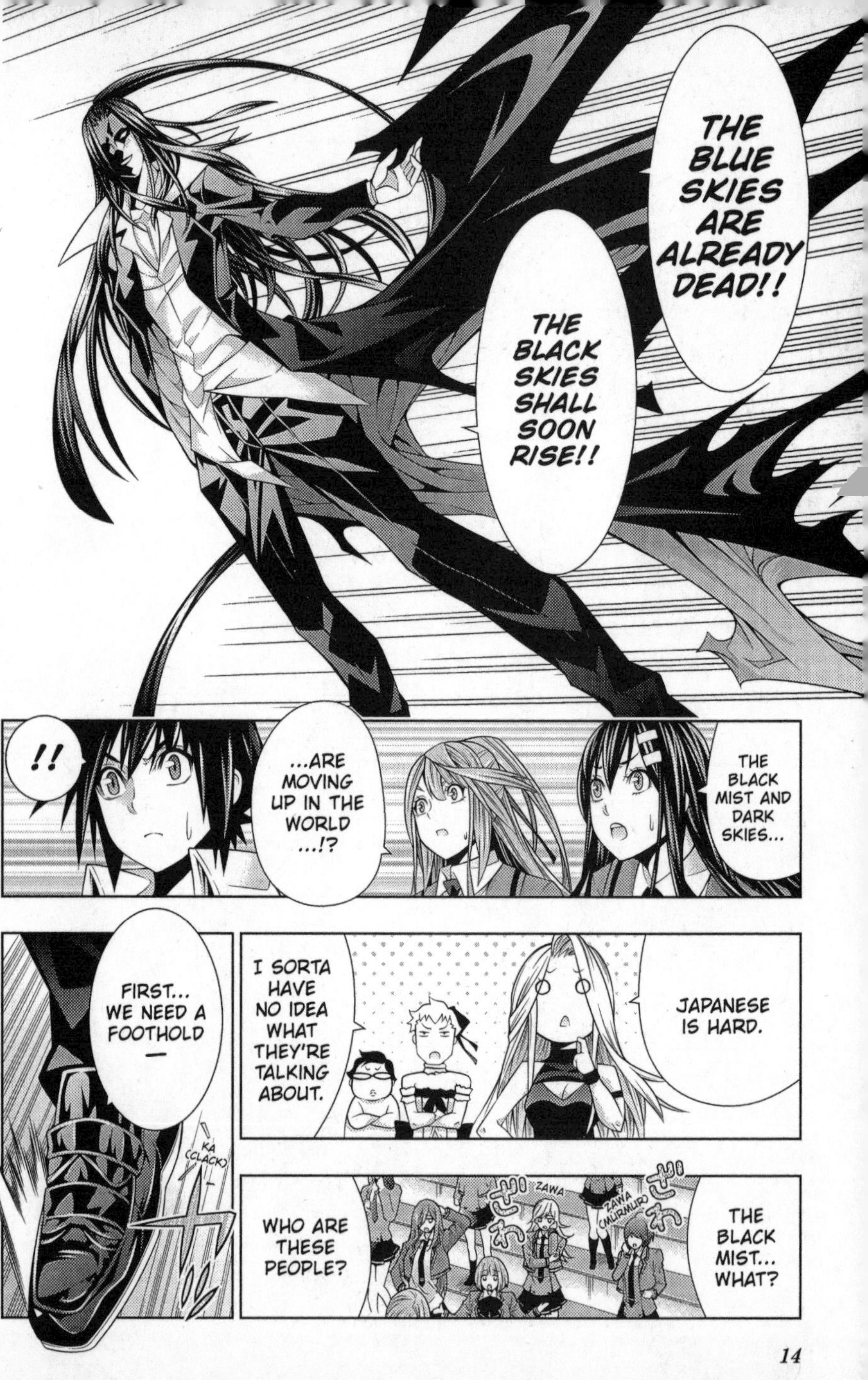
THE BLUE SKIES ARE ALREADY DEAD!!
THE BLACK SKIES SHALL SOON RISE!!
THE BLACK MIST AND DARK SKIES...
...ARE MOVING UP IN THE WORLD ...!?
!!
JAPANESE IS HARD.
I SORTA HAVE NO IDEA WHAT THEY'RE TALKING ABOUT.
THE BLACK MIST... WHAT?
ZAWA (MURMUR)
ZAWA
WHO ARE THESE PEOPLE?
FIRST... WE NEED A FOOTHOLD —
KA (CLACK)

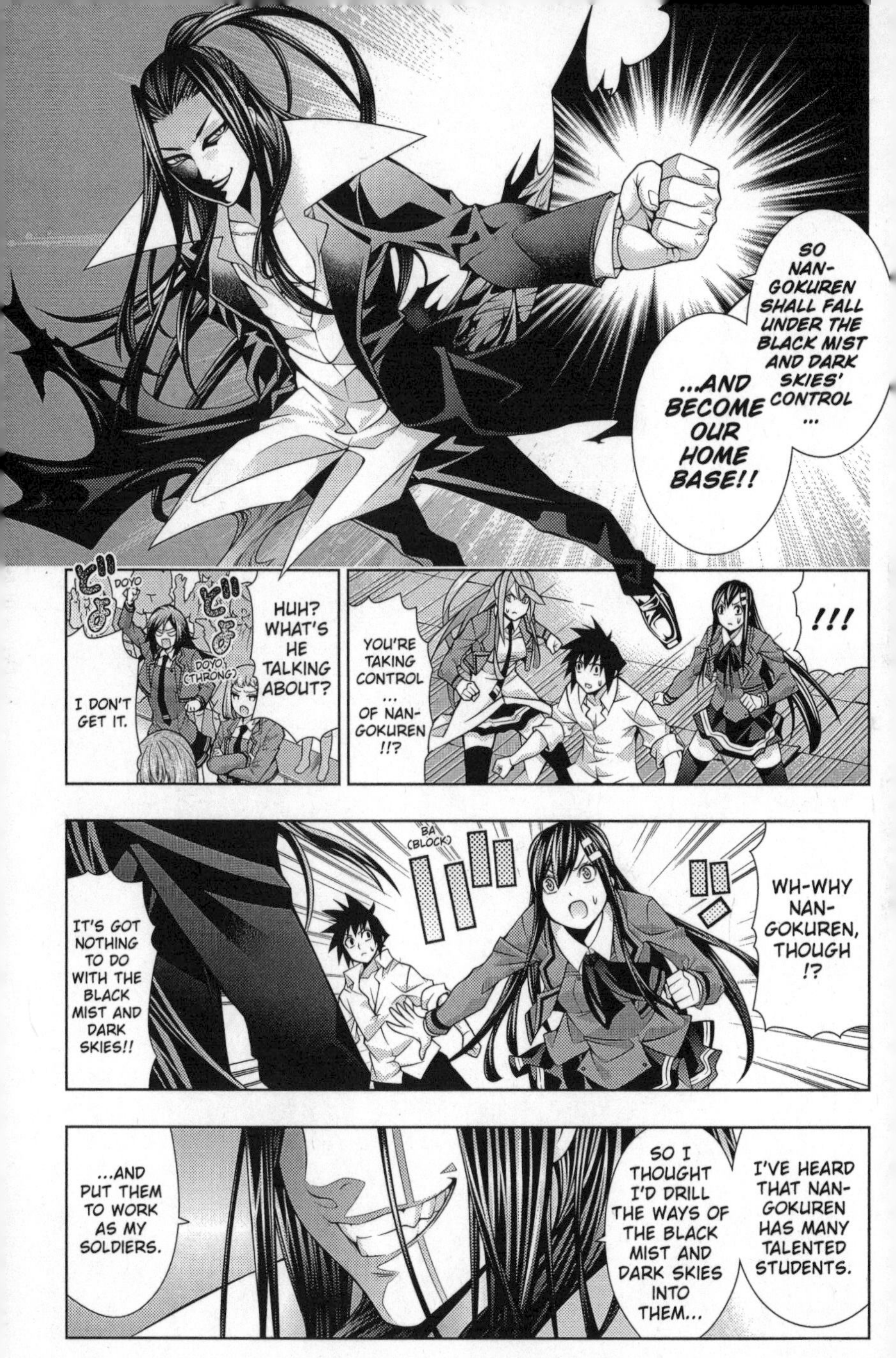
SO NAN-GOKUREN SHALL FALL UNDER THE BLACK MIST AND DARK SKIES' CONTROL ...
...AND BECOME OUR HOME BASE!!
!!!
YOU'RE TAKING CONTROL ... OF NAN-GOKUREN !!?
HUH? WHAT'S HE TALKING ABOUT?
DOYO
DOYO (THRONG)
I DON'T GET IT.
WH-WHY NAN-GOKUREN, THOUGH !?
BA (BLOCK)
IT'S GOT NOTHING TO DO WITH THE BLACK MIST AND DARK SKIES!!
I'VE HEARD THAT NAN-GOKUREN HAS MANY TALENTED STUDENTS.
SO I THOUGHT I'D DRILL THE WAYS OF THE BLACK MIST AND DARK SKIES INTO THEM...
...AND PUT THEM TO WORK AS MY SOLDIERS.

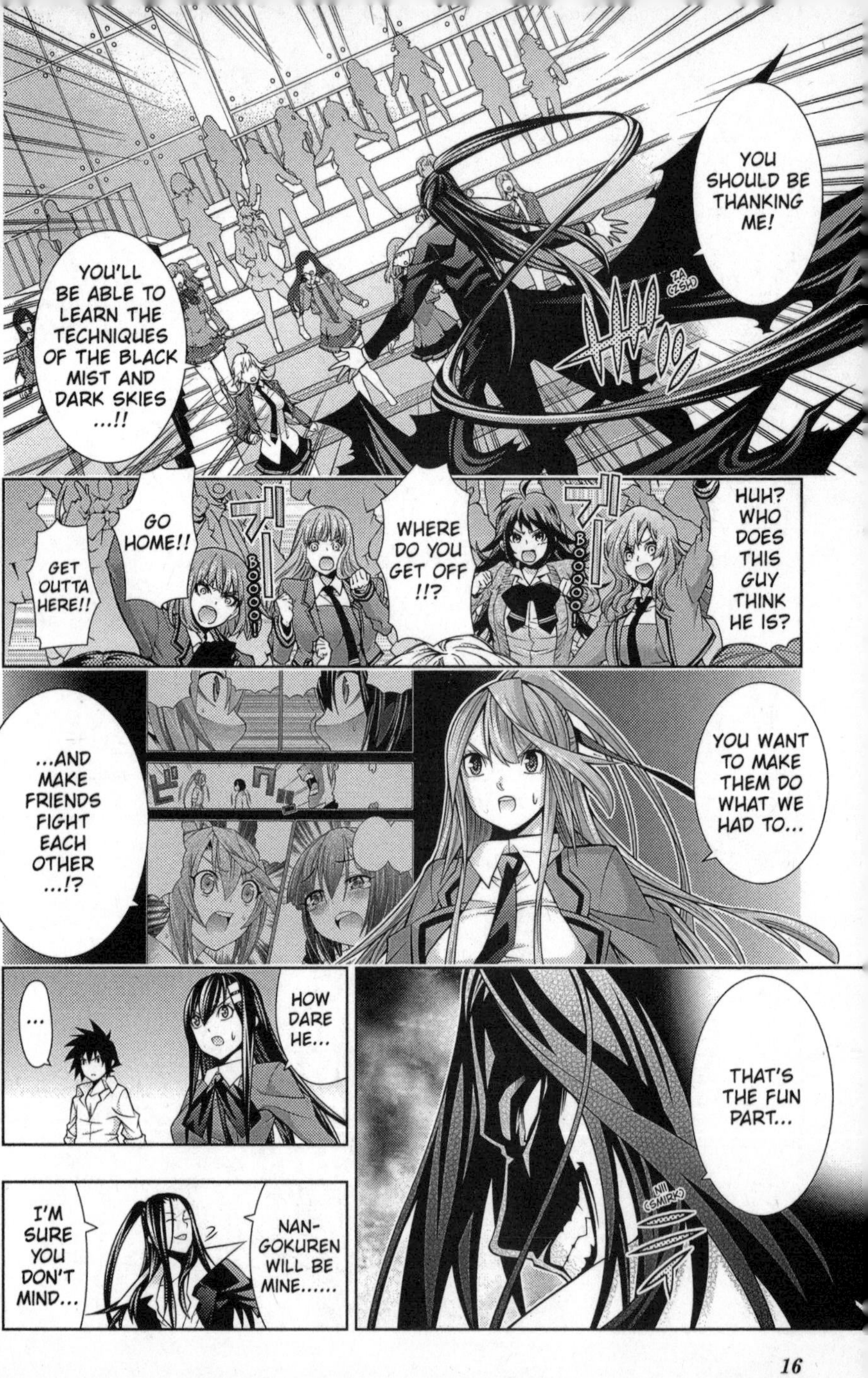

YOU SHOULD BE THANKING ME!
ZA (ZSH)
YOU'LL BE ABLE TO LEARN THE TECHNIQUES OF THE BLACK MIST AND DARK SKIES ...!!
HUH? WHO DOES THIS GUY THINK HE IS?
WHERE DO YOU GET OFF !!?
GO HOME!!
GET OUTTA HERE!!
YOU WANT TO MAKE THEM DO WHAT WE HAD TO...
...AND MAKE FRIENDS FIGHT EACH OTHER ...!?
THAT'S THE FUN PART...
NII (SMIRK)
HOW DARE HE...
...
NAN-GOKUREN WILL BE MINE......
I'M SURE YOU DON'T MIND...

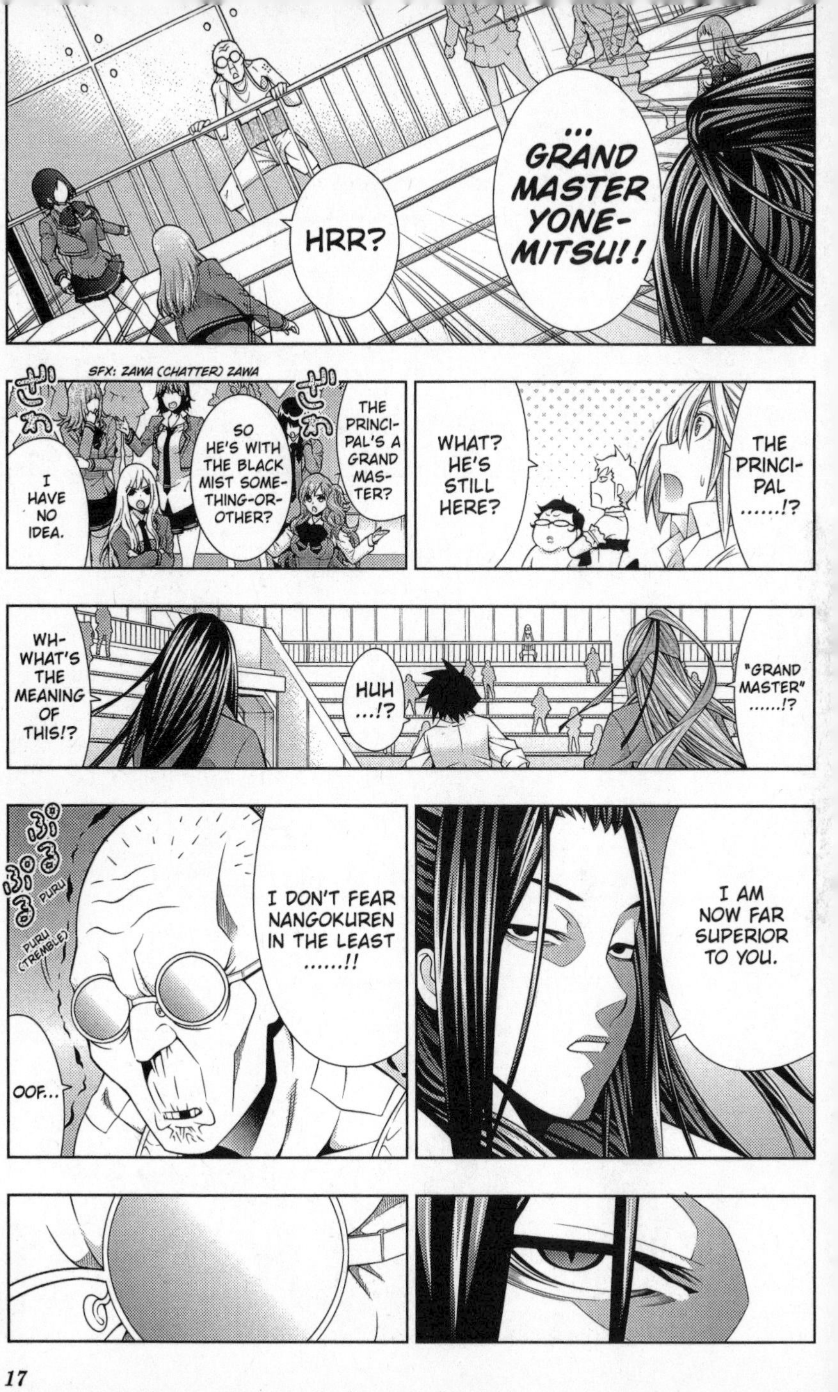
...GRAND MASTER YONE-MITSU!!
HRR?
THE PRINCI-PAL ......!?
WHAT? HE'S STILL HERE?
SFX: ZAWA (CHATTER) ZAWA
ざわ
THE PRINCI-PAL'S A GRAND MAS-TER?
SO HE'S WITH THE BLACK MIST SOME-THING-OR-OTHER?
ざわ
I HAVE NO IDEA.
"GRAND MASTER" ......!?
HUH ...!?
WH-WHAT'S THE MEANING OF THIS!?
I AM NOW FAR SUPERIOR TO YOU.
I DON'T FEAR NANGOKUREN IN THE LEAST ......!!
ぷるぷる
PURU PURU (TREMBLE)
OOF...

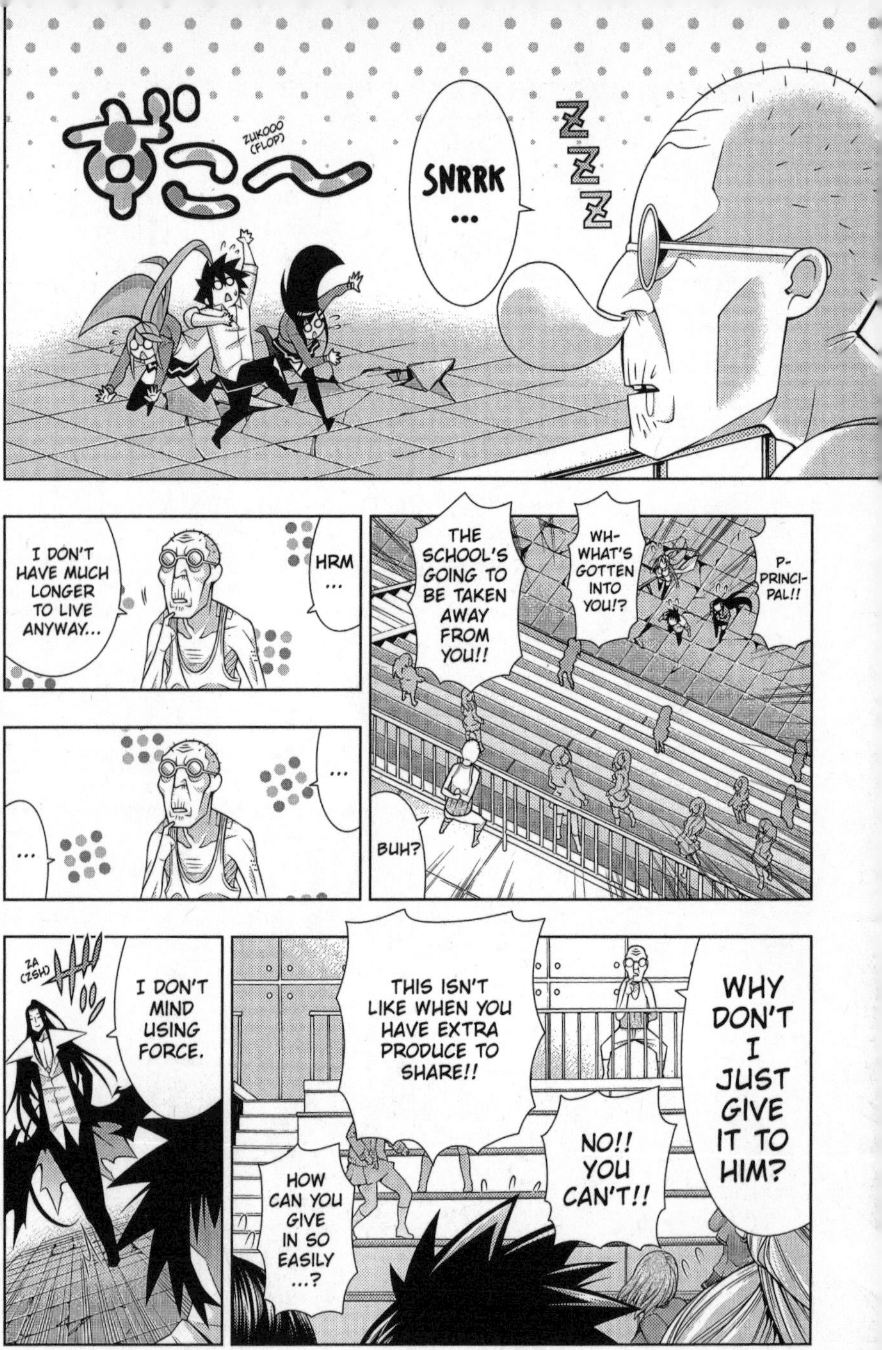
Z Z Z
SNRRK ...
ZUKOOO (FLOP)
P-PRINCIPAL!!
WH-WHAT'S GOTTEN INTO YOU!?
THE SCHOOL'S GOING TO BE TAKEN AWAY FROM YOU!!
BUH?
HRM ...
I DON'T HAVE MUCH LONGER TO LIVE ANYWAY...
...
...
WHY DON'T I JUST GIVE IT TO HIM?
NO!! YOU CAN'T!!
THIS ISN'T LIKE WHEN YOU HAVE EXTRA PRODUCE TO SHARE!!
HOW CAN YOU GIVE IN SO EASILY ...?
ZA (ZSH)
I DON'T MIND USING FORCE.

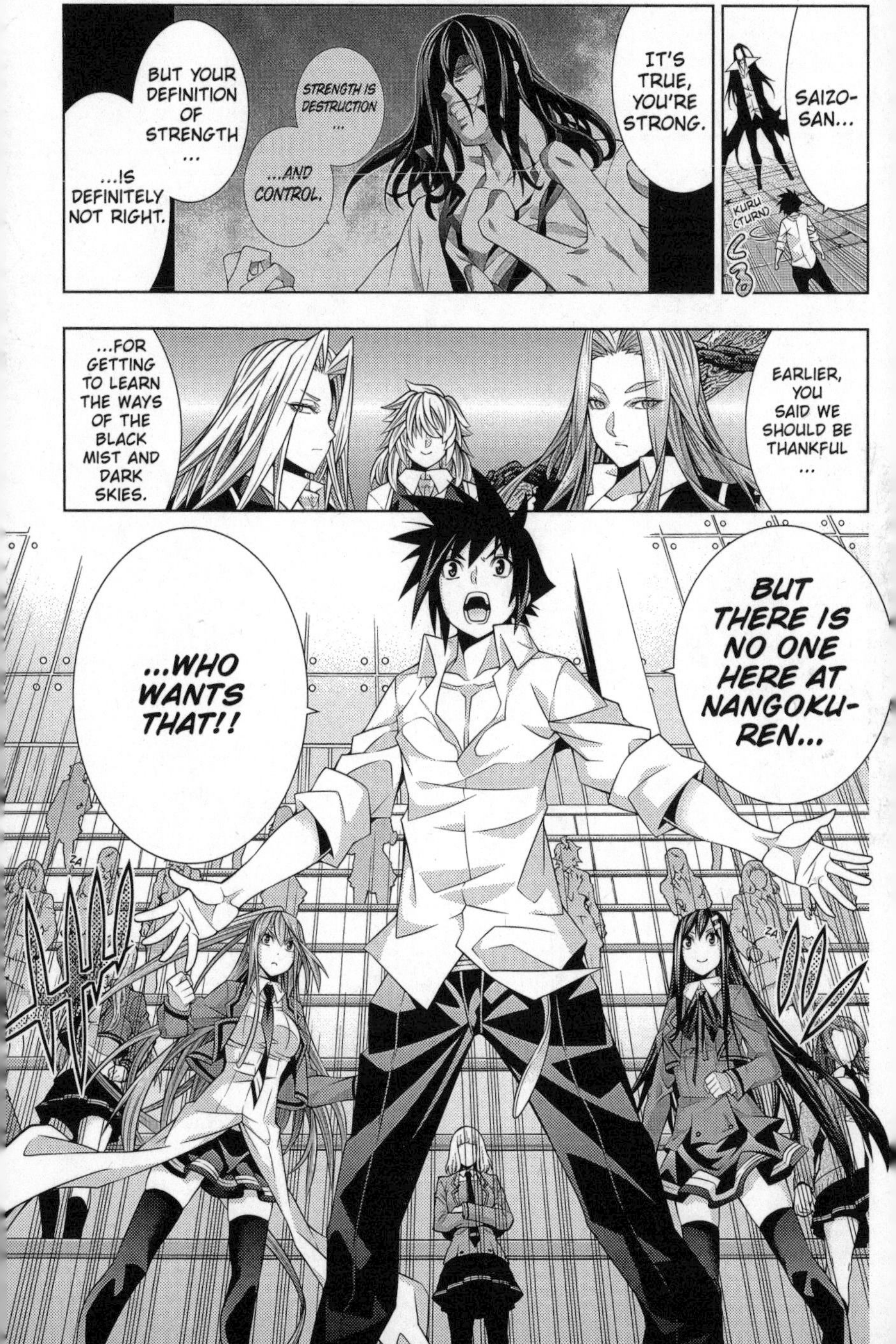
SAIZO-SAN...
KURU (TURN)
IT'S TRUE, YOU'RE STRONG.
STRENGTH IS DESTRUCTION ...
...AND CONTROL.
BUT YOUR DEFINITION OF STRENGTH ...
...IS DEFINITELY NOT RIGHT.
EARLIER, YOU SAID WE SHOULD BE THANKFUL ...
...FOR GETTING TO LEARN THE WAYS OF THE BLACK MIST AND DARK SKIES.
BUT THERE IS NO ONE HERE AT NANGOKU-REN...
...WHO WANTS THAT!!
ZA
ZA

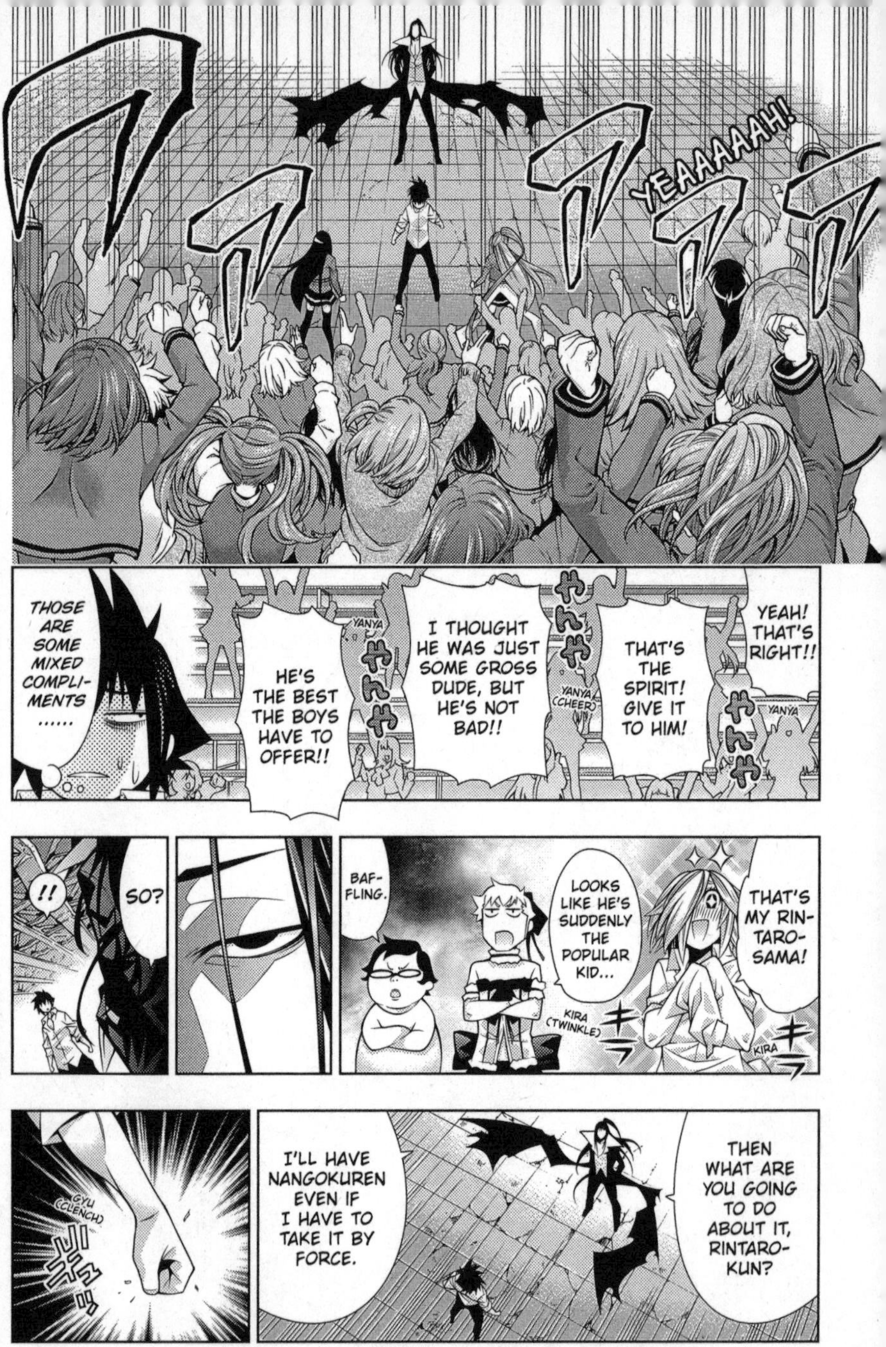
YEAAAAAH!
YEAH! THAT'S RIGHT!!
YANYA
THAT'S THE SPIRIT! GIVE IT TO HIM!
YANYA (CHEER)
I THOUGHT HE WAS JUST SOME GROSS DUDE, BUT HE'S NOT BAD!!
YANYA
HE'S THE BEST THE BOYS HAVE TO OFFER!!
THOSE ARE SOME MIXED COMPLIMENTS......
THAT'S MY RINTARO-SAMA!
KIRA
LOOKS LIKE HE'S SUDDENLY THE POPULAR KID...
KIRA (TWINKLE)
BAFFLING.
SO?
!!
THEN WHAT ARE YOU GOING TO DO ABOUT IT, RINTARO-KUN?
I'LL HAVE NANGOKUREN EVEN IF I HAVE TO TAKE IT BY FORCE.
GYU (CLENCH)

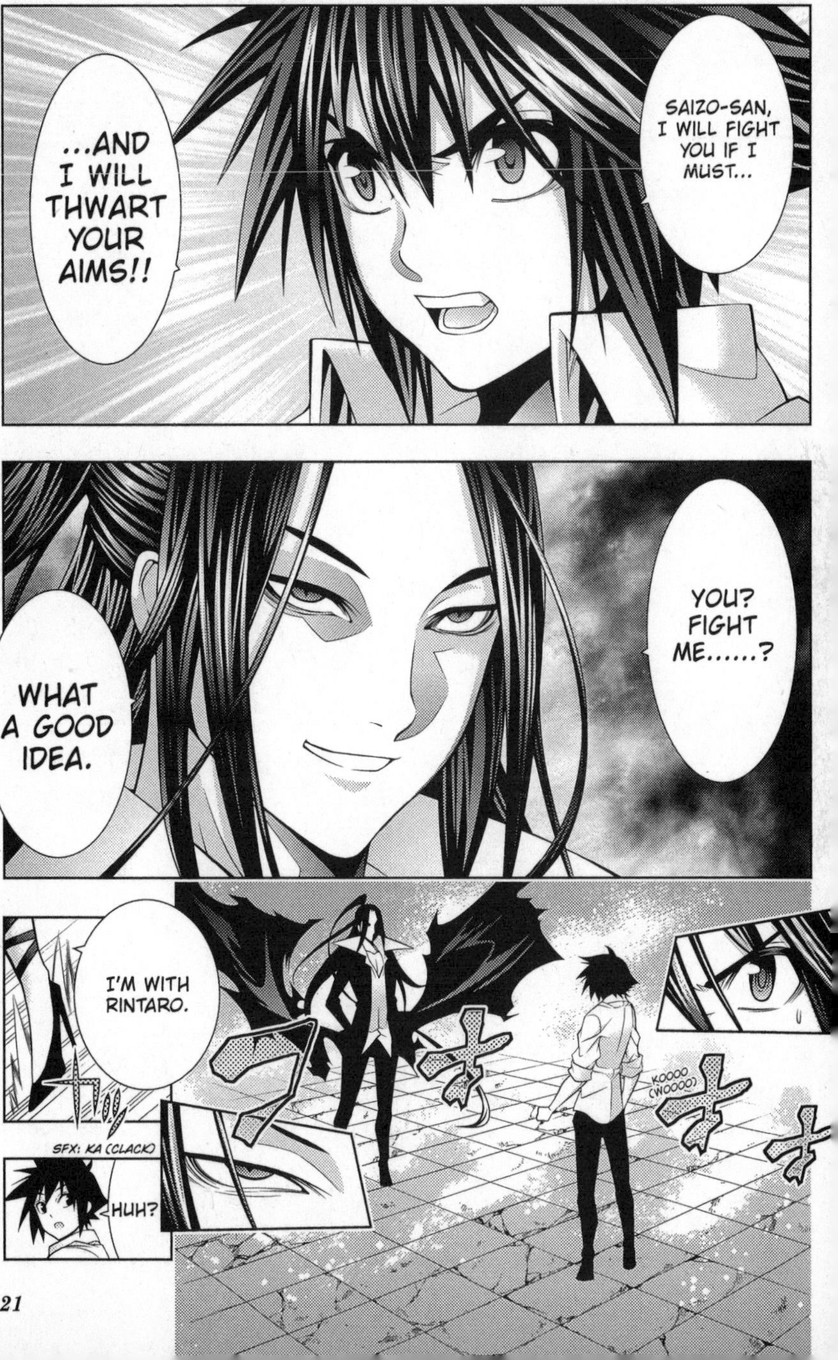
SAIZO-SAN, I WILL FIGHT YOU IF I MUST...
...AND I WILL THWART YOUR AIMS!!
YOU? FIGHT ME......?
WHAT A GOOD IDEA.
KOOOO (WOOOO)
I'M WITH RINTARO.
SFX: KA (CLACK)
HUH?

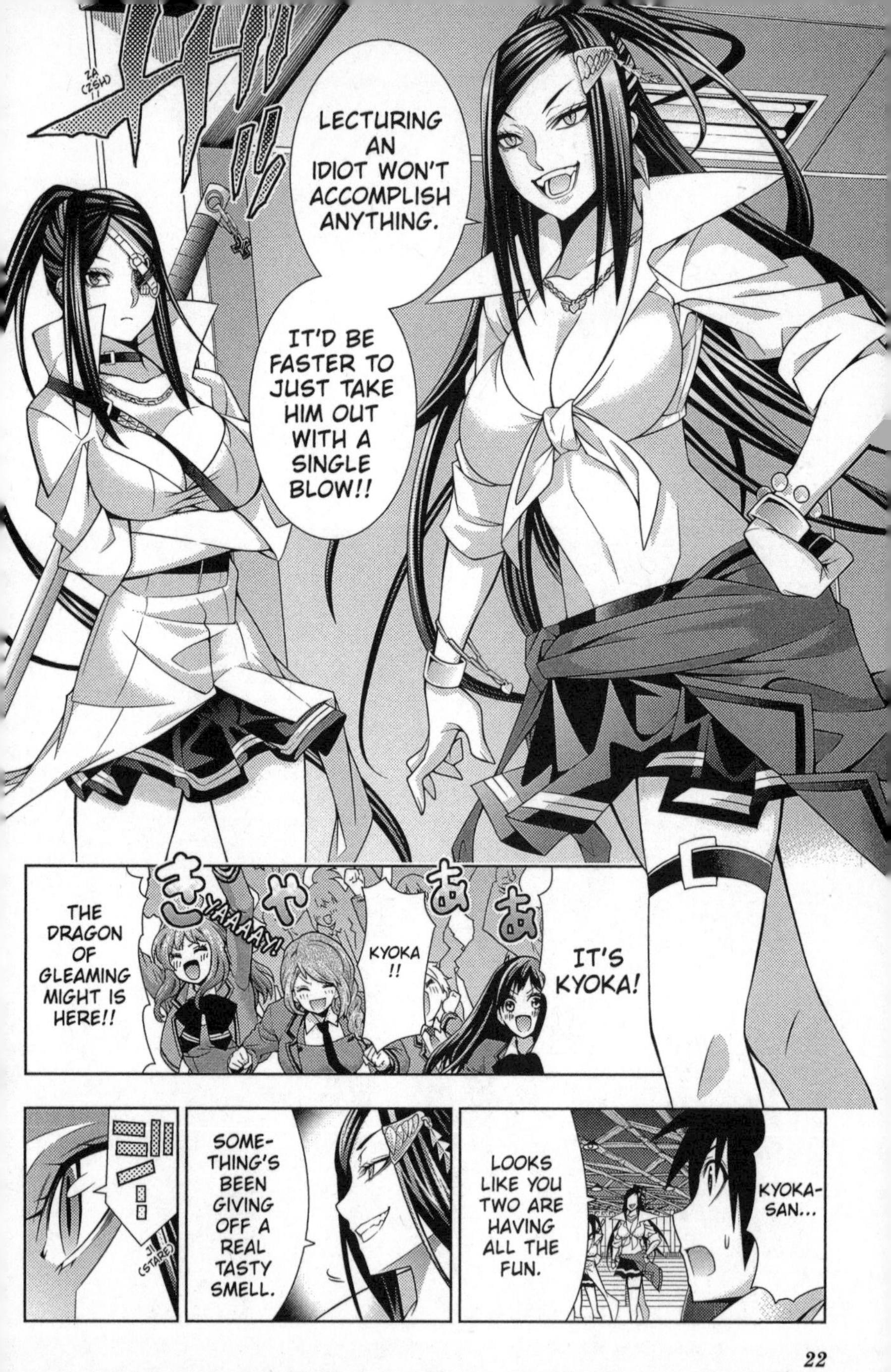
ZA (ZSH)
LECTURING AN IDIOT WON'T ACCOMPLISH ANYTHING.
IT'D BE FASTER TO JUST TAKE HIM OUT WITH A SINGLE BLOW!!
IT'S KYOKA!
KYOKA!!
YAAAAAY!
THE DRAGON OF GLEAMING MIGHT IS HERE!!
KYOKA-SAN...
LOOKS LIKE YOU TWO ARE HAVING ALL THE FUN.
SOME-THING'S BEEN GIVING OFF A REAL TASTY SMELL.
JI (STARE)

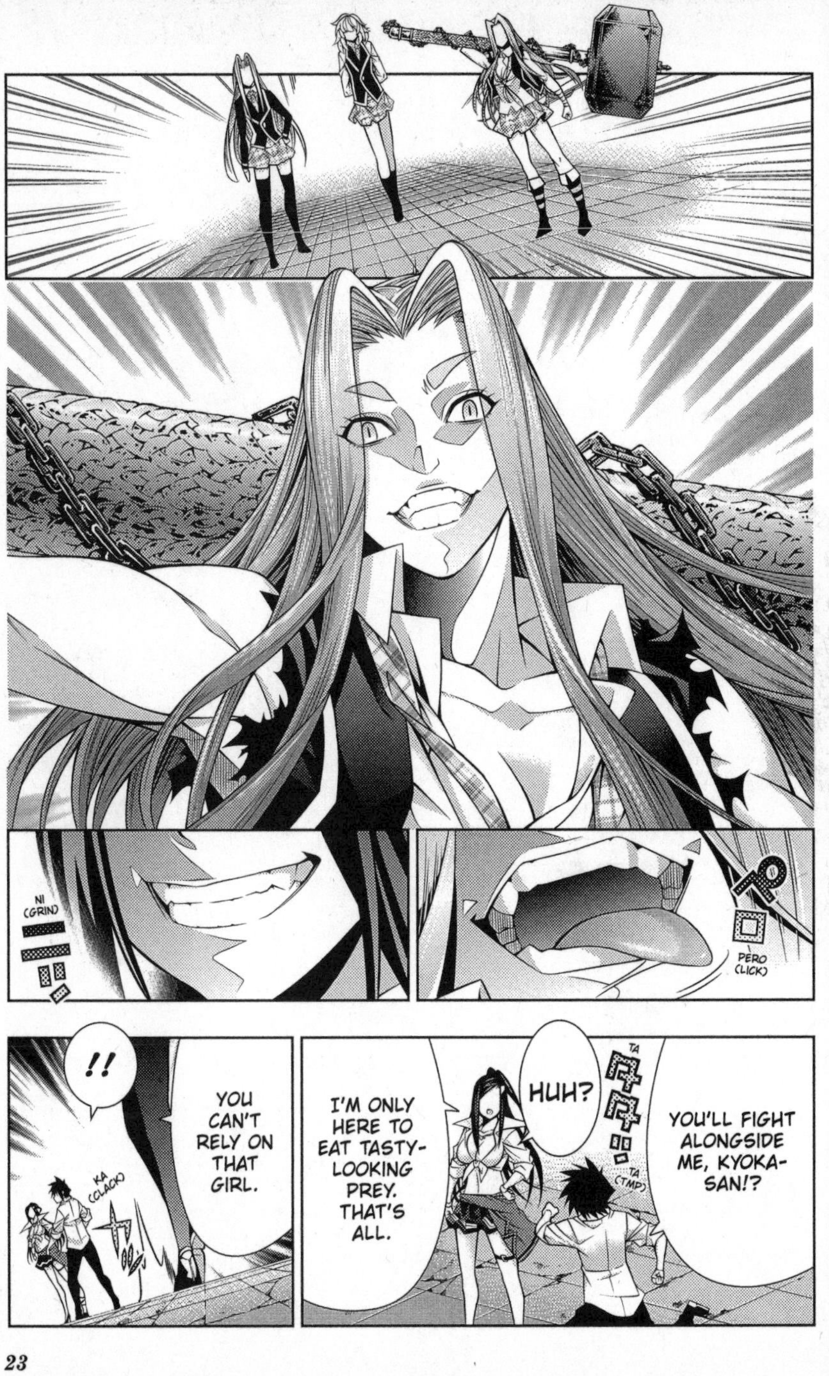
PERO (LICK)
NI (GRIN)
YOU'LL FIGHT ALONGSIDE ME, KYOKA-SAN!?
TA TA (TMP)
HUH?
I'M ONLY HERE TO EAT TASTY-LOOKING PREY. THAT'S ALL.
!!
YOU CAN'T RELY ON THAT GIRL.
KA (CLACK)

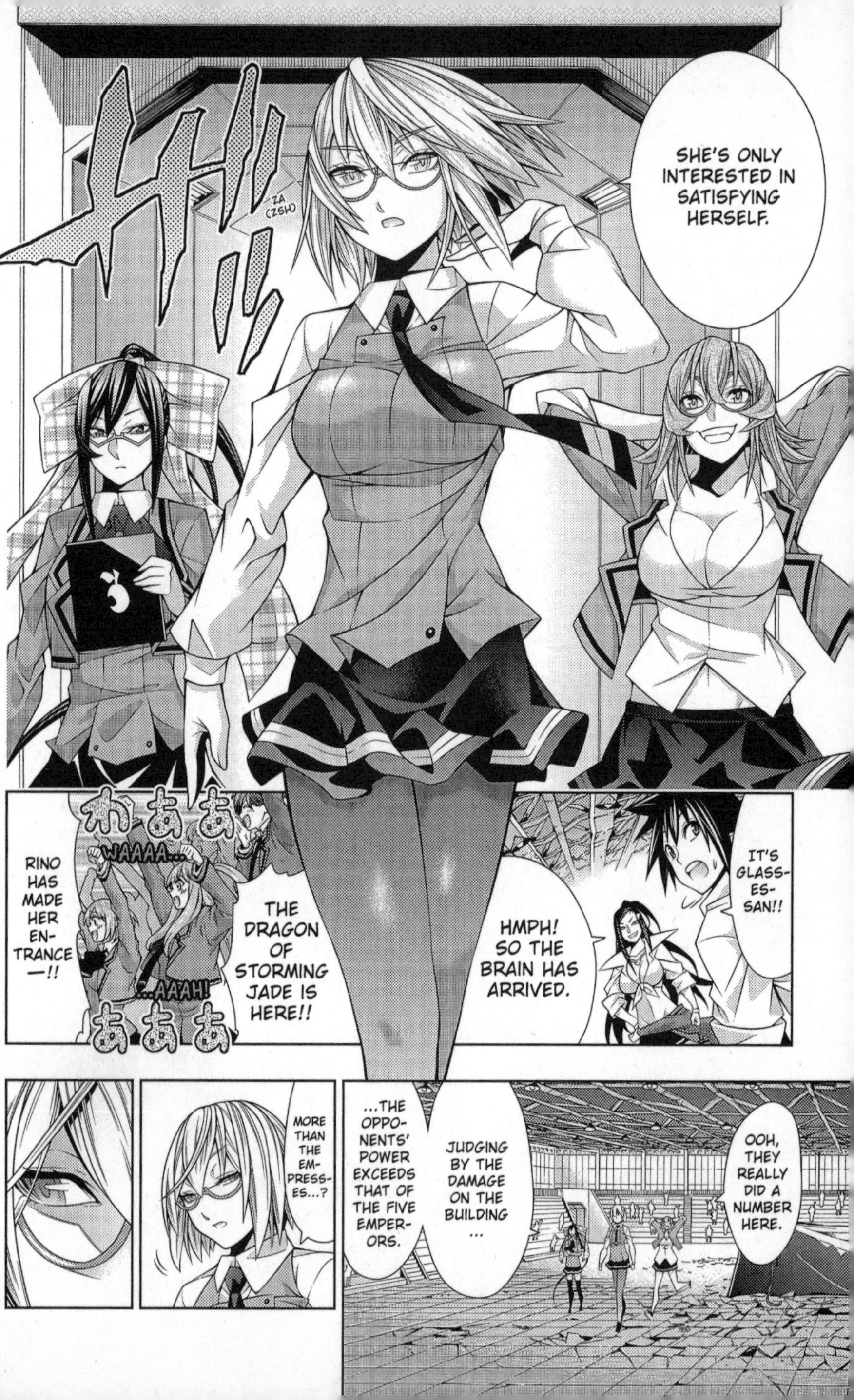
ZA (ZSH)
SHE'S ONLY INTERESTED IN SATISFYING HERSELF.
IT'S GLASSES-SAN!!
HMPH! SO THE BRAIN HAS ARRIVED.
THE DRAGON OF STORMING JADE IS HERE!!
RINO HAS MADE HER ENTRANCE—!!
わああ
WAAAA...
...AAAH!
あああ
OOH, THEY REALLY DID A NUMBER HERE.
JUDGING BY THE DAMAGE ON THE BUILDING...
...THE OPPONENTS' POWER EXCEEDS THAT OF THE FIVE EMPERORS.
MORE THAN THE EMPRESSES...?

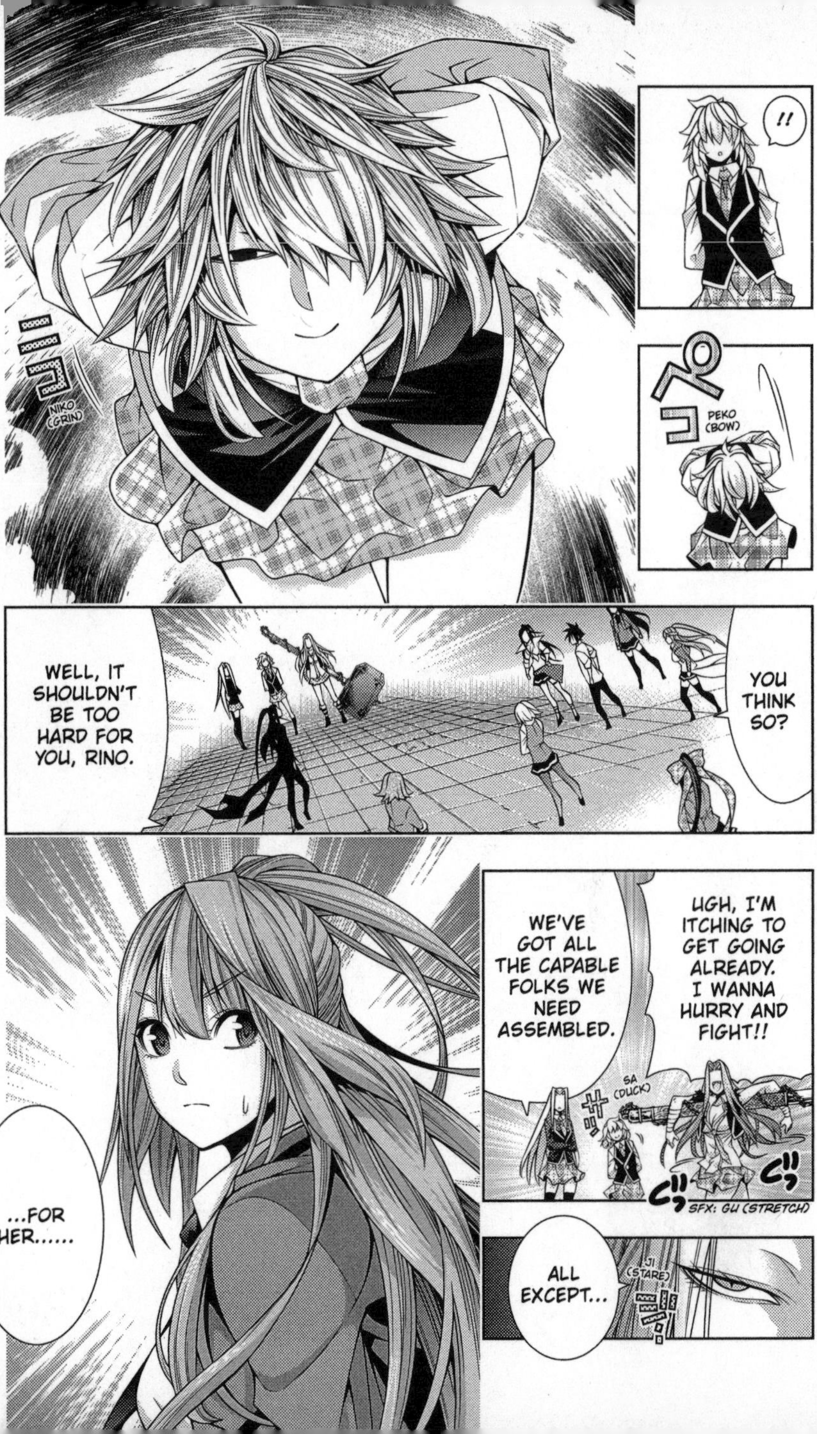
!!
PEKO (BOW)
NIKO (GRIN)
YOU THINK SO?
WELL, IT SHOULDN'T BE TOO HARD FOR YOU, RINO.
UGH, I'M ITCHING TO GET GOING ALREADY. I WANNA HURRY AND FIGHT!!
WE'VE GOT ALL THE CAPABLE FOLKS WE NEED ASSEMBLED.
SA (DUCK)
SFX: GU (STRETCH)
ALL EXCEPT...
JI (STARE)
...FOR HER......

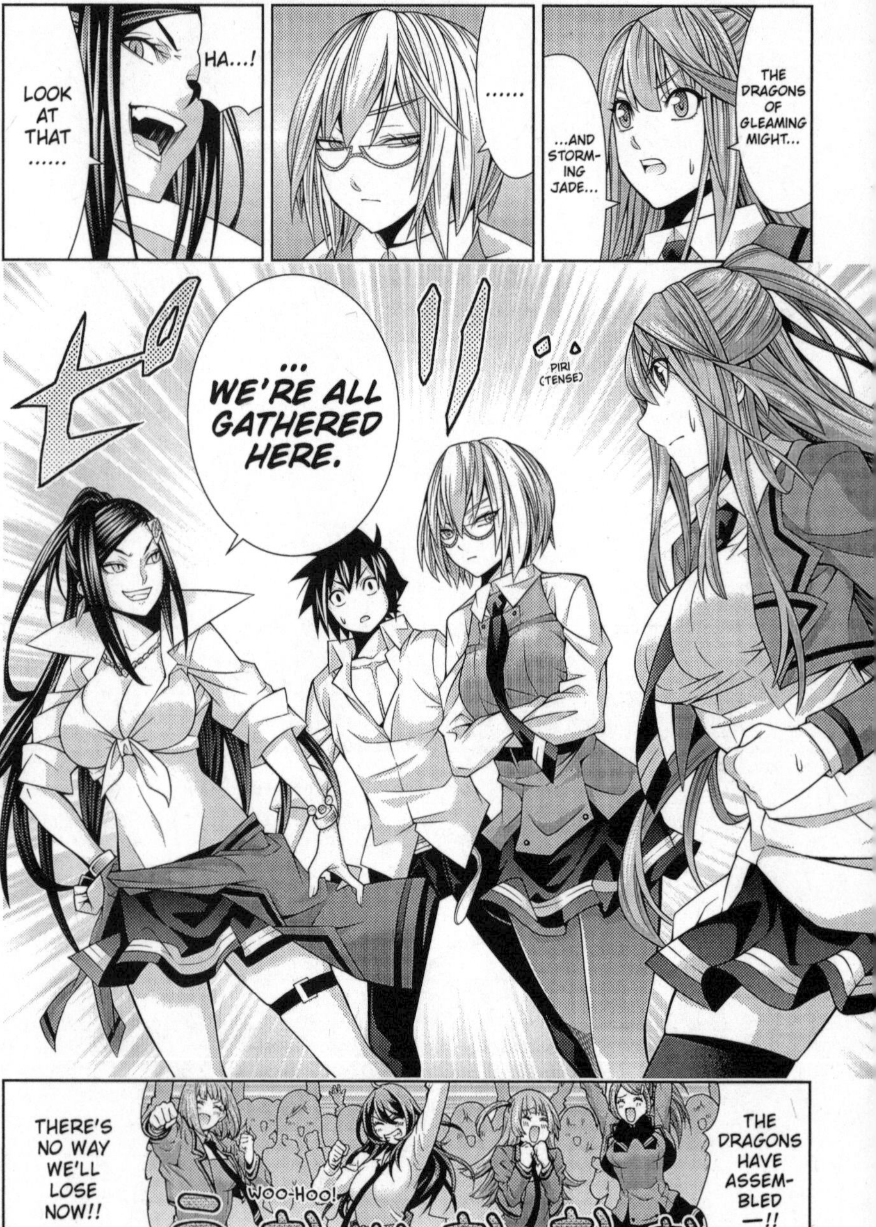
THE DRAGONS OF GLEAMING MIGHT...
...AND STORMING-ING JADE...
......
HA...!
LOOK AT THAT ......
PIRI (TENSE)
... WE'RE ALL GATHERED HERE.
THE DRAGONS HAVE ASSEM-BLED —!!
WOO-HOO!
うおおおおお
THERE'S NO WAY WE'LL LOSE NOW!!

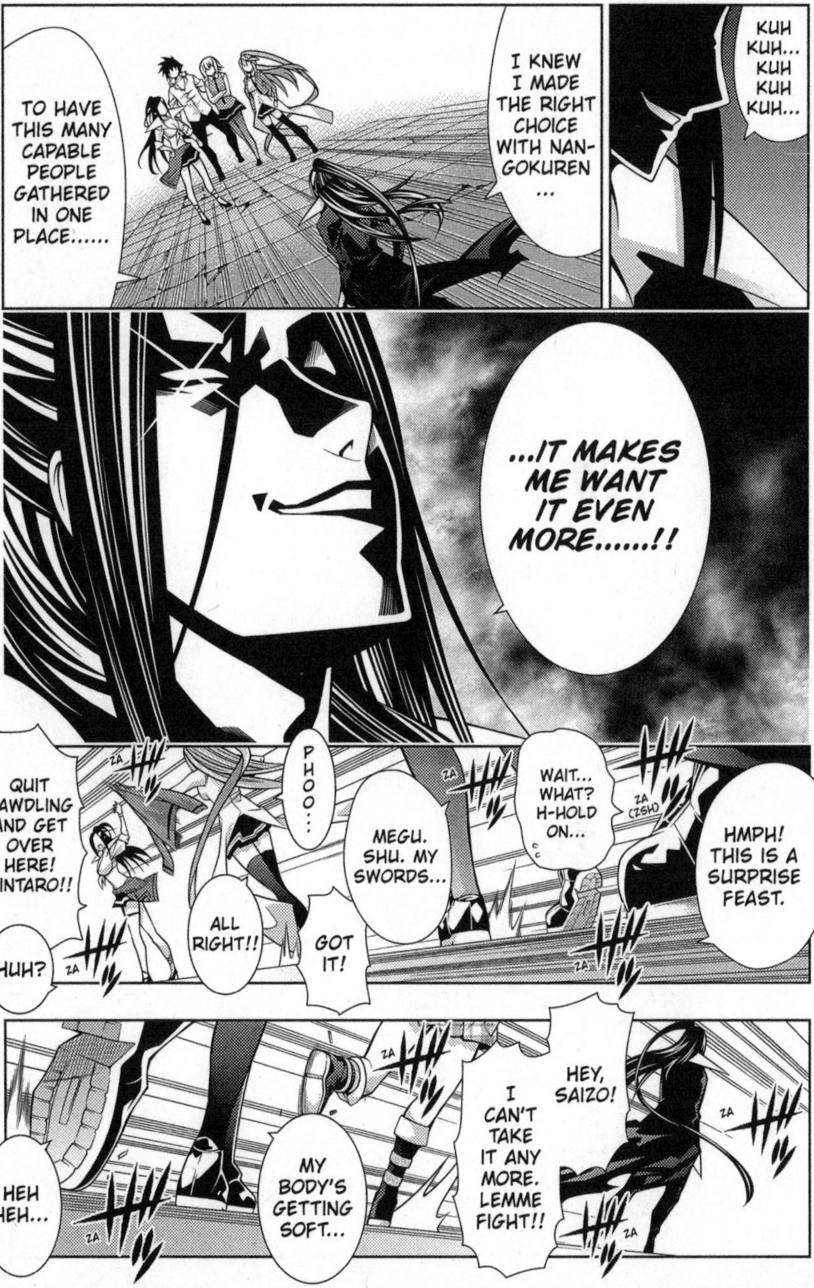
KUH KUH... KUH KUH KUH...
I KNEW I MADE THE RIGHT CHOICE WITH NAN-GOKUREN ...
TO HAVE THIS MANY CAPABLE PEOPLE GATHERED IN ONE PLACE......
...IT MAKES ME WANT IT EVEN MORE......!!
ZA
HMPH! THIS IS A SURPRISE FEAST.
ZA (ZSH)
WAIT... WHAT? H-HOLD ON...
ZA
MEGU. SHU. MY SWORDS...
GOT IT!
PHOOO...
ALL RIGHT!!
ZA
QUIT DAWDLING AND GET OVER HERE! RINTARO!!
ZA
HUH?
ZA
HEY, SAIZO!
ZA
ZA
I CAN'T TAKE IT ANY MORE. LEMME FIGHT!!
ZA
MY BODY'S GETTING SOFT...
ZA
HEH HEH...

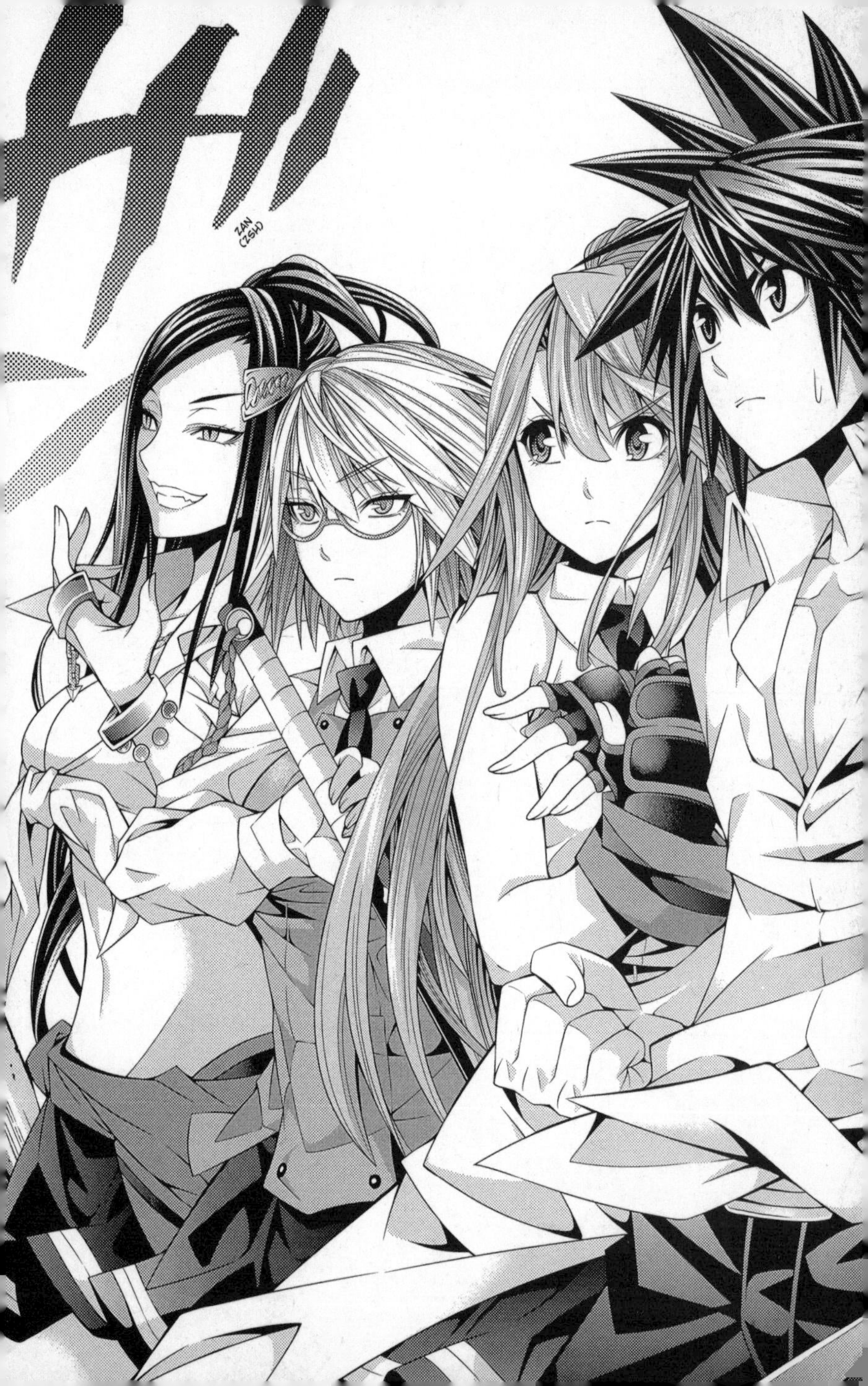
ZAN
(ZSH)

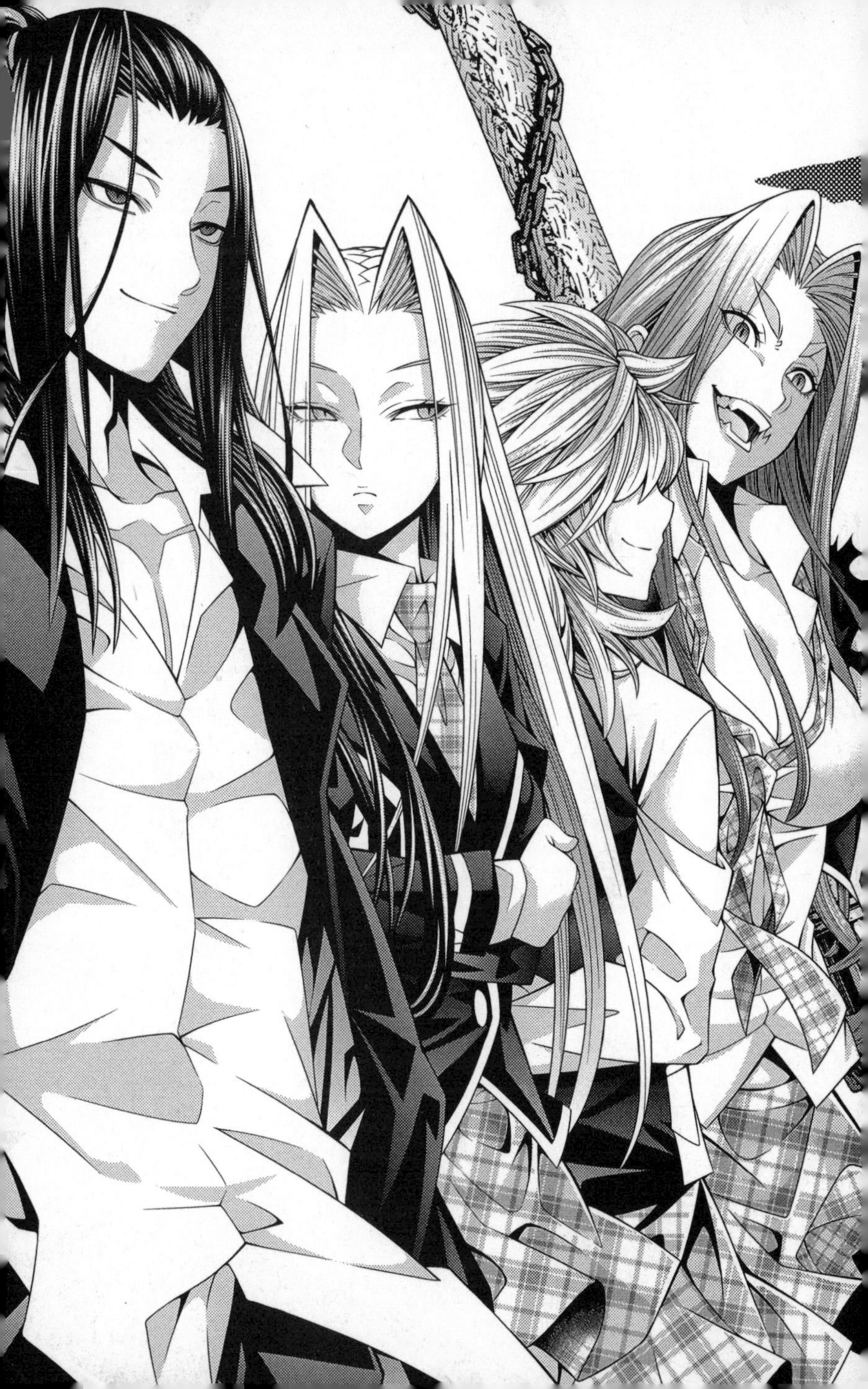

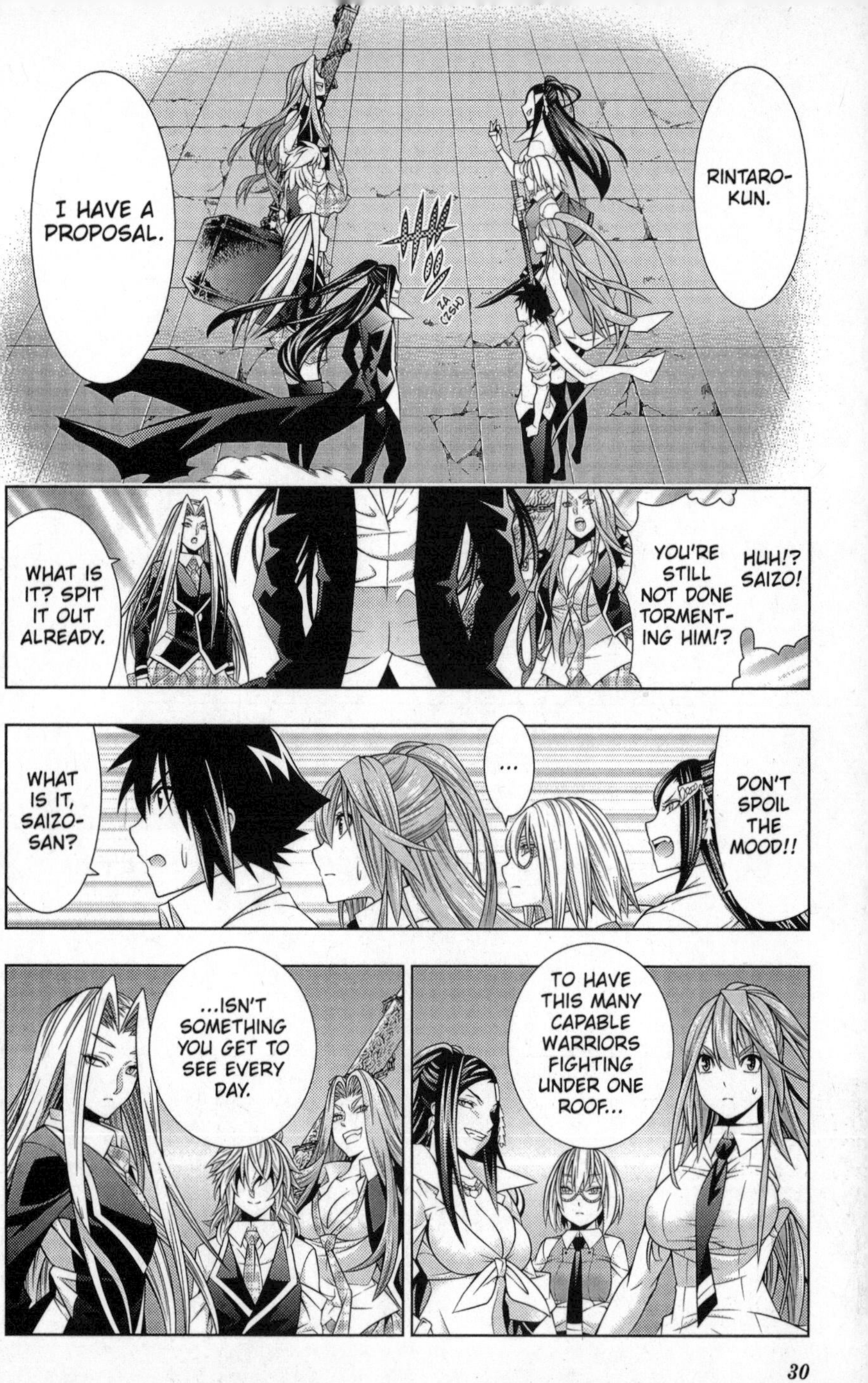
RINTARO-KUN.
I HAVE A PROPOSAL.
ZA (ZSH)
HUH!? SAIZO!
YOU'RE STILL NOT DONE TORMENT-ING HIM!?
WHAT IS IT? SPIT IT OUT ALREADY.
DON'T SPOIL THE MOOD!!
...
WHAT IS IT, SAIZO-SAN?
TO HAVE THIS MANY CAPABLE WARRIORS FIGHTING UNDER ONE ROOF...
...ISN'T SOMETHING YOU GET TO SEE EVERY DAY.

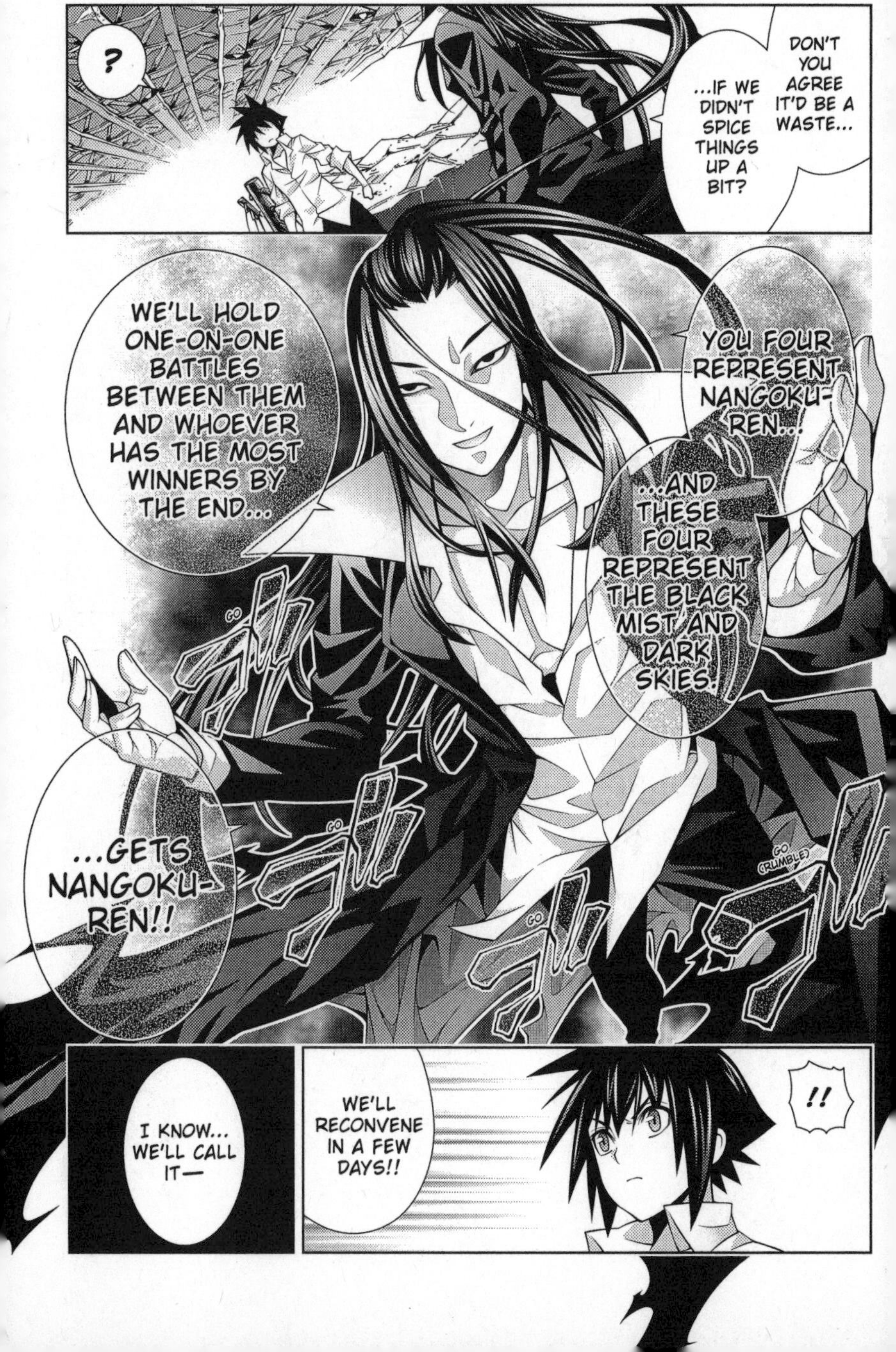
DON'T YOU AGREE IT'D BE A WASTE...
...IF WE DIDN'T SPICE THINGS UP A BIT?
?
YOU FOUR REPRESENT NANGOKU-REN...
...AND THESE FOUR REPRESENT THE BLACK MIST AND DARK SKIES.
WE'LL HOLD ONE-ON-ONE BATTLES BETWEEN THEM AND WHOEVER HAS THE MOST WINNERS BY THE END...
...GETS NANGOKU-REN!!
GO
GO
GO (RUMBLE)
GO
!!
WE'LL RECONVENE IN A FEW DAYS!!
I KNOW... WE'LL CALL IT—

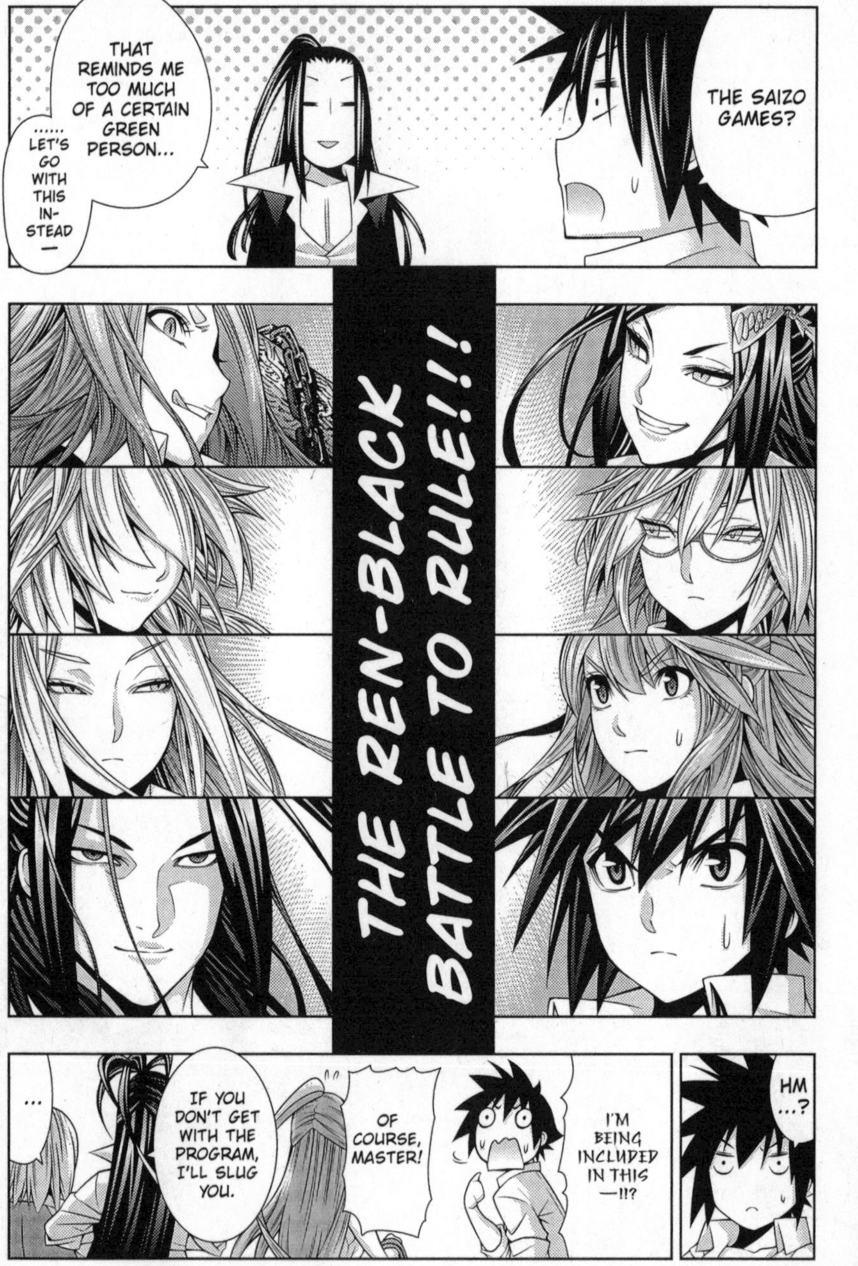
THE SAIZO GAMES?
THAT REMINDS ME TOO MUCH OF A CERTAIN GREEN PERSON...
......LET'S GO WITH THIS IN-STEAD—
THE REN-BLACK BATTLE TO RULE!!!
HM ...?
I'M BEING INCLUDED IN THIS —!!?
OF COURSE, MASTER!
IF YOU DON'T GET WITH THE PROGRAM, I'LL SLUG YOU.
...

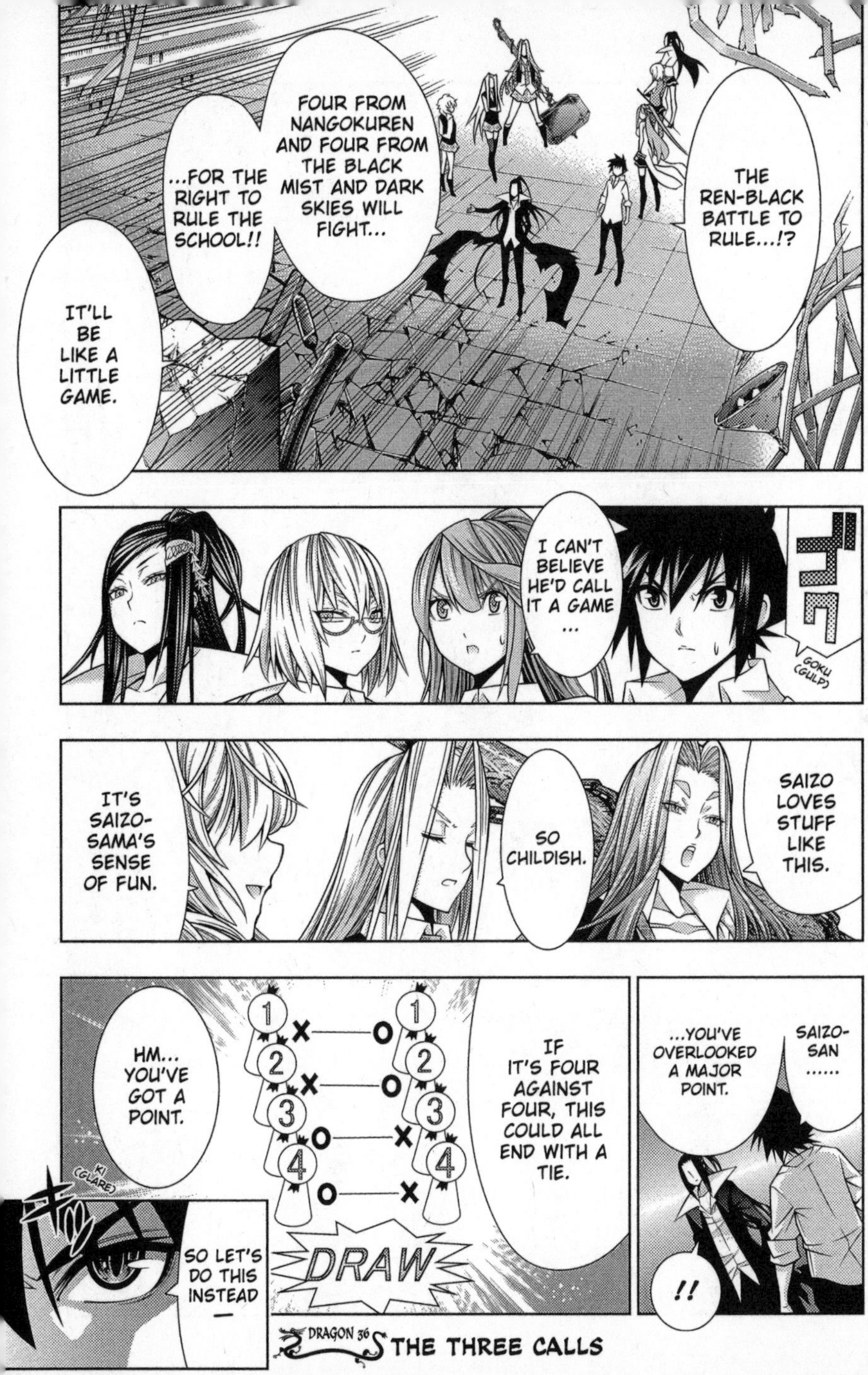
THE REN-BLACK BATTLE TO RULE...!?
FOUR FROM NANGOKUREN AND FOUR FROM THE BLACK MIST AND DARK SKIES WILL FIGHT...
...FOR THE RIGHT TO RULE THE SCHOOL!!
IT'LL BE LIKE A LITTLE GAME.
GOKU (GULP)
I CAN'T BELIEVE HE'D CALL IT A GAME ...
SAIZO LOVES STUFF LIKE THIS.
SO CHILDISH.
IT'S SAIZO-SAMA'S SENSE OF FUN.
SAIZO-SAN ......
...YOU'VE OVERLOOKED A MAJOR POINT.
!!
IF IT'S FOUR AGAINST FOUR, THIS COULD ALL END WITH A TIE.
1
2
3
4
DRAW
HM... YOU'VE GOT A POINT.
KI (GLARE)
SO LET'S DO THIS INSTEAD —

DRAGON 36 THE THREE CALLS

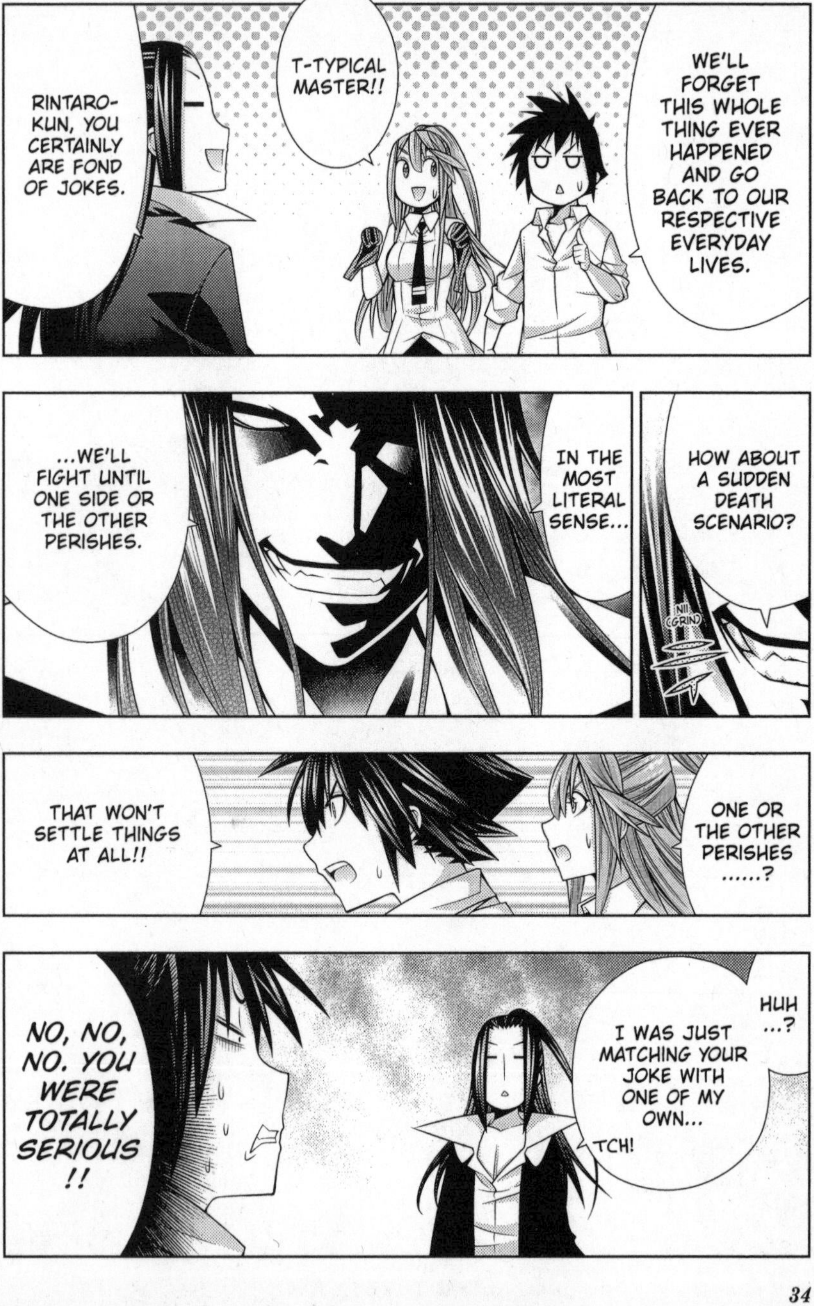
WE'LL FORGET THIS WHOLE THING EVER HAPPENED AND GO BACK TO OUR RESPECTIVE EVERYDAY LIVES.
T-TYPICAL MASTER!!
RINTARO-KUN, YOU CERTAINLY ARE FOND OF JOKES.
HOW ABOUT A SUDDEN DEATH SCENARIO?
NII (GRIN)
IN THE MOST LITERAL SENSE...
...WE'LL FIGHT UNTIL ONE SIDE OR THE OTHER PERISHES.
ONE OR THE OTHER PERISHES ......?
THAT WON'T SETTLE THINGS AT ALL!!
HUH ...?
I WAS JUST MATCHING YOUR JOKE WITH ONE OF MY OWN...
TCH!
NO, NO, NO. YOU WERE TOTALLY SERIOUS !!

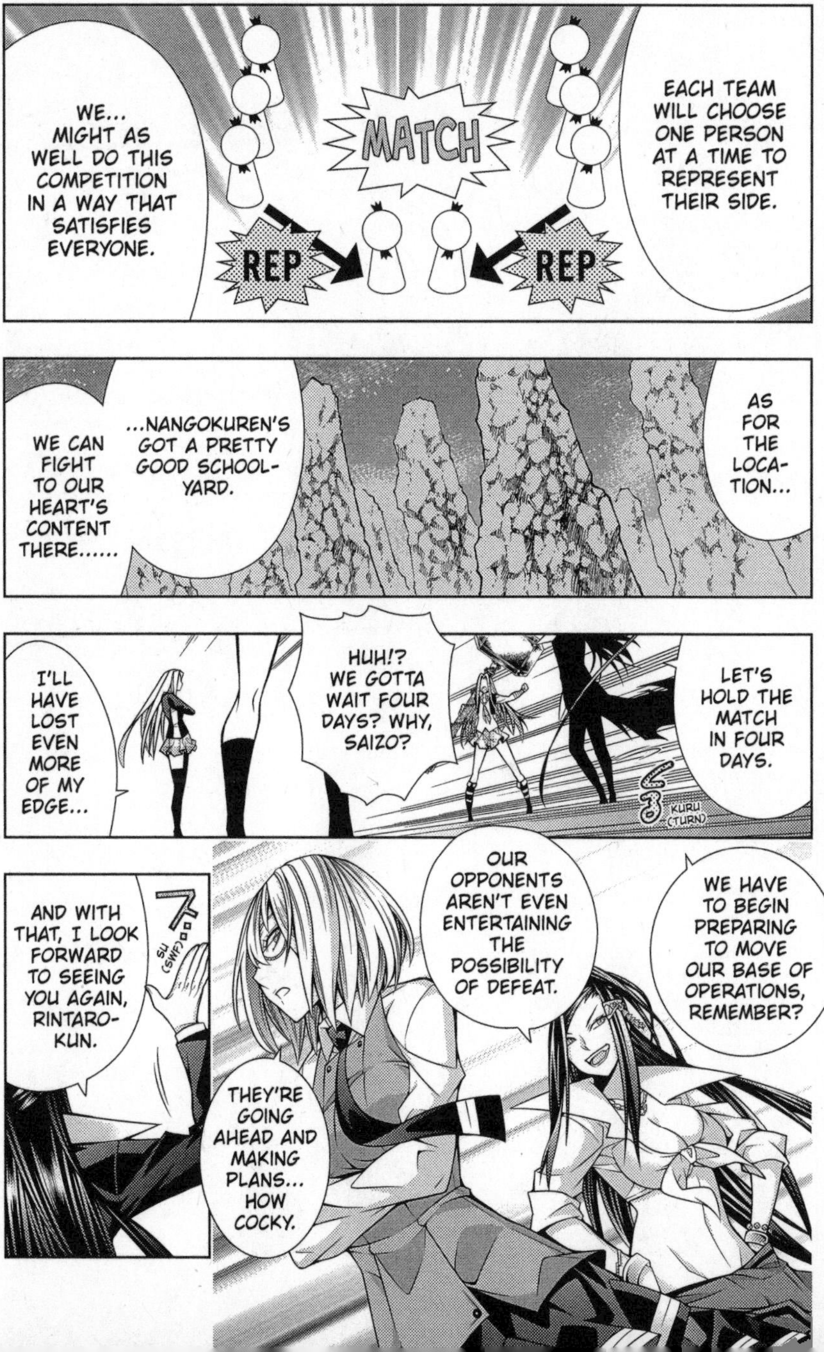
EACH TEAM WILL CHOOSE ONE PERSON AT A TIME TO REPRESENT THEIR SIDE.
MATCH
REP
REP
WE... MIGHT AS WELL DO THIS COMPETITION IN A WAY THAT SATISFIES EVERYONE.
AS FOR THE LOCA-TION...
...NANGOKUREN'S GOT A PRETTY GOOD SCHOOL-YARD.
WE CAN FIGHT TO OUR HEART'S CONTENT THERE......
LET'S HOLD THE MATCH IN FOUR DAYS.
KURU (TURN)
HUH!? WE GOTTA WAIT FOUR DAYS? WHY, SAIZO?
I'LL HAVE LOST EVEN MORE OF MY EDGE...
WE HAVE TO BEGIN PREPARING TO MOVE OUR BASE OF OPERATIONS, REMEMBER?
OUR OPPONENTS AREN'T EVEN ENTERTAINING THE POSSIBILITY OF DEFEAT.
THEY'RE GOING AHEAD AND MAKING PLANS... HOW COCKY.
AND WITH THAT, I LOOK FORWARD TO SEEING YOU AGAIN, RINTARO-KUN.
SU (SWF)

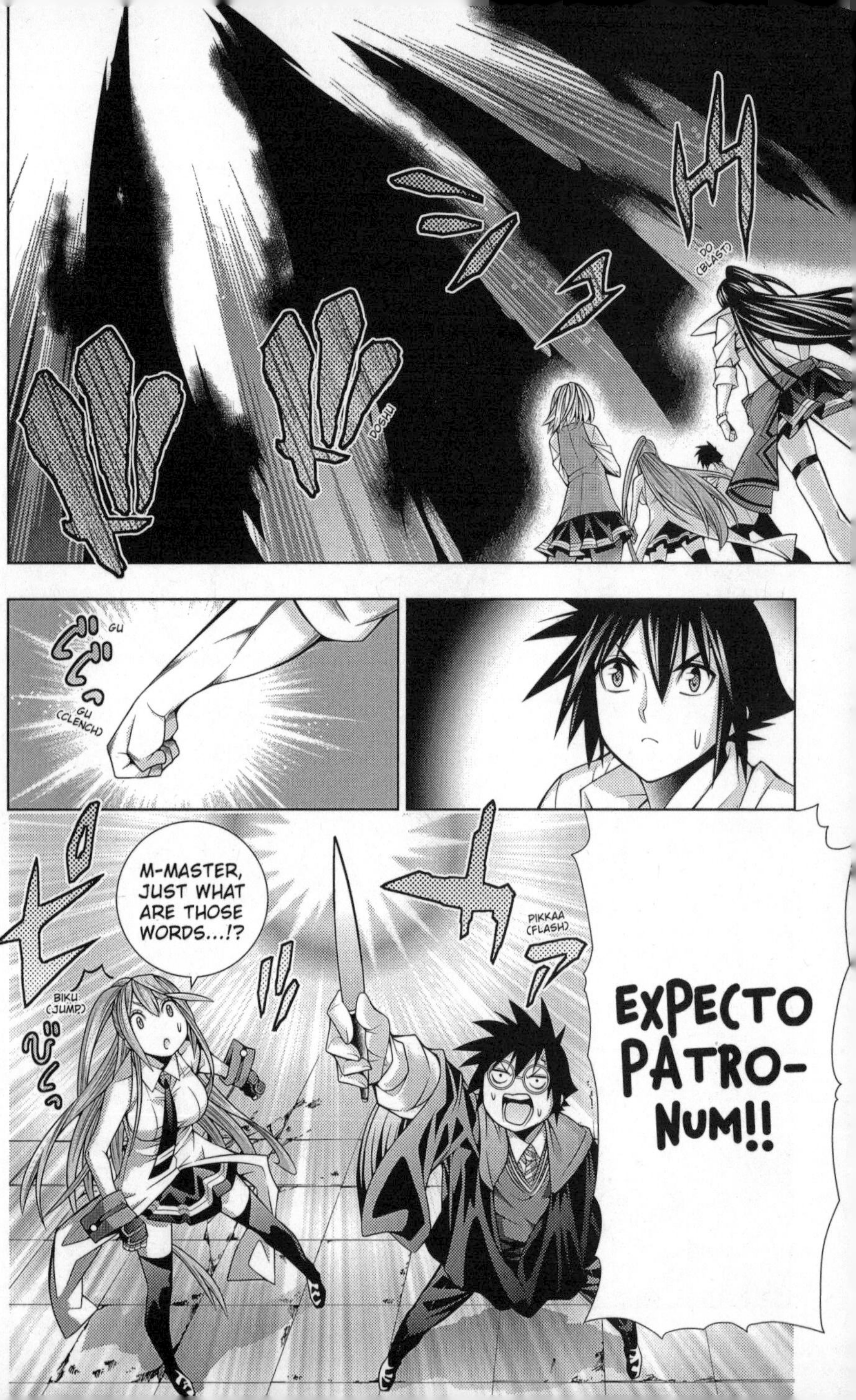
DO (BLAST)
DOSHU
GU
GU (CLENCH)
EXPECTO PATRO-NUM!!
PIKKAA (FLASH)
M-MASTER, JUST WHAT ARE THOSE WORDS...!?
BIKU (JUMP)

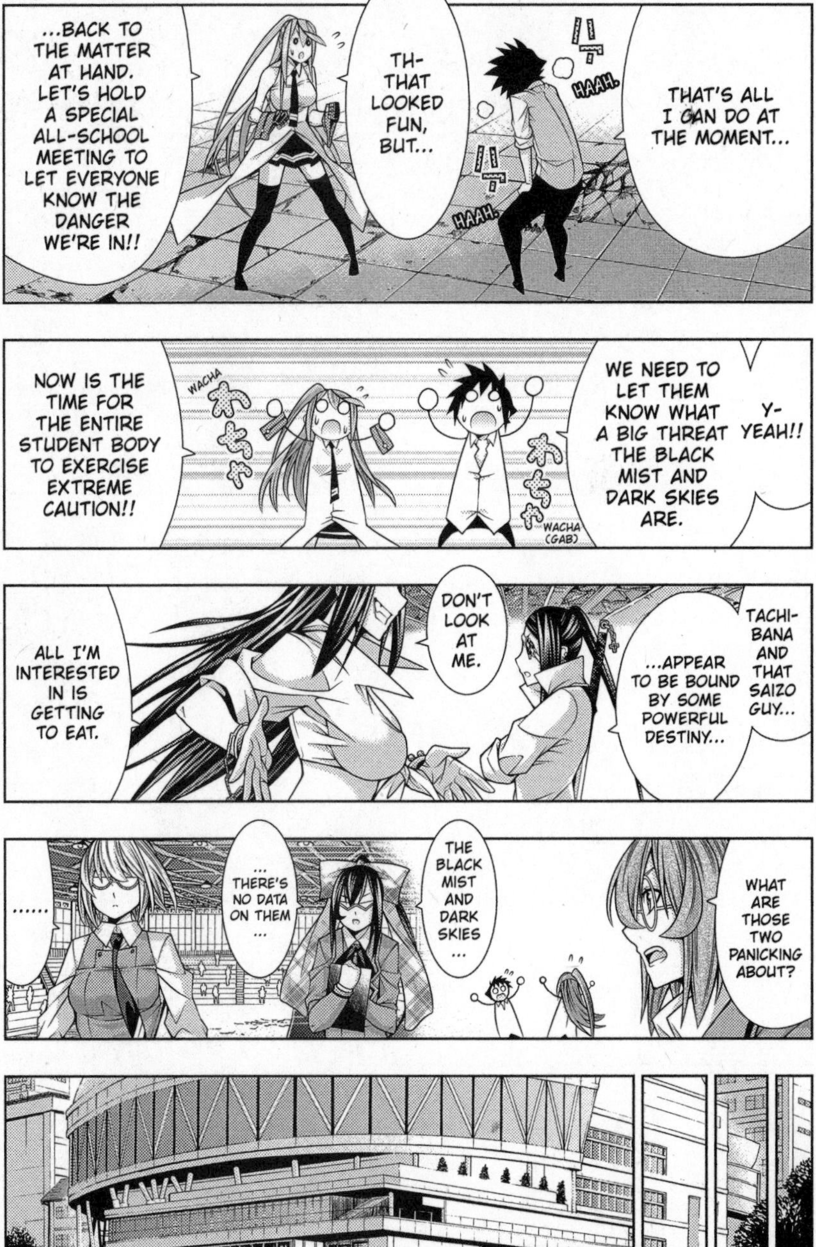
THAT'S ALL I CAN DO AT THE MOMENT...
HAAH.
HAAH.
TH- THAT LOOKED FUN, BUT...
...BACK TO THE MATTER AT HAND. LET'S HOLD A SPECIAL ALL-SCHOOL MEETING TO LET EVERYONE KNOW THE DANGER WE'RE IN!!
Y-YEAH!!
WE NEED TO LET THEM KNOW WHAT A BIG THREAT THE BLACK MIST AND DARK SKIES ARE.
WACHA (GAB)
WACHA
NOW IS THE TIME FOR THE ENTIRE STUDENT BODY TO EXERCISE EXTREME CAUTION!!
TACHIBANA AND THAT SAIZO GUY...
...APPEAR TO BE BOUND BY SOME POWERFUL DESTINY...
DON'T LOOK AT ME.
ALL I'M INTERESTED IN IS GETTING TO EAT.
WHAT ARE THOSE TWO PANICKING ABOUT?
THE BLACK MIST AND DARK SKIES...
...THERE'S NO DATA ON THEM...
......

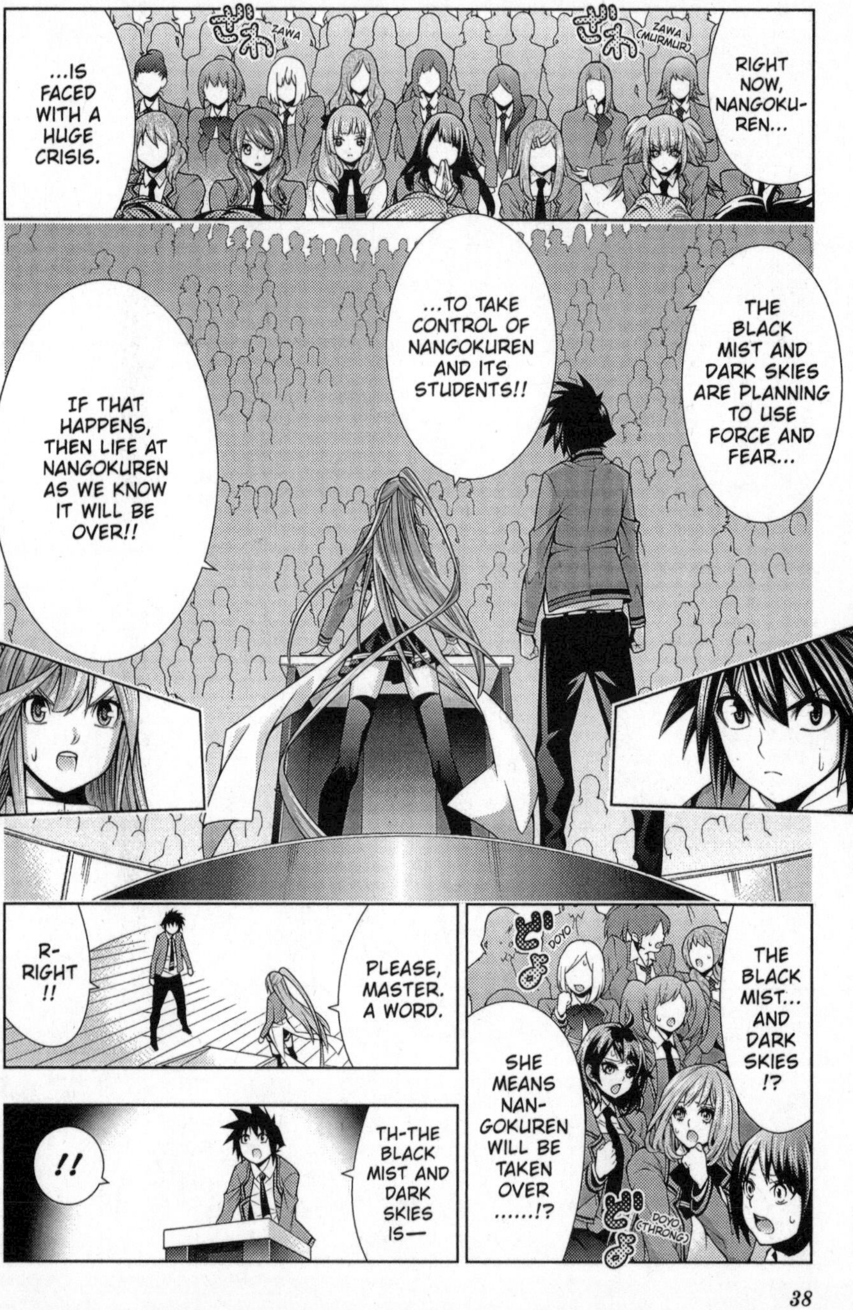
ざわ ZAWA (MURMUR)
ざわ ZAWA
RIGHT NOW, NANGOKU-REN...
...IS FACED WITH A HUGE CRISIS.
THE BLACK MIST AND DARK SKIES ARE PLANNING TO USE FORCE AND FEAR...
...TO TAKE CONTROL OF NANGOKUREN AND ITS STUDENTS!!
IF THAT HAPPENS, THEN LIFE AT NANGOKUREN AS WE KNOW IT WILL BE OVER!!
どよ DOYO
THE BLACK MIST... AND DARK SKIES !?
SHE MEANS NAN-GOKUREN WILL BE TAKEN OVER ......!?
どよ DOYO (THRONG)
PLEASE, MASTER. A WORD.
R-RIGHT !!
TH-THE BLACK MIST AND DARK SKIES IS—
!!

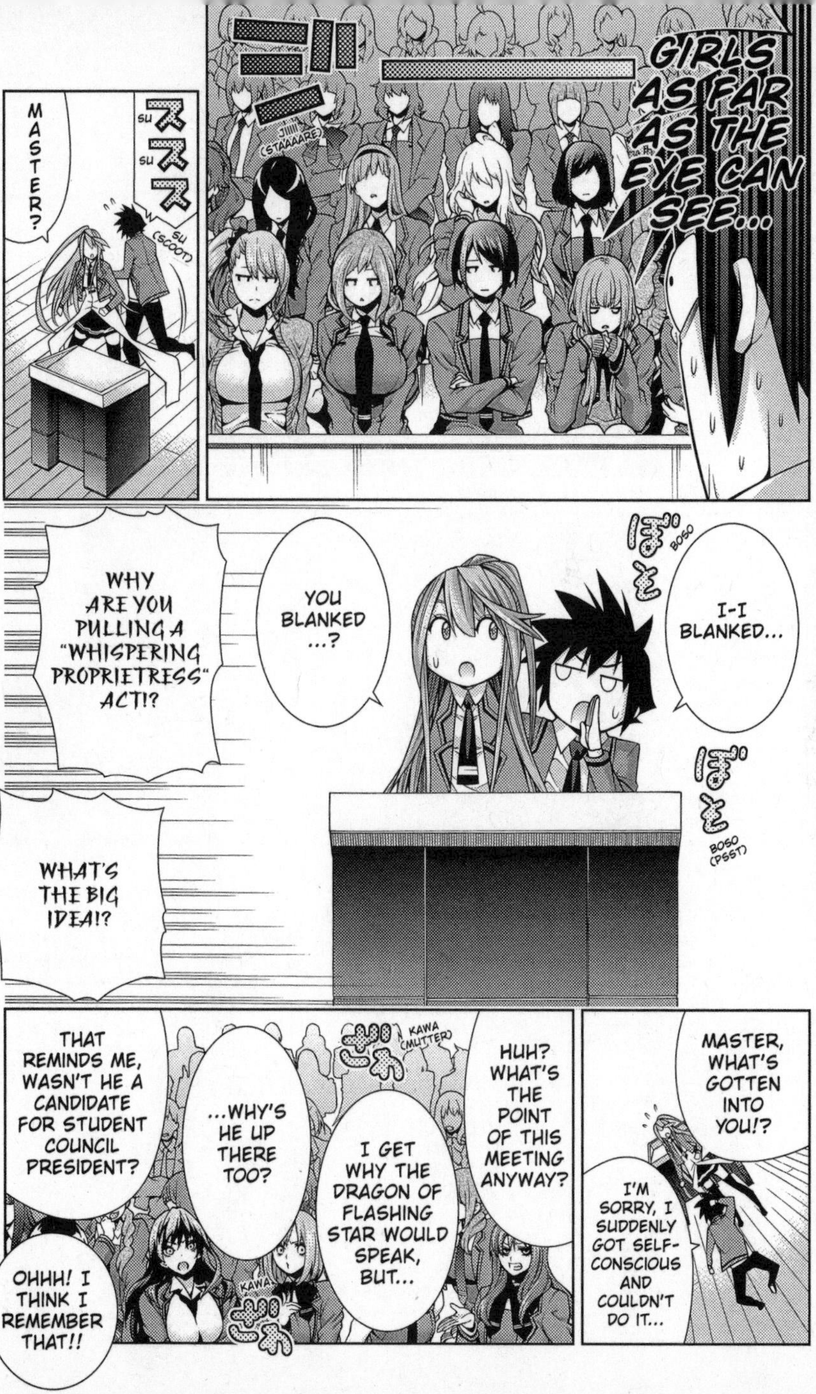
GIRLS AS FAR AS THE EYE CAN SEE...
JIIIII (STAAAARE)
SU SU SU (SCOOT)
MASTER?
BOSO
I-I BLANKED...
YOU BLANKED ...?
BOSO (PSST)
WHY ARE YOU PULLING A "WHISPERING PROPRIETRESS" ACT!?
WHAT'S THE BIG IDEA!?
MASTER, WHAT'S GOTTEN INTO YOU!?
I'M SORRY, I SUDDENLY GOT SELF-CONSCIOUS AND COULDN'T DO IT...
KAWA (MUTTER)
HUH? WHAT'S THE POINT OF THIS MEETING ANYWAY?
I GET WHY THE DRAGON OF FLASHING STAR WOULD SPEAK, BUT...
...WHY'S HE UP THERE TOO?
THAT REMINDS ME, WASN'T HE A CANDIDATE FOR STUDENT COUNCIL PRESIDENT?
OHHH! I THINK I REMEMBER THAT!!
KAWA

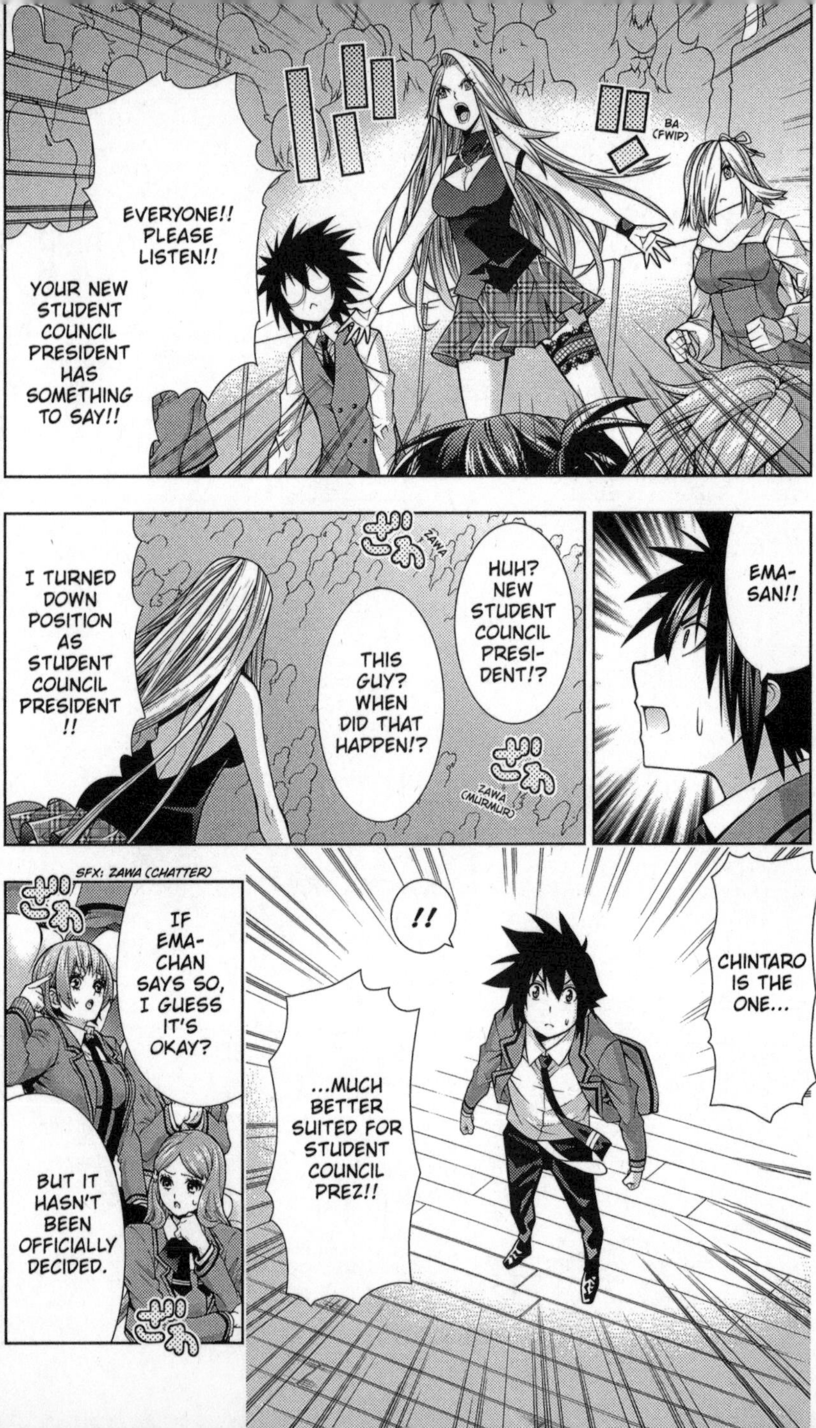
BA (FWIP)
EVERYONE!! PLEASE LISTEN!!
YOUR NEW STUDENT COUNCIL PRESIDENT HAS SOMETHING TO SAY!!
EMA-SAN!!
ZAWA
HUH? NEW STUDENT COUNCIL PRESI-DENT!?
THIS GUY? WHEN DID THAT HAPPEN!?
ZAWA (MURMUR)
I TURNED DOWN POSITION AS STUDENT COUNCIL PRESIDENT!!
CHINTARO IS THE ONE...
!!
...MUCH BETTER SUITED FOR STUDENT COUNCIL PREZ!!
SFX: ZAWA (CHATTER)
IF EMA-CHAN SAYS SO, I GUESS IT'S OKAY?
BUT IT HASN'T BEEN OFFICIALLY DECIDED.

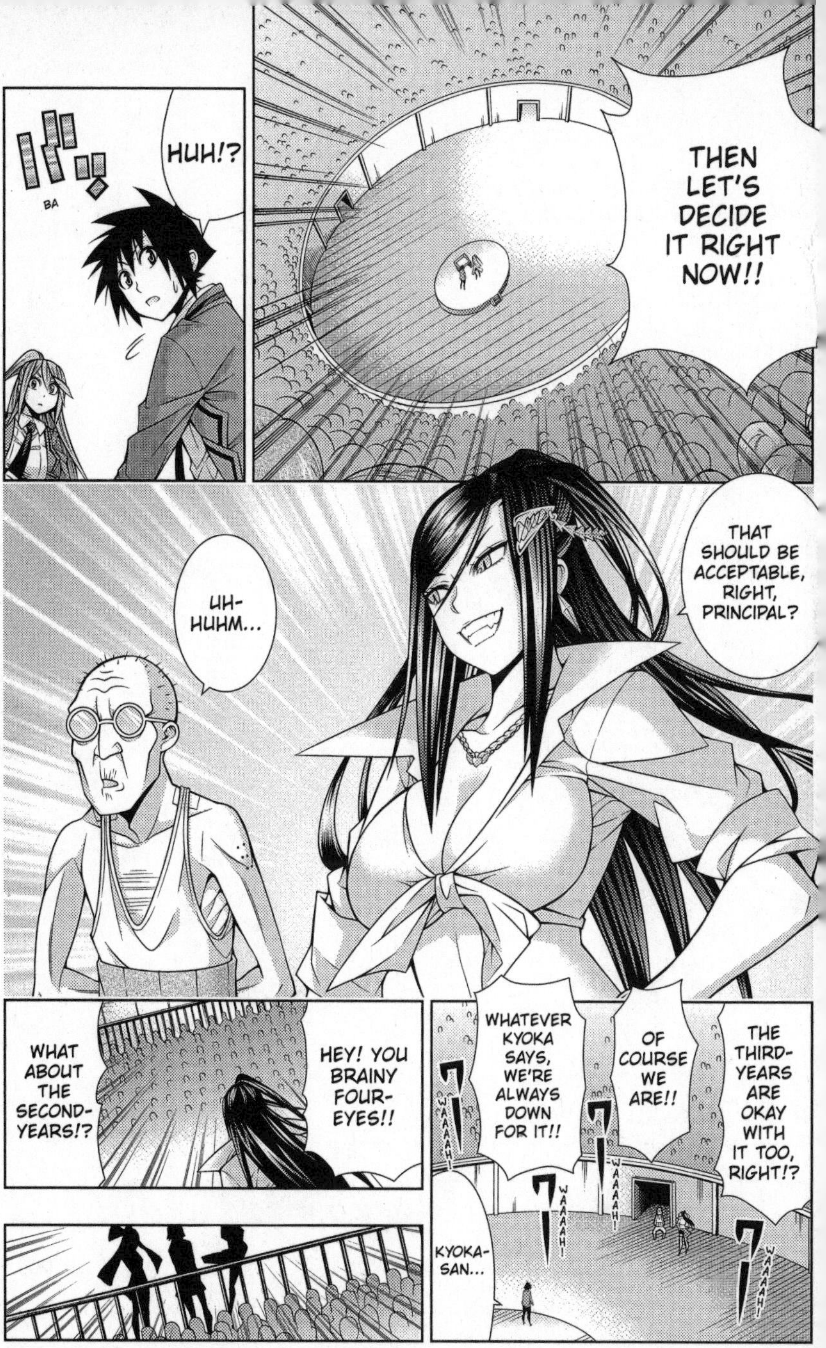
THEN LET'S DECIDE IT RIGHT NOW!!
HUH!?
BA
THAT SHOULD BE ACCEPTABLE, RIGHT, PRINCIPAL?
UH-HUHM...
THE THIRD-YEARS ARE OKAY WITH IT TOO, RIGHT!?
WAAAAH!
OF COURSE WE ARE!!
WAAAAH!
WAAAAH!
WHATEVER KYOKA SAYS, WE'RE ALWAYS DOWN FOR IT!!
WAAAAH!
KYOKA-SAN...
HEY! YOU BRAINY FOUR-EYES!!
WHAT ABOUT THE SECOND-YEARS!?

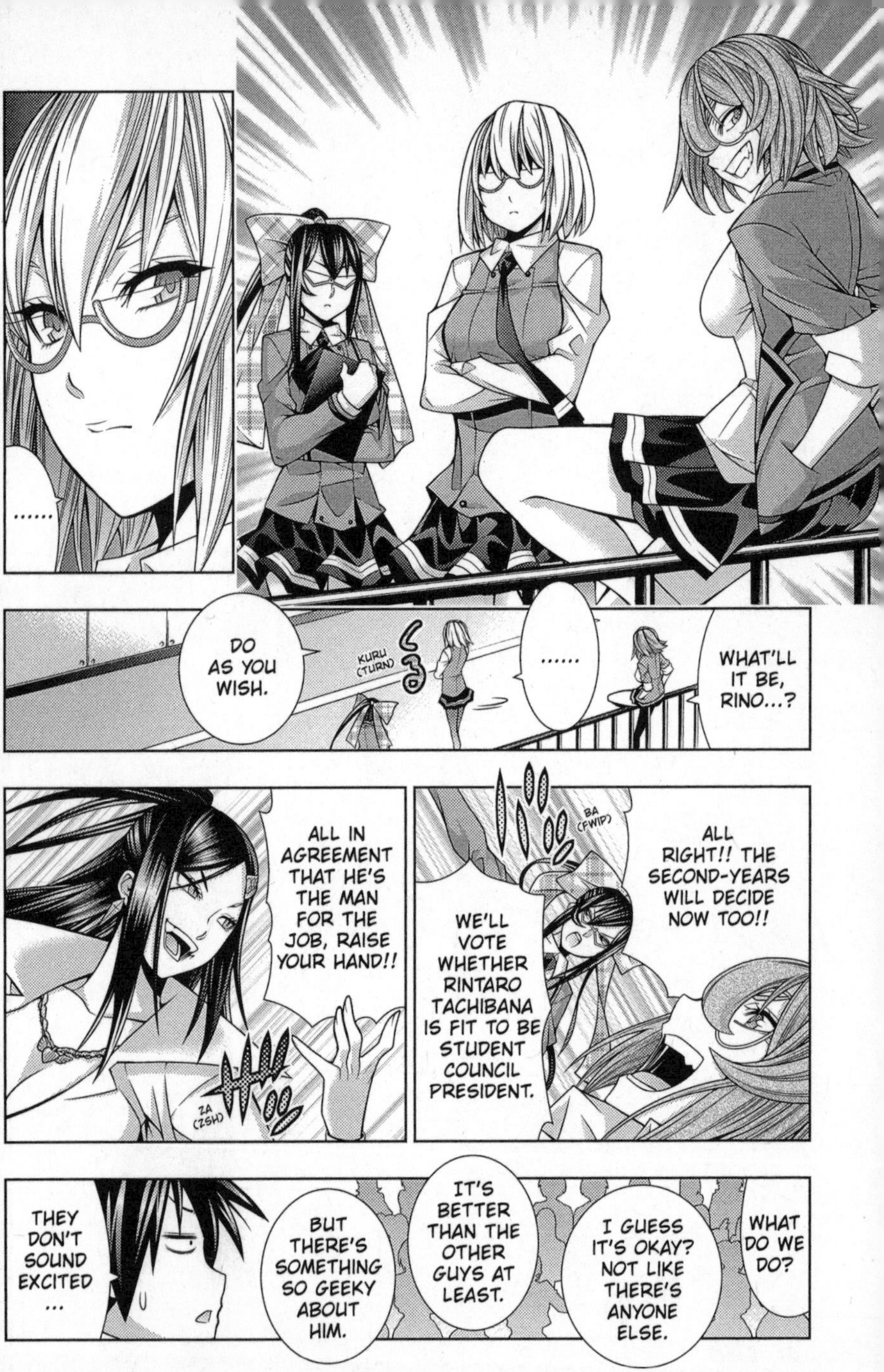

......
WHAT'LL IT BE, RINO...?
......
KURU (TURN)
DO AS YOU WISH.
BA (FWIP)
ALL RIGHT!! THE SECOND-YEARS WILL DECIDE NOW TOO!!
WE'LL VOTE WHETHER RINTARO TACHIBANA IS FIT TO BE STUDENT COUNCIL PRESIDENT.
ALL IN AGREEMENT THAT HE'S THE MAN FOR THE JOB, RAISE YOUR HAND!!
ZA (ZSH)
WHAT DO WE DO?
I GUESS IT'S OKAY? NOT LIKE THERE'S ANYONE ELSE.
IT'S BETTER THAN THE OTHER GUYS AT LEAST.
BUT THERE'S SOMETHING SO GEEKY ABOUT HIM.
THEY DON'T SOUND EXCITED ...

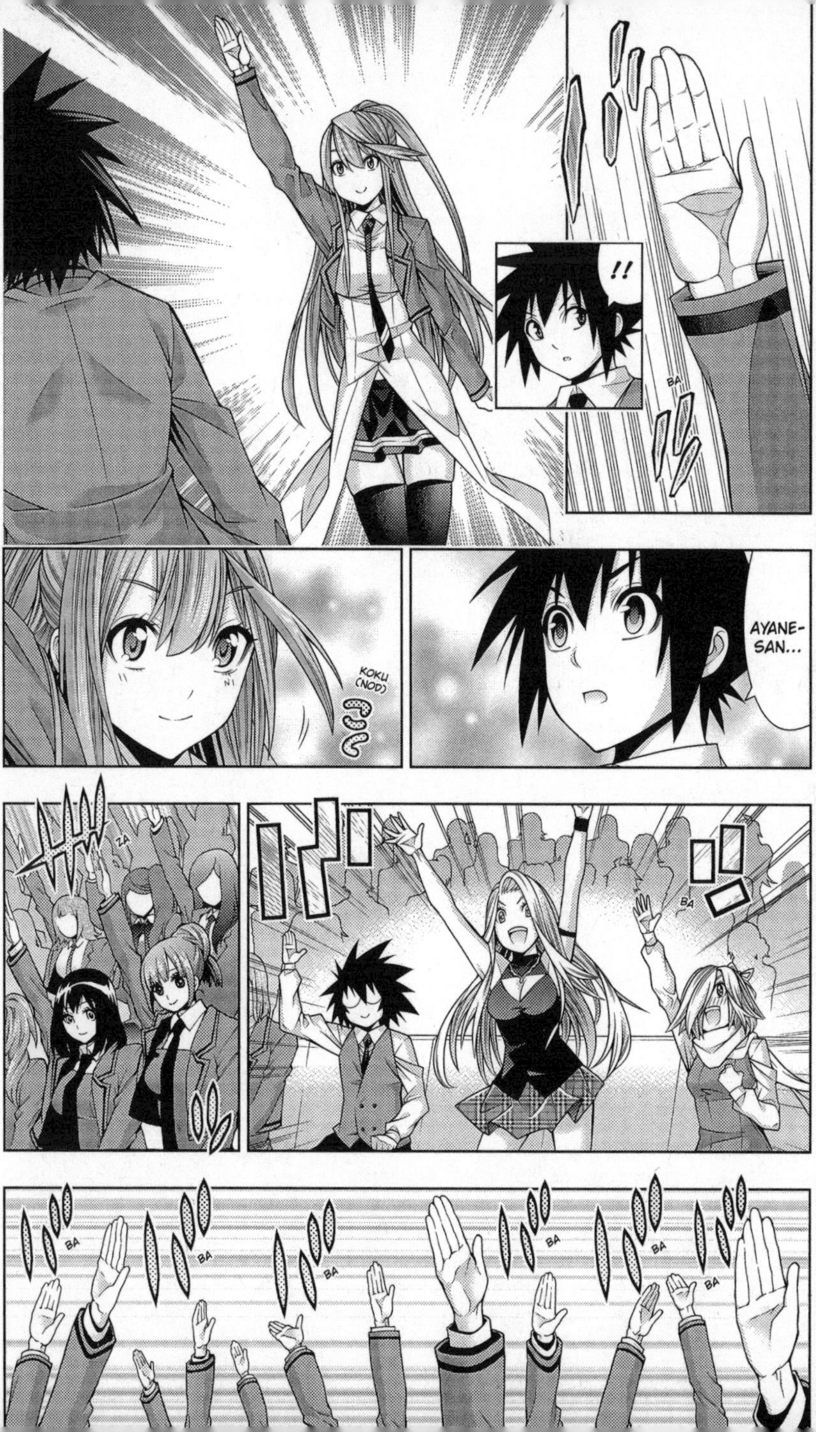
BA
!!
AYANE-SAN...
KOKU (NOD)
BA
ZA
BA
BA
BA
BA
BA
BA

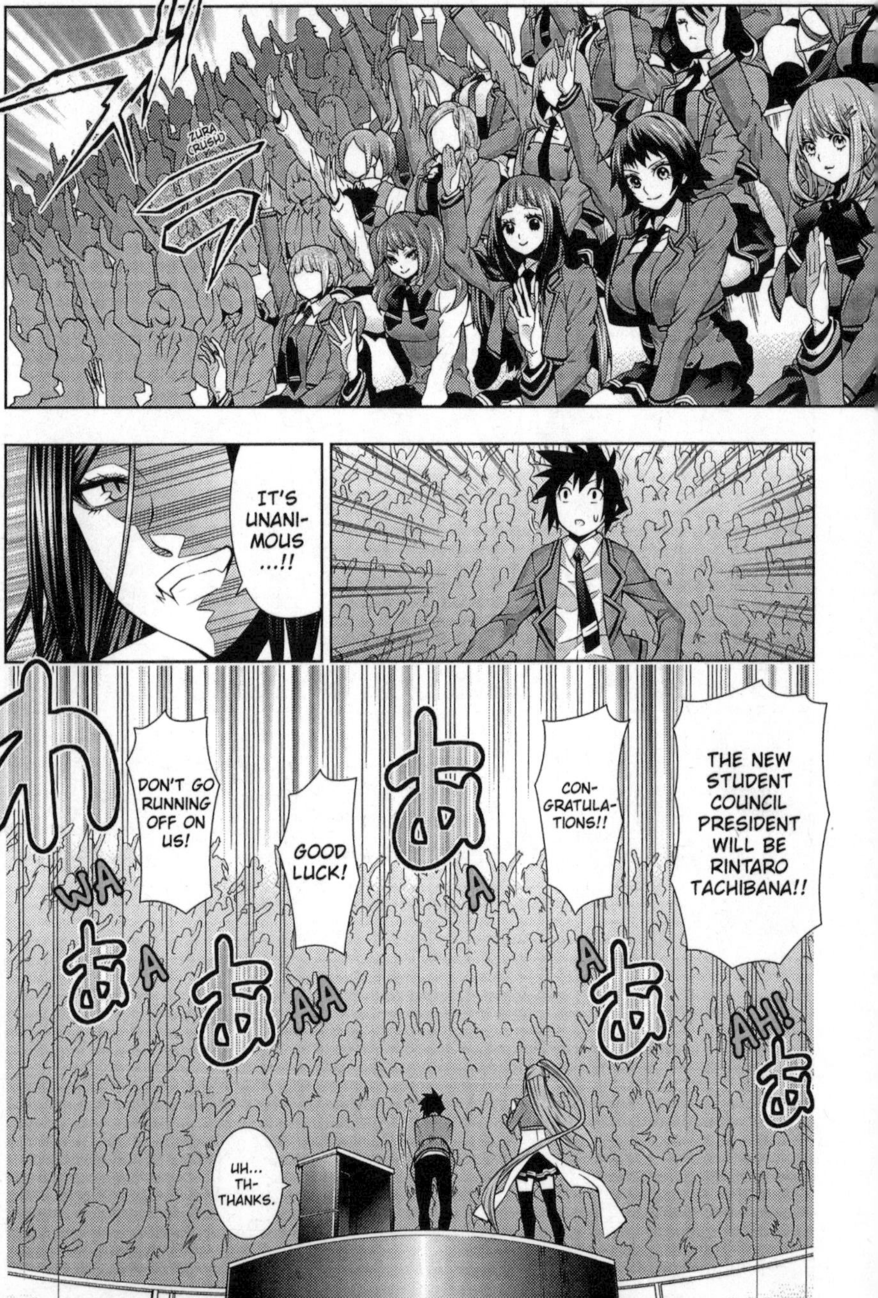
ZURA (CRUSH)
IT'S UNANIMOUS...!!
THE NEW STUDENT COUNCIL PRESIDENT WILL BE RINTARO TACHIBANA!!
CON-GRATULATIONS!!
GOOD LUCK!
DON'T GO RUNNING OFF ON US!
WA A AA A AH!
UH... TH-THANKS.

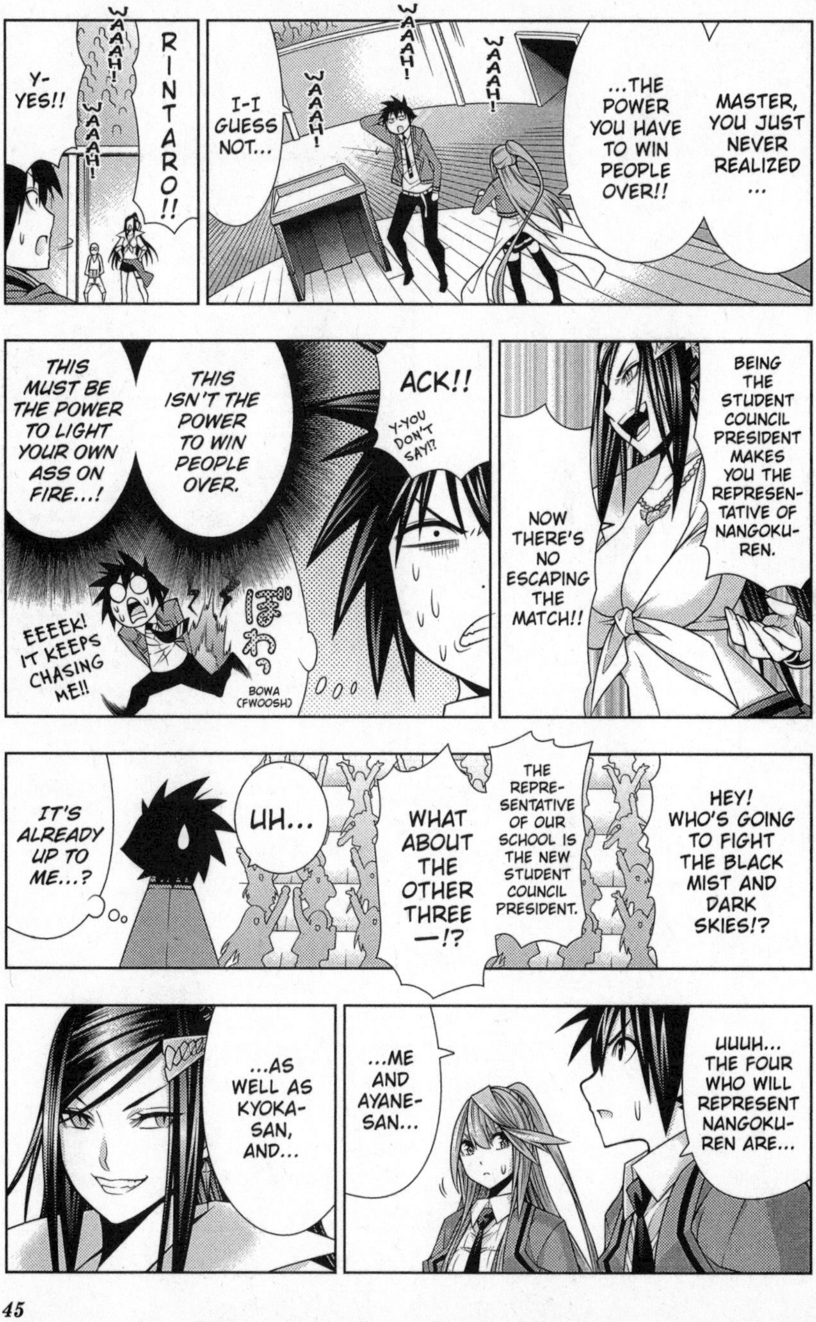
MASTER, YOU JUST NEVER REALIZED...
...THE POWER YOU HAVE TO WIN PEOPLE OVER!!
WAAAAH!
WAAAAH!
WAAAAH!
I-I GUESS NOT...
RINTARO!!
WAAAAH!
WAAAAH!
Y-YES!!
BEING THE STUDENT COUNCIL PRESIDENT MAKES YOU THE REPRESENTATIVE OF NANGOKUREN.
NOW THERE'S NO ESCAPING THE MATCH!!
ACK!!
Y-YOU DON'T SAY!?
THIS ISN'T THE POWER TO WIN PEOPLE OVER.
THIS MUST BE THE POWER TO LIGHT YOUR OWN ASS ON FIRE...!
ぼわっ
BOWA (FWOOSH)
EEEEK! IT KEEPS CHASING ME!!
HEY! WHO'S GOING TO FIGHT THE BLACK MIST AND DARK SKIES!?
THE REPRESENTATIVE OF OUR SCHOOL IS THE NEW STUDENT COUNCIL PRESIDENT.
WHAT ABOUT THE OTHER THREE—!?
UH...
IT'S ALREADY UP TO ME...?
UUUH... THE FOUR WHO WILL REPRESENT NANGOKUREN ARE...
...ME AND AYANE-SAN...
...AS WELL AS KYOKA-SAN, AND...

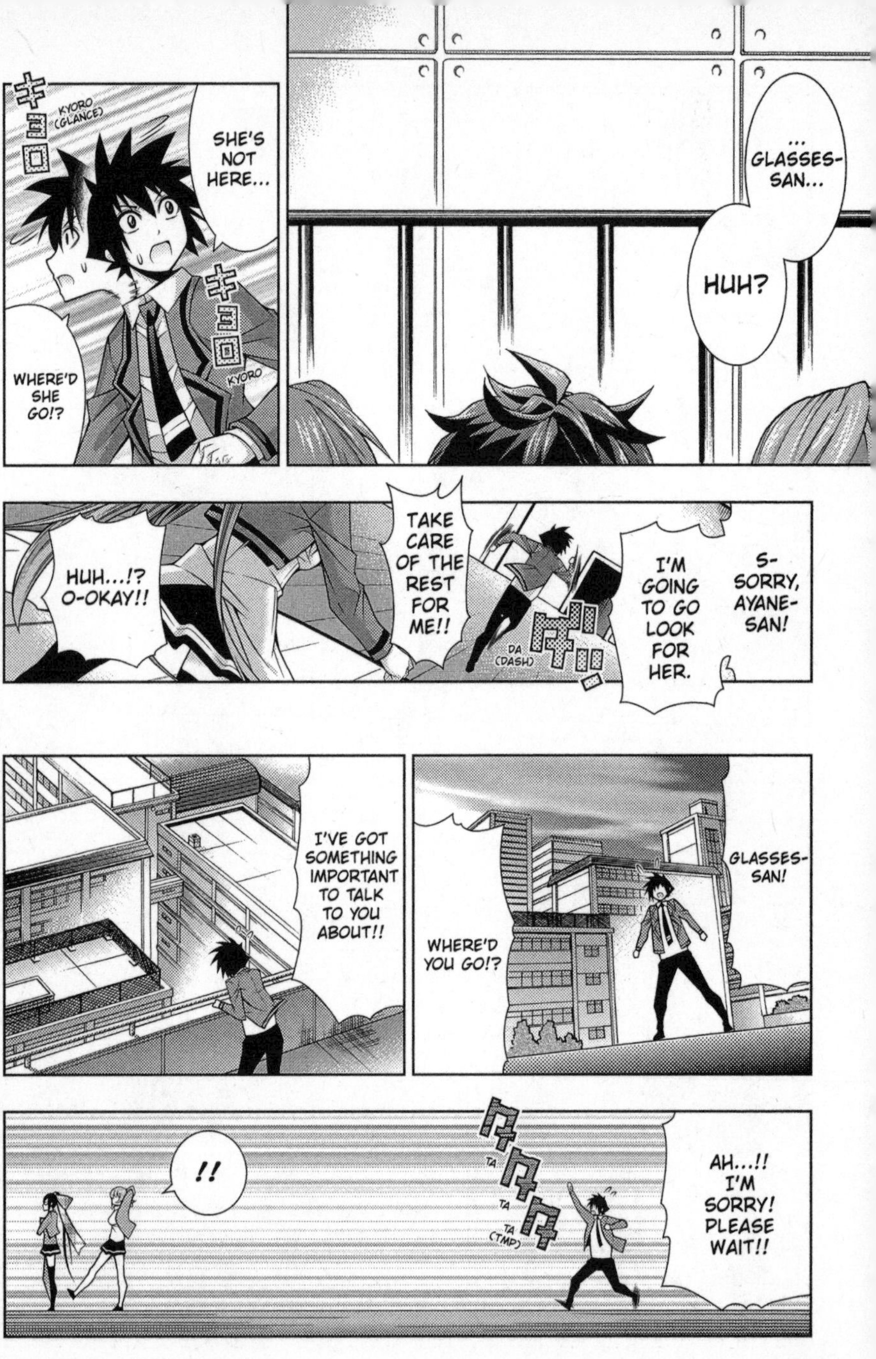
...GLASSES-SAN...
HUH?
KYORO (GLANCE)
SHE'S NOT HERE...
KYORO
WHERE'D SHE GO!?
S-SORRY, AYANE-SAN!
I'M GOING TO GO LOOK FOR HER.
DA (DASH)
TAKE CARE OF THE REST FOR ME!!
HUH...!? O-OKAY!!
GLASSES-SAN!
WHERE'D YOU GO!?
I'VE GOT SOMETHING IMPORTANT TO TALK TO YOU ABOUT!!
AH...!! I'M SORRY! PLEASE WAIT!!
TA TA TA (TMP)
!!

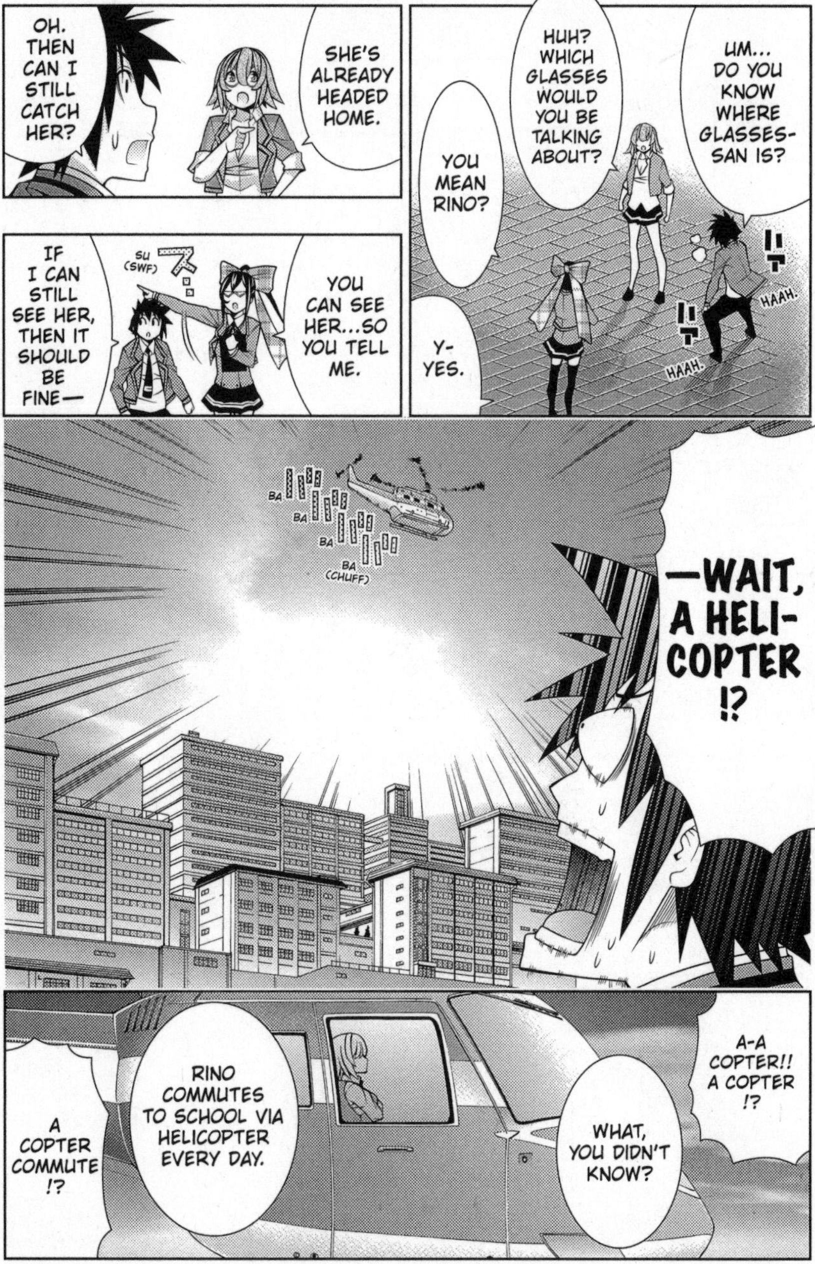
UM... DO YOU KNOW WHERE GLASSES-SAN IS?
HAAH. HAAH.
HUH? WHICH GLASSES WOULD YOU BE TALKING ABOUT?
YOU MEAN RINO?
Y-YES.
SHE'S ALREADY HEADED HOME.
OH. THEN CAN I STILL CATCH HER?
YOU CAN SEE HER...SO YOU TELL ME.
SU (SWF)
IF I CAN STILL SEE HER, THEN IT SHOULD BE FINE—
—WAIT, A HELICOPTER!?
BA BA BA BA (CHUFF)
A-A COPTER!! A COPTER!?
WHAT, YOU DIDN'T KNOW?
RINO COMMUTES TO SCHOOL VIA HELICOPTER EVERY DAY.
A COPTER COMMUTE!?

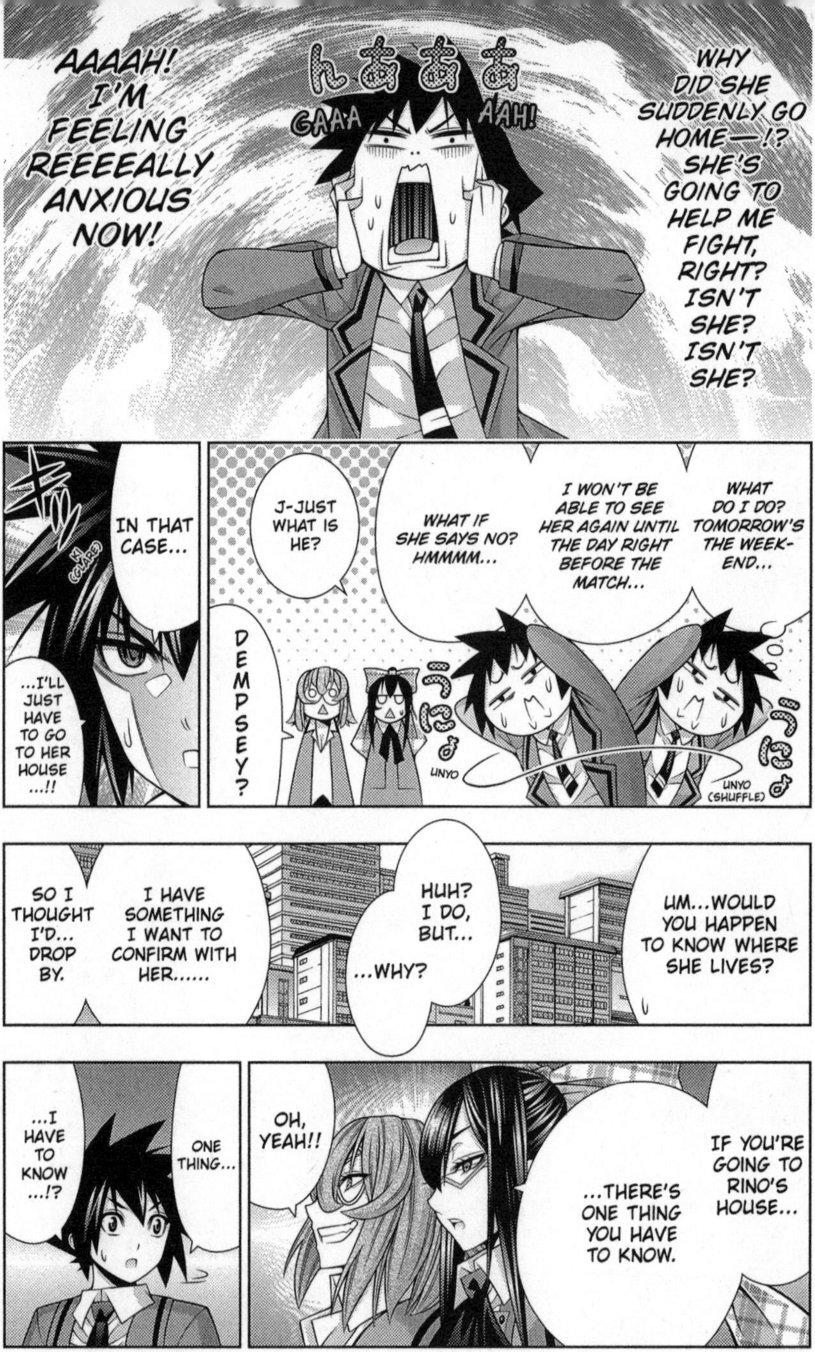
WHY DID SHE SUDDENLY GO HOME—!? SHE'S GOING TO HELP ME FIGHT, RIGHT? ISN'T SHE? ISN'T SHE?
んあああ
GAAAAAH!
AAAAH! I'M FEELING REEEEALLY ANXIOUS NOW!
WHAT DO I DO? TOMORROW'S THE WEEK-END...
I WON'T BE ABLE TO SEE HER AGAIN UNTIL THE DAY RIGHT BEFORE THE MATCH...
WHAT IF SHE SAYS NO? HMMMM...
J-JUST WHAT IS HE?
DEMPSEY?
うにょ
UNYO (SHUFFLE)
うにょ
UNYO
ギッ
KI (GLARE)
IN THAT CASE...
...I'LL JUST HAVE TO GO TO HER HOUSE ...!!
UM...WOULD YOU HAPPEN TO KNOW WHERE SHE LIVES?
HUH? I DO, BUT...
...WHY?
I HAVE SOMETHING I WANT TO CONFIRM WITH HER......
SO I THOUGHT I'D... DROP BY.
IF YOU'RE GOING TO RINO'S HOUSE...
...THERE'S ONE THING YOU HAVE TO KNOW.
OH, YEAH!!
ONE THING...
...I HAVE TO KNOW ...!?

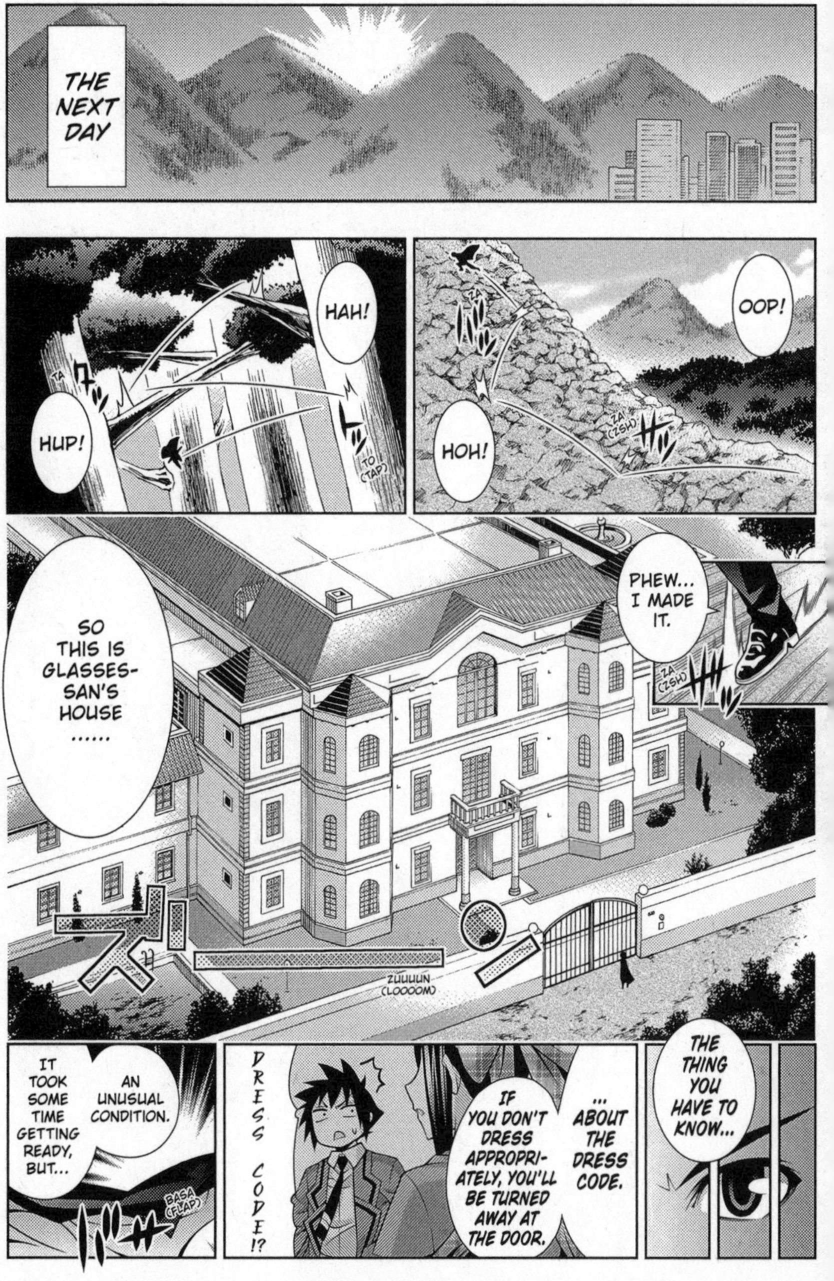
THE NEXT DAY
OOP!
ZA
ZA (ZSH)
HOH!
HAH!
TA
HUP!
TO (TAP)
PHEW... I MADE IT.
ZA (ZSH)
SO THIS IS GLASSES-SAN'S HOUSE ......
ZUUUUN (LOOOOM)
THE THING YOU HAVE TO KNOW...
... ABOUT THE DRESS CODE.
IF YOU DON'T DRESS APPROPRI-ATELY, YOU'LL BE TURNED AWAY AT THE DOOR.
DRESS CODE!?
AN UNUSUAL CONDITION.
IT TOOK SOME TIME GETTING READY, BUT...
BASA (FLAP)

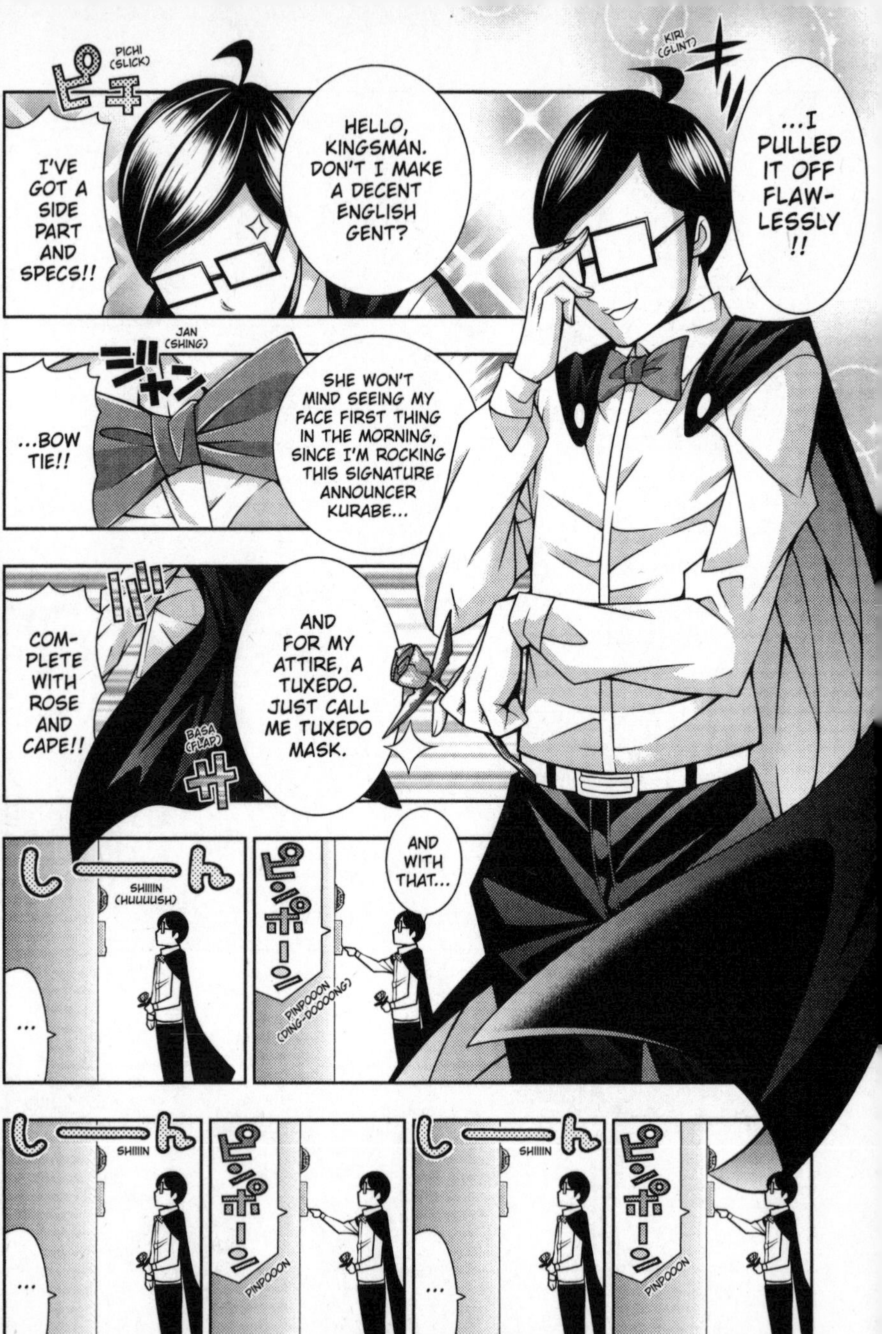

KIRI (GLINT)
...I PULLED IT OFF FLAWLESSLY!!
PICHI (SLICK)
I'VE GOT A SIDE PART AND SPECS!!
HELLO, KINGSMAN. DON'T I MAKE A DECENT ENGLISH GENT?
JAN (SHING)
...BOW TIE!!
SHE WON'T MIND SEEING MY FACE FIRST THING IN THE MORNING, SINCE I'M ROCKING THIS SIGNATURE ANNOUNCER KURABE...
COMPLETE WITH ROSE AND CAPE!!
BASA (FLAP)
AND FOR MY ATTIRE, A TUXEDO. JUST CALL ME TUXEDO MASK.
AND WITH THAT...
PINPOOON (DING-DOOOONG)
SHIIIN (HUUUUUSH)
...
PINPOOON
SHIIIN
...
PINPOOON
SHIIIN
...

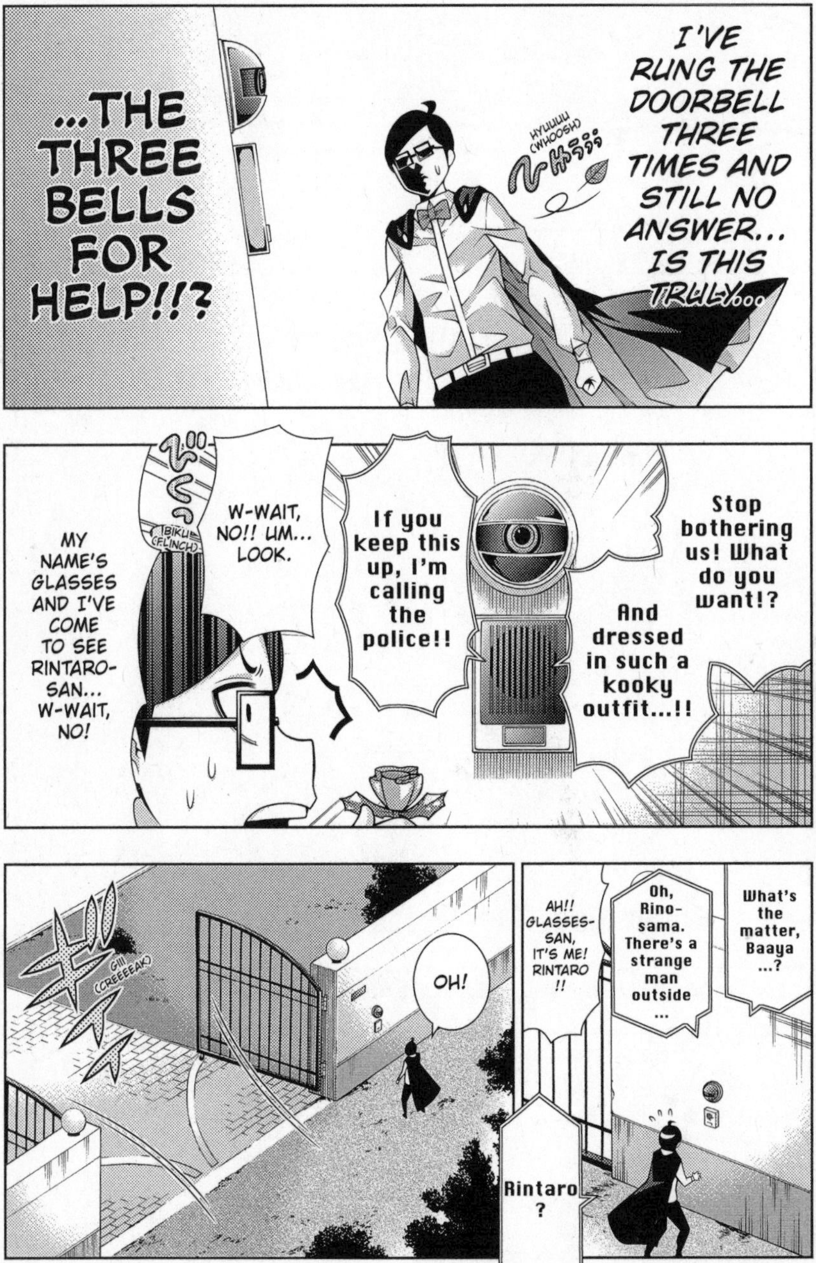
I'VE RUNG THE DOORBELL THREE TIMES AND STILL NO ANSWER... IS THIS TRULY...
HYUUUU (WHOOSH)
...THE THREE BELLS FOR HELP!!?
Stop bothering us! What do you want!?
And dressed in such a kooky outfit...!!
If you keep this up, I'm calling the police!!
W-WAIT, NO!! UM... LOOK.
BIKU (FLINCH)
MY NAME'S GLASSES AND I'VE COME TO SEE RINTARO-SAN... W-WAIT, NO!
What's the matter, Baaya ...?
Oh, Rino-sama. There's a strange man outside ...
AH!! GLASSES-SAN, IT'S ME! RINTARO !!
Rintaro ?
OH!
GIII (CREEEEAK)

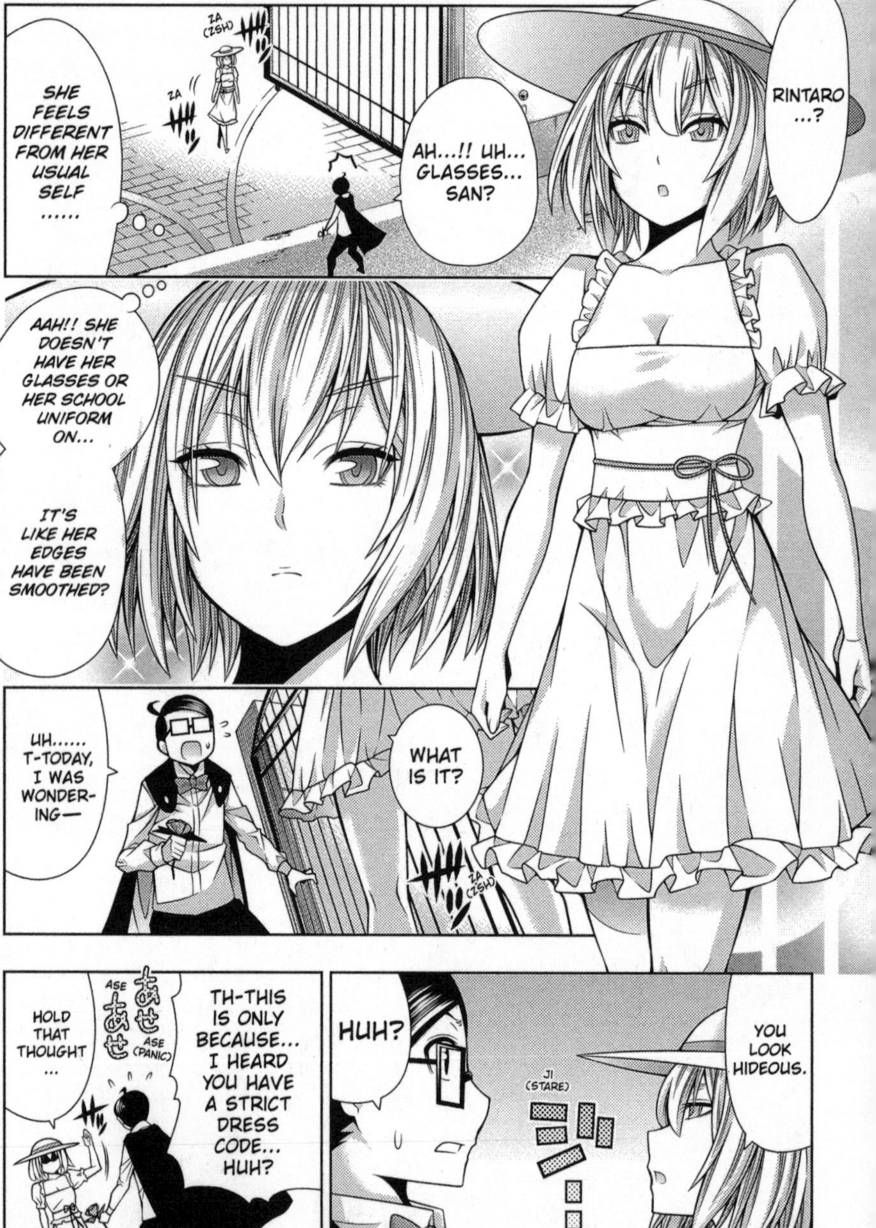
RINTARO ...?
AH...!! UH... GLASSES... SAN?
ZA (ZSH)
ZA
SHE FEELS DIFFERENT FROM HER USUAL SELF ......
AAH!! SHE DOESN'T HAVE HER GLASSES OR HER SCHOOL UNIFORM ON...
IT'S LIKE HER EDGES HAVE BEEN SMOOTHED?
WHAT IS IT?
ZA (ZSH)
UH...... T-TODAY, I WAS WONDER-ING—
YOU LOOK HIDEOUS.
JI (STARE)
HUH?
TH-THIS IS ONLY BECAUSE... I HEARD YOU HAVE A STRICT DRESS CODE... HUH?
あせ ASE
あせ ASE (PANIC)
HOLD THAT THOUGHT ...
SFX: SA (SWISH)

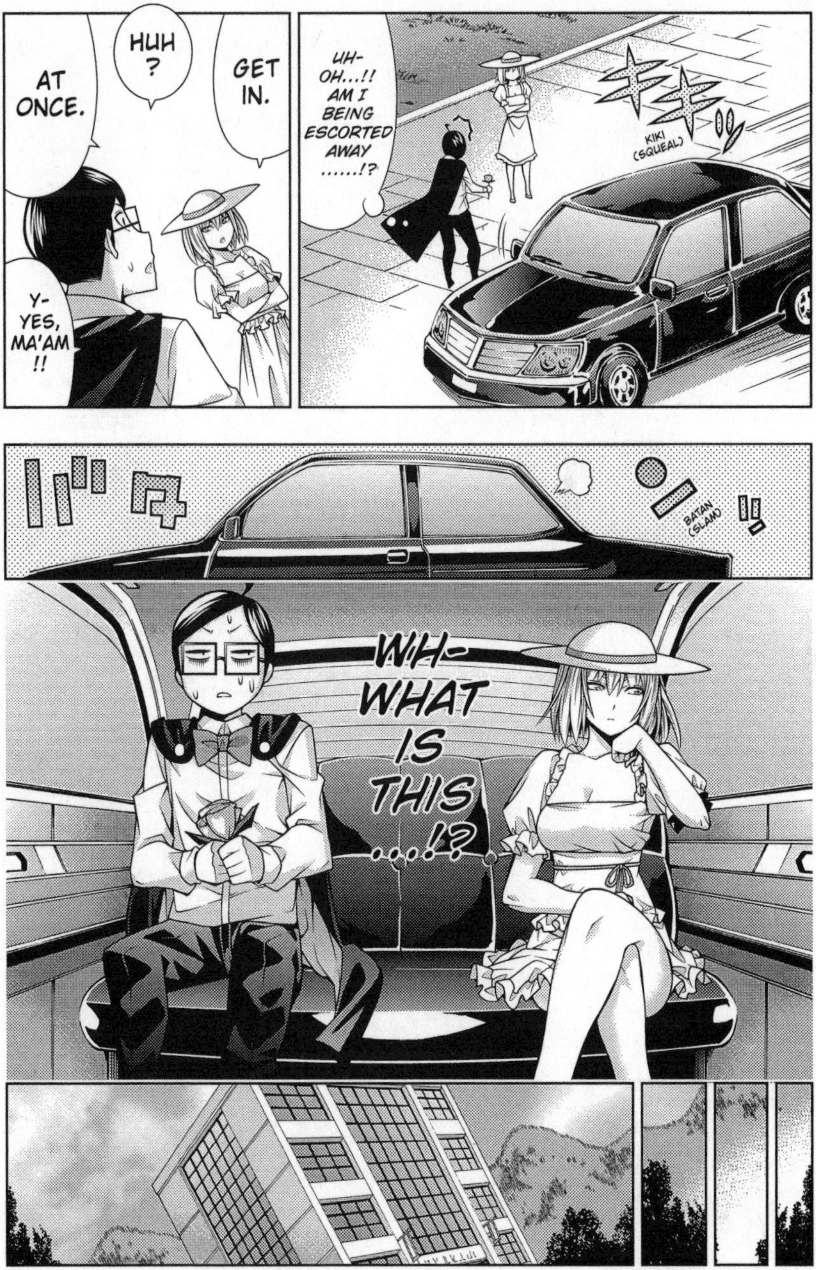
UH-OH...!! AM I BEING ESCORTED AWAY ......!?
KIKI (SQUEAL)
GET IN.
HUH?
AT ONCE.
Y-YES, MA'AM!!
BATAN (SLAM)
WH-WHAT IS THIS ...!?

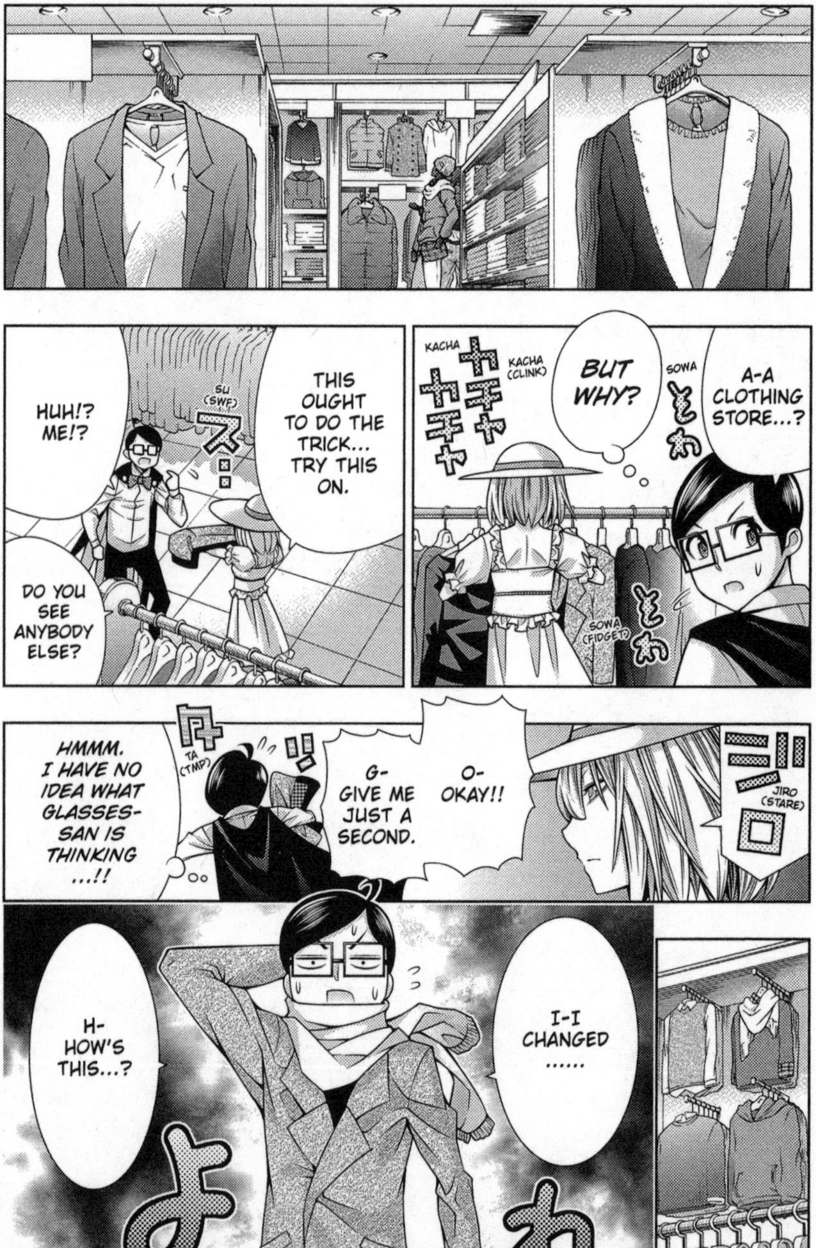
A-A CLOTHING STORE...?
SOWA
BUT WHY?
KACHA
KACHA (CLINK)
SOWA (FIDGET)
THIS OUGHT TO DO THE TRICK... TRY THIS ON.
SU (SWF)
HUH!? ME!?
DO YOU SEE ANYBODY ELSE?
JIRO (STARE)
O-OKAY!!
G-GIVE ME JUST A SECOND.
TA (TMP)
HMMM. I HAVE NO IDEA WHAT GLASSES-SAN IS THINKING ...!!
I-I CHANGED ......
H-HOW'S THIS...?
YORE (SHABBY)

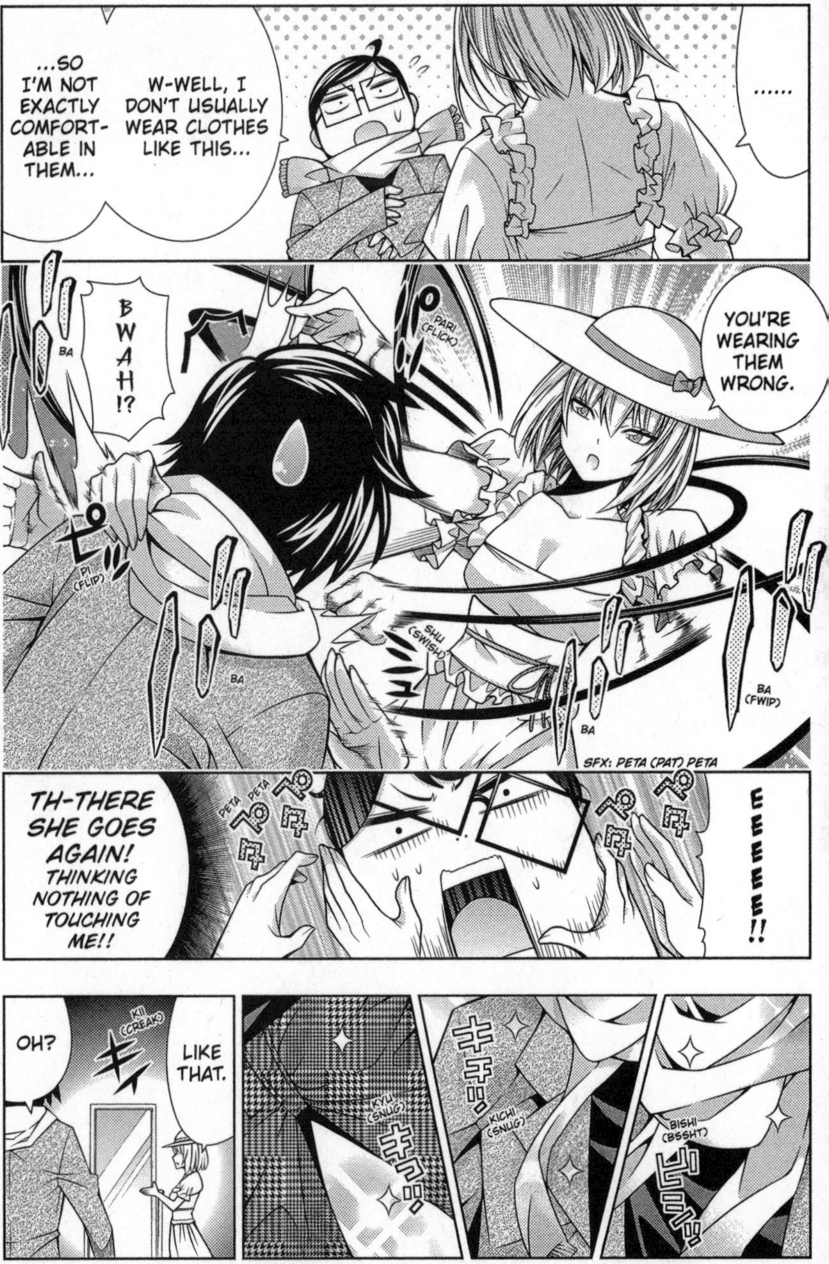
......
W-WELL, I DON'T USUALLY WEAR CLOTHES LIKE THIS...
...SO I'M NOT EXACTLY COMFORT-ABLE IN THEM...
YOU'RE WEARING THEM WRONG.
PARI (FLICK)
BWAH!?
BA
PI (FLIP)
SHU (SWISH)
BA
BA (FWIP)
BA
SFX: PETA (PAT) PETA
EEEEEE!!
PETA PETA
TH-THERE SHE GOES AGAIN! THINKING NOTHING OF TOUCHING ME!!
BISHI (BSSHT)
KICHI (SNUG)
KYU (SNUG)
LIKE THAT.
KII (CREAK)
OH?

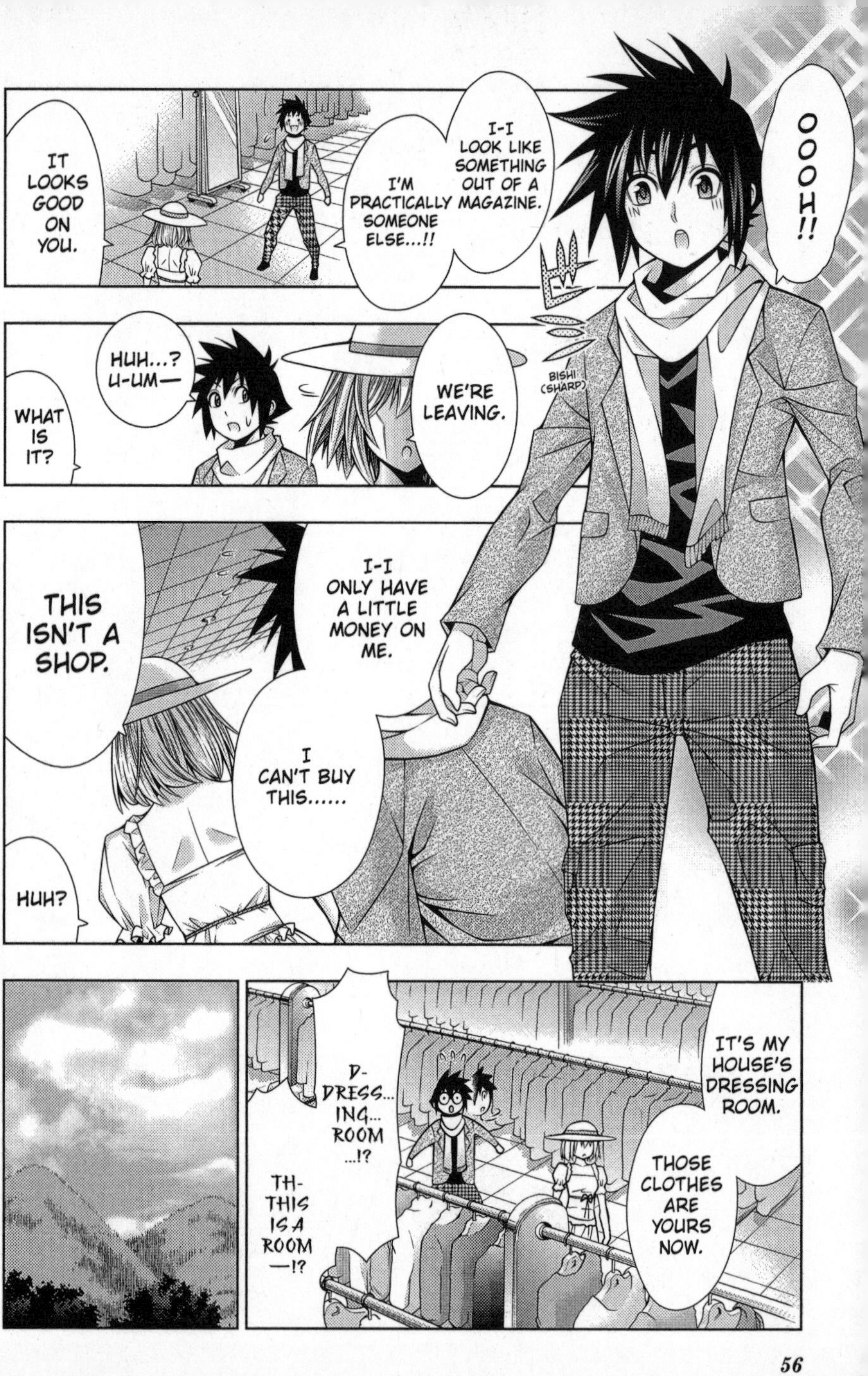
OOOH!!
BISHI (SHARP)
I-I LOOK LIKE SOMETHING OUT OF A MAGAZINE.
I'M PRACTICALLY SOMEONE ELSE...!!
IT LOOKS GOOD ON YOU.
WE'RE LEAVING.
HUH...? U-UM—
WHAT IS IT?
I-I ONLY HAVE A LITTLE MONEY ON ME.
I CAN'T BUY THIS......
THIS ISN'T A SHOP.
HUH?
IT'S MY HOUSE'S DRESSING ROOM.
THOSE CLOTHES ARE YOURS NOW.
D-DRESS... ING... ROOM ...!?
TH-THIS IS A ROOM —!?

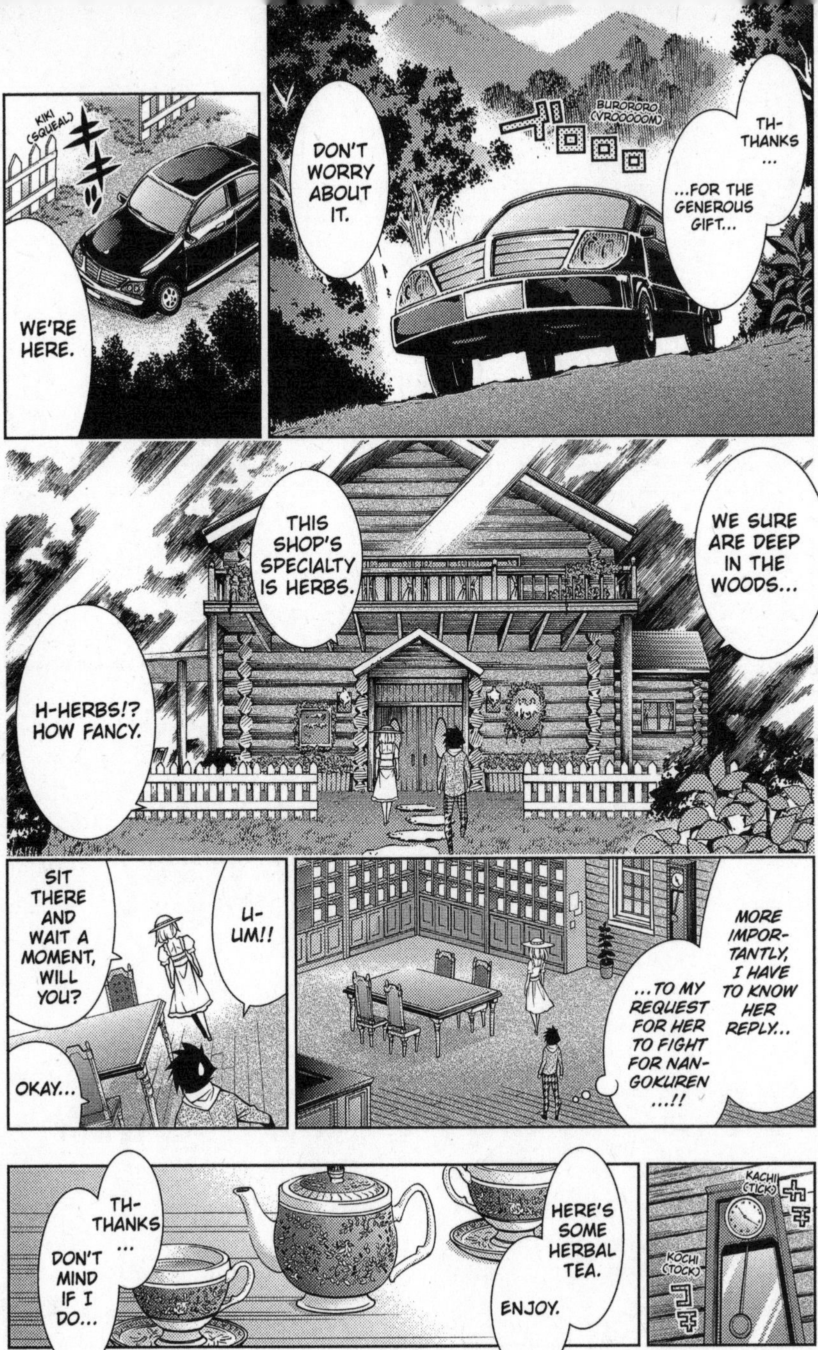
TH-THANKS...
...FOR THE GENEROUS GIFT...
BURORORO (VROOOOOM)
DON'T WORRY ABOUT IT.
KIKI (SQUEAL)
WE'RE HERE.
WE SURE ARE DEEP IN THE WOODS...
THIS SHOP'S SPECIALTY IS HERBS.
H-HERBS!? HOW FANCY.
MORE IMPORTANTLY, I HAVE TO KNOW HER REPLY...
...TO MY REQUEST FOR HER TO FIGHT FOR NANGOKUREN...!!
SIT THERE AND WAIT A MOMENT, WILL YOU?
U-UM!!
OKAY...
KACHI (TICK)
KOCHI (TOCK)
HERE'S SOME HERBAL TEA.
ENJOY.
TH-THANKS...
DON'T MIND IF I DO...

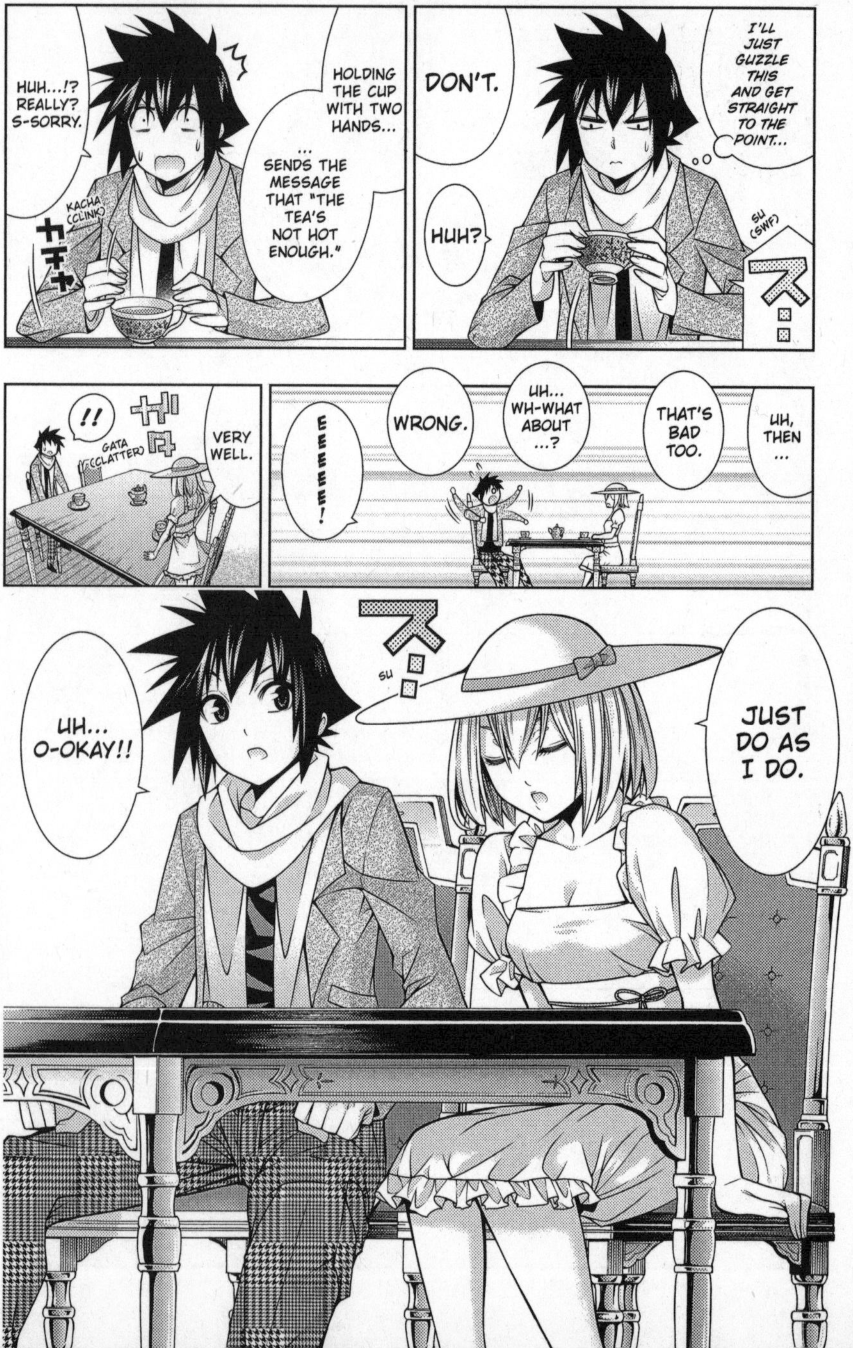
I'LL JUST GUZZLE THIS AND GET STRAIGHT TO THE POINT...
SU (SWF)
ス
HUH?
DON'T.
HOLDING THE CUP WITH TWO HANDS...
... SENDS THE MESSAGE THAT "THE TEA'S NOT HOT ENOUGH."
HUH...!? REALLY? S-SORRY.
KACHA (CLINK)
カチャ
UH, THEN ...
THAT'S BAD TOO.
UH... WH-WHAT ABOUT ...?
WRONG.
EEEEEE!
VERY WELL.
GATA (CLATTER)
!!
JUST DO AS I DO.
SU
ス
UH... O-OKAY!!

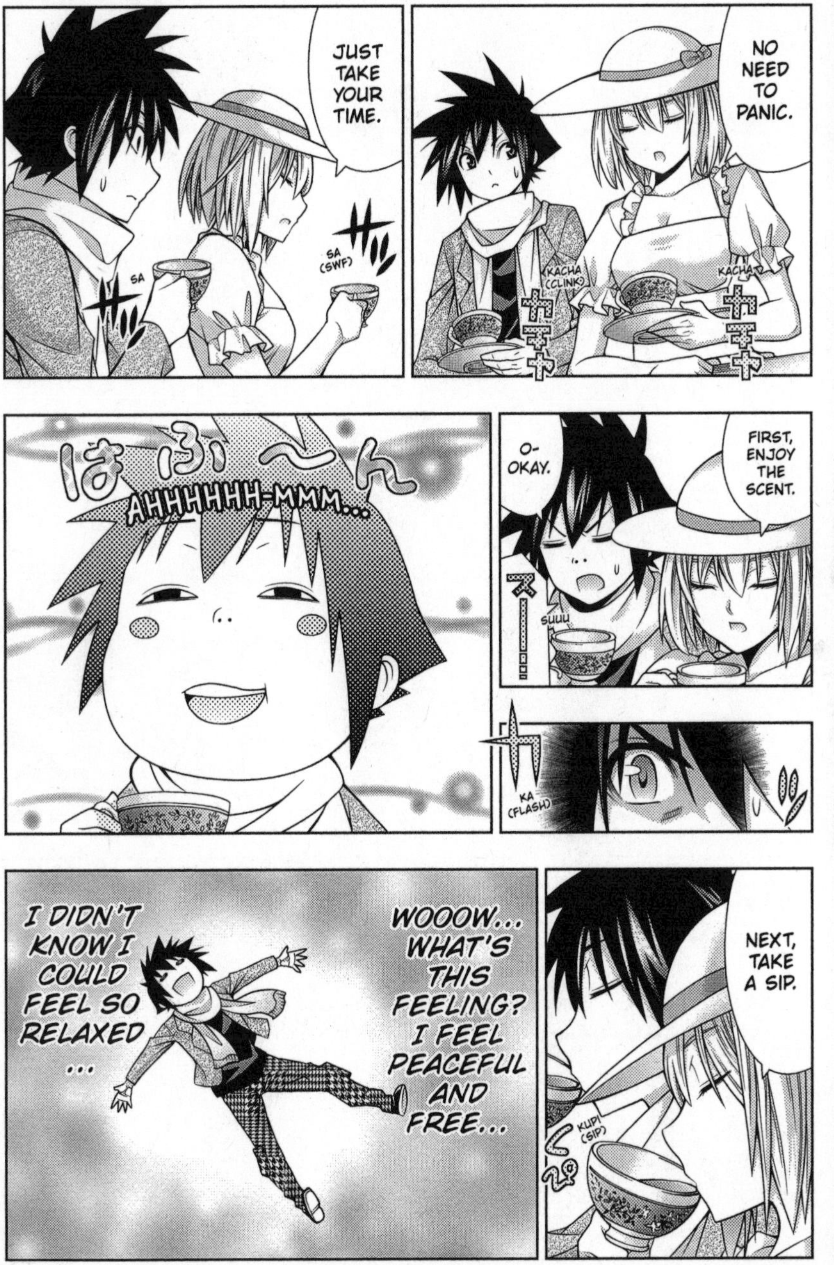
NO NEED TO PANIC.
KACHA (CLINK)
KACHA
JUST TAKE YOUR TIME.
SA (SWF)
SA
FIRST, ENJOY THE SCENT.
O-OKAY.
SUUU
KA (FLASH)
AHHHHHH-MMM...
NEXT, TAKE A SIP.
KUPI (SIP)
WOOOW... WHAT'S THIS FEELING? I FEEL PEACEFUL AND FREE...
I DIDN'T KNOW I COULD FEEL SO RELAXED...

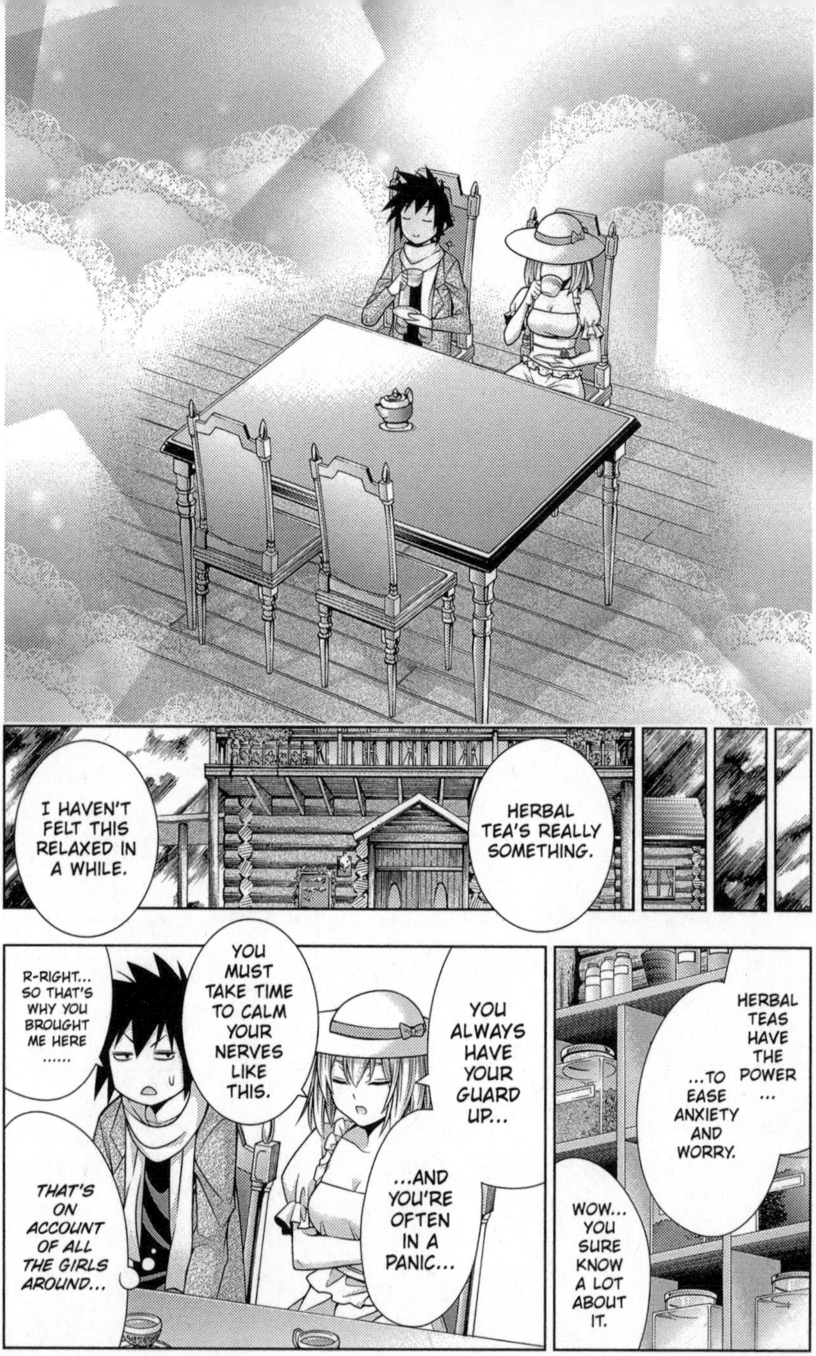
HERBAL TEA'S REALLY SOMETHING.
I HAVEN'T FELT THIS RELAXED IN A WHILE.
HERBAL TEAS HAVE THE POWER ...
...TO EASE ANXIETY AND WORRY.
WOW... YOU SURE KNOW A LOT ABOUT IT.
YOU ALWAYS HAVE YOUR GUARD UP...
...AND YOU'RE OFTEN IN A PANIC...
YOU MUST TAKE TIME TO CALM YOUR NERVES LIKE THIS.
R-RIGHT... SO THAT'S WHY YOU BROUGHT ME HERE ......
THAT'S ON ACCOUNT OF ALL THE GIRLS AROUND...

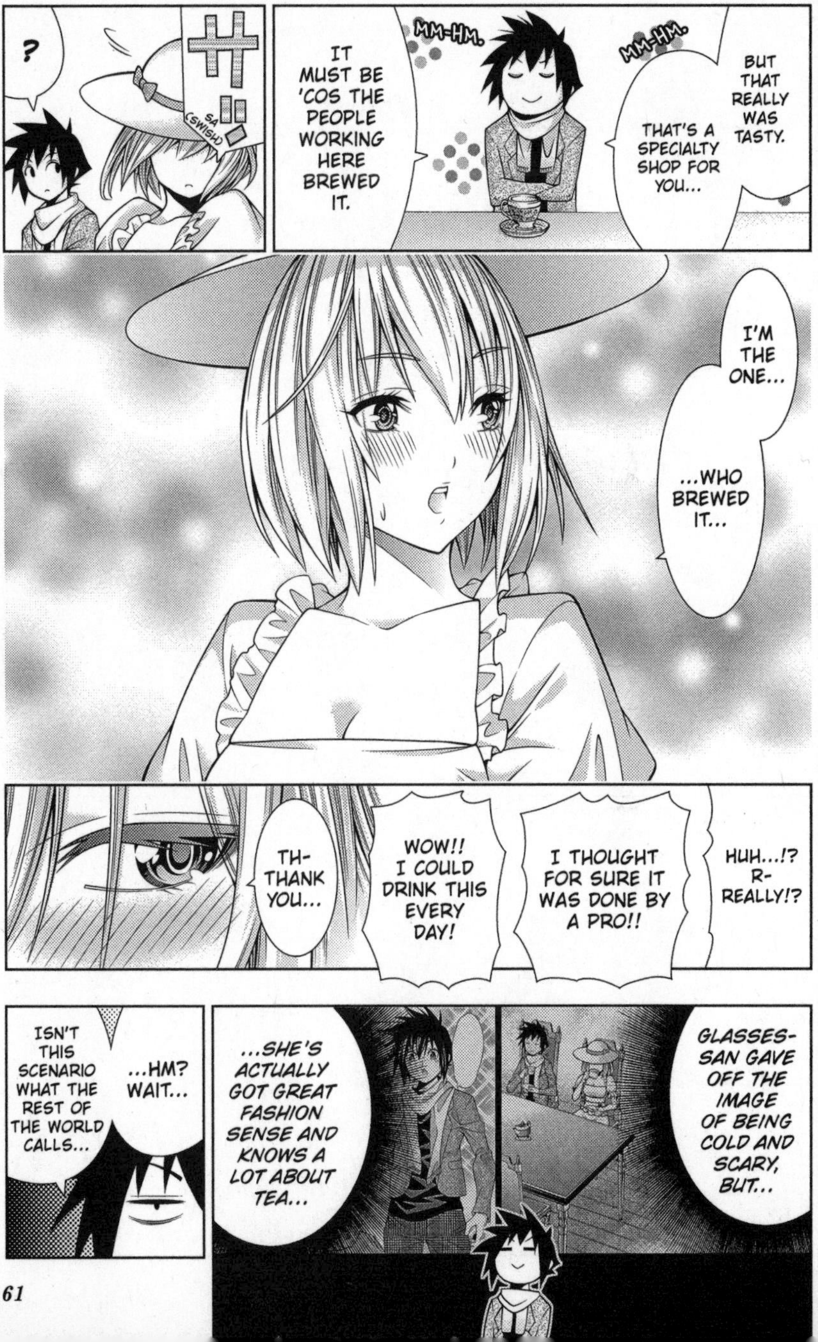
MM-HM.
BUT THAT REALLY WAS TASTY.
THAT'S A SPECIALTY SHOP FOR YOU...
MM-HM.
IT MUST BE 'COS THE PEOPLE WORKING HERE BREWED IT.
SA (SWISH)
?
I'M THE ONE...
...WHO BREWED IT...
HUH...!? R-REALLY!?
I THOUGHT FOR SURE IT WAS DONE BY A PRO!!
WOW!! I COULD DRINK THIS EVERY DAY!
TH-THANK YOU...
GLASSES-SAN GAVE OFF THE IMAGE OF BEING COLD AND SCARY, BUT...
...SHE'S ACTUALLY GOT GREAT FASHION SENSE AND KNOWS A LOT ABOUT TEA...
...HM? WAIT...
ISN'T THIS SCENARIO WHAT THE REST OF THE WORLD CALLS...

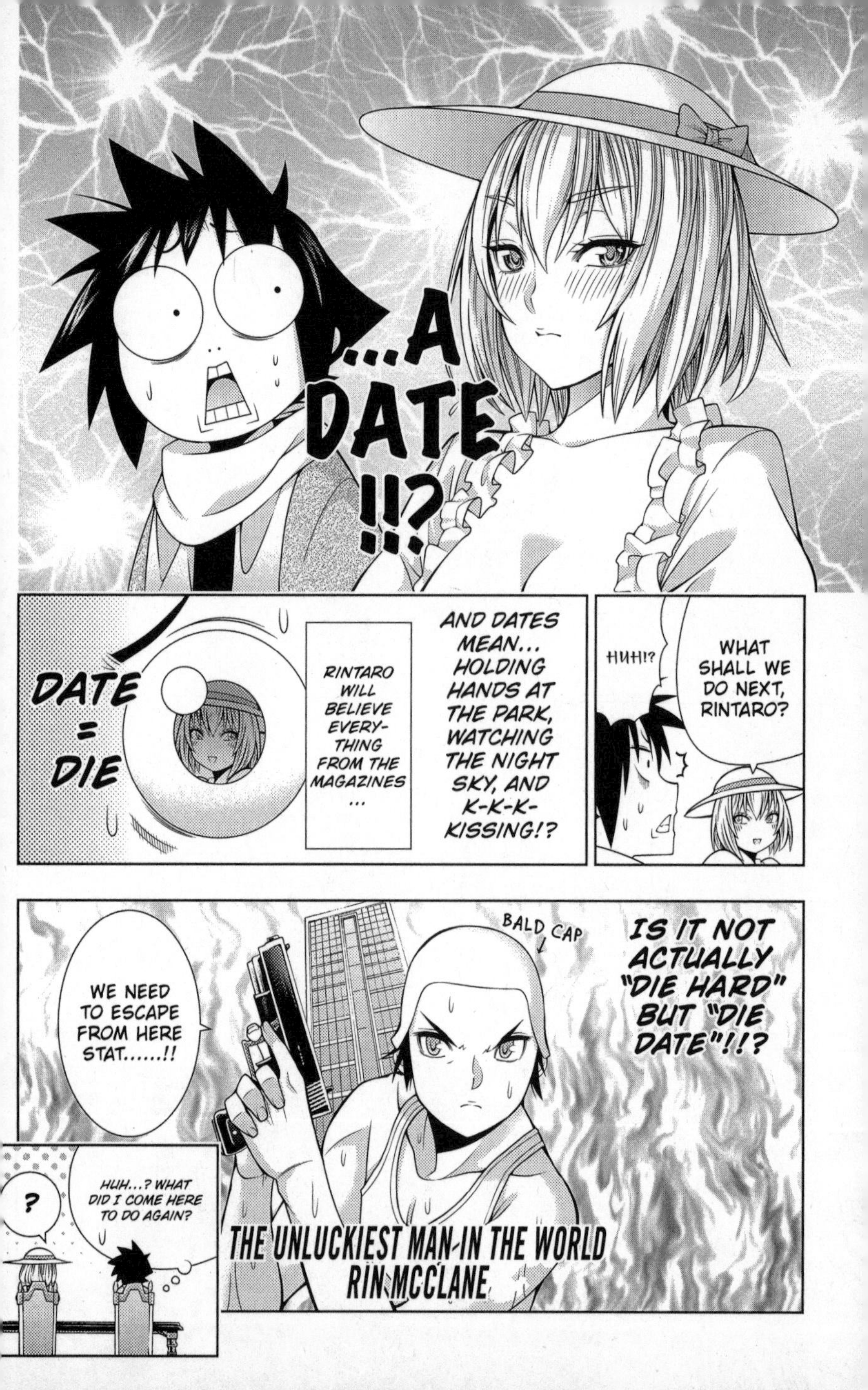
...A DATE!!?
WHAT SHALL WE DO NEXT, RINTARO?
HUH!?
AND DATES MEAN... HOLDING HANDS AT THE PARK, WATCHING THE NIGHT SKY, AND K-K-K-KISSING!?
RINTARO WILL BELIEVE EVERY-THING FROM THE MAGAZINES ...
DATE = DIE
IS IT NOT ACTUALLY "DIE HARD" BUT "DIE DATE"!!?
BALD CAP
WE NEED TO ESCAPE FROM HERE STAT......!!
THE UNLUCKIEST MAN IN THE WORLD
RIN MCCLANE
HUH...? WHAT DID I COME HERE TO DO AGAIN?
?

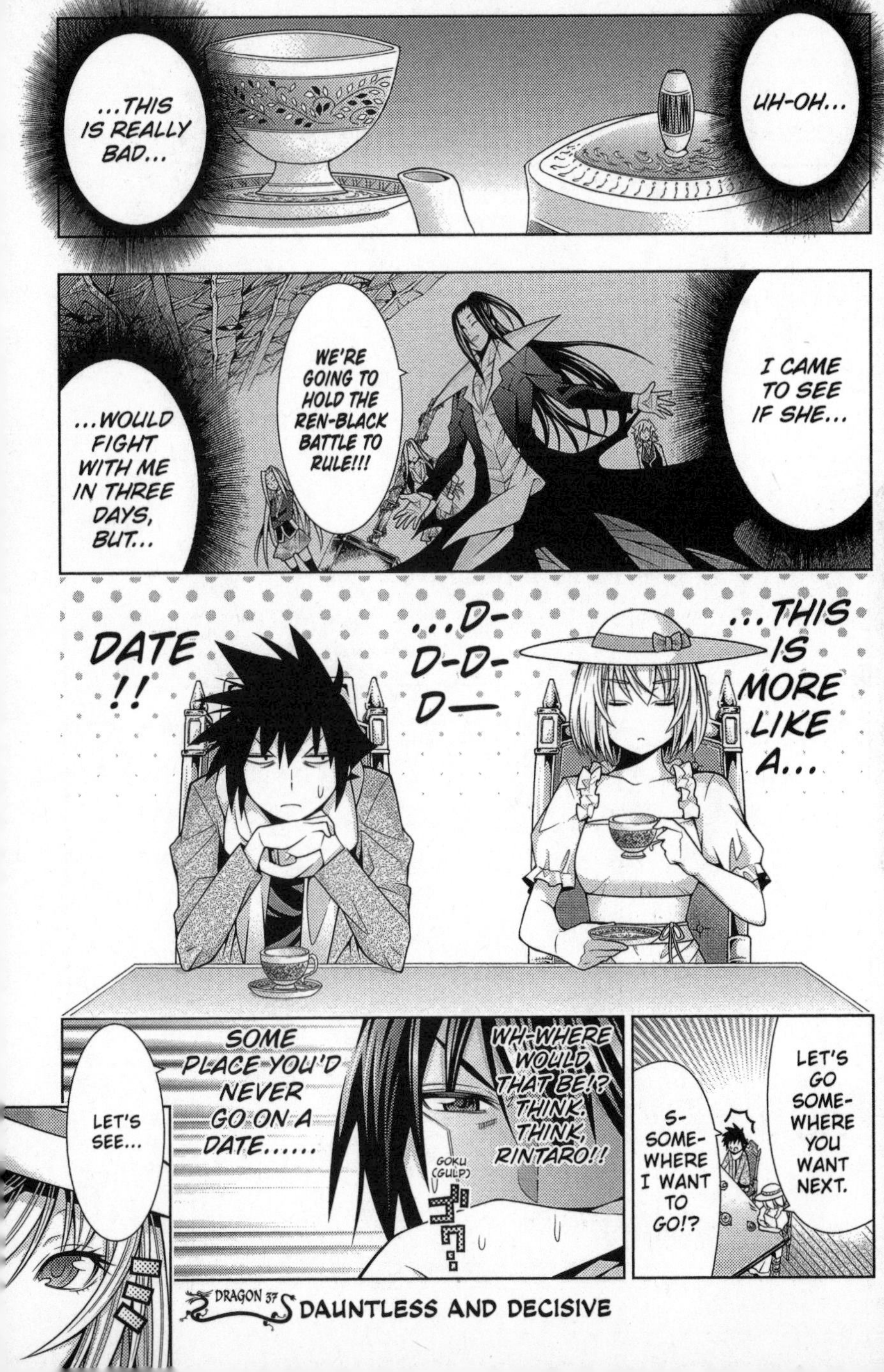
UH-OH...
...THIS IS REALLY BAD...
I CAME TO SEE IF SHE...
WE'RE GOING TO HOLD THE REN-BLACK BATTLE TO RULE!!!
...WOULD FIGHT WITH ME IN THREE DAYS, BUT...
...THIS IS MORE LIKE A...
...D-D-D-D—
DATE!!
LET'S GO SOMEWHERE YOU WANT NEXT.
S-SOMEWHERE I WANT TO GO!?
WH-WHERE WOULD THAT BE!? THINK, THINK, RINTARO!!
GOKU (GULP)
SOME PLACE YOU'D NEVER GO ON A DATE......
LET'S SEE...
DRAGON 37 DAUNTLESS AND DECISIVE

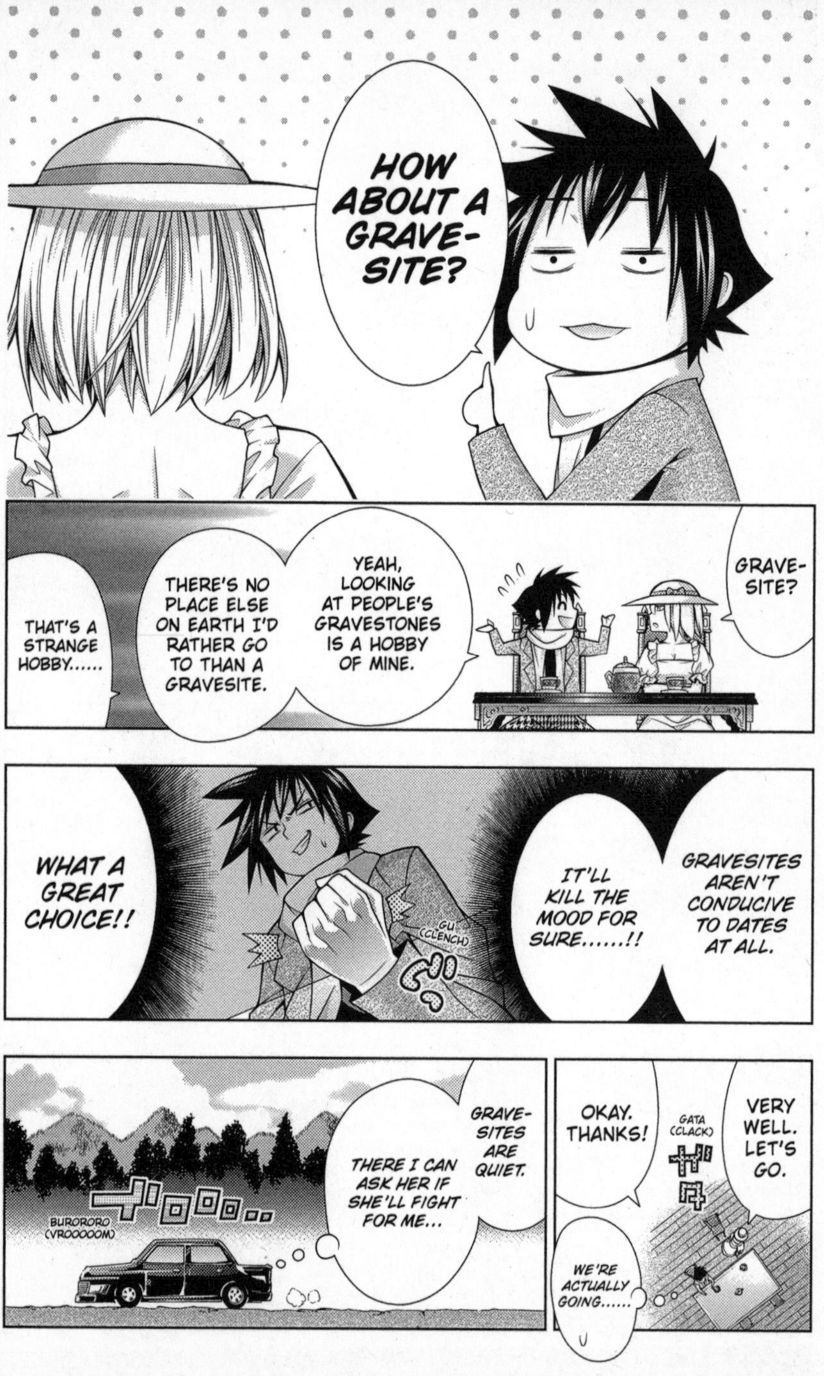
HOW ABOUT A GRAVE-SITE?
GRAVE-SITE?
YEAH, LOOKING AT PEOPLE'S GRAVESTONES IS A HOBBY OF MINE.
THERE'S NO PLACE ELSE ON EARTH I'D RATHER GO TO THAN A GRAVESITE.
THAT'S A STRANGE HOBBY......
GRAVESITES AREN'T CONDUCIVE TO DATES AT ALL.
IT'LL KILL THE MOOD FOR SURE......!!
GU (CLENCH)
WHAT A GREAT CHOICE!!
VERY WELL. LET'S GO.
GATA (CLACK)
OKAY. THANKS!
WE'RE ACTUALLY GOING......
GRAVE-SITES ARE QUIET.
THERE I CAN ASK HER IF SHE'LL FIGHT FOR ME...
BURORORO (VROOOOOM)

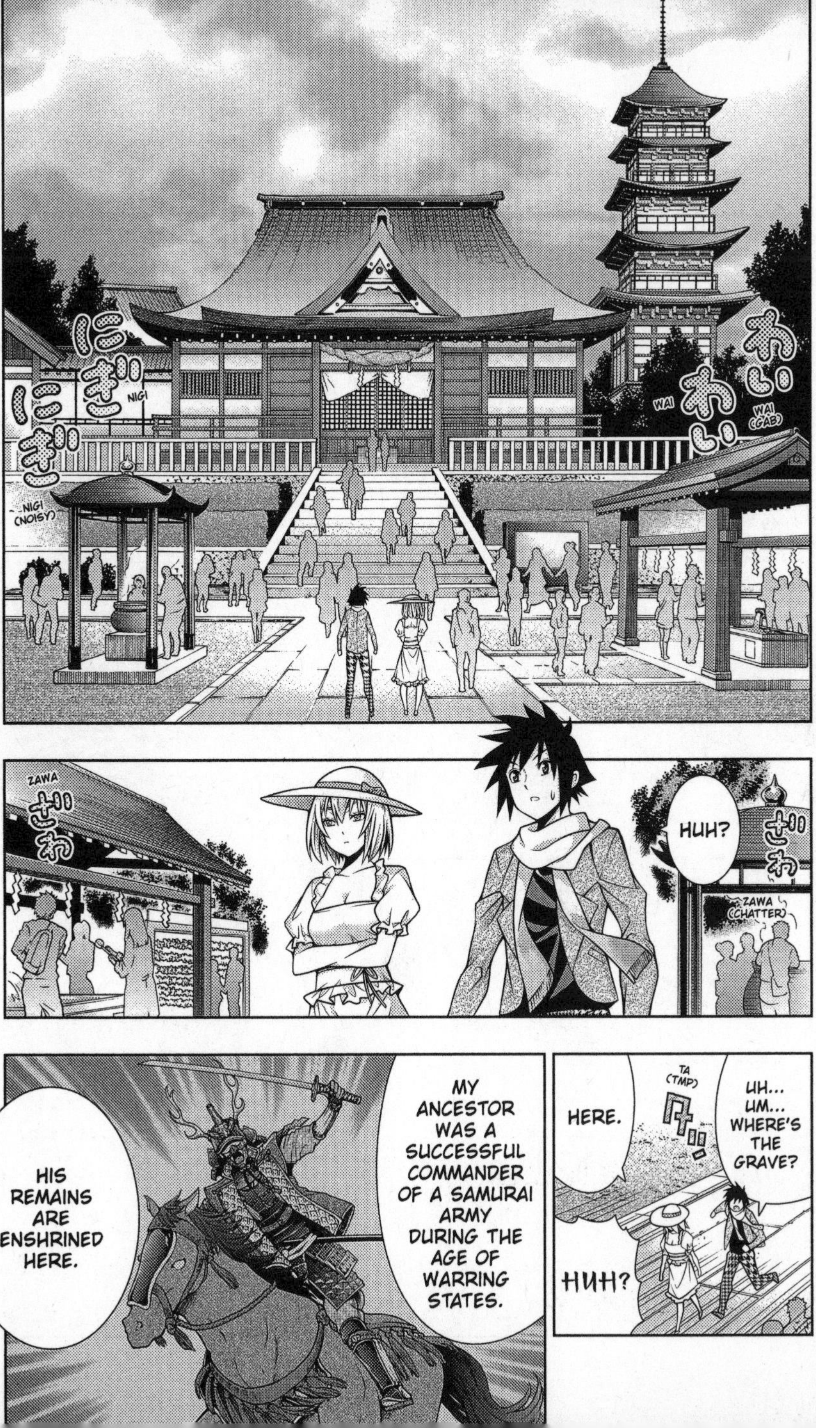
わい わい
WAI WAI (GAB)
にぎ にぎ
NIGI NIGI (NOISY)
HUH?
ざわ
ZAWA (CHATTER)
ZAWA
ざわ
UH... UM... WHERE'S THE GRAVE?
TA (TMP)
タッ
HERE.
HUH?
MY ANCESTOR WAS A SUCCESSFUL COMMANDER OF A SAMURAI ARMY DURING THE AGE OF WARRING STATES.
HIS REMAINS ARE ENSHRINED HERE.

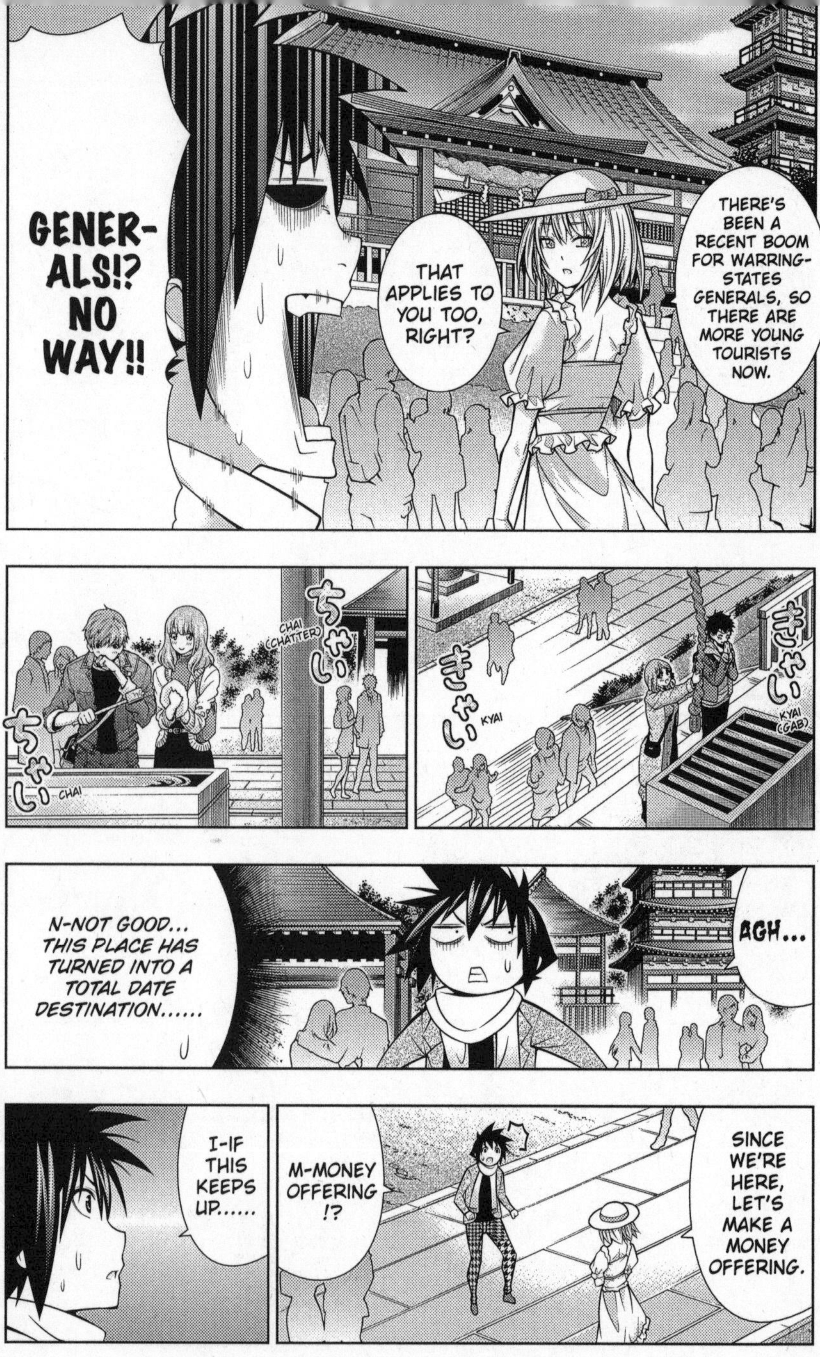
THERE'S BEEN A RECENT BOOM FOR WARRING-STATES GENERALS, SO THERE ARE MORE YOUNG TOURISTS NOW.
THAT APPLIES TO YOU TOO, RIGHT?
GENER-ALS!? NO WAY!!
きゃい
KYAI (GAB)
きゃい
KYAI
ちゃい
CHAI (CHATTER)
ちゃい
CHAI
AGH...
N-NOT GOOD... THIS PLACE HAS TURNED INTO A TOTAL DATE DESTINATION......
SINCE WE'RE HERE, LET'S MAKE A MONEY OFFERING.
M-MONEY OFFERING!?
I-IF THIS KEEPS UP......

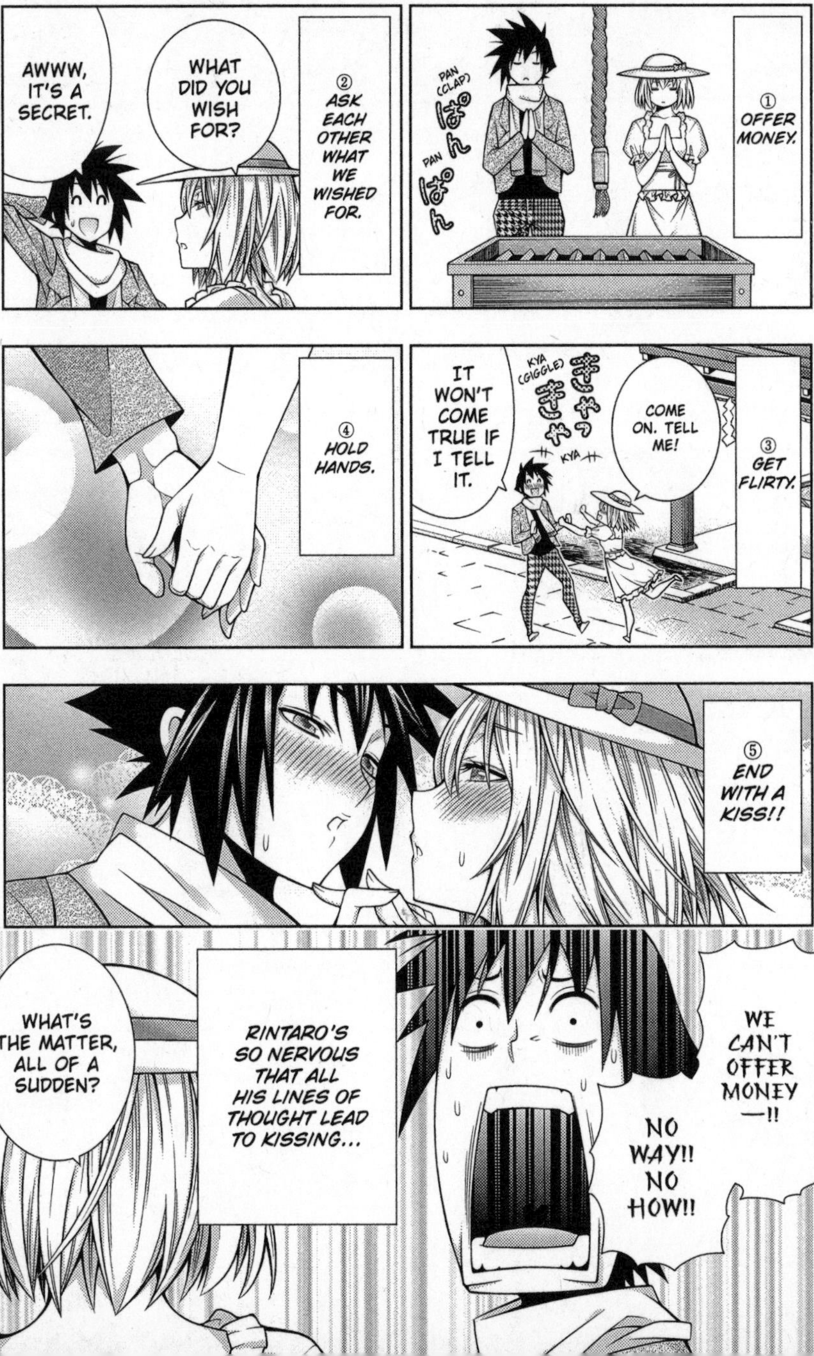
① OFFER MONEY.
PAN (CLAP) ぱん
PAN ぱん
② ASK EACH OTHER WHAT WE WISHED FOR.
WHAT DID YOU WISH FOR?
AWWW, IT'S A SECRET.
③ GET FLIRTY.
COME ON. TELL ME!
KYA (GIGGLE) きゃっきゃっ
KYA
IT WON'T COME TRUE IF I TELL IT.
④ HOLD HANDS.
⑤ END WITH A KISS!!
WE CAN'T OFFER MONEY—!!
NO WAY!! NO HOW!!
RINTARO'S SO NERVOUS THAT ALL HIS LINES OF THOUGHT LEAD TO KISSING...
WHAT'S THE MATTER, ALL OF A SUDDEN?

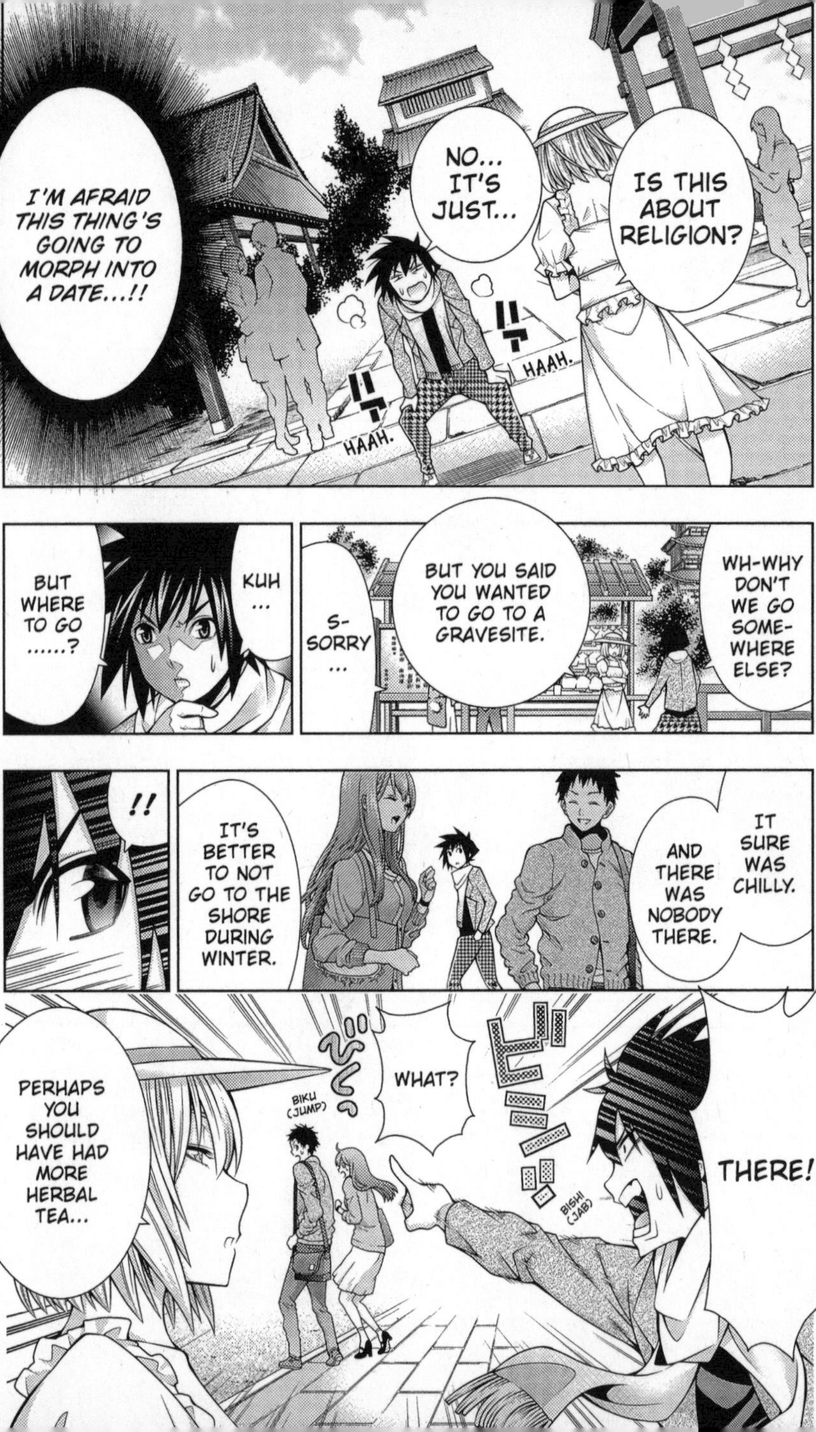
IS THIS ABOUT RELIGION?
NO... IT'S JUST...
HAAH.
HAAH.
I'M AFRAID THIS THING'S GOING TO MORPH INTO A DATE...!!
WH-WHY DON'T WE GO SOME-WHERE ELSE?
BUT YOU SAID YOU WANTED TO GO TO A GRAVESITE.
S-SORRY ...
KUH ...
BUT WHERE TO GO ......?
IT SURE WAS CHILLY.
AND THERE WAS NOBODY THERE.
IT'S BETTER TO NOT GO TO THE SHORE DURING WINTER.
!!
THERE!!
BISHI (JAB)
WHAT?
BIKU (JUMP)
PERHAPS YOU SHOULD HAVE HAD MORE HERBAL TEA...

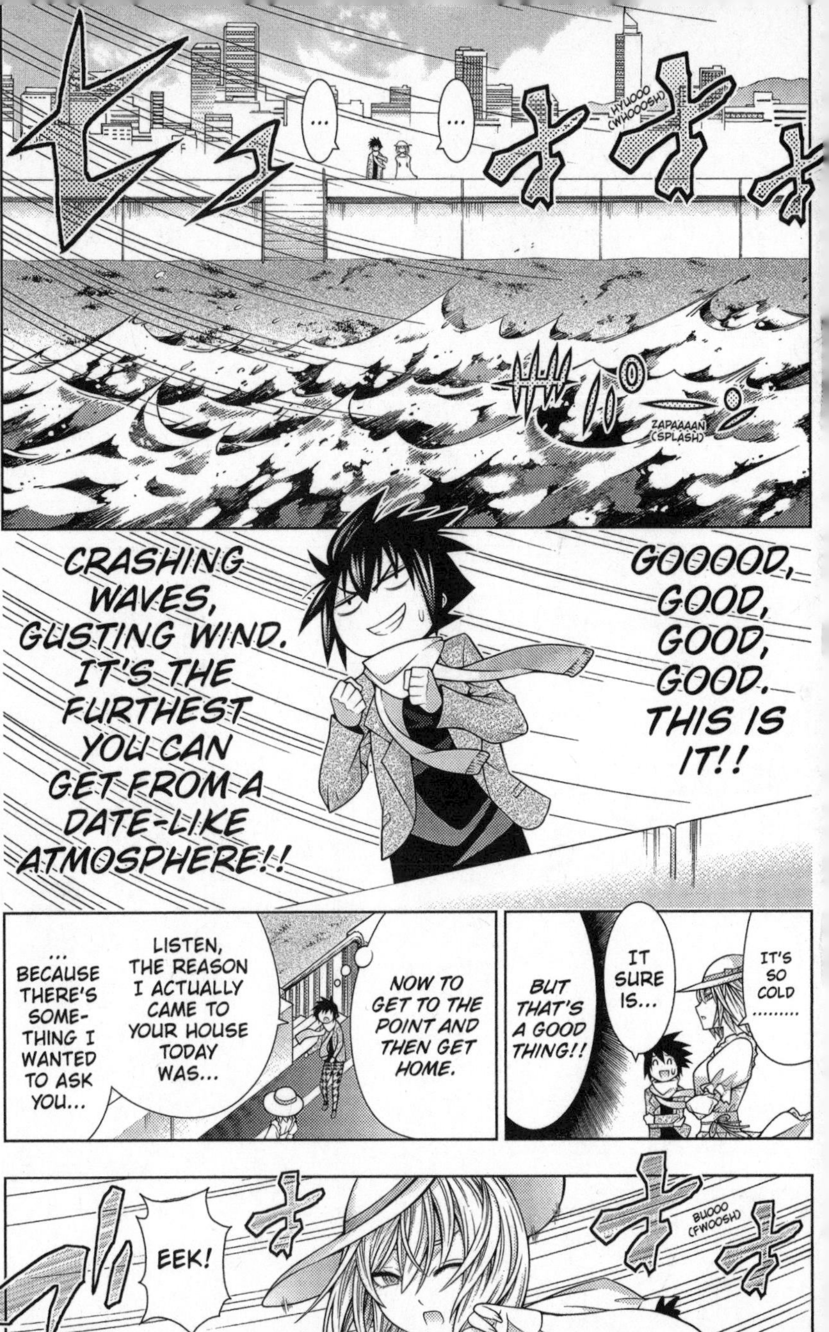
HYUOOO (WHOOOSH)
...
...
ZAPAAAAN (SPLASH)
GOOOOD, GOOD, GOOD, GOOD. THIS IS IT!!
CRASHING WAVES, GUSTING WIND. IT'S THE FURTHEST YOU CAN GET FROM A DATE-LIKE ATMOSPHERE!!
IT'S SO COLD.........
IT SURE IS...
BUT THAT'S A GOOD THING!!
NOW TO GET TO THE POINT AND THEN GET HOME.
LISTEN, THE REASON I ACTUALLY CAME TO YOUR HOUSE TODAY WAS...
... BECAUSE THERE'S SOME-THING I WANTED TO ASK YOU...
BUOOO (FWOOSH)
EEK!

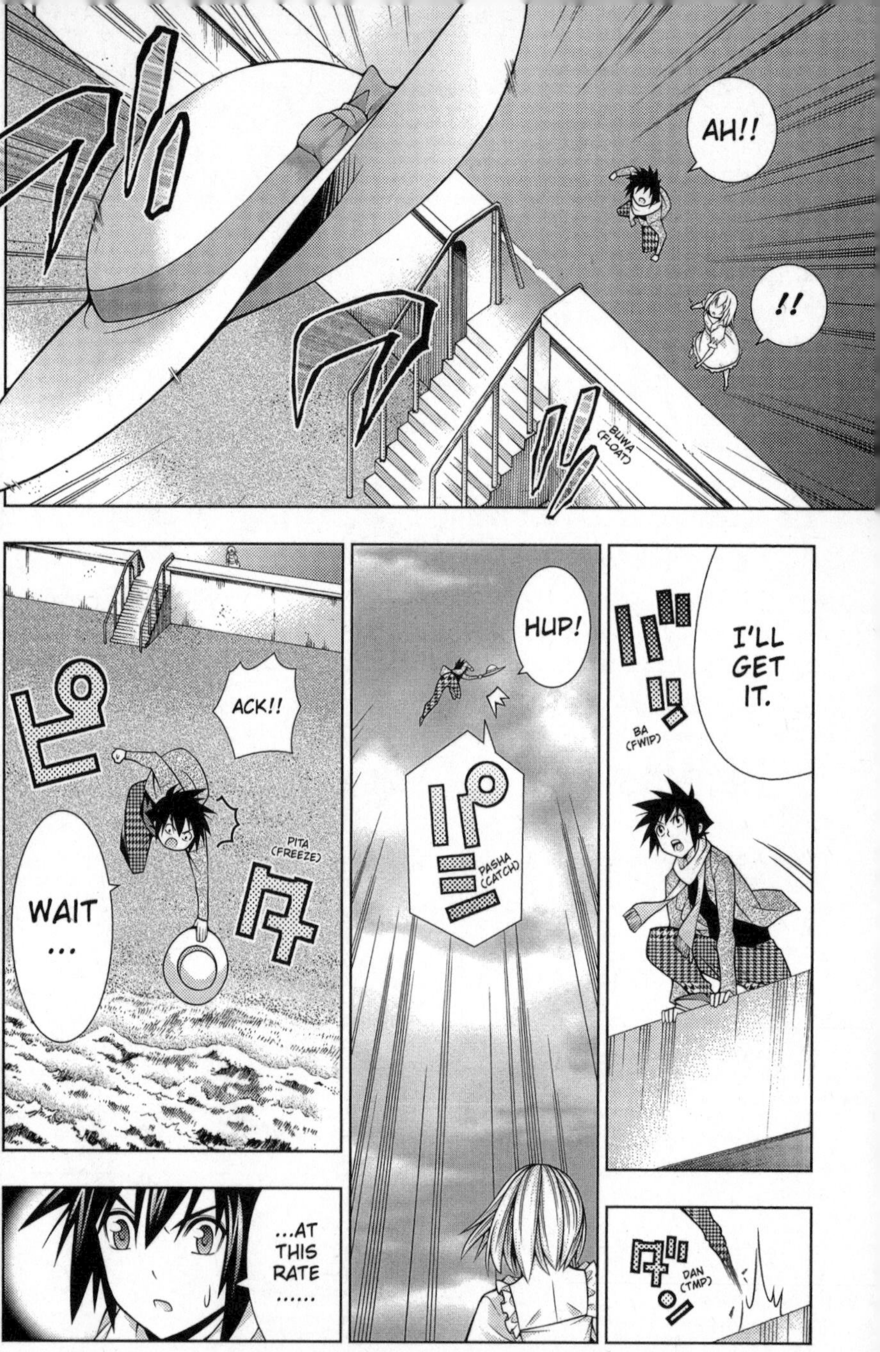
AH!!
!!
BUWA (FLOAT)
I'LL GET IT.
BA (FWIP)
DAN (TMP)
HUP!
PASHA (CATCH)
ACK!!
PITA (FREEZE)
WAIT ...
...AT THIS RATE ......

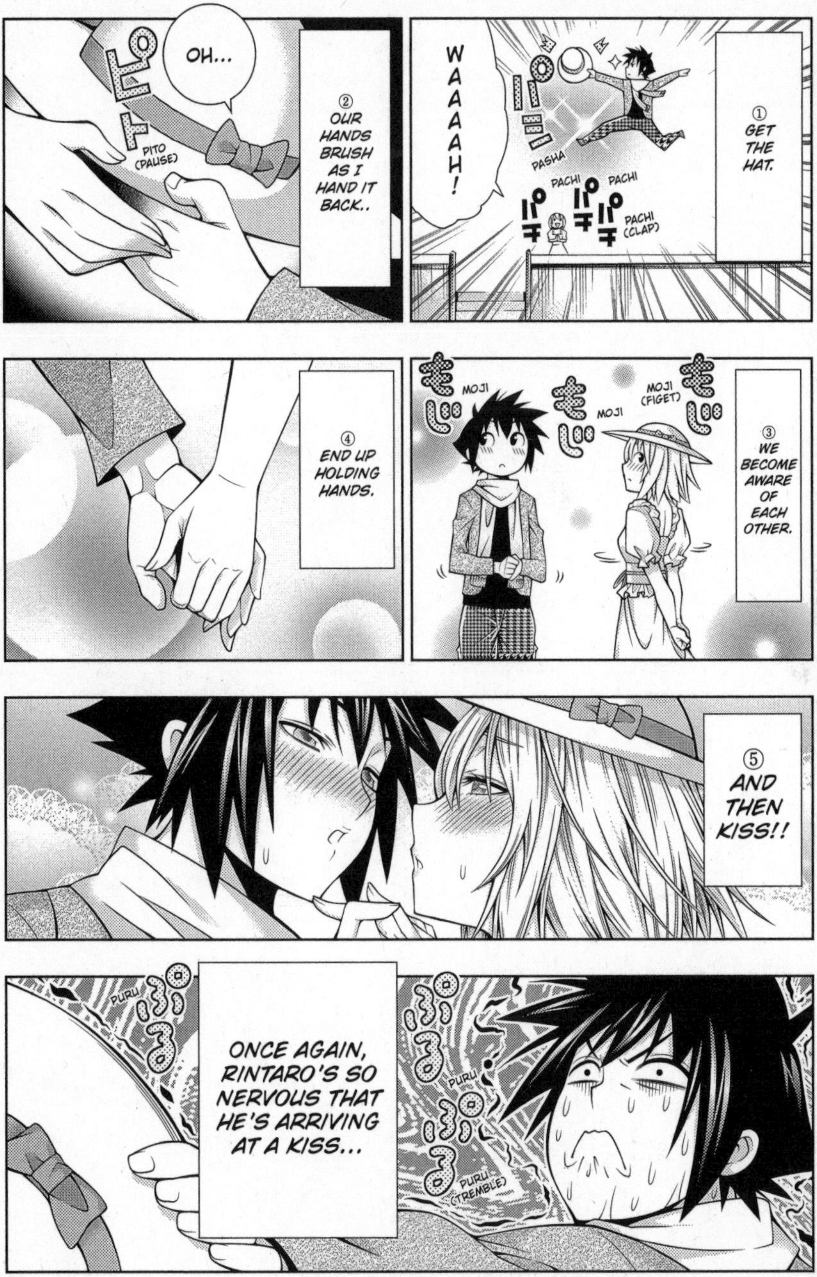
① GET THE HAT.
WAAAAAH!
PASHA
PACHI PACHI PACHI (CLAP)
② OUR HANDS BRUSH AS I HAND IT BACK..
OH...
PITO (PAUSE)
③ WE BECOME AWARE OF EACH OTHER.
MOJI (FIGET)
MOJI
MOJI
④ END UP HOLDING HANDS.
⑤ AND THEN KISS!!
PURU
PURU
PURU (TREMBLE)
ONCE AGAIN, RINTARO'S SO NERVOUS THAT HE'S ARRIVING AT A KISS...

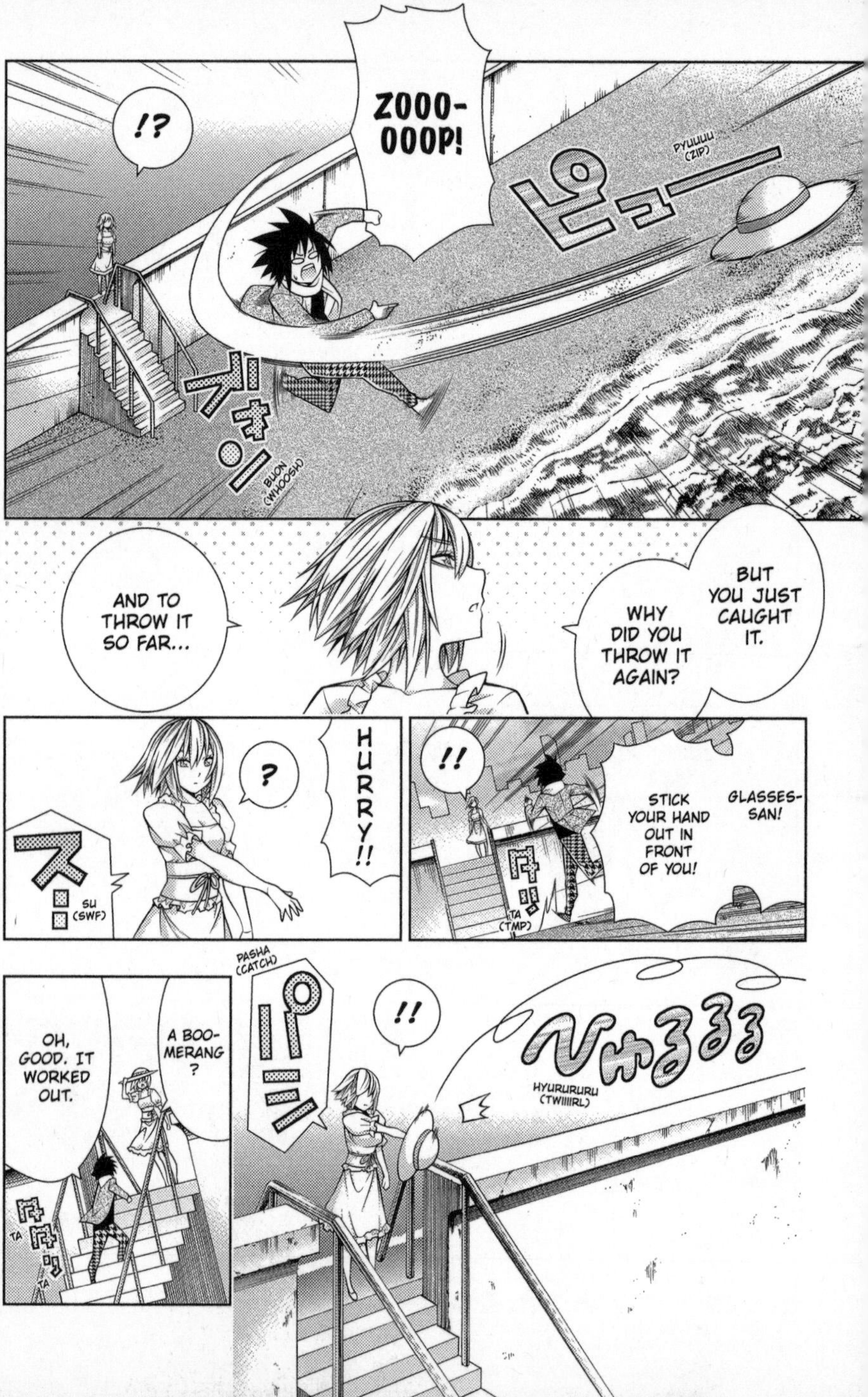
ZOOO-OOOP!
PYUUUU (ZIP)
!?
BUON (WHOOSH)
BUT YOU JUST CAUGHT IT.
WHY DID YOU THROW IT AGAIN?
AND TO THROW IT SO FAR...
GLASSES-SAN!
STICK YOUR HAND OUT IN FRONT OF YOU!
!!
TA (TMP)
HURRY!!
?
SU (SWF)
HYURURURU (TWIIIIRL)
!!
PASHA (CATCH)
A BOO-MERANG?
OH, GOOD. IT WORKED OUT.
TA
TA

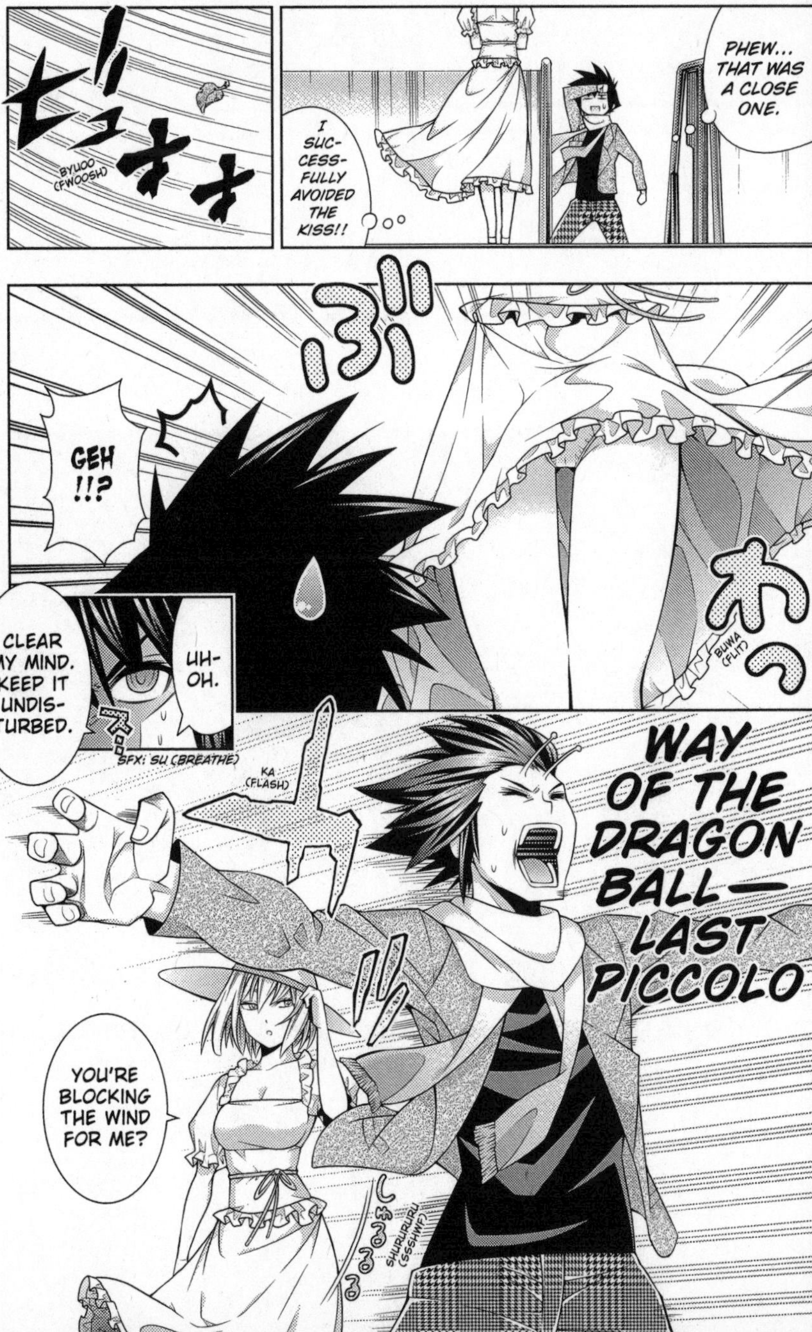
PHEW... THAT WAS A CLOSE ONE.
I SUCCESSFULLY AVOIDED THE KISS!!
BYUOO (FWOOSH)
BUWA (FLIT)
GEH!!?
UH-OH.
CLEAR MY MIND. KEEP IT UNDISTURBED.
SFX: SU (BREATHE)
WAY OF THE DRAGON BALL— LAST PICCOLO
KA (FLASH)
SHURURURU (SSSHWF)
YOU'RE BLOCKING THE WIND FOR ME?

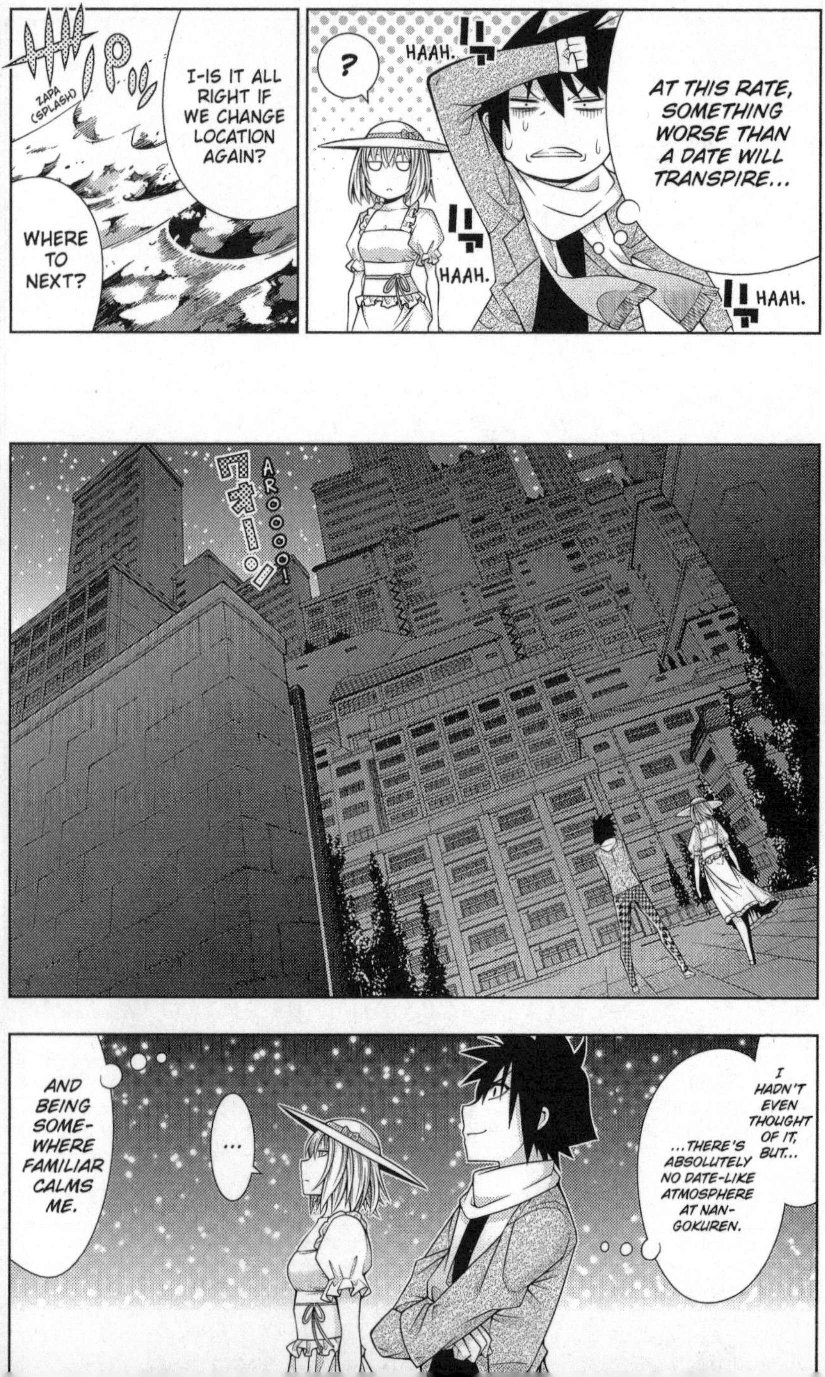
HAAH.
AT THIS RATE, SOMETHING WORSE THAN A DATE WILL TRANSPIRE...
?
HAAH.
HAAH.
I-IS IT ALL RIGHT IF WE CHANGE LOCATION AGAIN?
ZAPA (SPLASH)
WHERE TO NEXT?
AROOOOO!
I HADN'T EVEN THOUGHT OF IT, BUT...
...THERE'S ABSOLUTELY NO DATE-LIKE ATMOSPHERE AT NAN-GOKUREN.
...
AND BEING SOME-WHERE FAMILIAR CALMS ME.

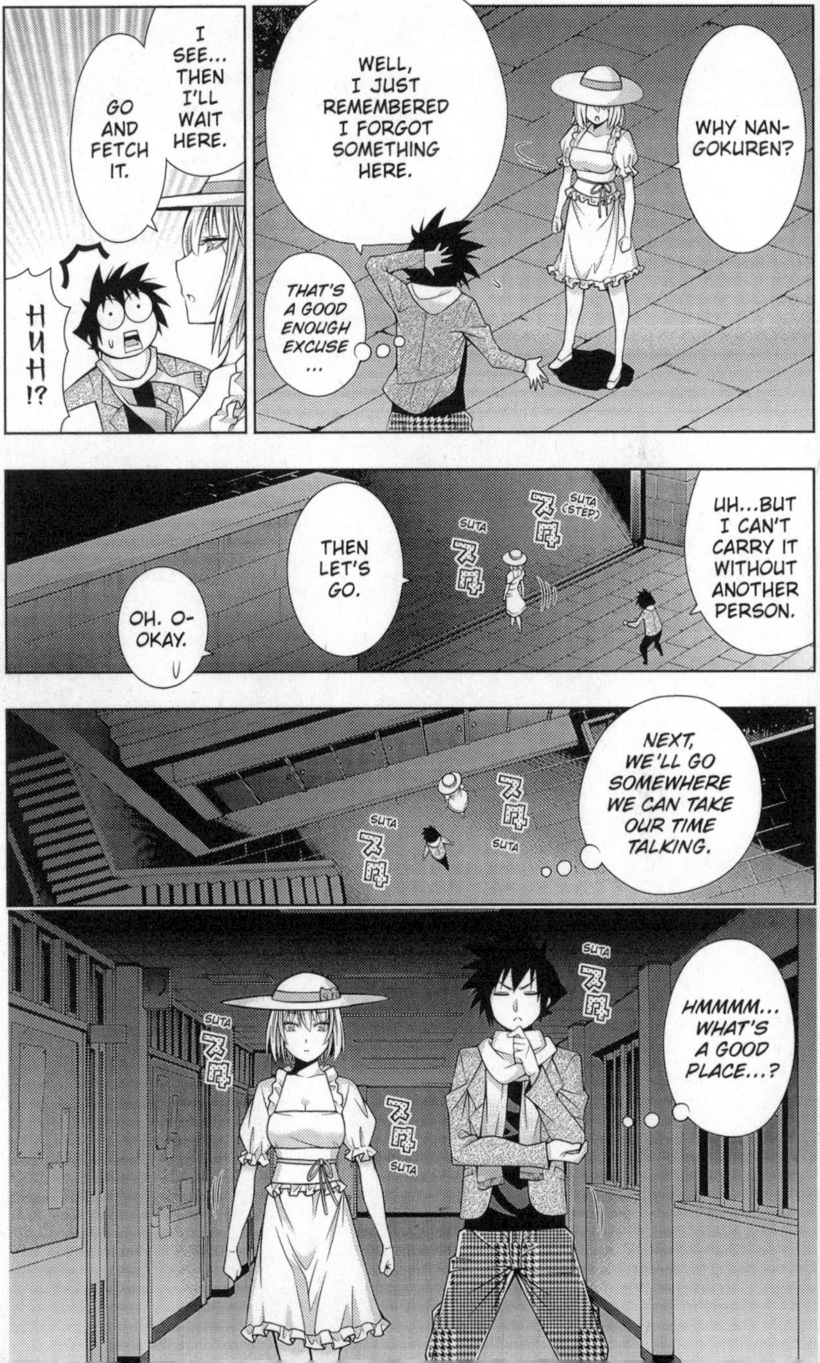
WHY NAN-GOKUREN?
WELL, I JUST REMEMBERED I FORGOT SOMETHING HERE.
THAT'S A GOOD ENOUGH EXCUSE ...
I SEE... THEN I'LL WAIT HERE.
GO AND FETCH IT.
HUH!?
UH...BUT I CAN'T CARRY IT WITHOUT ANOTHER PERSON.
SUTA (STEP)
SUTA
THEN LET'S GO.
OH. O-OKAY.
NEXT, WE'LL GO SOMEWHERE WE CAN TAKE OUR TIME TALKING.
SUTA
SUTA
HMMMM... WHAT'S A GOOD PLACE...?
SUTA
SUTA
SUTA

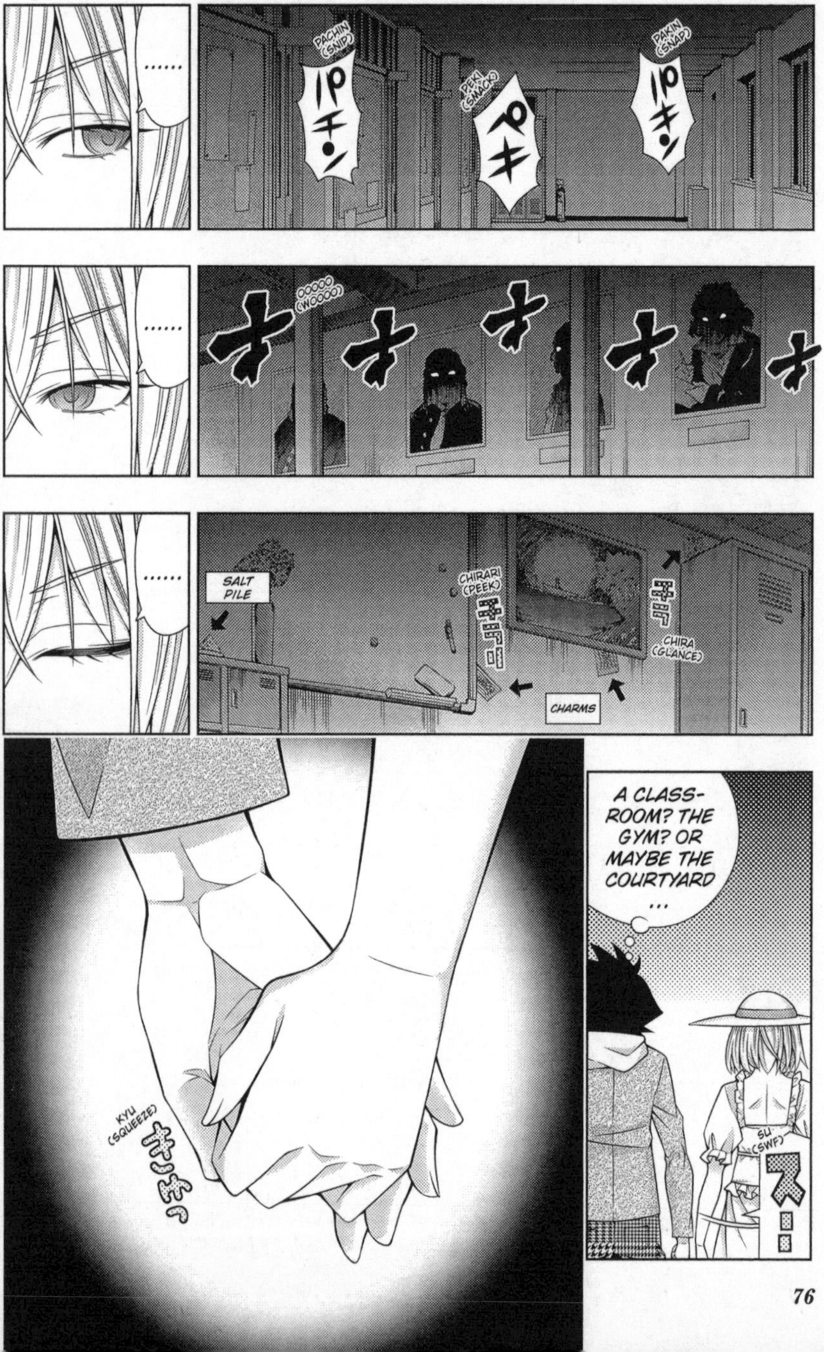
PAKIN (SNAP)
パキン
PEKI (SMACK)
ペキ
PACHIN (SNIP)
パチン
......
OOOOO (WOOOO)
オオオオオオ
......
CHIRA (GLANCE)
CHARMS
CHIRARI (PEEK)
SALT PILE
......
A CLASS-ROOM? THE GYM? OR MAYBE THE COURTYARD ...
SU (SWF)
ス…
KYU (SQUEEZE)

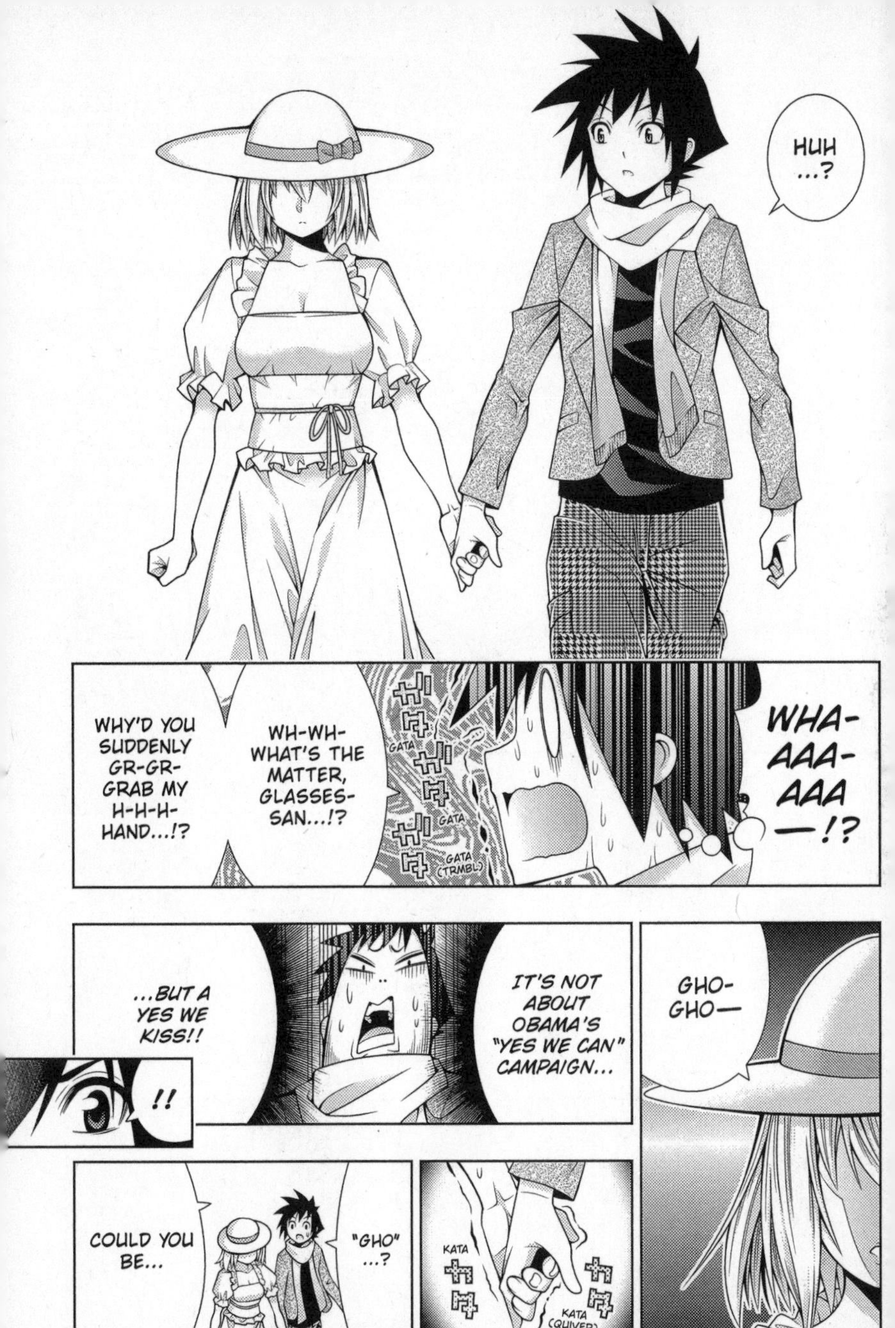
HUH ...?
WHA-AAA-AAA—!?
GATA GATA GATA (TRMBL)
WH-WH-WHAT'S THE MATTER, GLASSES-SAN...!?
WHY'D YOU SUDDENLY GR-GR-GRAB MY H-H-H-HAND...!?
GHO-GHO—
IT'S NOT ABOUT OBAMA'S "YES WE CAN" CAMPAIGN...
...BUT A YES WE KISS!!
!!
KATA KATA (QUIVER)
"GHO" ...?
COULD YOU BE...

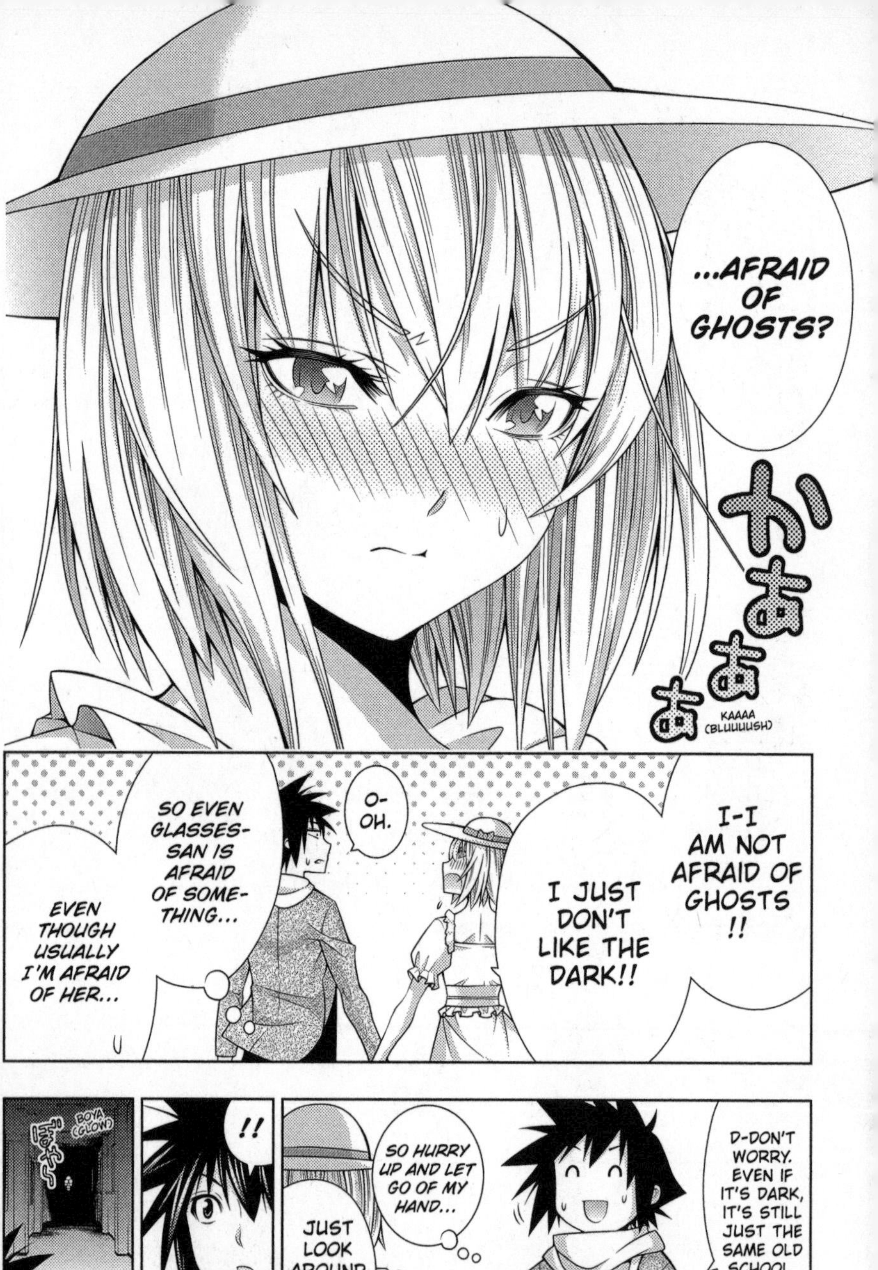
...AFRAID OF GHOSTS?
かぁぁぁ
KAAAA (BLUUUUSH)
I-I AM NOT AFRAID OF GHOSTS!!
I JUST DON'T LIKE THE DARK!!
O-OH.
SO EVEN GLASSES-SAN IS AFRAID OF SOME-THING...
EVEN THOUGH USUALLY I'M AFRAID OF HER...
D-DON'T WORRY. EVEN IF IT'S DARK, IT'S STILL JUST THE SAME OLD SCHOOL.
SO HURRY UP AND LET GO OF MY HAND...
JUST LOOK AROUND...
!!
ぼや
BOYA (GLOW)

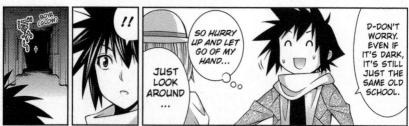

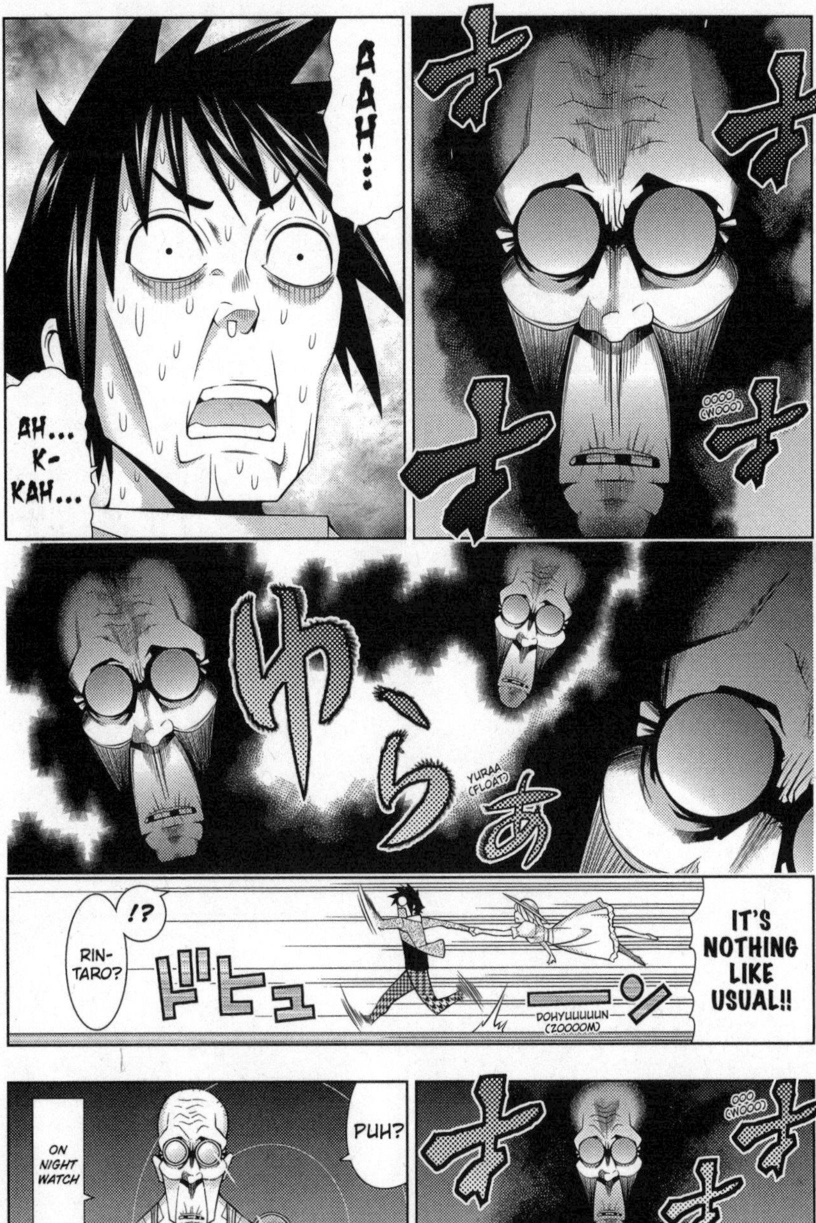
OOOO (WOOO)
AAH..
AH... K-KAH...
YURAA (FLOAT)
IT'S NOTHING LIKE USUAL!!
DOHYUUUUUN (ZOOOOM)
!?
RIN-TARO?
OOO (WOOO)
PUH?
ON NIGHT WATCH

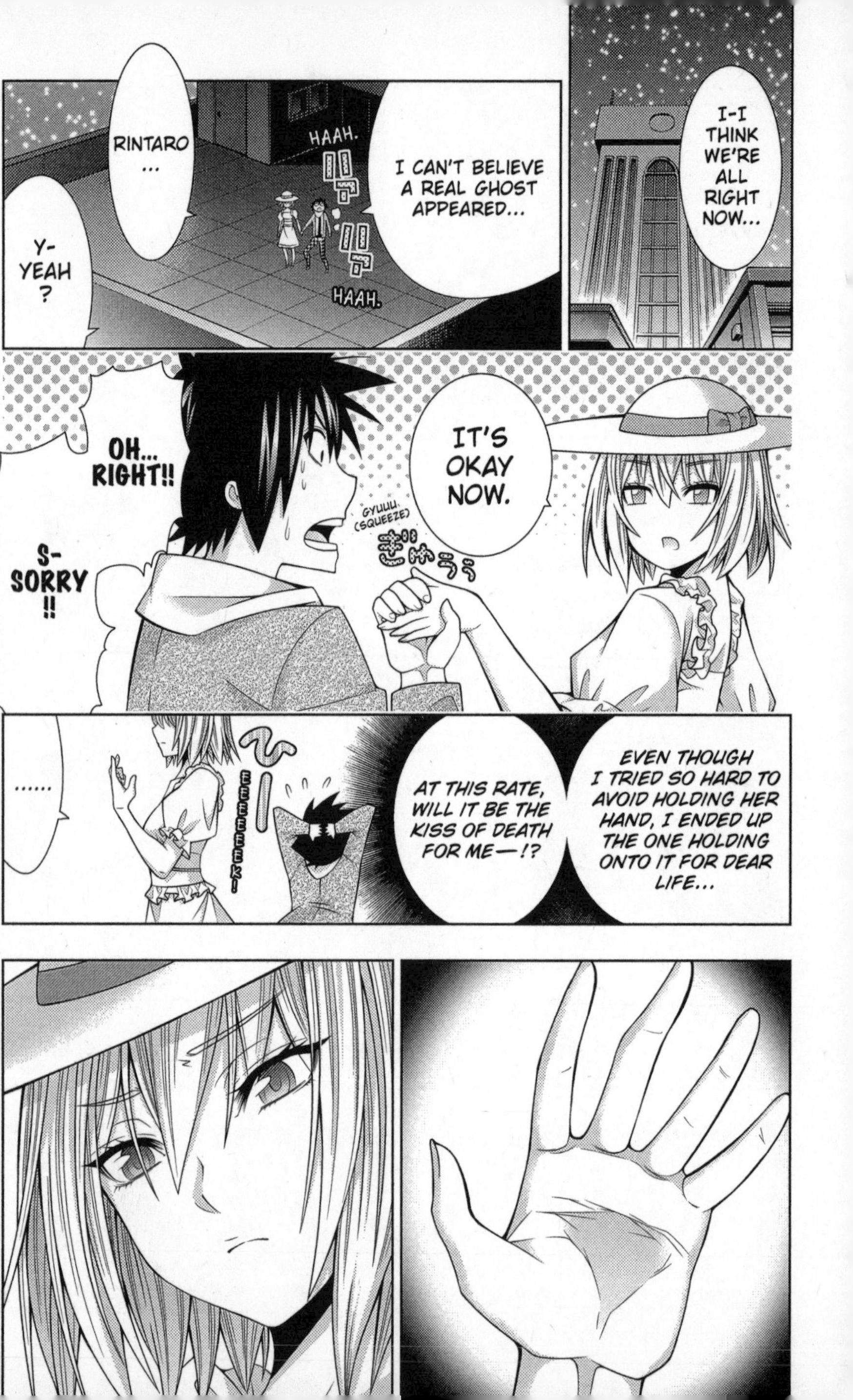
I-I THINK WE'RE ALL RIGHT NOW...
I CAN'T BELIEVE A REAL GHOST APPEARED...
HAAH.
HAAH.
RINTARO ...
Y-YEAH?
IT'S OKAY NOW.
GYUUU (SQUEEZE)
OH... RIGHT!!
S-SORRY!!
EVEN THOUGH I TRIED SO HARD TO AVOID HOLDING HER HAND, I ENDED UP THE ONE HOLDING ONTO IT FOR DEAR LIFE...
AT THIS RATE, WILL IT BE THE KISS OF DEATH FOR ME—!?
EEEEEEEEK!
......

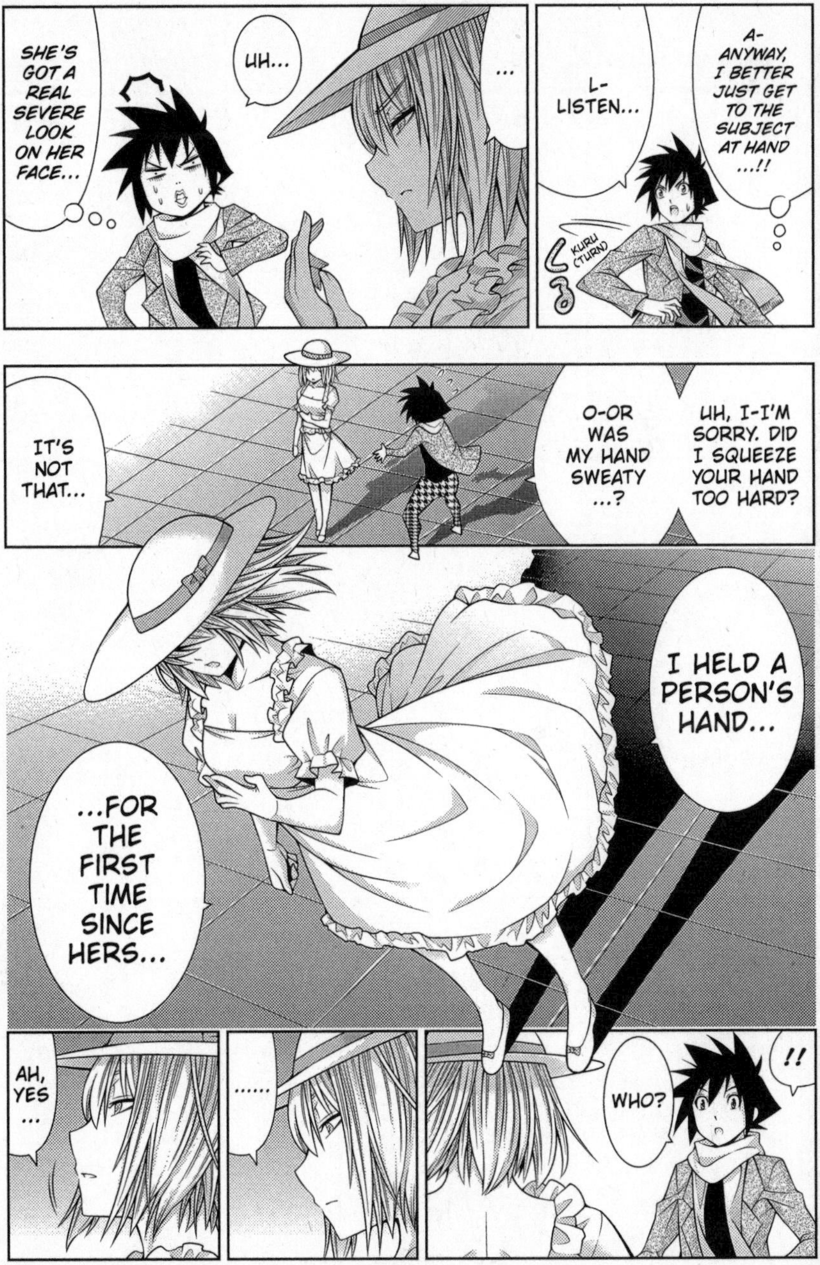
A- ANYWAY, I BETTER JUST GET TO THE SUBJECT AT HAND ...!!
L- LISTEN...
KURU (TURN)
...
UH...
SHE'S GOT A REAL SEVERE LOOK ON HER FACE...
UH, I-I'M SORRY. DID I SQUEEZE YOUR HAND TOO HARD?
O-OR WAS MY HAND SWEATY ...?
IT'S NOT THAT...
I HELD A PERSON'S HAND...
...FOR THE FIRST TIME SINCE HERS...
!!
WHO?
......
AH, YES ...

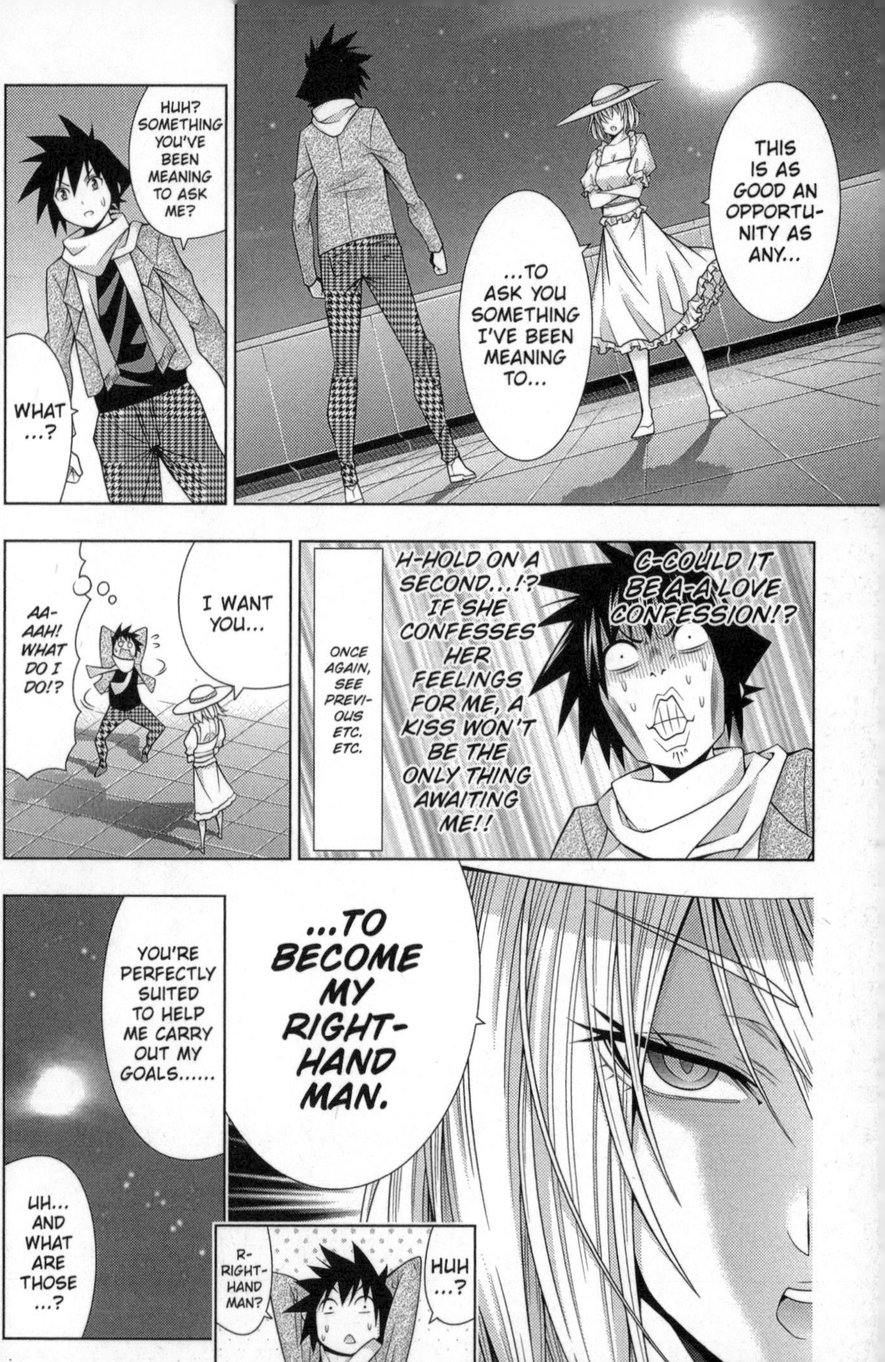
THIS IS AS GOOD AN OPPORTUNITY AS ANY...
...TO ASK YOU SOMETHING I'VE BEEN MEANING TO...
HUH? SOMETHING YOU'VE BEEN MEANING TO ASK ME?
WHAT...?
C-COULD IT BE A-A LOVE CONFESSION!?
H-HOLD ON A SECOND...!? IF SHE CONFESSES HER FEELINGS FOR ME, A KISS WON'T BE THE ONLY THING AWAITING ME!!
ONCE AGAIN, SEE PREVIOUS ETC. ETC.
I WANT YOU...
AA-AAH! WHAT DO I DO!?
...TO BECOME MY RIGHT-HAND MAN.
YOU'RE PERFECTLY SUITED TO HELP ME CARRY OUT MY GOALS......
HUH...?
R-RIGHT-HAND MAN?
UH... AND WHAT ARE THOSE...?

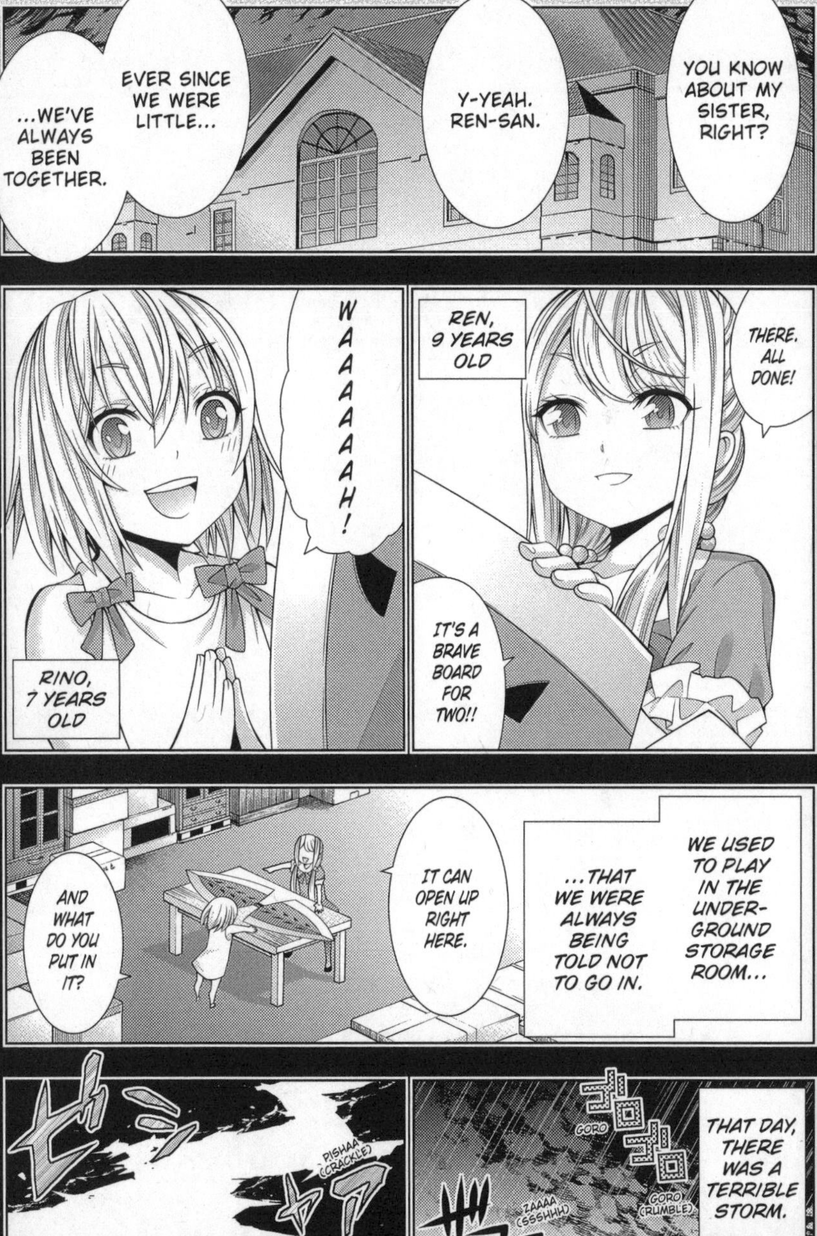
YOU KNOW ABOUT MY SISTER, RIGHT?
Y-YEAH. REN-SAN.
EVER SINCE WE WERE LITTLE...
...WE'VE ALWAYS BEEN TOGETHER.
REN, 9 YEARS OLD
THERE. ALL DONE!
IT'S A BRAVE BOARD FOR TWO!!
WAAAAAAAH!
RINO, 7 YEARS OLD
WE USED TO PLAY IN THE UNDER-GROUND STORAGE ROOM...
...THAT WE WERE ALWAYS BEING TOLD NOT TO GO IN.
IT CAN OPEN UP RIGHT HERE.
AND WHAT DO YOU PUT IN IT?
THAT DAY, THERE WAS A TERRIBLE STORM.
GORO
GORO (RUMBLE)
ZAAAA (SSSHHH)
PISHAA (CRACKLE)

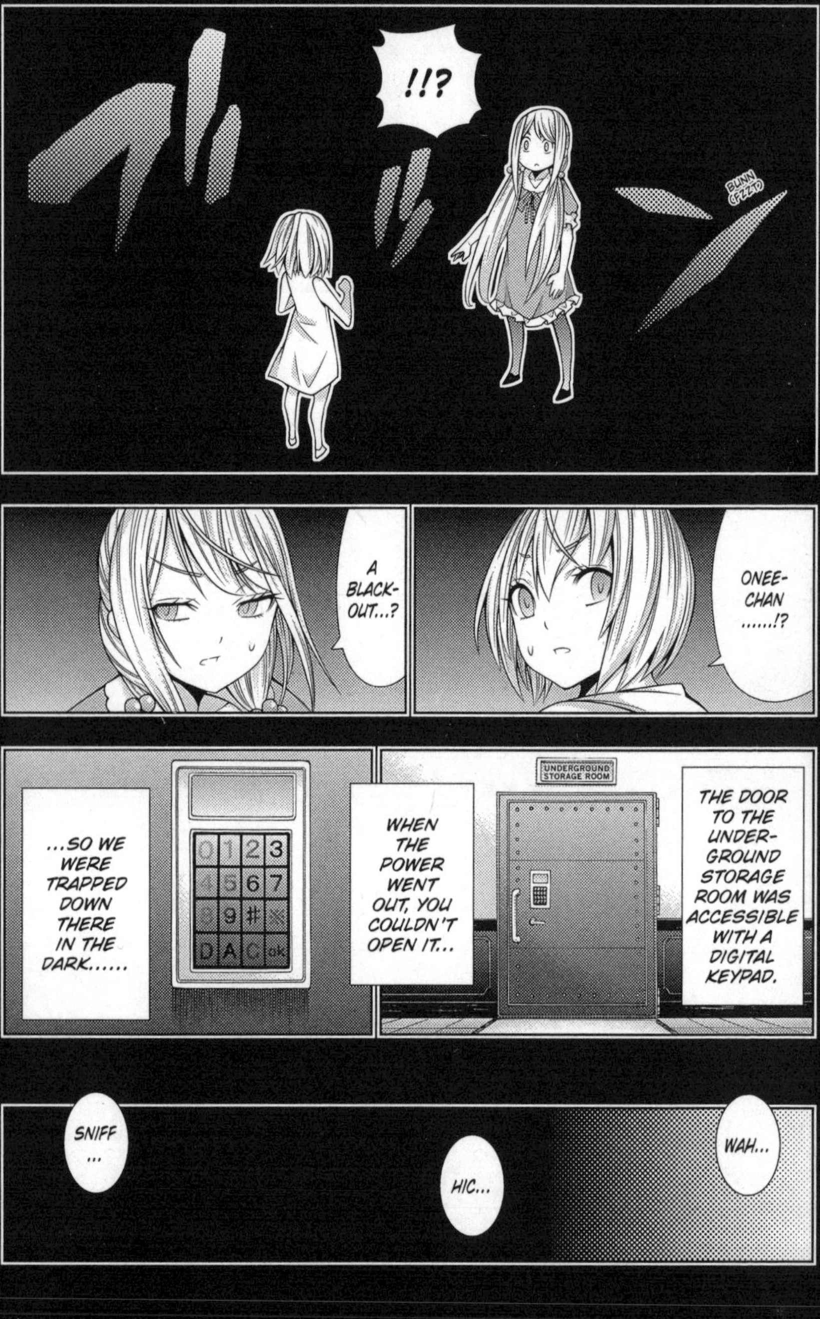
BUNN (FZZT)
!!?
ONEE-CHAN ......!?
A BLACK-OUT...?
THE DOOR TO THE UNDERGROUND STORAGE ROOM WAS ACCESSIBLE WITH A DIGITAL KEYPAD.
UNDERGROUND STORAGE ROOM
WHEN THE POWER WENT OUT, YOU COULDN'T OPEN IT...
...SO WE WERE TRAPPED DOWN THERE IN THE DARK......
WAH...
HIC...
SNIFF ...

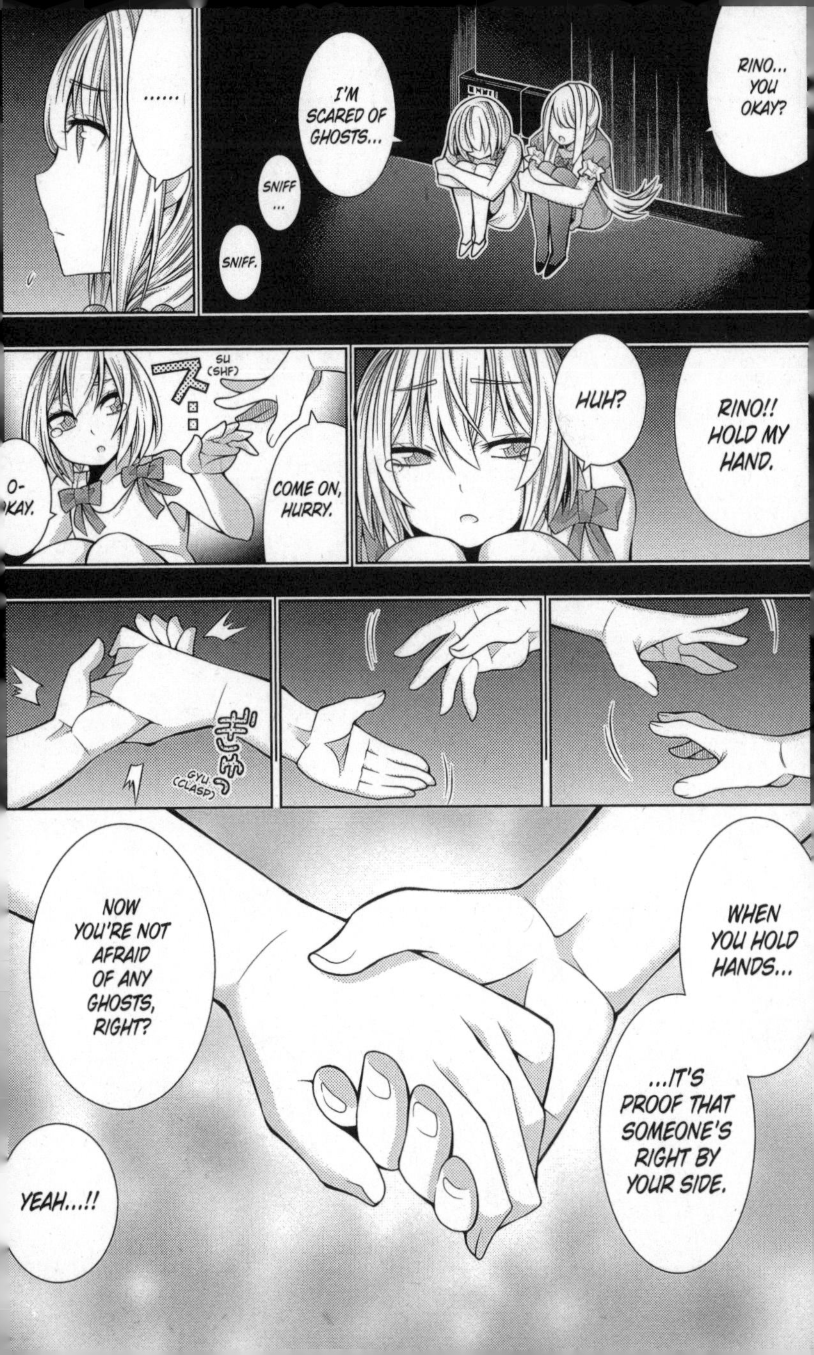
RINO... YOU OKAY?
I'M SCARED OF GHOSTS...
SNIFF...
SNIFF.
......
RINO!! HOLD MY HAND.
HUH?
SU (SHF)
COME ON, HURRY.
O- KAY.
GYU (CLASP)
WHEN YOU HOLD HANDS...
...IT'S PROOF THAT SOMEONE'S RIGHT BY YOUR SIDE.
NOW YOU'RE NOT AFRAID OF ANY GHOSTS, RIGHT?
YEAH...!!

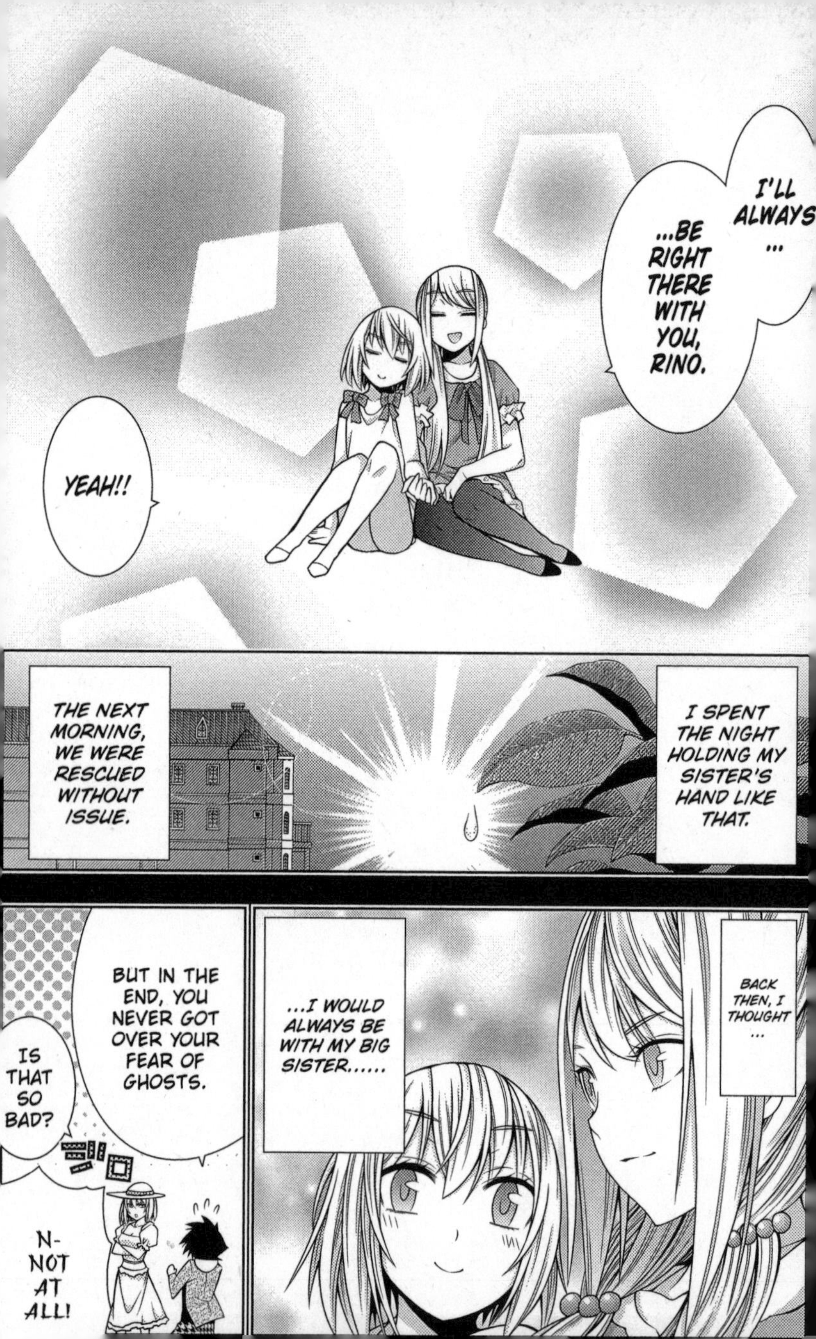
I'LL ALWAYS ...
...BE RIGHT THERE WITH YOU, RINO.
YEAH!!
I SPENT THE NIGHT HOLDING MY SISTER'S HAND LIKE THAT.
THE NEXT MORNING, WE WERE RESCUED WITHOUT ISSUE.
BACK THEN, I THOUGHT ...
...I WOULD ALWAYS BE WITH MY BIG SISTER......
BUT IN THE END, YOU NEVER GOT OVER YOUR FEAR OF GHOSTS.
IS THAT SO BAD?
N-NOT AT ALL!

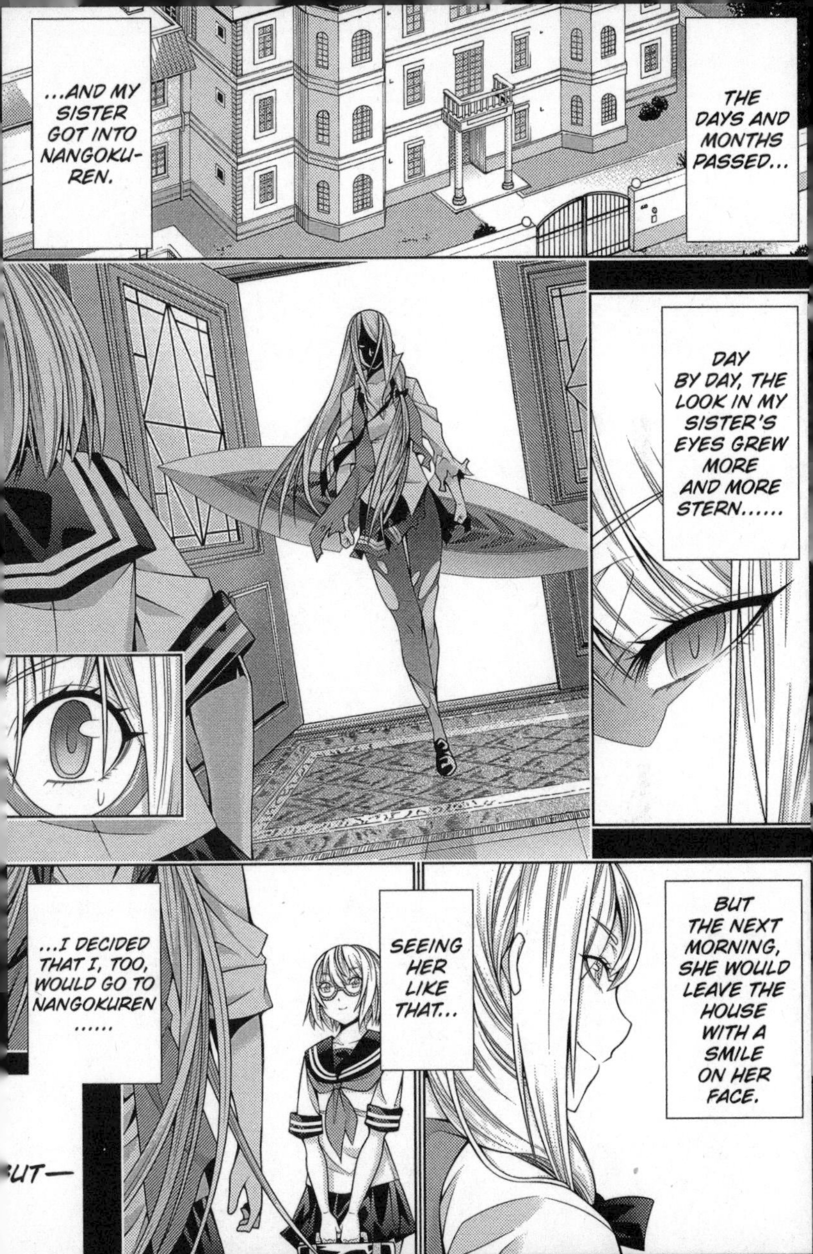
THE DAYS AND MONTHS PASSED...
...AND MY SISTER GOT INTO NANGOKU-REN.
DAY BY DAY, THE LOOK IN MY SISTER'S EYES GREW MORE AND MORE STERN......
BUT THE NEXT MORNING, SHE WOULD LEAVE THE HOUSE WITH A SMILE ON HER FACE.
SEEING HER LIKE THAT...
...I DECIDED THAT I, TOO, WOULD GO TO NANGOKUREN ......

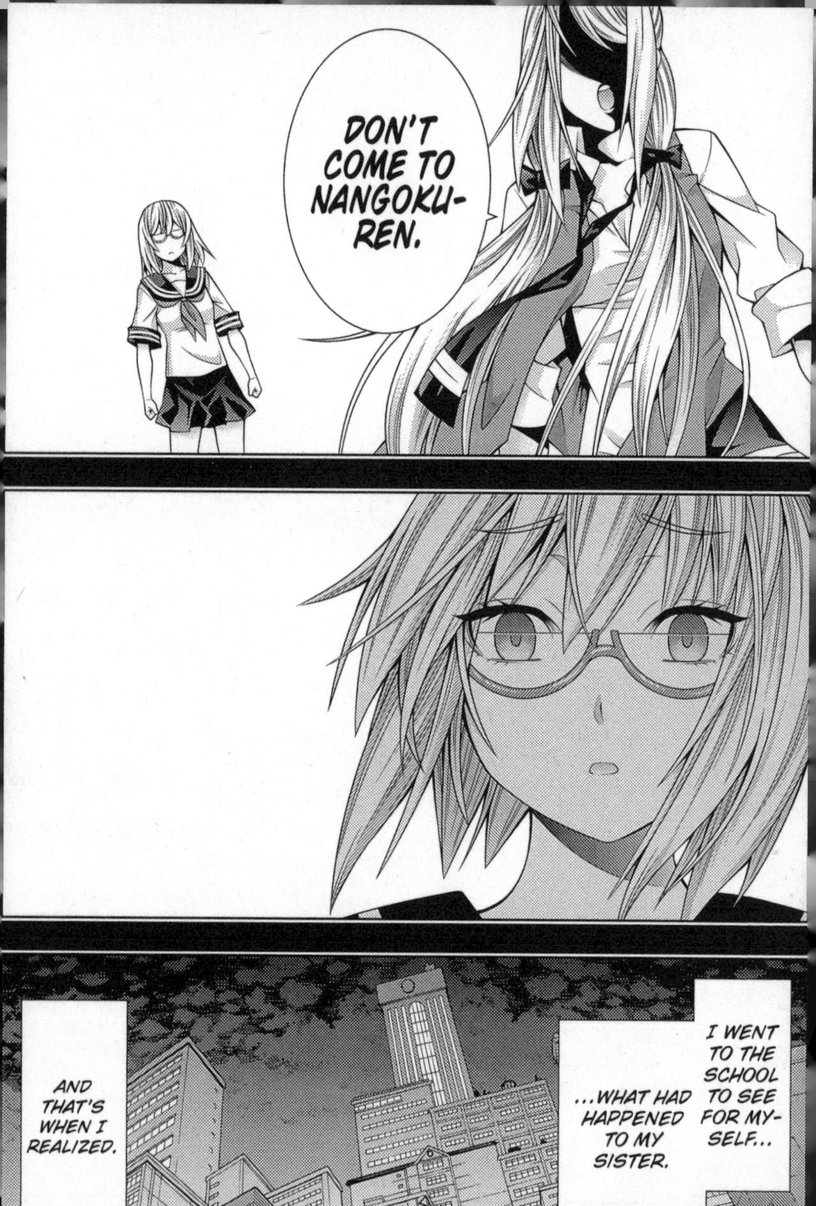
DON'T COME TO NANGOKU-REN.
I WENT TO THE SCHOOL TO SEE FOR MY-SELF...
...WHAT HAD HAPPENED TO MY SISTER.
AND THAT'S WHEN I REALIZED.

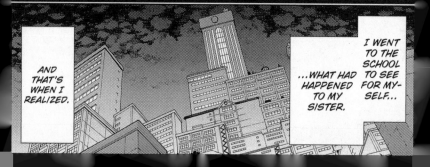

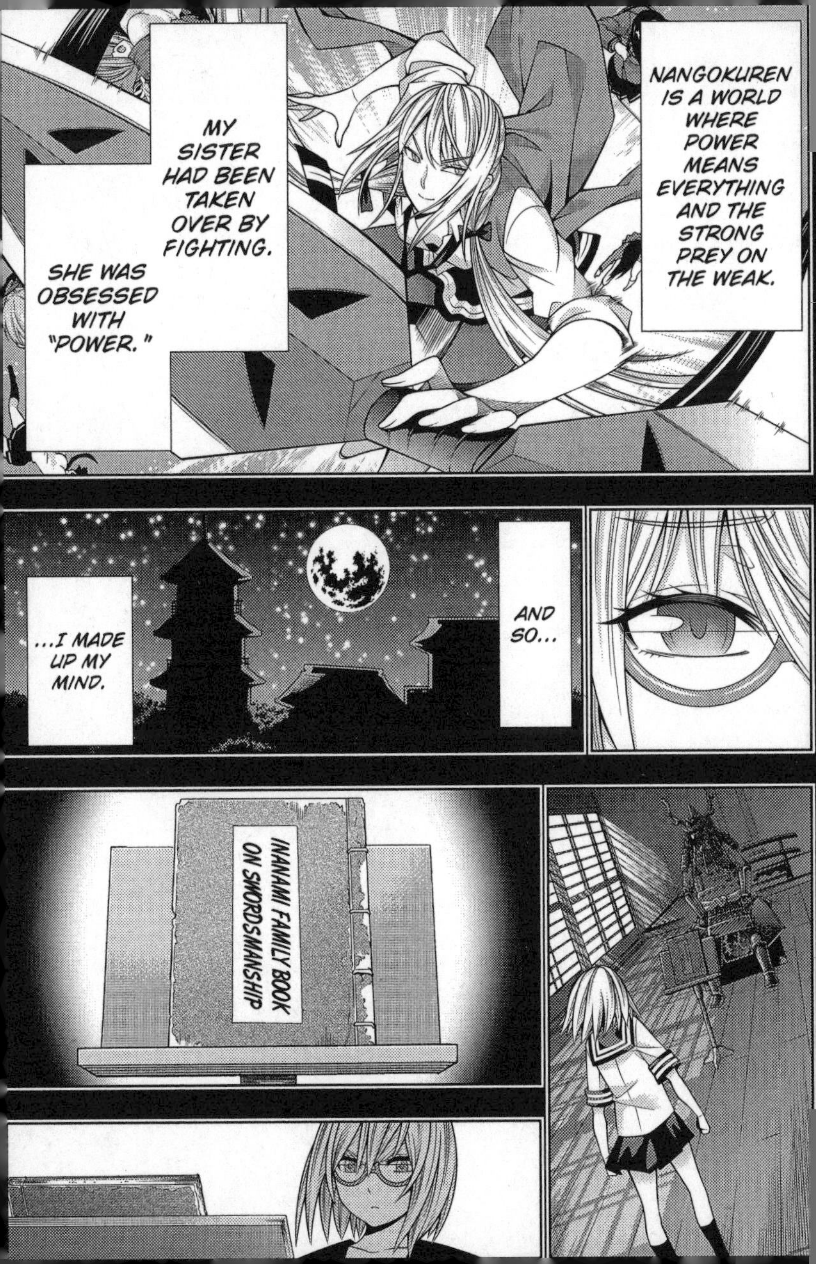
NANGOKUREN IS A WORLD WHERE POWER MEANS EVERYTHING AND THE STRONG PREY ON THE WEAK.
MY SISTER HAD BEEN TAKEN OVER BY FIGHTING.
SHE WAS OBSESSED WITH "POWER."
AND SO...
...I MADE UP MY MIND.
INANAMI FAMILY BOOK ON SWORDSMANSHIP

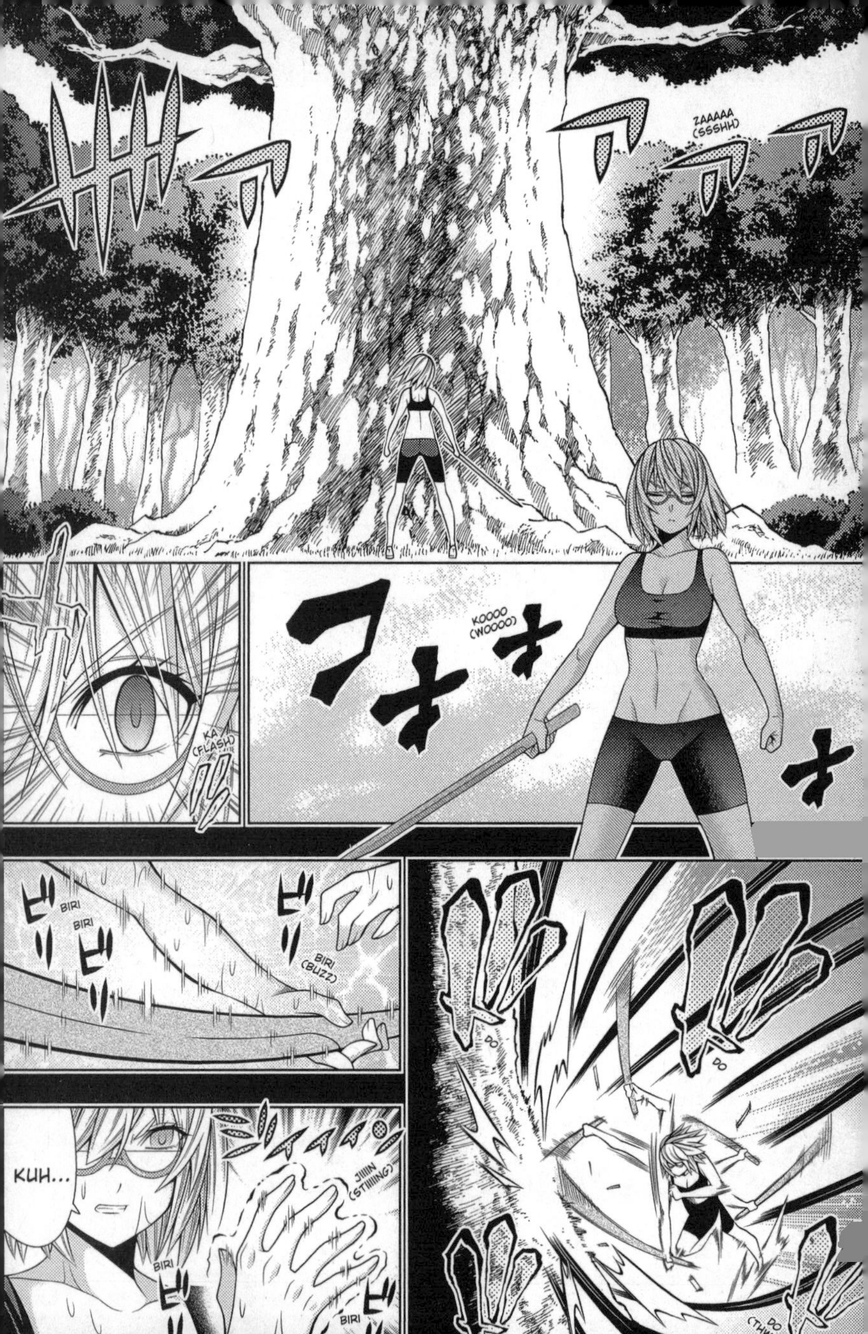
ZAAAAA (SSSHH)
KOOOO (WOOOO)
KA (FLASH)
DO
DO
DO
BIRI (BUZZ)
BIRI
BIRI
JIIIN (STIIIING)
KUH...
BIRI
BIRI

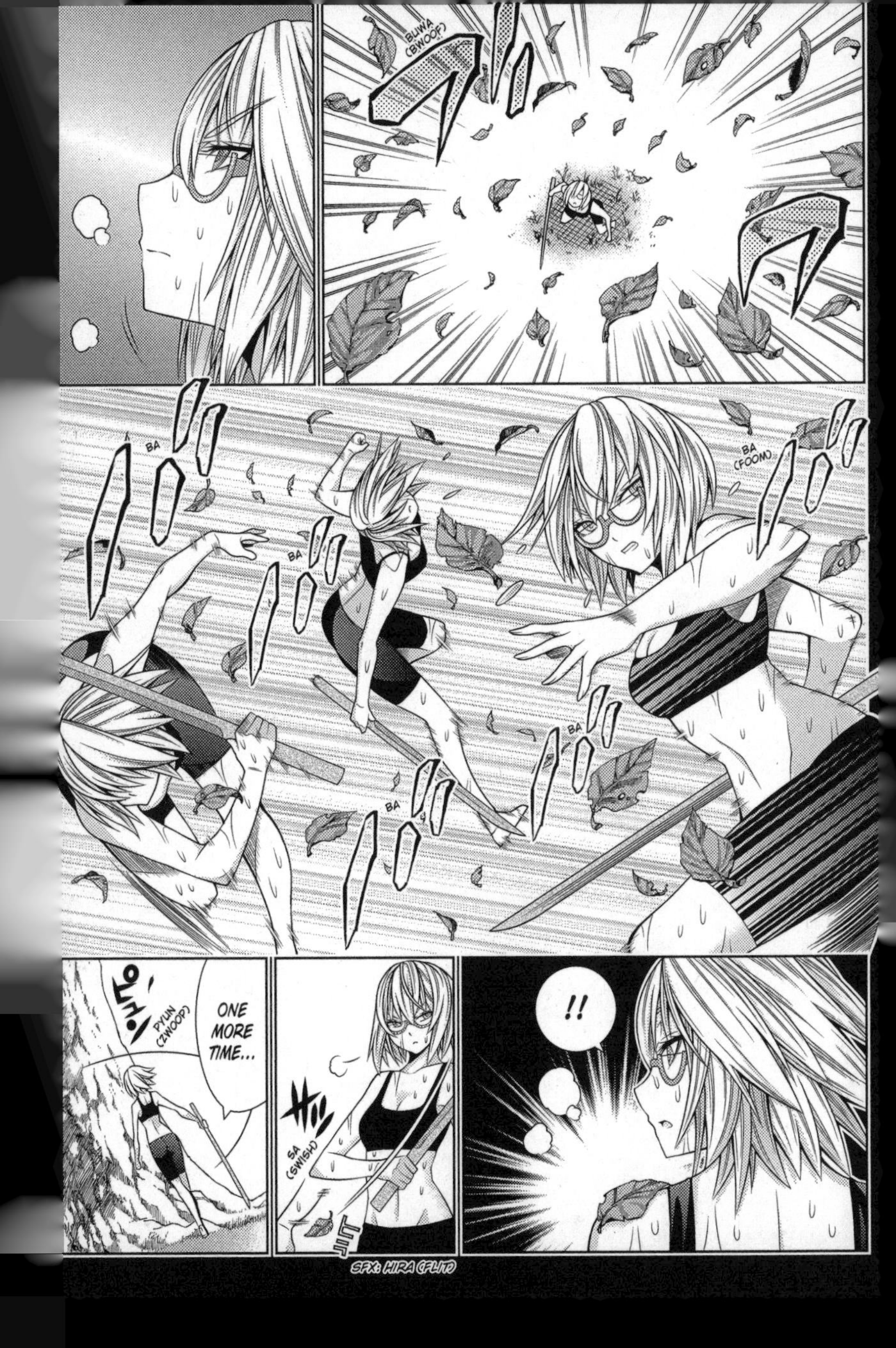
BUWA (BWOOF)
BA (FOOM)
BA
BA
BA
BA
!!
SA (SWISH)
PYUN (ZWOOP)
ONE MORE TIME...
SFX: HIRA (FLIT)

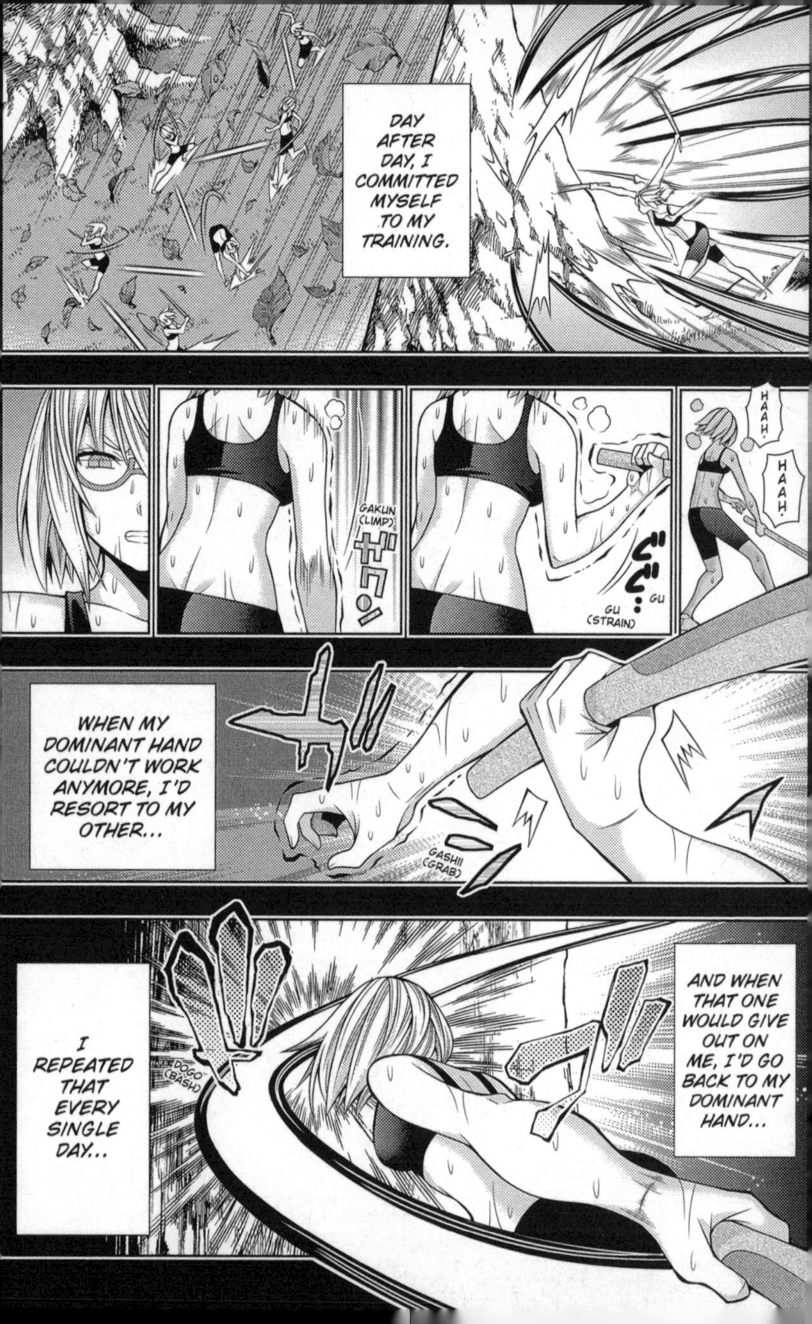
DAY AFTER DAY, I COMMITTED MYSELF TO MY TRAINING.
HAAH.
HAAH.
GU
GU (STRAIN)
GAKUN (LIMP)
WHEN MY DOMINANT HAND COULDN'T WORK ANYMORE, I'D RESORT TO MY OTHER...
GASHII (GRAB)
AND WHEN THAT ONE WOULD GIVE OUT ON ME, I'D GO BACK TO MY DOMINANT HAND...
DOGO (BASH)
I REPEATED THAT EVERY SINGLE DAY...

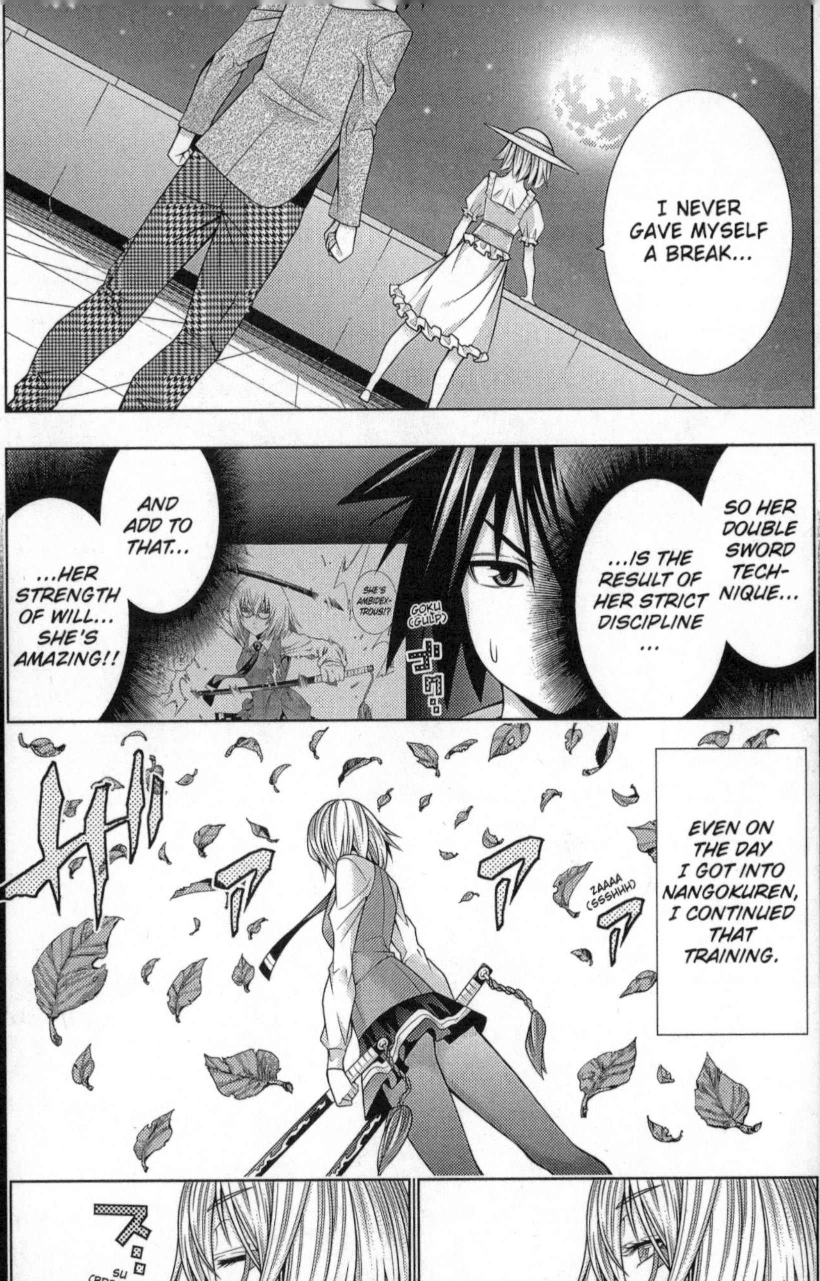
I NEVER GAVE MYSELF A BREAK...
SO HER DOUBLE SWORD TECH-NIQUE...
...IS THE RESULT OF HER STRICT DISCIPLINE ...
GOKU (GULP)
SHE'S AMBIDEX-TROUS!?
AND ADD TO THAT...
...HER STRENGTH OF WILL... SHE'S AMAZING!!
EVEN ON THE DAY I GOT INTO NANGOKUREN, I CONTINUED THAT TRAINING.
ZAAAA (SSSHHH)
SU (BREATHE)

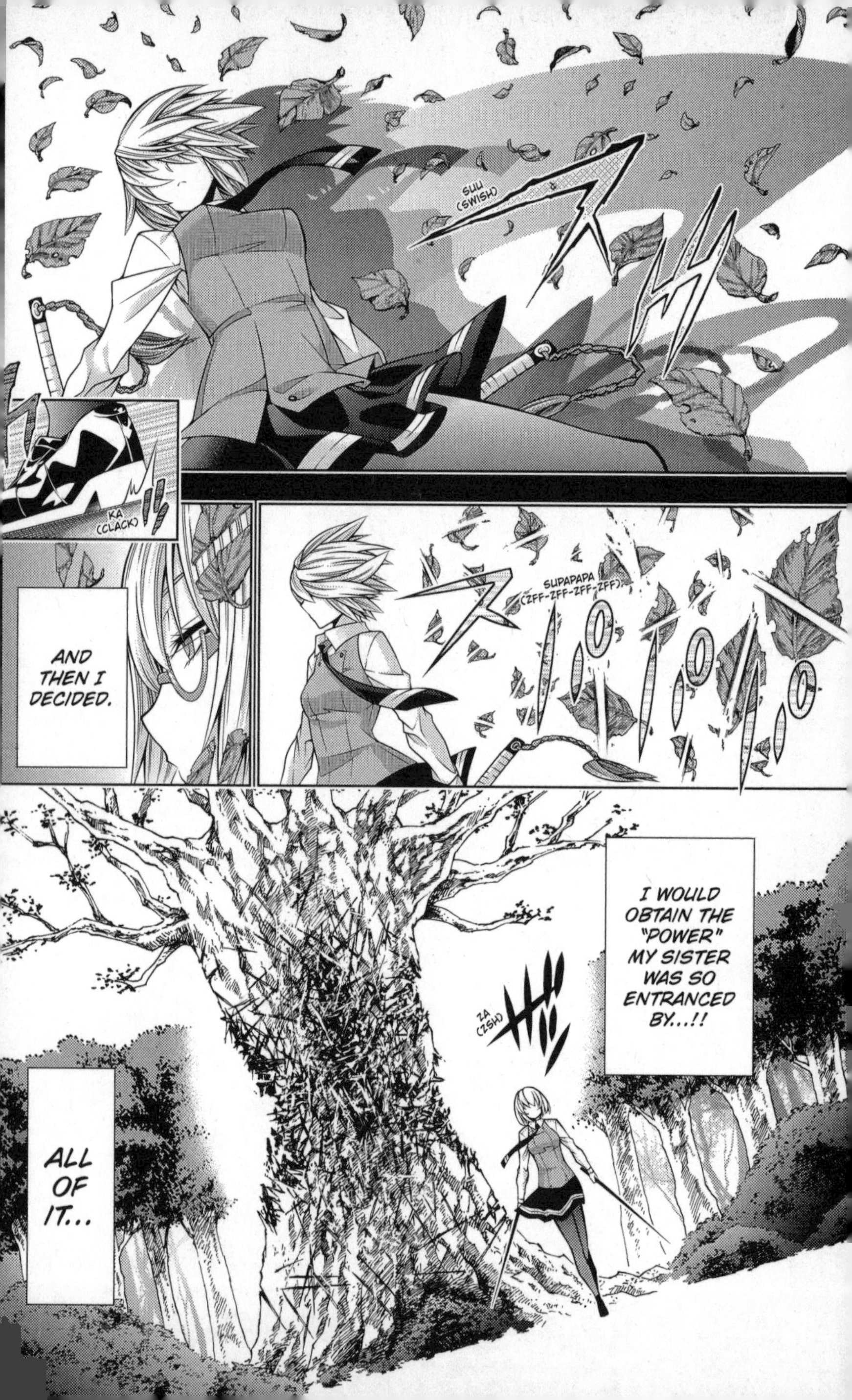
SUU (SWISH)
KA (CLACK)
SUPAPAPA (ZFF-ZFF-ZFF-ZFF)
AND THEN I DECIDED.
I WOULD OBTAIN THE "POWER" MY SISTER WAS SO ENTRANCED BY...!!
ZA (ZSH)
ALL OF IT...

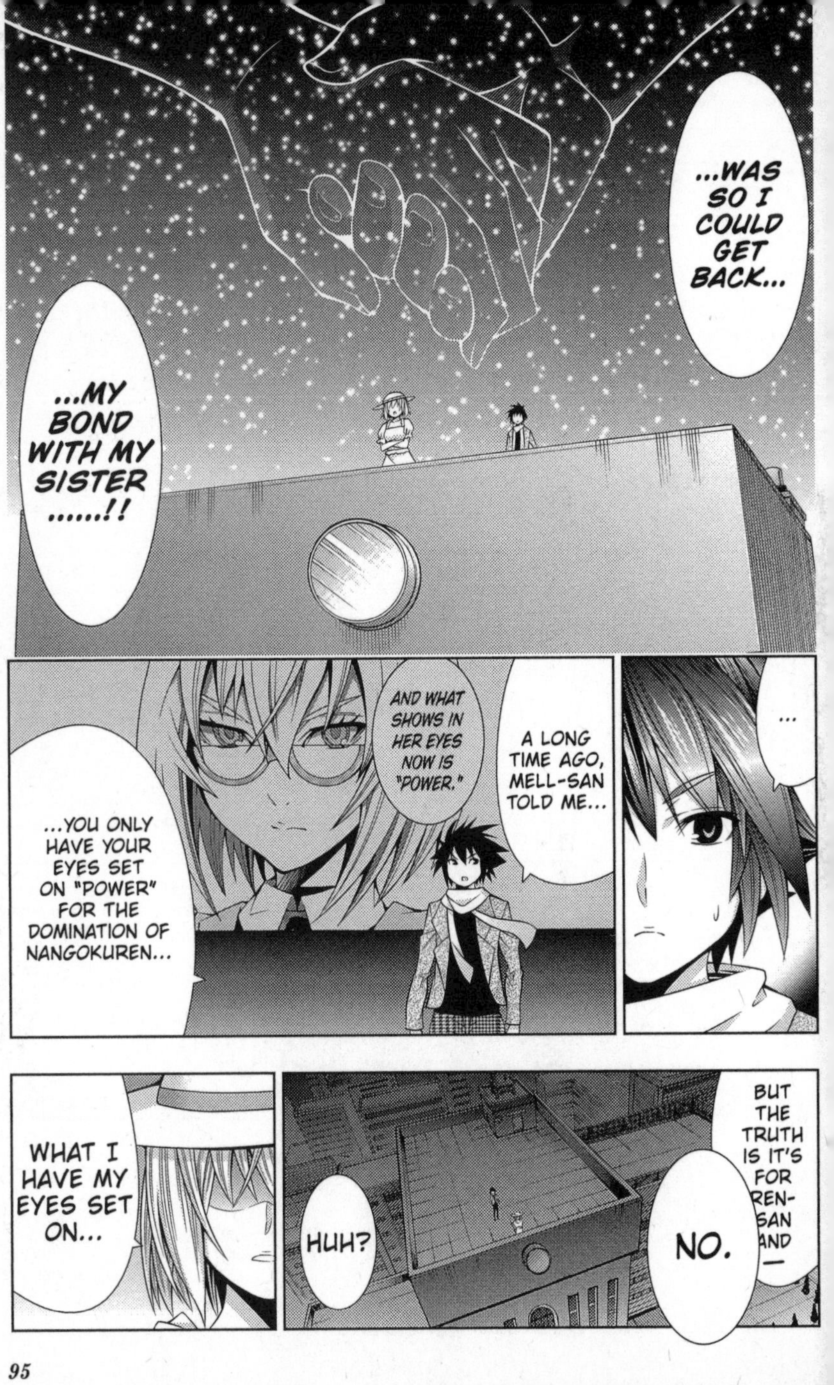
...WAS SO I COULD GET BACK...
...MY BOND WITH MY SISTER ......!!
...
A LONG TIME AGO, MELL-SAN TOLD ME...
AND WHAT SHOWS IN HER EYES NOW IS "POWER."
...YOU ONLY HAVE YOUR EYES SET ON "POWER" FOR THE DOMINATION OF NANGOKUREN...
BUT THE TRUTH IS IT'S FOR REN-SAN AND—
NO.
HUH?
WHAT I HAVE MY EYES SET ON...

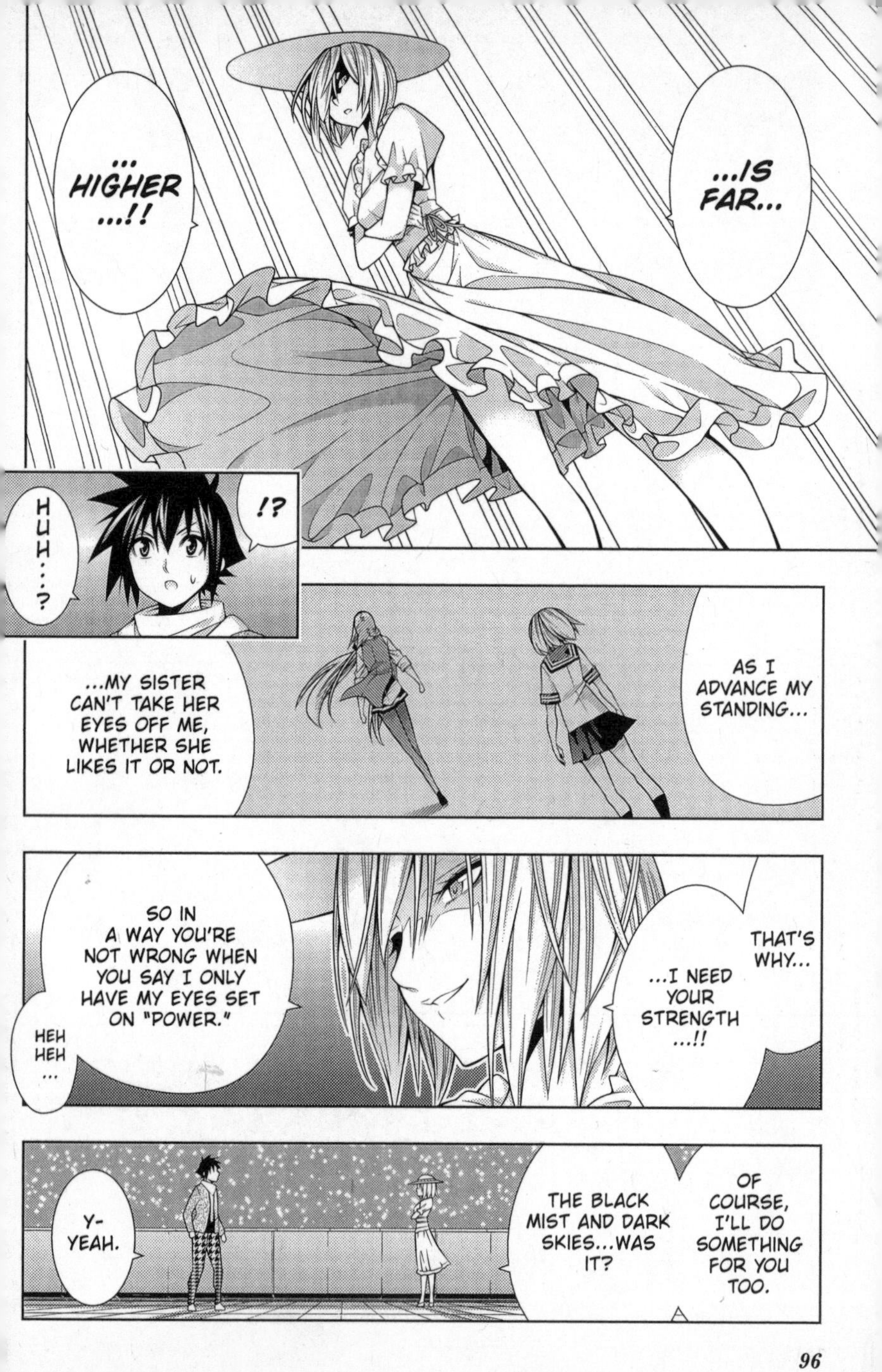
...IS FAR...
...HIGHER...!!
!?
HUH...?
AS I ADVANCE MY STANDING...
...MY SISTER CAN'T TAKE HER EYES OFF ME, WHETHER SHE LIKES IT OR NOT.
SO IN A WAY YOU'RE NOT WRONG WHEN YOU SAY I ONLY HAVE MY EYES SET ON "POWER."
HEH HEH...
THAT'S WHY...
...I NEED YOUR STRENGTH...!!
OF COURSE, I'LL DO SOMETHING FOR YOU TOO.
THE BLACK MIST AND DARK SKIES...WAS IT?
Y-YEAH.

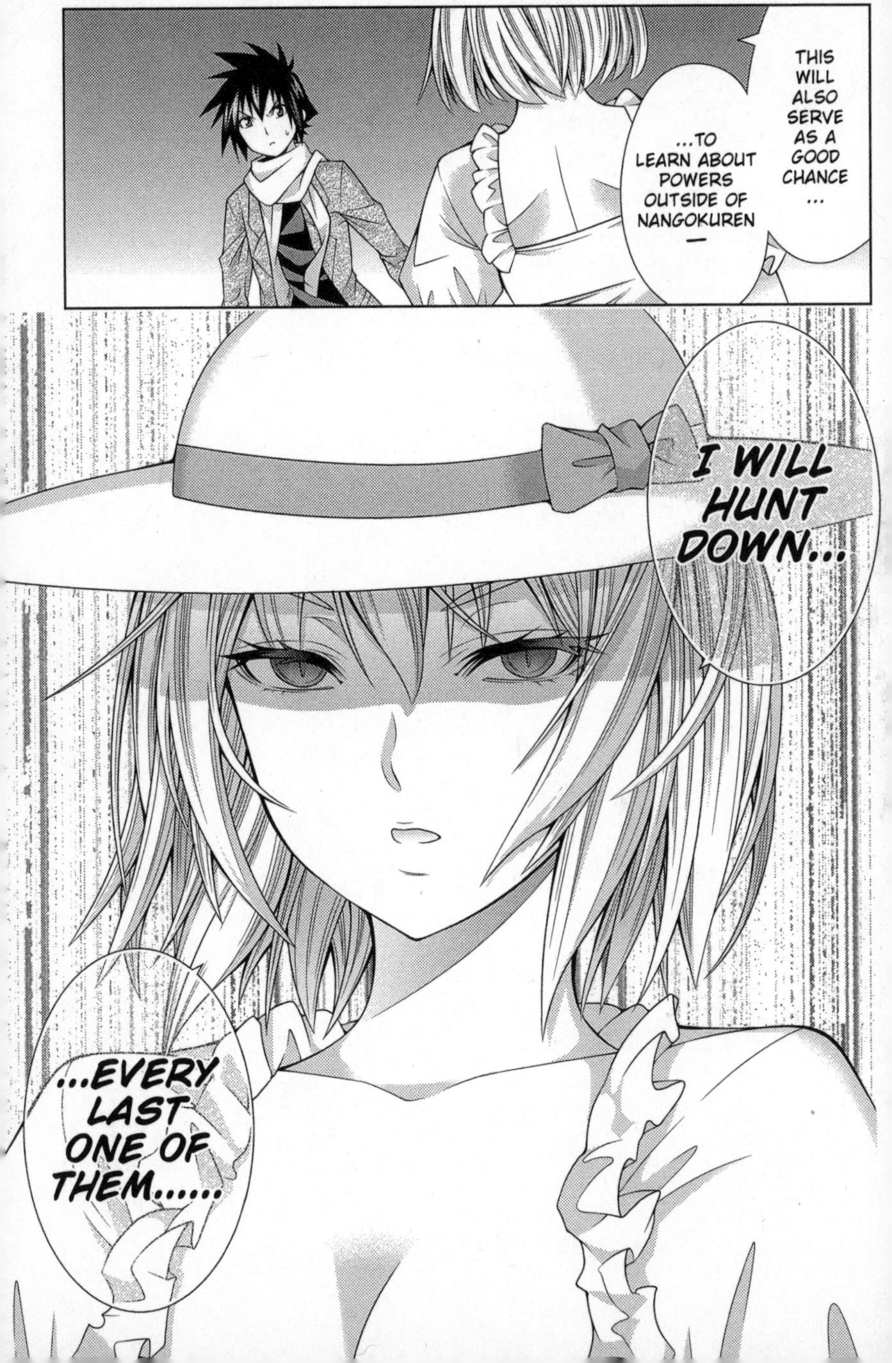
THIS WILL ALSO SERVE AS A GOOD CHANCE...
...TO LEARN ABOUT POWERS OUTSIDE OF NANGOKUREN—
I WILL HUNT DOWN...
...EVERY LAST ONE OF THEM......

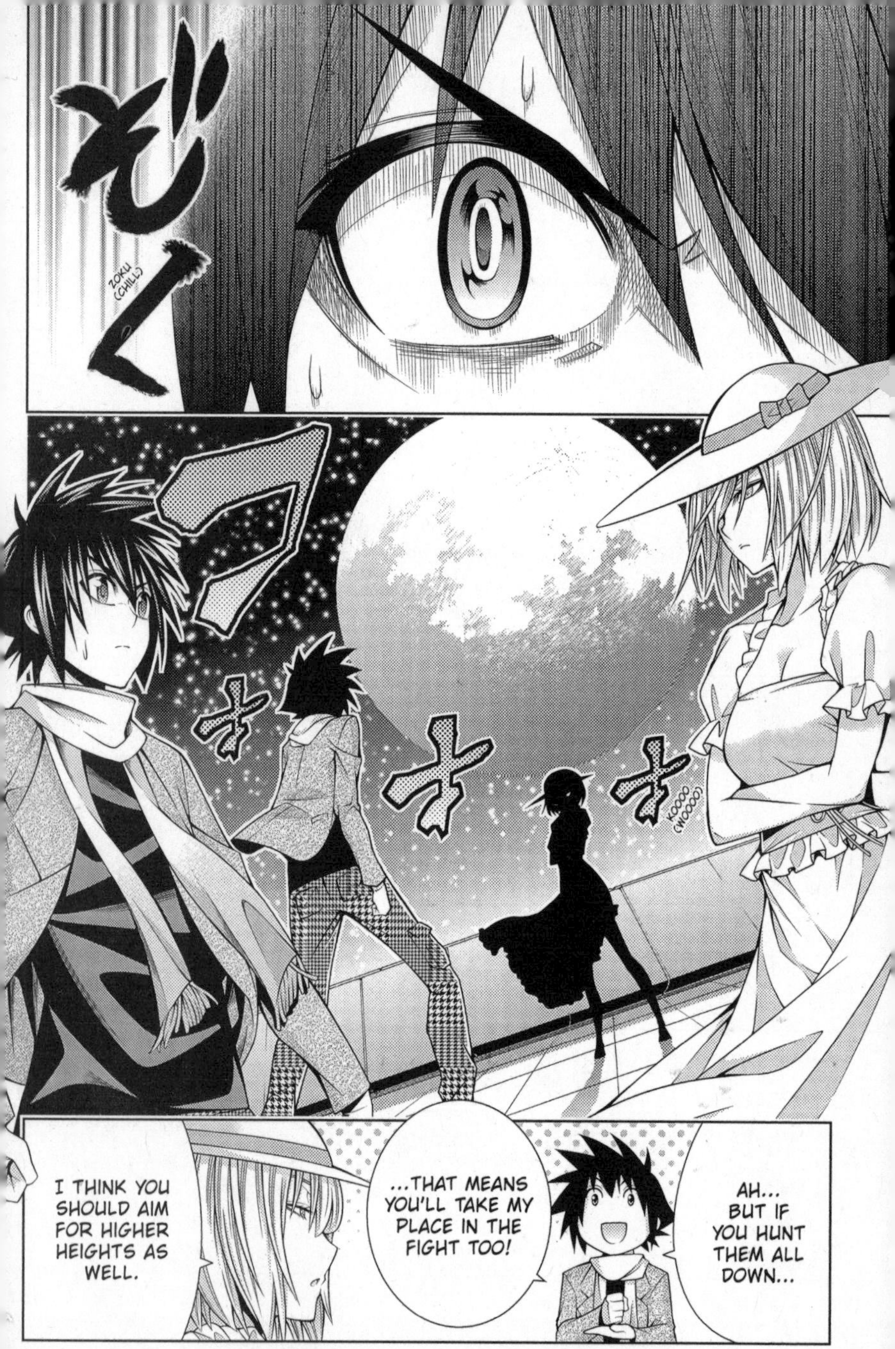
ZOKU (CHILL)
KOOOO (WOOOO)
AH... BUT IF YOU HUNT THEM ALL DOWN...
...THAT MEANS YOU'LL TAKE MY PLACE IN THE FIGHT TOO!
I THINK YOU SHOULD AIM FOR HIGHER HEIGHTS AS WELL.

DRAGON 38 MAX-POWER STRIKE

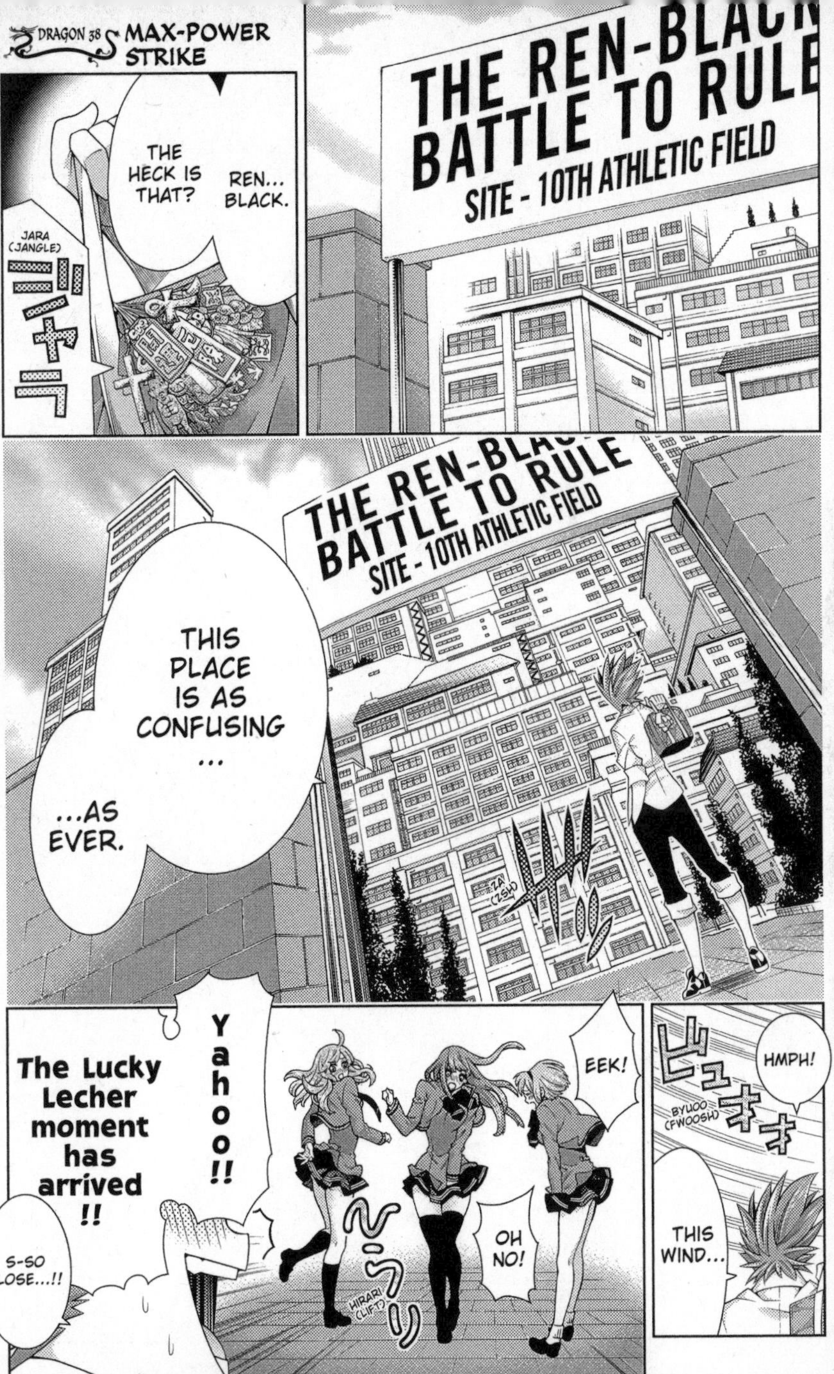
THE REN-BLAC
BATTLE TO RULE
SITE - 10TH ATHLETIC FIELD
REN... BLACK.
THE HECK IS THAT?
JARA (JANGLE)
THE REN-BLAC
BATTLE TO RULE
SITE - 10TH ATHLETIC FIELD
THIS PLACE IS AS CONFUSING ...
...AS EVER.
ZA (ZSH)
HMPH!
BYUOO (FWOOSH)
THIS WIND...
EEK!
Yahoo!!
The Lucky Lecher moment has arrived!!
OH NO!
HIRARI (LIFT)
S-SO CLOSE...!!

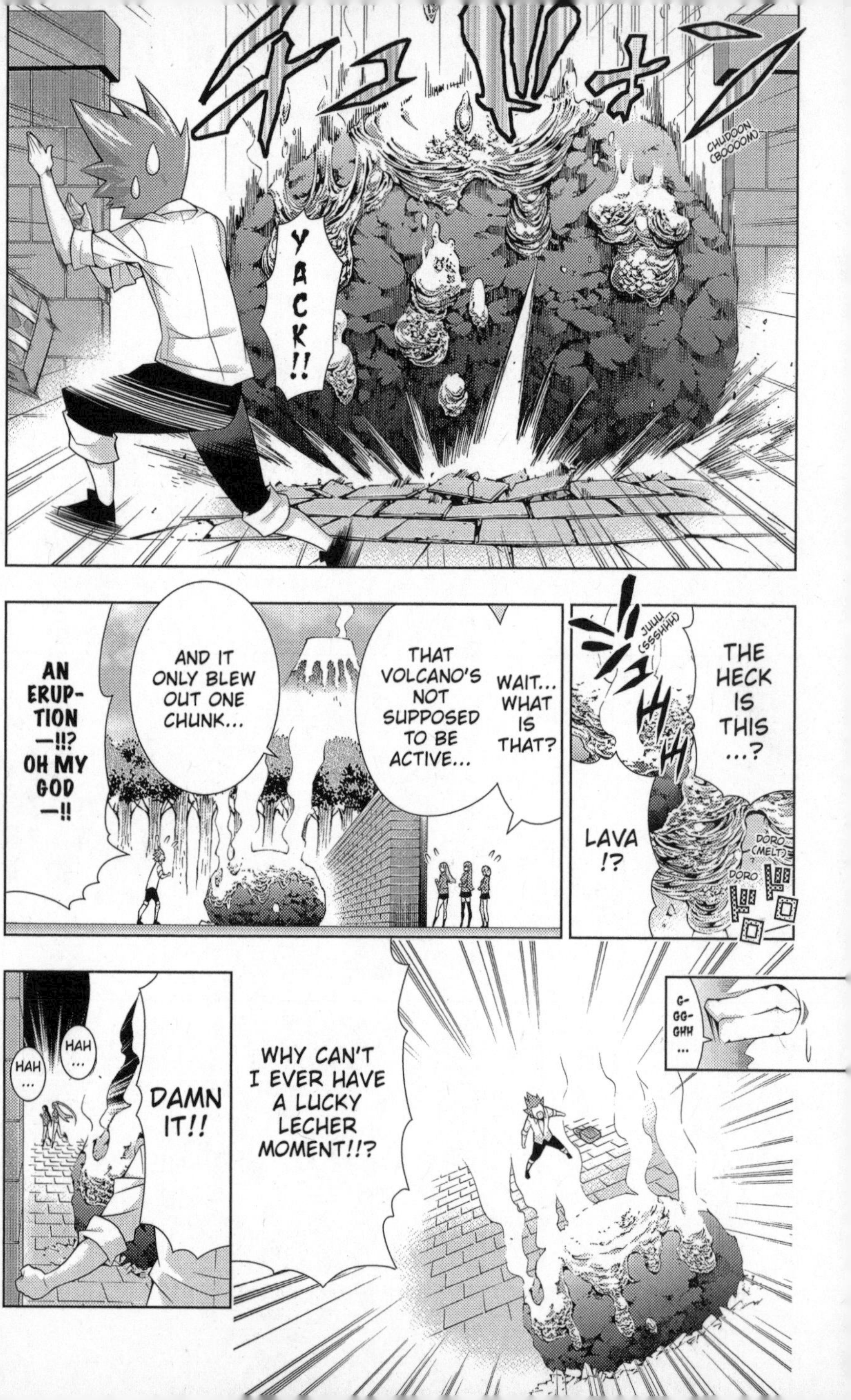
CHUDOON (BOOOOM)
YACK!!
JUUU (SSSHHH)
THE HECK IS THIS...?
LAVA!?
DORO (MELT) DORO
WAIT... WHAT IS THAT?
THAT VOLCANO'S NOT SUPPOSED TO BE ACTIVE...
AND IT ONLY BLEW OUT ONE CHUNK...
AN ERUPTION—!!? OH MY GOD—!!
G-GG-GHH...
WHY CAN'T I EVER HAVE A LUCKY LECHER MOMENT!!?
HAH...
HAH...
DAMN IT!!

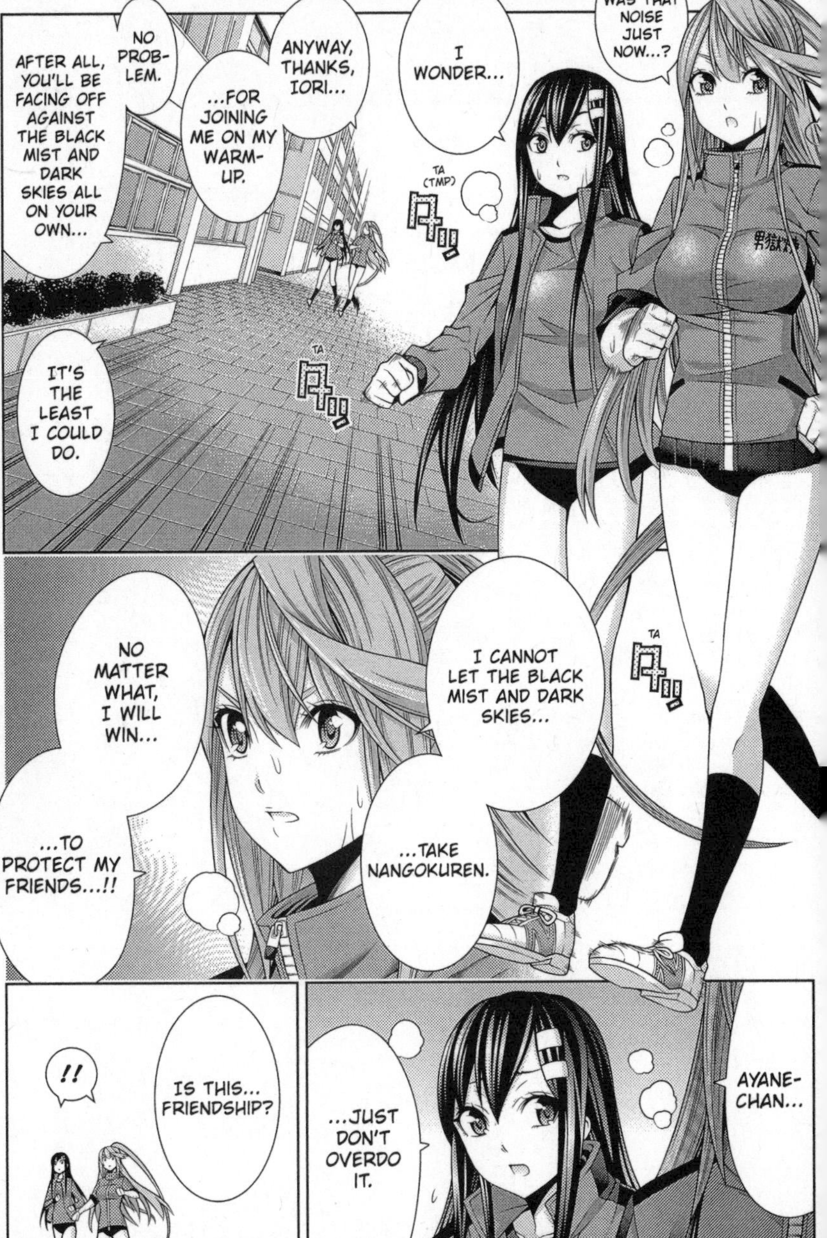
WHAT WAS THAT NOISE JUST NOW...?
I WONDER...
TA (TMP)
ANYWAY, THANKS, IORI...
...FOR JOINING ME ON MY WARM-UP.
NO PROB-LEM.
AFTER ALL, YOU'LL BE FACING OFF AGAINST THE BLACK MIST AND DARK SKIES ALL ON YOUR OWN...
TA
IT'S THE LEAST I COULD DO.
TA
I CANNOT LET THE BLACK MIST AND DARK SKIES...
...TAKE NANGOKUREN.
NO MATTER WHAT, I WILL WIN...
...TO PROTECT MY FRIENDS...!!
AYANE-CHAN...
...JUST DON'T OVERDO IT.
IS THIS... FRIENDSHIP?
!!

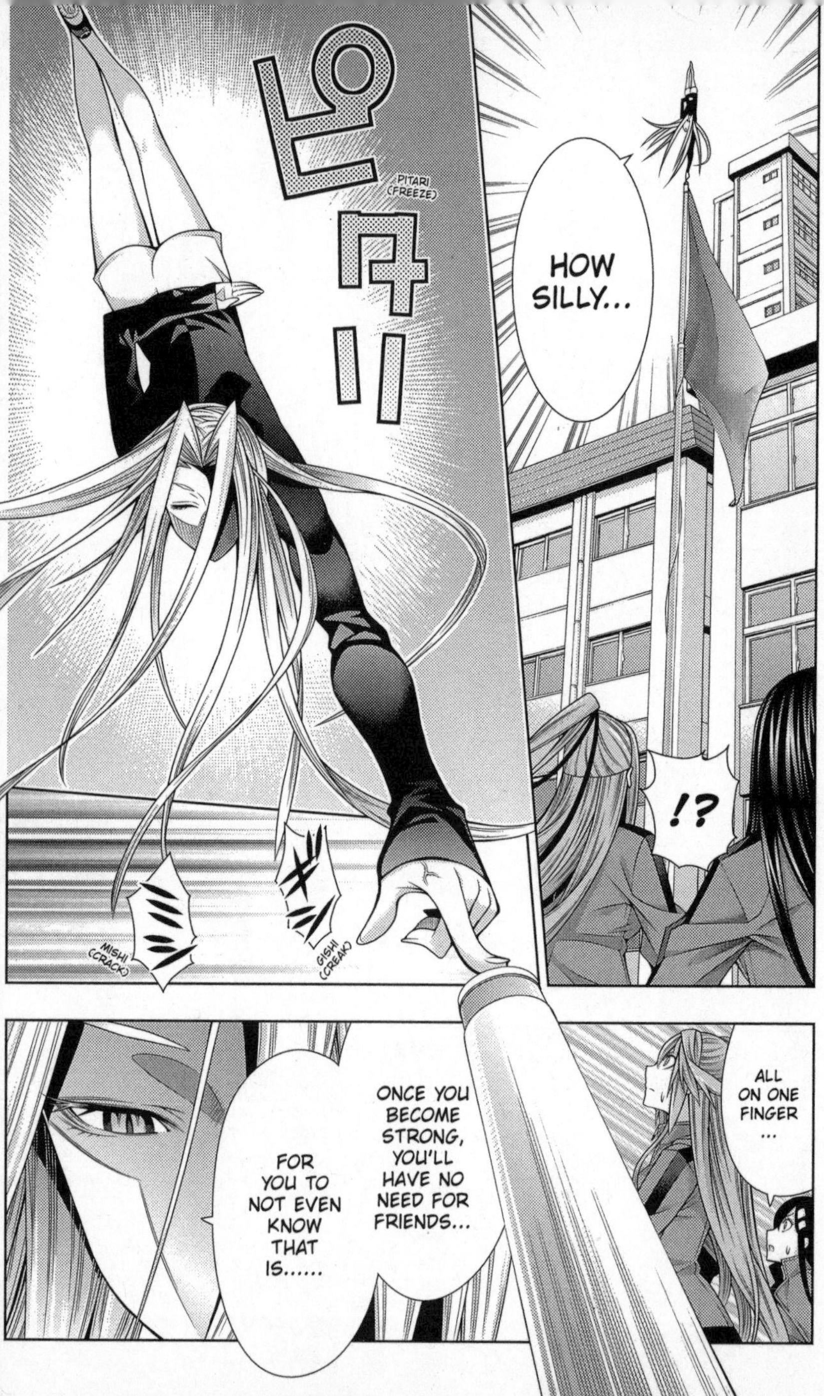
HOW SILLY...
!?
PITARI (FREEZE)
GISHI (CREAK)
MISHI (CRACK)
ALL ON ONE FINGER ...
ONCE YOU BECOME STRONG, YOU'LL HAVE NO NEED FOR FRIENDS...
FOR YOU TO NOT EVEN KNOW THAT IS......

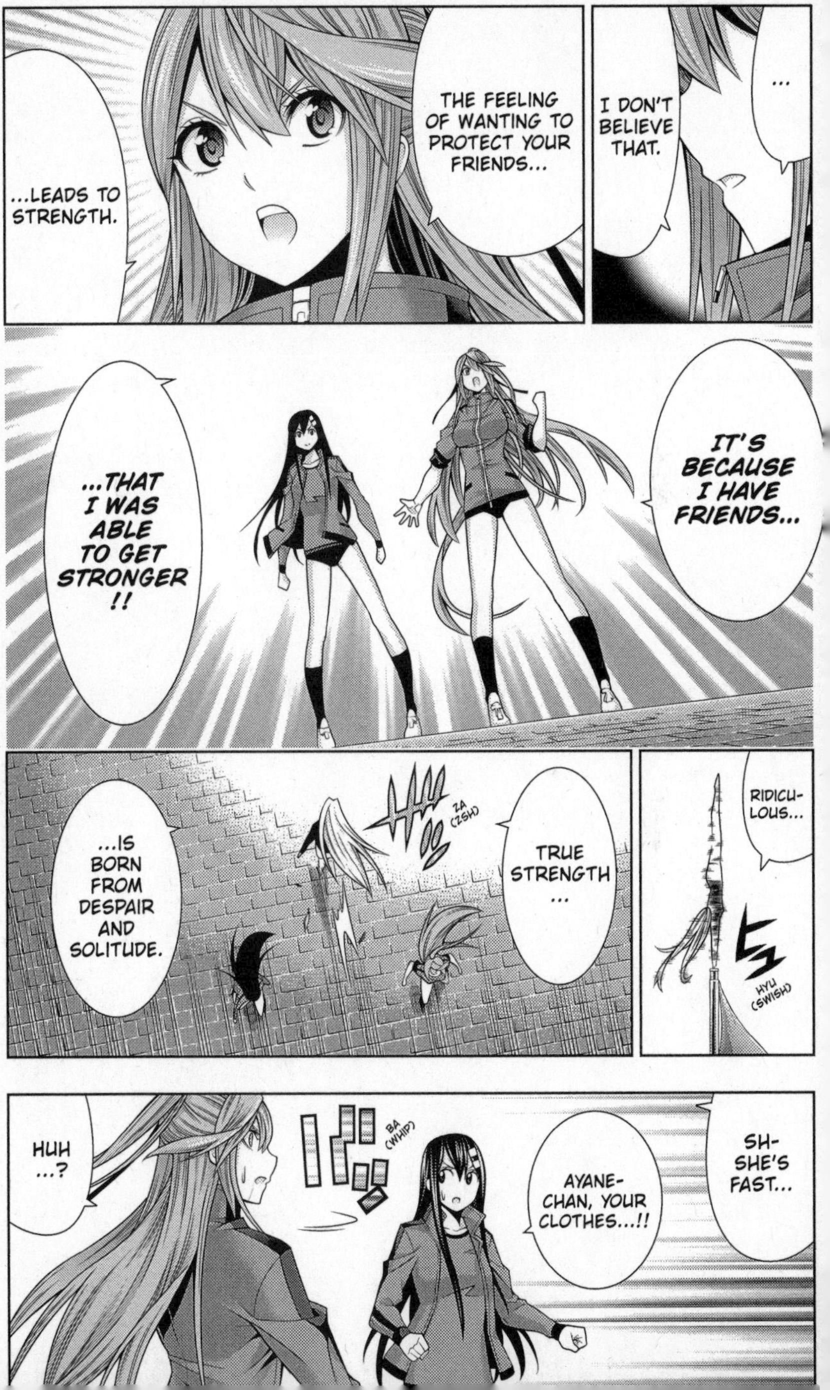
...
I DON'T BELIEVE THAT.
THE FEELING OF WANTING TO PROTECT YOUR FRIENDS...
...LEADS TO STRENGTH.
IT'S BECAUSE I HAVE FRIENDS...
...THAT I WAS ABLE TO GET STRONGER!!
RIDICULOUS...
HYU (SWISH)
ZA (ZSH)
TRUE STRENGTH...
...IS BORN FROM DESPAIR AND SOLITUDE.
SH-SHE'S FAST...
AYANE-CHAN, YOUR CLOTHES...!!
BA (WHIP)
HUH...?

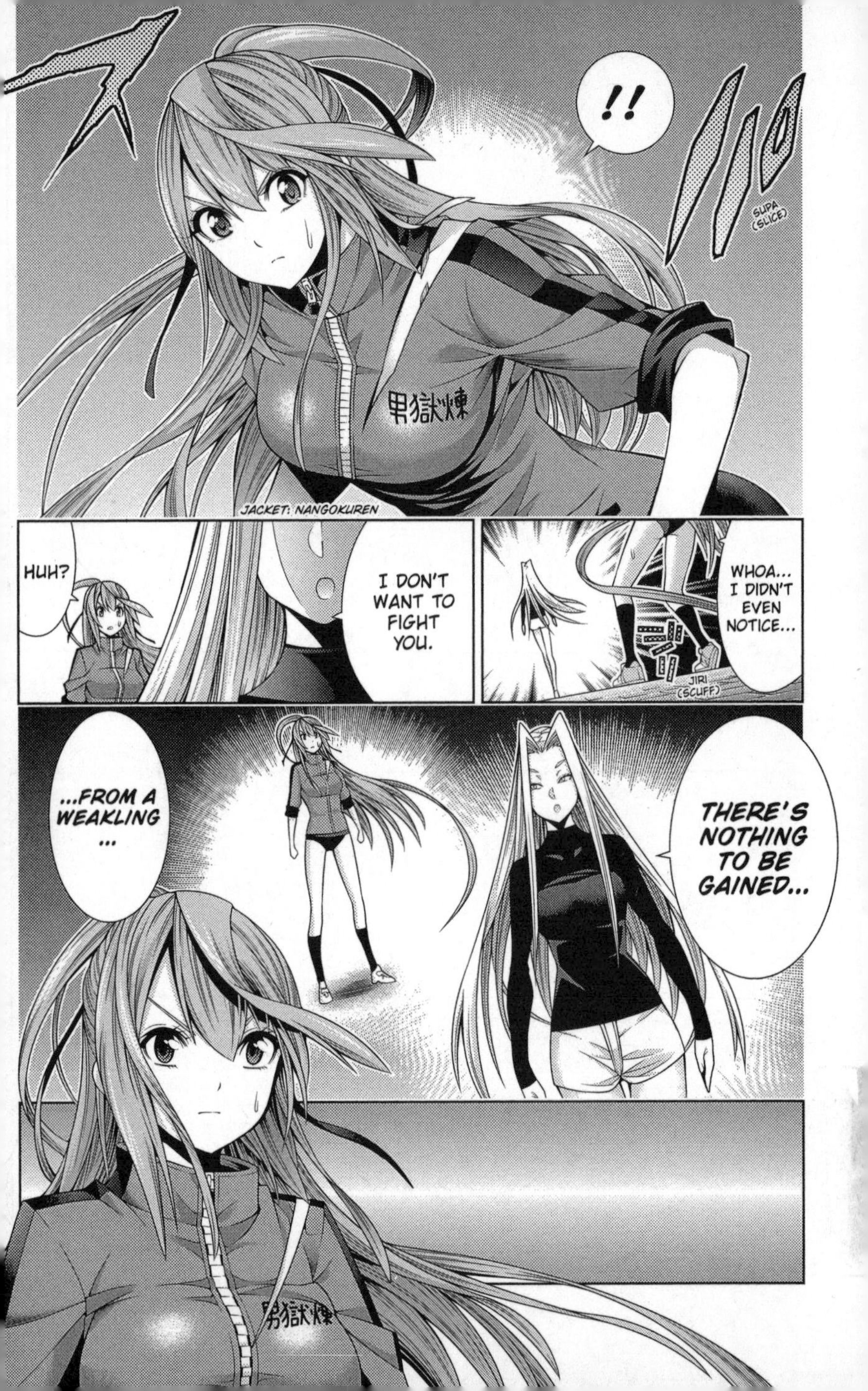
!!
SUPA (SLICE)
JACKET: NANGOKUREN
WHOA... I DIDN'T EVEN NOTICE...
JIRI (SCUFF)
I DON'T WANT TO FIGHT YOU.
HUH?
THERE'S NOTHING TO BE GAINED...
...FROM A WEAKLING ...

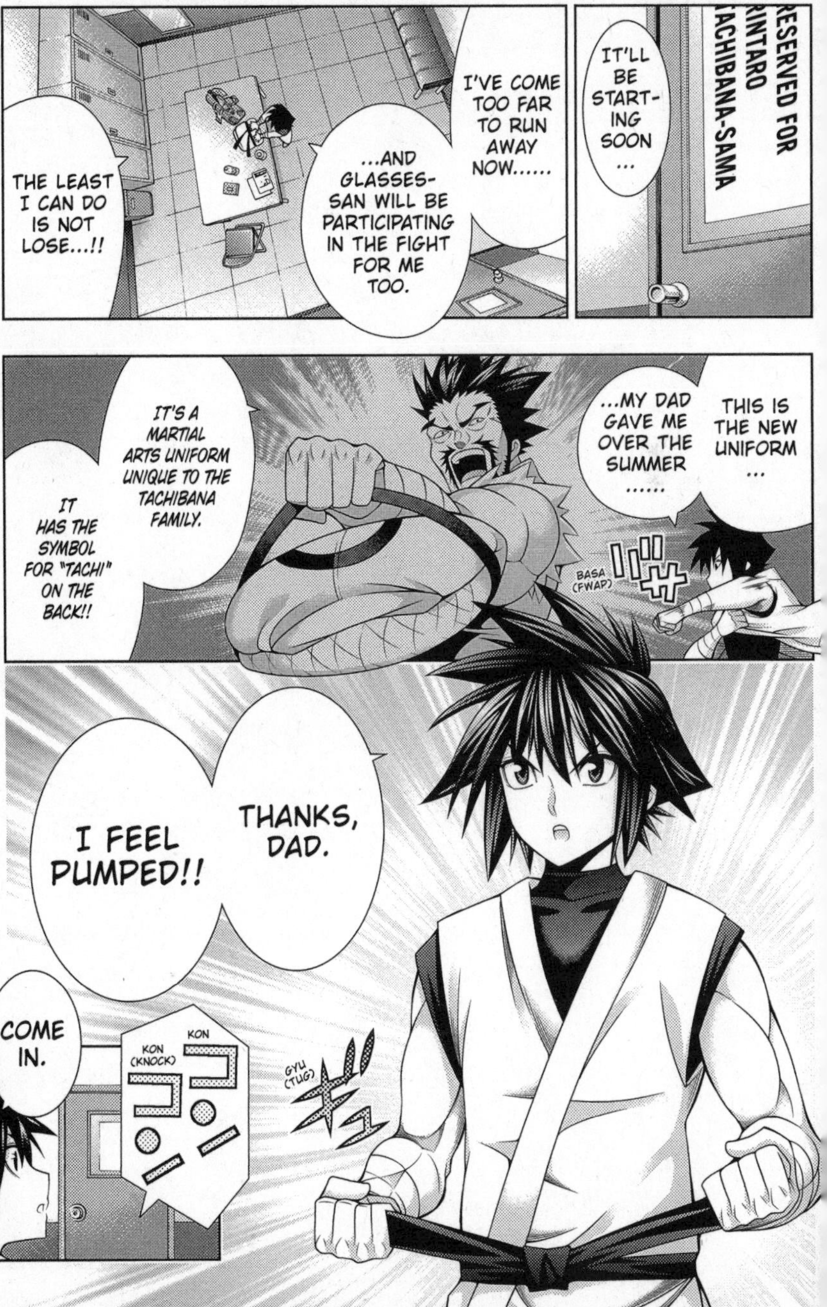
RESERVED FOR RINTARO TACHIBANA-SAMA
IT'LL BE START-ING SOON ...
I'VE COME TOO FAR TO RUN AWAY NOW......
...AND GLASSES-SAN WILL BE PARTICIPATING IN THE FIGHT FOR ME TOO.
THE LEAST I CAN DO IS NOT LOSE...!!
THIS IS THE NEW UNIFORM ...
...MY DAD GAVE ME OVER THE SUMMER ......
BASA (FWAP)
IT'S A MARTIAL ARTS UNIFORM UNIQUE TO THE TACHIBANA FAMILY.
IT HAS THE SYMBOL FOR "TACHI" ON THE BACK!!
THANKS, DAD.
I FEEL PUMPED!!
GYU (TUG)
KON KON (KNOCK)
COME IN.

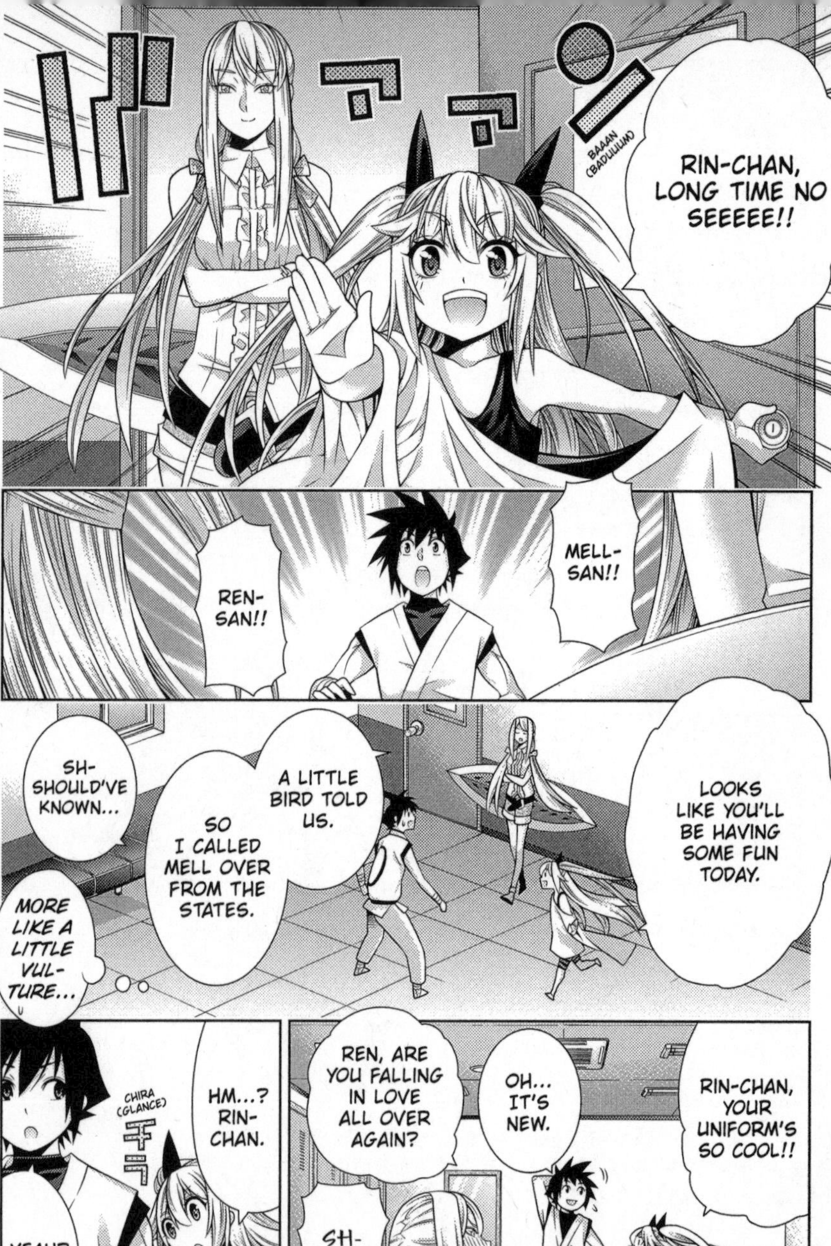
RIN-CHAN, LONG TIME NO SEEEEE!!
BAAAN (BADUUUM)
MELL-SAN!!
REN-SAN!!
LOOKS LIKE YOU'LL BE HAVING SOME FUN TODAY.
A LITTLE BIRD TOLD US.
SO I CALLED MELL OVER FROM THE STATES.
SH-SHOULD'VE KNOWN...
MORE LIKE A LITTLE VULTURE...
RIN-CHAN, YOUR UNIFORM'S SO COOL!!
OH... IT'S NEW.
REN, ARE YOU FALLING IN LOVE ALL OVER AGAIN?
SH-SHUT UP!
HM...? RIN-CHAN.
CHIRA (GLANCE)
YEAH?

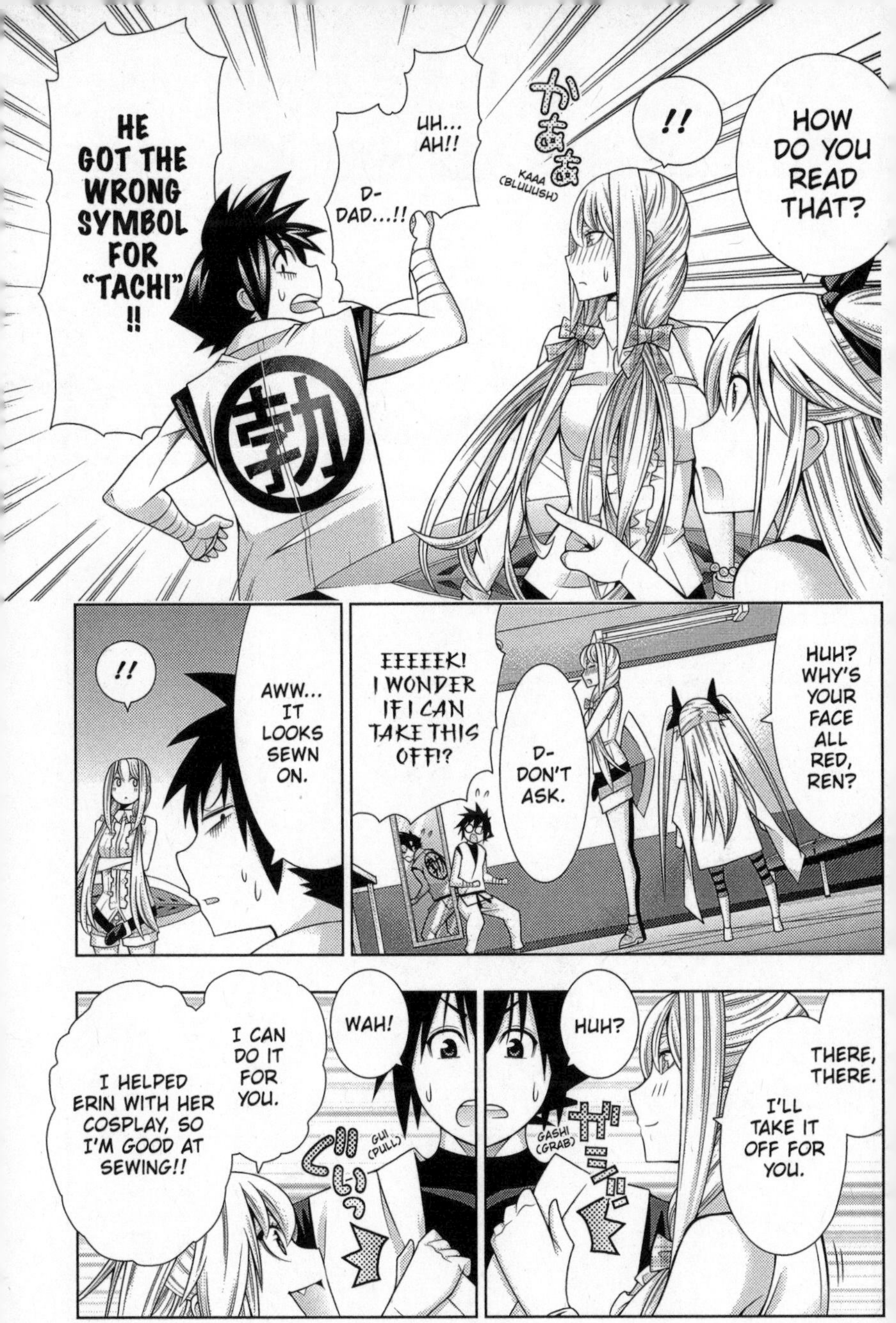
HOW DO YOU READ THAT?
!!
かぁぁ
KAAA (BLUUUSH)
UH... AH!!
D-DAD...!!
勃
HE GOT THE WRONG SYMBOL FOR "TACHI" !!
HUH? WHY'S YOUR FACE ALL RED, REN?
D- DON'T ASK.
EEEEEK! I WONDER IF I CAN TAKE THIS OFF!?
AWW... IT LOOKS SEWN ON.
!!
THERE, THERE.
I'LL TAKE IT OFF FOR YOU.
HUH?
ガッ
GASHI (GRAB)
WAH!
I CAN DO IT FOR YOU.
I HELPED ERIN WITH HER COSPLAY, SO I'M GOOD AT SEWING!!
ぐいっ
GUI (PULL)

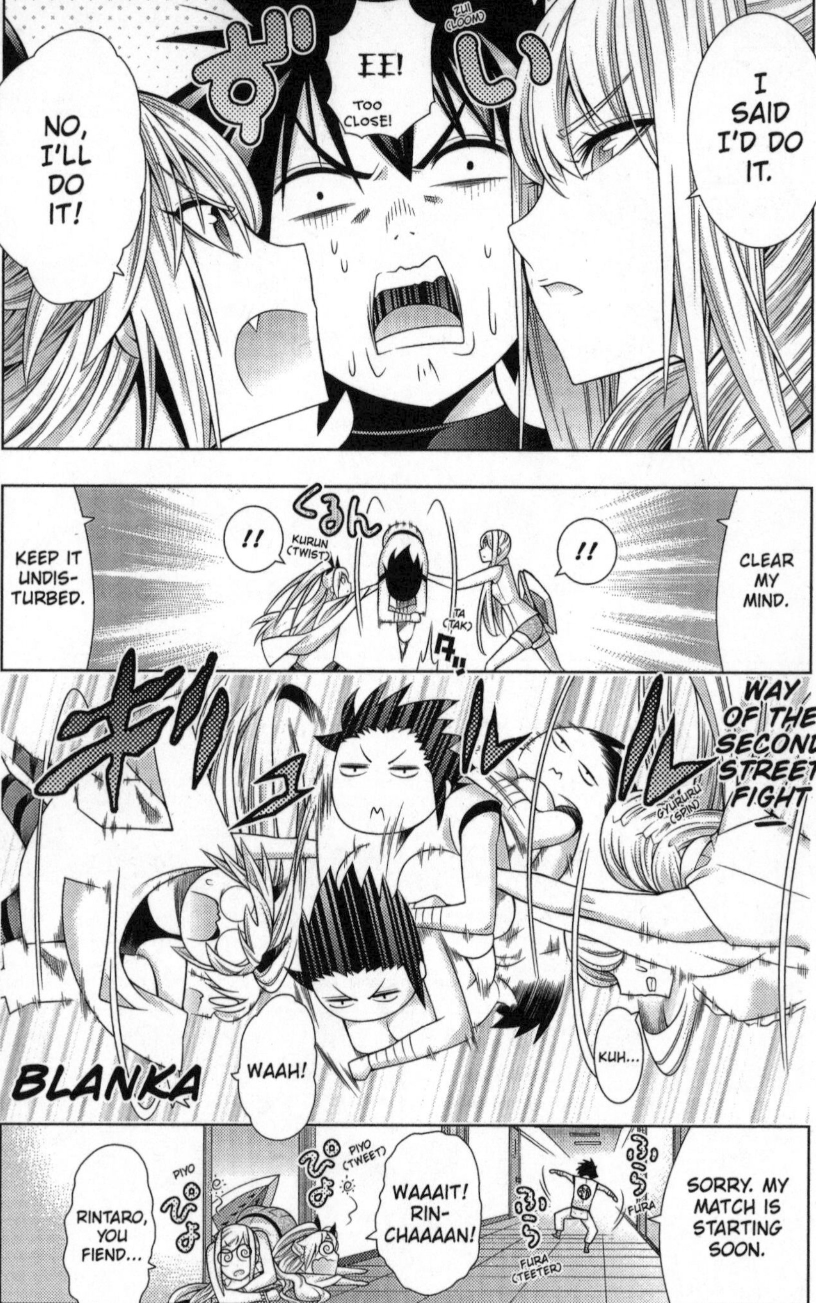
I SAID I'D DO IT.
ZUI (LOOM)
EE!
TOO CLOSE!
NO, I'LL DO IT!
CLEAR MY MIND.
!!
TA (TAK)
KURUN (TWIST)
!!
KEEP IT UNDIS-TURBED.
WAY OF THE SECOND STREET FIGHT
GYURURU (SPIN)
KUH...
WAAH!
BLANKA
SORRY. MY MATCH IS STARTING SOON.
FURA
FURA (TEETER)
WAAAIT! RIN-CHAAAAN!
PIYO (TWEET)
PIYO
RINTARO, YOU FIEND...

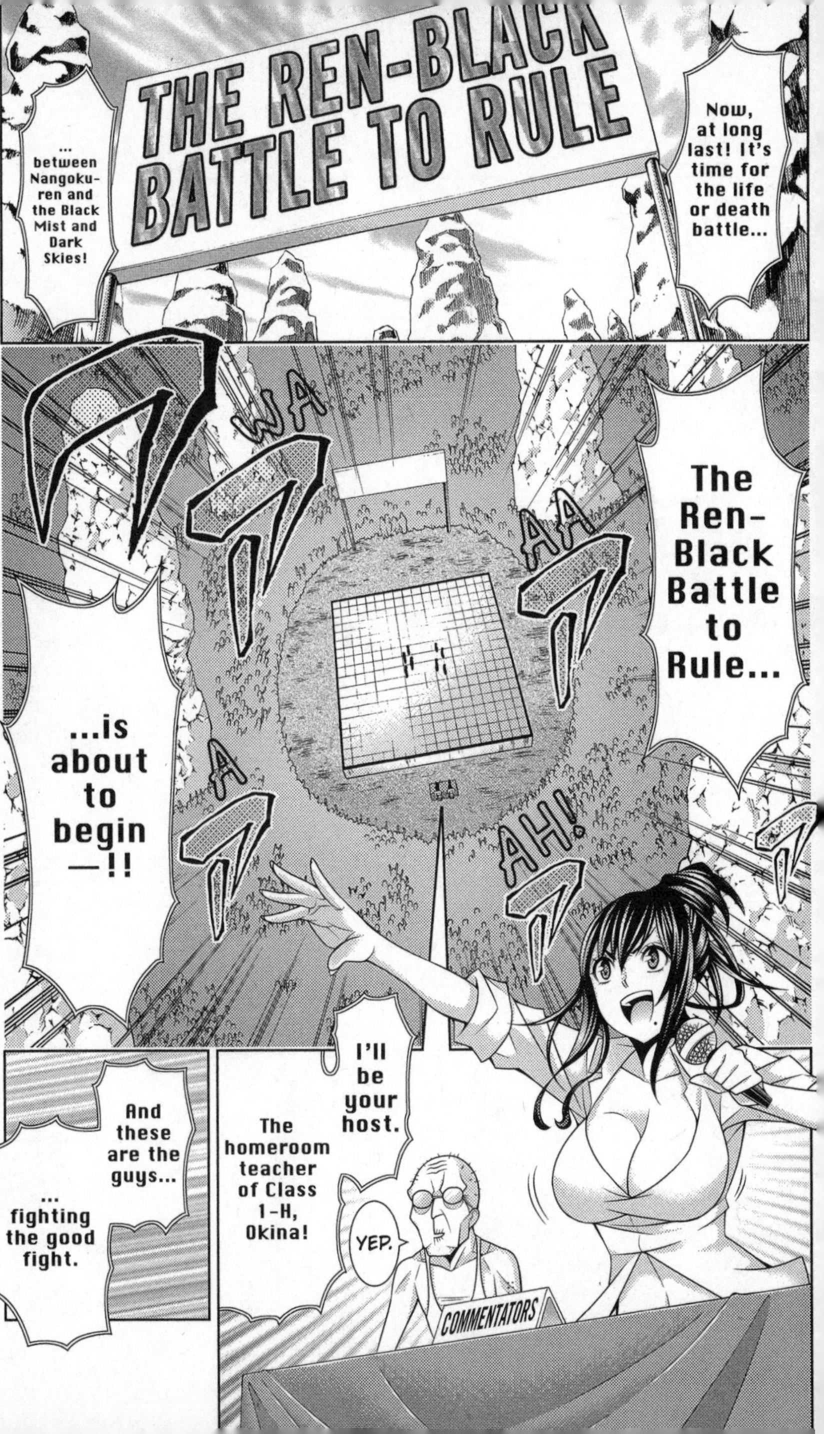
Now, at long last! It's time for the life or death battle...
THE REN-BLACK BATTLE TO RULE
... between Nangoku-ren and the Black Mist and Dark Skies!
The Ren-Black Battle to Rule...
AA
AH!
WA
A
...is about to begin—!!
I'll be your host.
The homeroom teacher of Class 1-H, Okina!
YEP.
COMMENTATORS
And these are the guys...
... fighting the good fight.

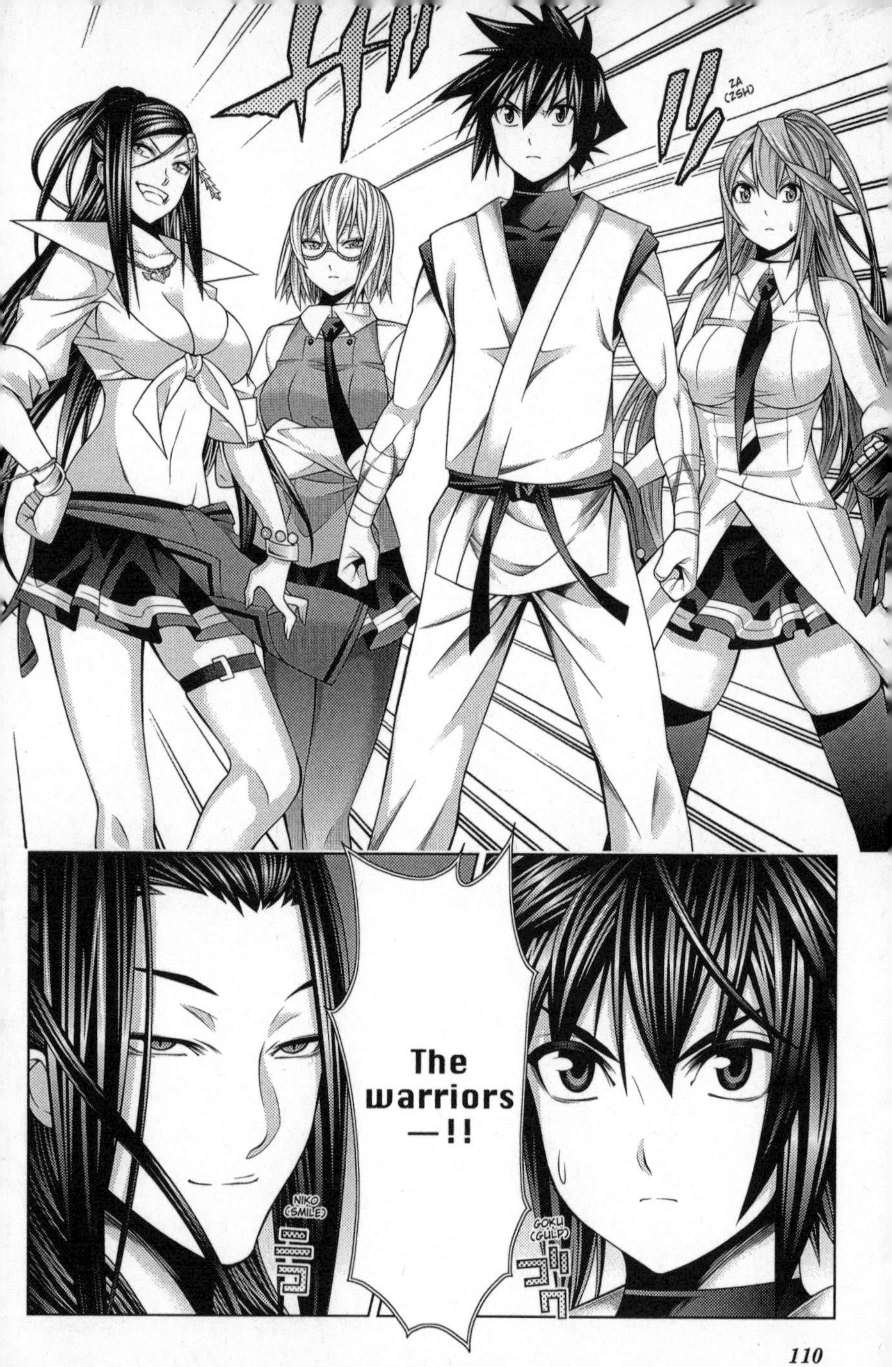
ZA (ZSH)
The warriors—!!
GOKU (GULP)
NIKO (SMILE)

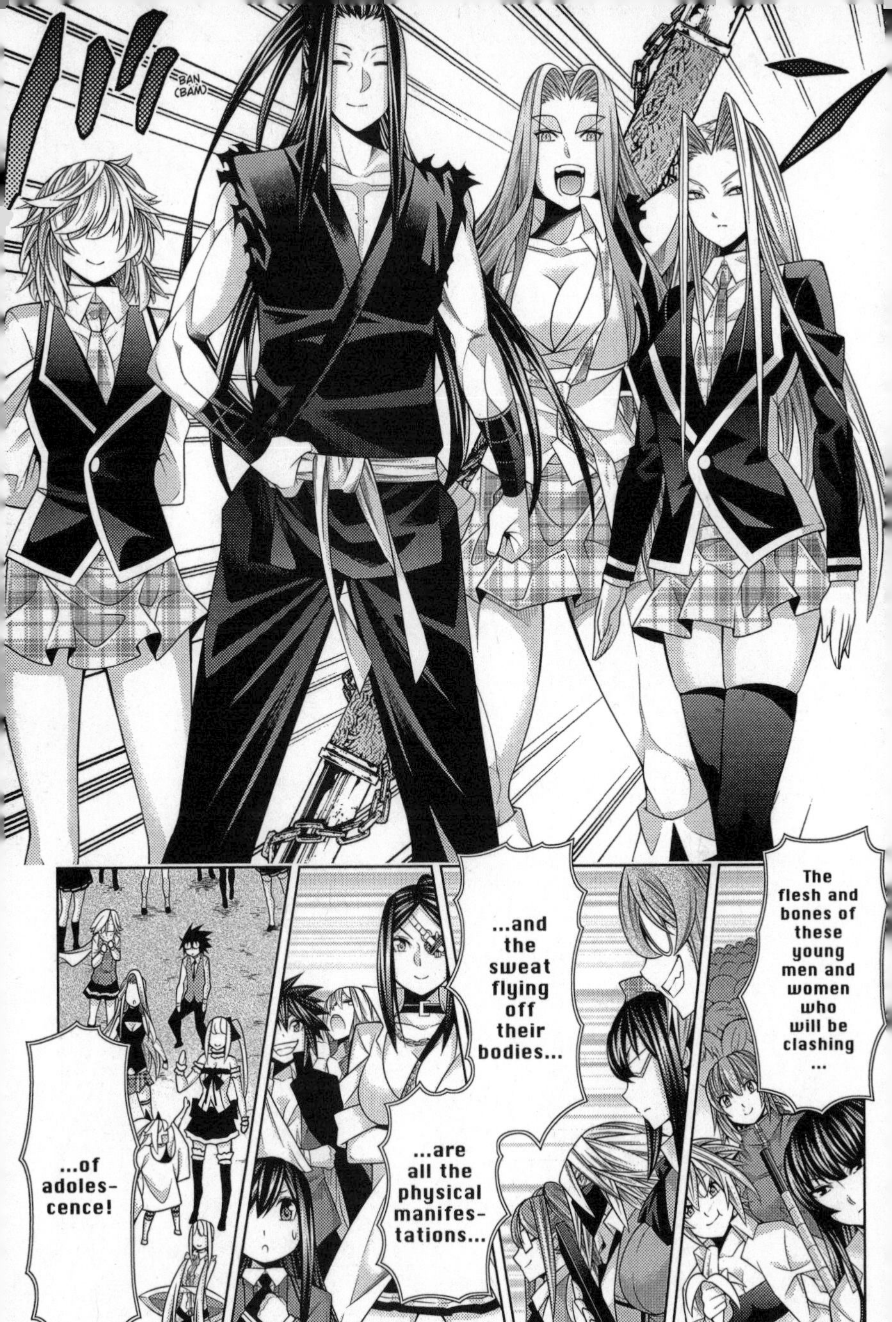

BAN (BAM)
The flesh and bones of these young men and women who will be clashing ...
...and the sweat flying off their bodies...
...are all the physical manifestations...
...of adolescence!

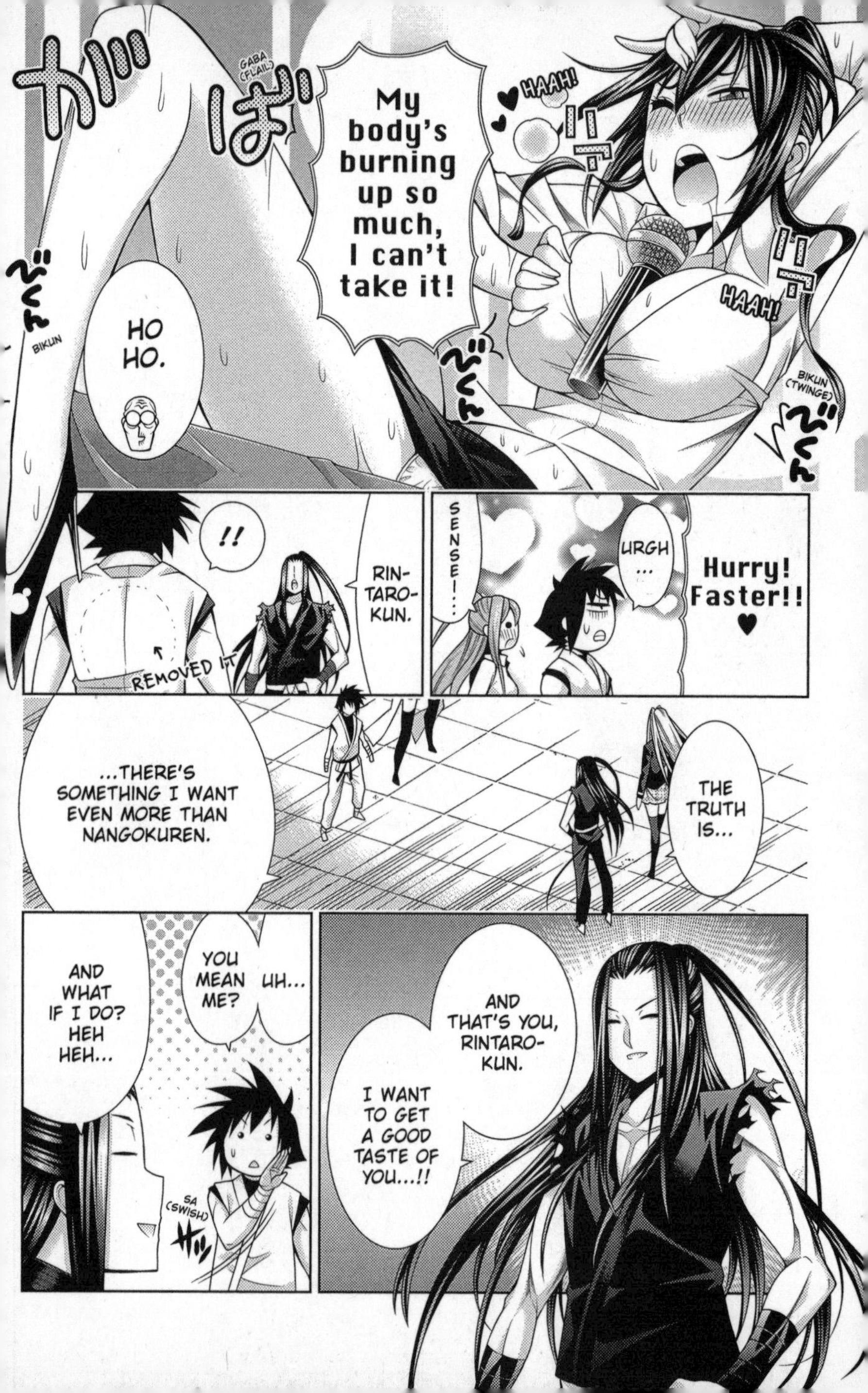
HAAH!
My body's burning up so much, I can't take it!
GABA (FLAIL)
HAAH!
BIKUN (TWINGE)
HO HO.
BIKUN
Hurry! Faster!!
URGH...
SENSE!...
RIN-TARO-KUN.
!!
REMOVED IT
THE TRUTH IS...
...THERE'S SOMETHING I WANT EVEN MORE THAN NANGOKUREN.
AND THAT'S YOU, RINTARO-KUN.
I WANT TO GET A GOOD TASTE OF YOU...!!
UH...
YOU MEAN ME?
AND WHAT IF I DO? HEH HEH...
SA (SWISH)

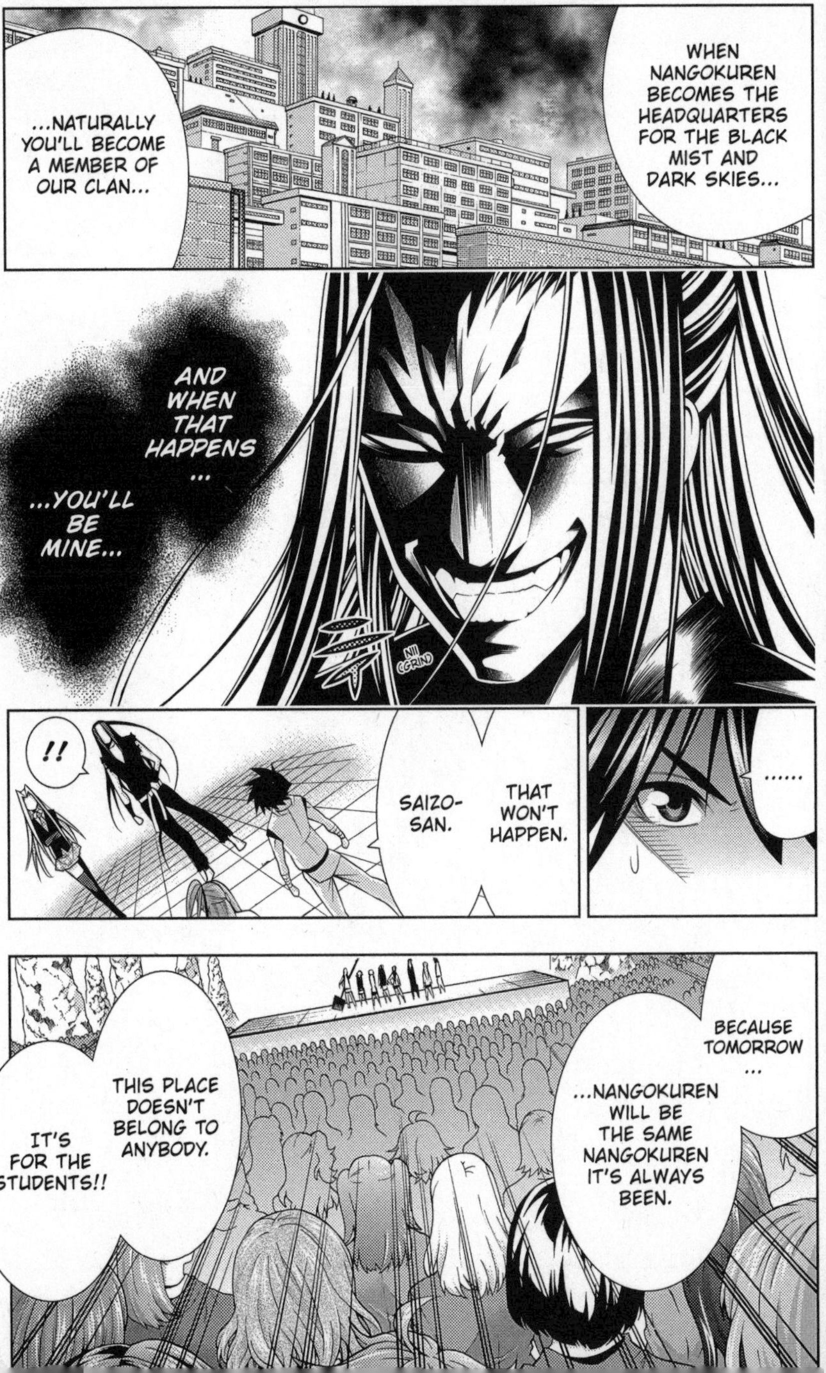

WHEN NANGOKUREN BECOMES THE HEADQUARTERS FOR THE BLACK MIST AND DARK SKIES...
...NATURALLY YOU'LL BECOME A MEMBER OF OUR CLAN...
AND WHEN THAT HAPPENS ...
...YOU'LL BE MINE...
NII (GRIN)
......
THAT WON'T HAPPEN.
SAIZO-SAN.
!!
BECAUSE TOMORROW ...
...NANGOKUREN WILL BE THE SAME NANGOKUREN IT'S ALWAYS BEEN.
THIS PLACE DOESN'T BELONG TO ANYBODY.
IT'S FOR THE STUDENTS!!

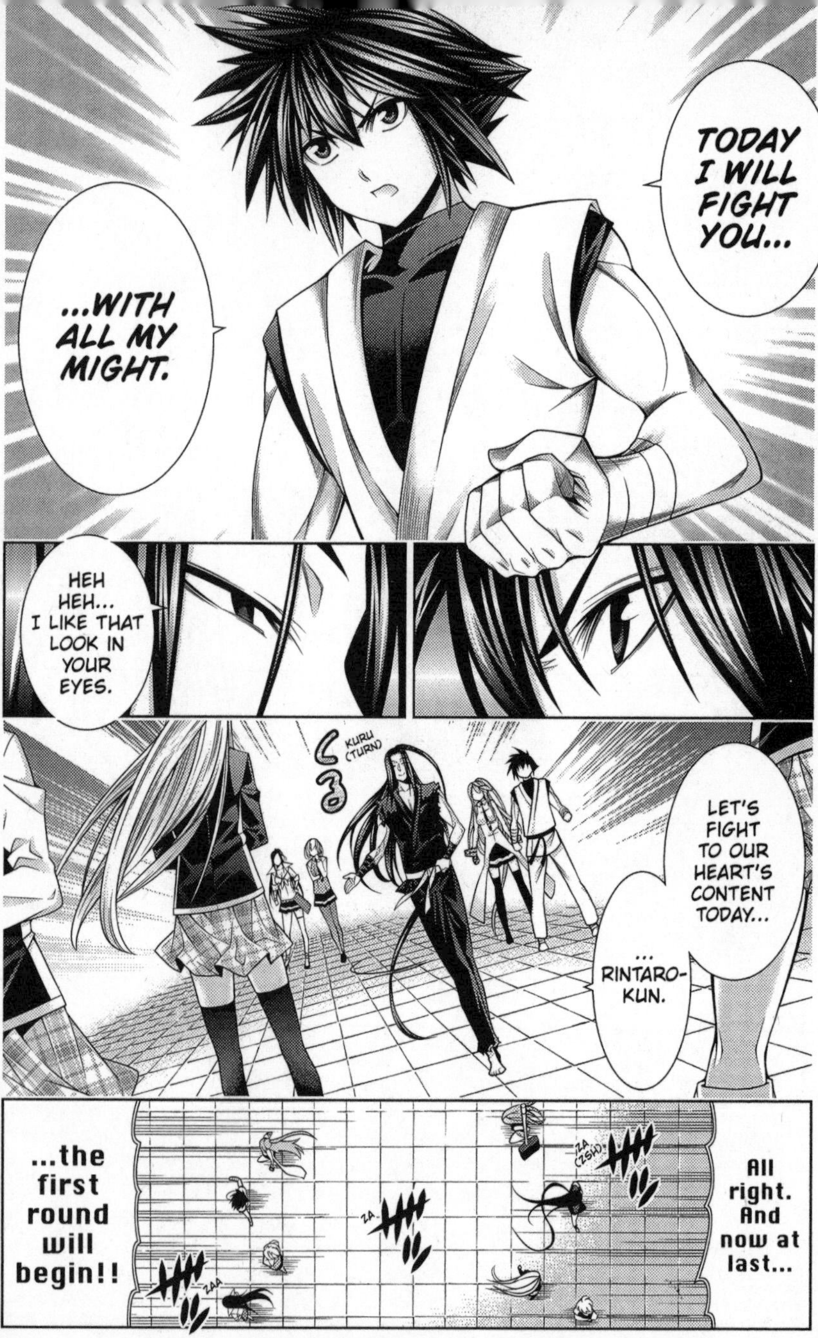
TODAY I WILL FIGHT YOU...
...WITH ALL MY MIGHT.
HEH HEH... I LIKE THAT LOOK IN YOUR EYES.
KURU (TURN)
LET'S FIGHT TO OUR HEART'S CONTENT TODAY...
...RINTARO-KUN.
All right. And now at last...
ZA (ZSHD)
ZA
ZAA
...the first round will begin!!

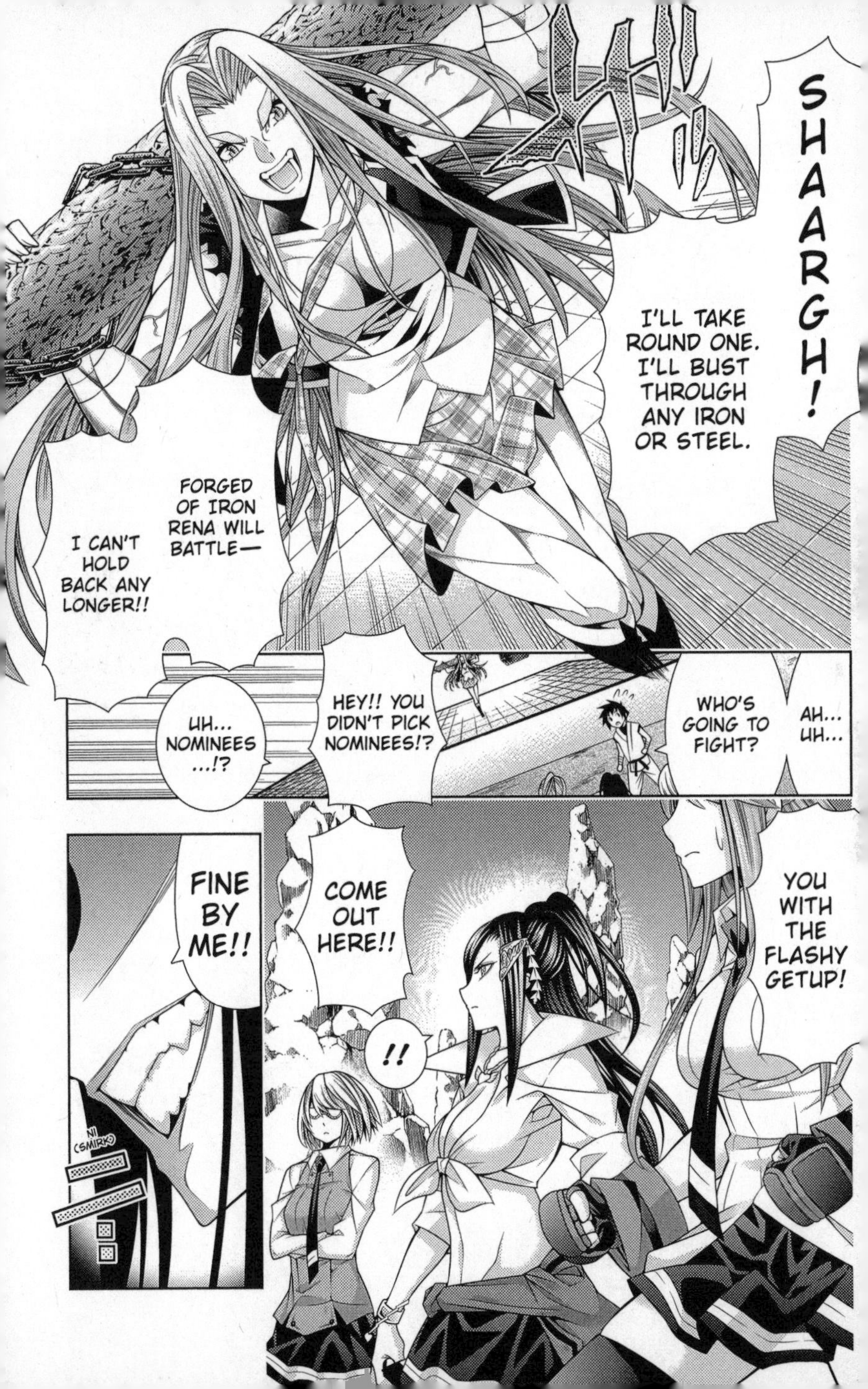
SHAARGH!
I'LL TAKE ROUND ONE. I'LL BUST THROUGH ANY IRON OR STEEL.
FORGED OF IRON RENA WILL BATTLE—
I CAN'T HOLD BACK ANY LONGER!!
AH... UH...
WHO'S GOING TO FIGHT?
HEY!! YOU DIDN'T PICK NOMINEES!?
UH... NOMINEES ...!?
YOU WITH THE FLASHY GETUP!
!!
COME OUT HERE!!
FINE BY ME!!
NI (SMIRK)

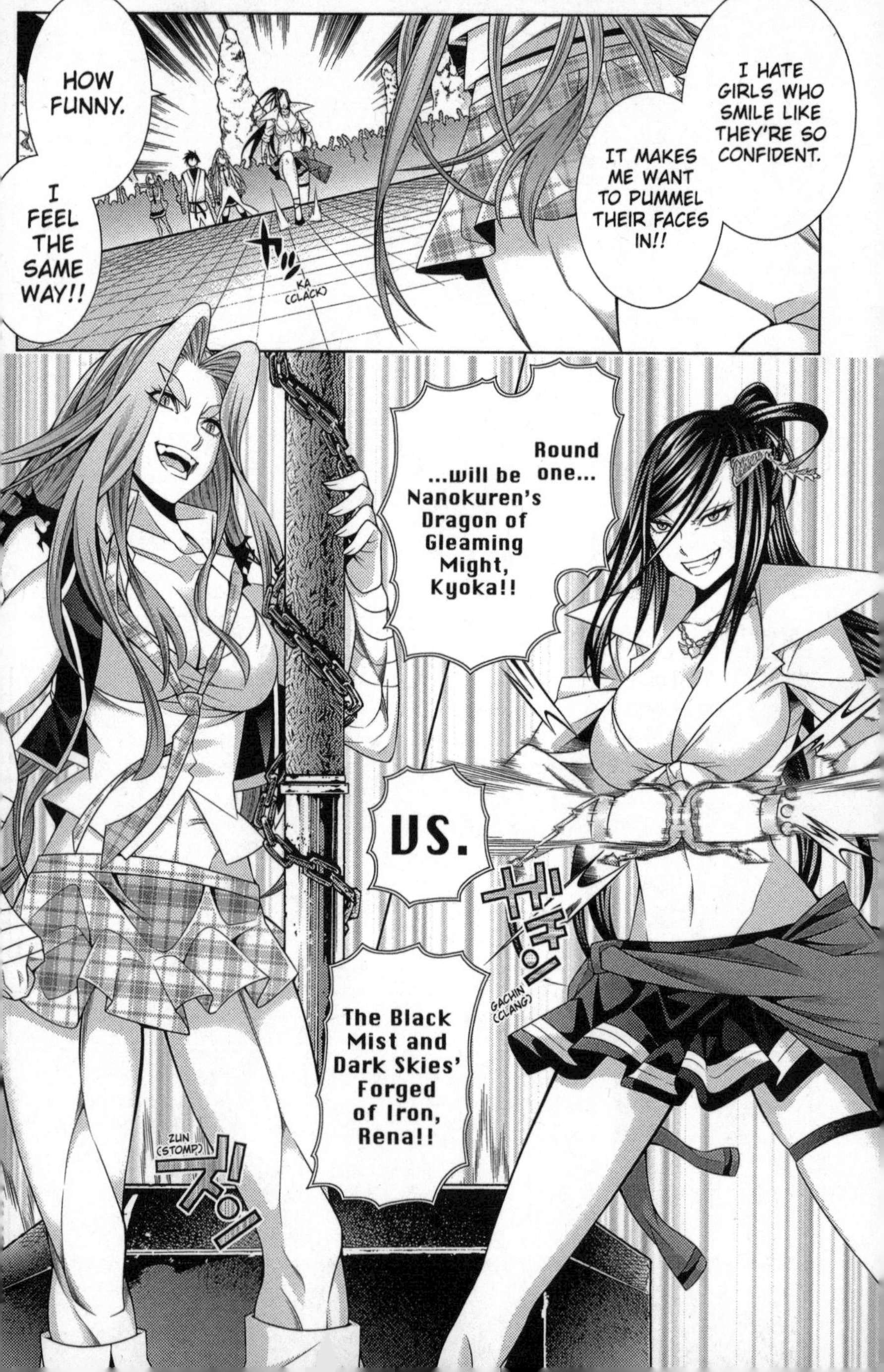
I HATE GIRLS WHO SMILE LIKE THEY'RE SO CONFIDENT.
IT MAKES ME WANT TO PUMMEL THEIR FACES IN!!
HOW FUNNY.
I FEEL THE SAME WAY!!
KA (CLACK)
Round one...
...will be Nanokuren's Dragon of Gleaming Might, Kyoka!!
VS.
GACHIN (CLANG)
The Black Mist and Dark Skies' Forged of Iron, Rena!!
ZUN (STOMP)

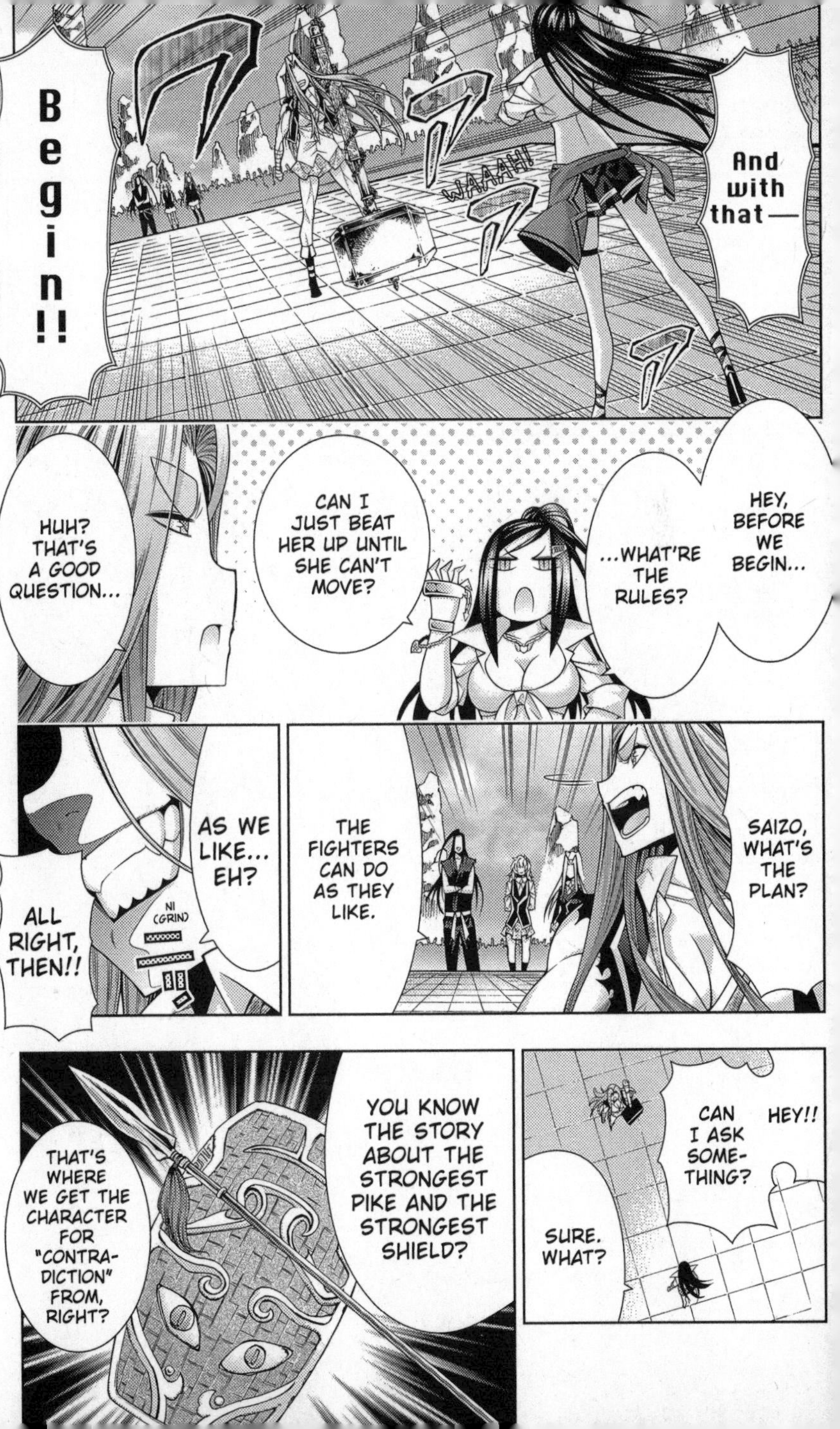
And with that—
WAAAH!
Begin!!
HEY, BEFORE WE BEGIN...
...WHAT'RE THE RULES?
CAN I JUST BEAT HER UP UNTIL SHE CAN'T MOVE?
HUH? THAT'S A GOOD QUESTION...
SAIZO, WHAT'S THE PLAN?
THE FIGHTERS CAN DO AS THEY LIKE.
AS WE LIKE... EH?
NI (GRIN)
ALL RIGHT, THEN!!
HEY!!
CAN I ASK SOME-THING?
SURE. WHAT?
YOU KNOW THE STORY ABOUT THE STRONGEST PIKE AND THE STRONGEST SHIELD?
THAT'S WHERE WE GET THE CHARACTER FOR "CONTRA-DICTION" FROM, RIGHT?

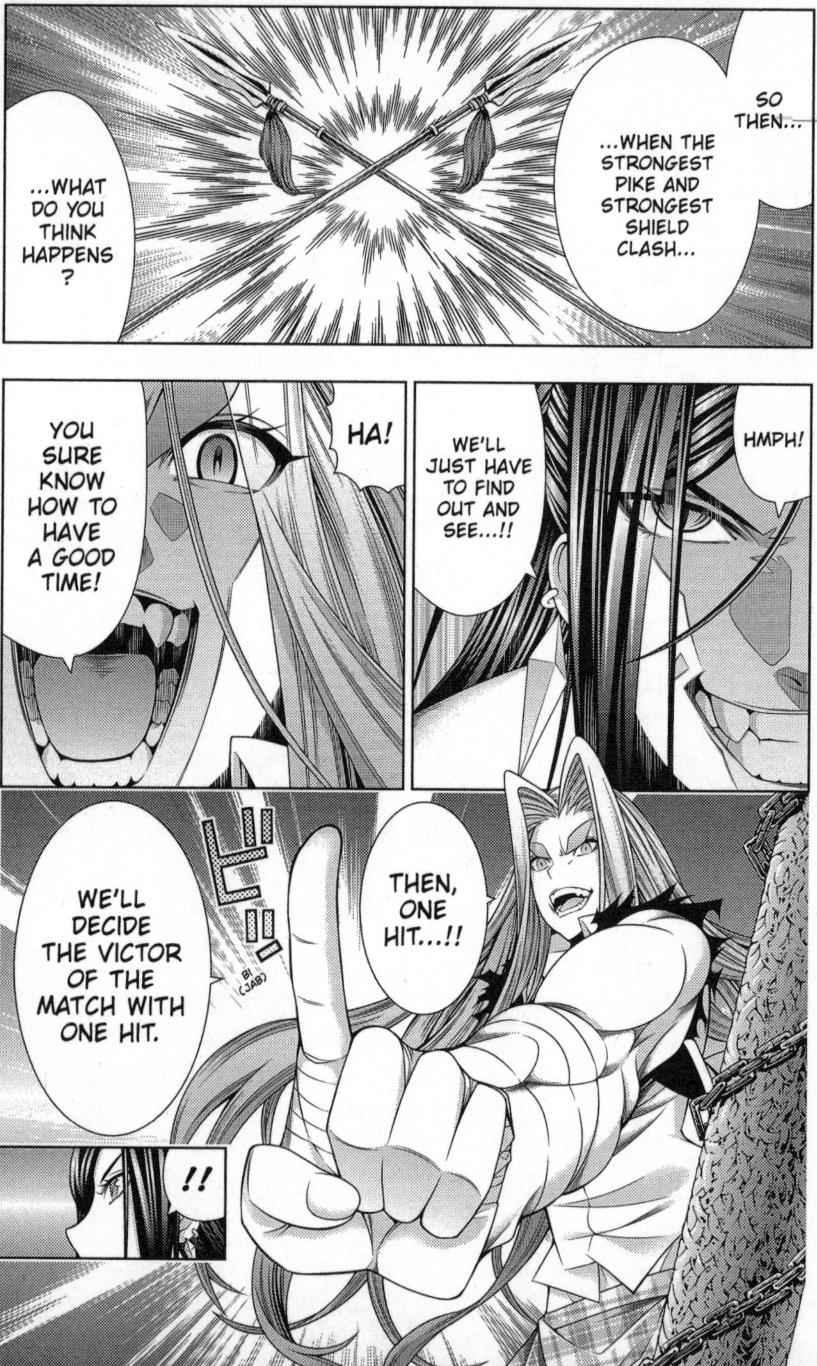
SO THEN...
...WHEN THE STRONGEST PIKE AND STRONGEST SHIELD CLASH...
...WHAT DO YOU THINK HAPPENS ?
HMPH!
WE'LL JUST HAVE TO FIND OUT AND SEE...!!
HA!
YOU SURE KNOW HOW TO HAVE A GOOD TIME!
THEN, ONE HIT...!!
BI (JAB)
WE'LL DECIDE THE VICTOR OF THE MATCH WITH ONE HIT.
!!

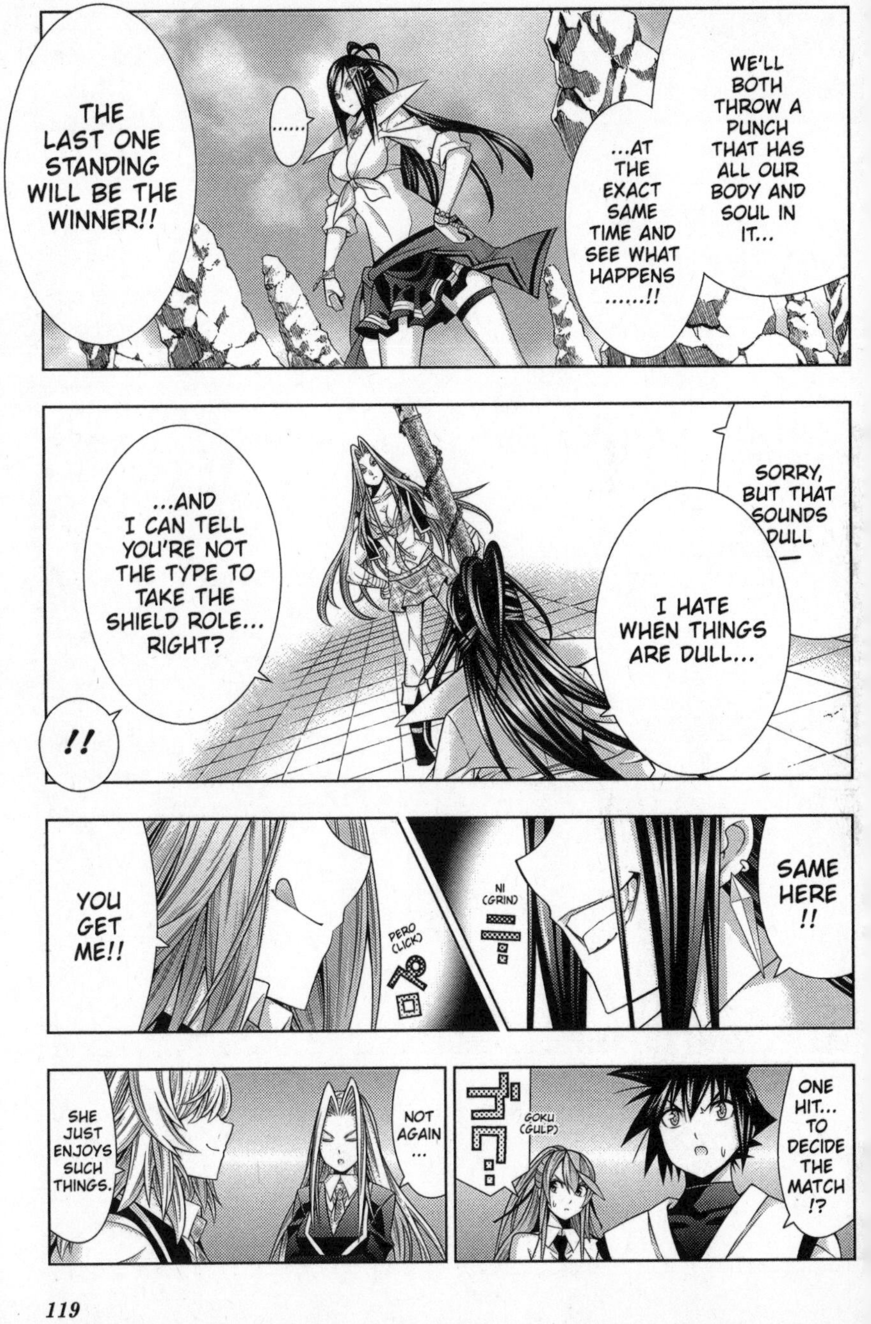
WE'LL BOTH THROW A PUNCH THAT HAS ALL OUR BODY AND SOUL IN IT...
...AT THE EXACT SAME TIME AND SEE WHAT HAPPENS ......!!
......
THE LAST ONE STANDING WILL BE THE WINNER!!
SORRY, BUT THAT SOUNDS DULL —
I HATE WHEN THINGS ARE DULL...
...AND I CAN TELL YOU'RE NOT THE TYPE TO TAKE THE SHIELD ROLE... RIGHT?
!!
SAME HERE !!
NI (GRIN)
PERO (LICK)
YOU GET ME!!
ONE HIT... TO DECIDE THE MATCH !?
GOKU (GULP)
NOT AGAIN ...
SHE JUST ENJOYS SUCH THINGS.

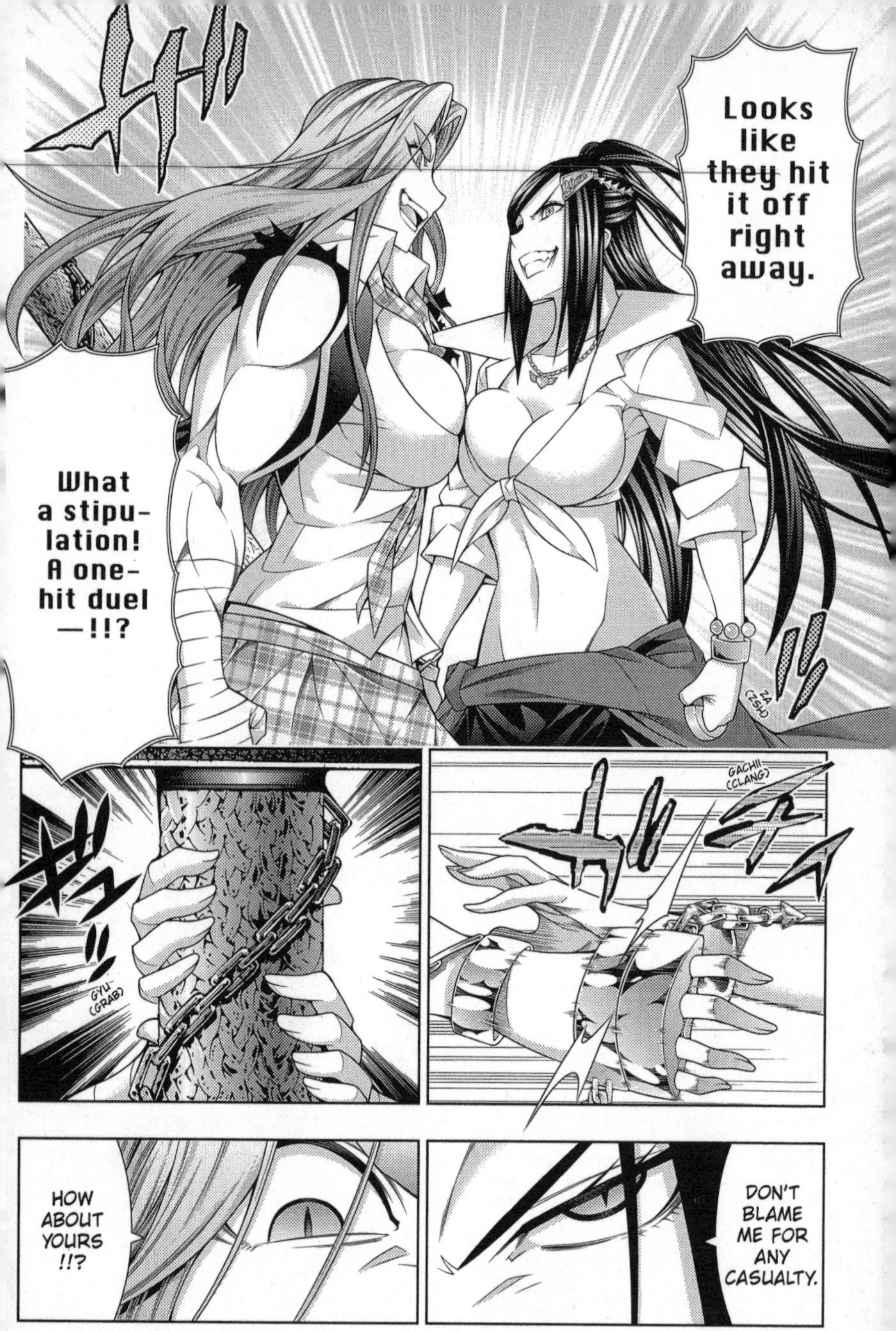
Looks like they hit it off right away.
What a stipu-lation! A one-hit duel—!!?
ZA (ZSH)
GACHII (CLANG)
GYU- (GRAB)
DON'T BLAME ME FOR ANY CASUALTY.
HOW ABOUT YOURS !!?

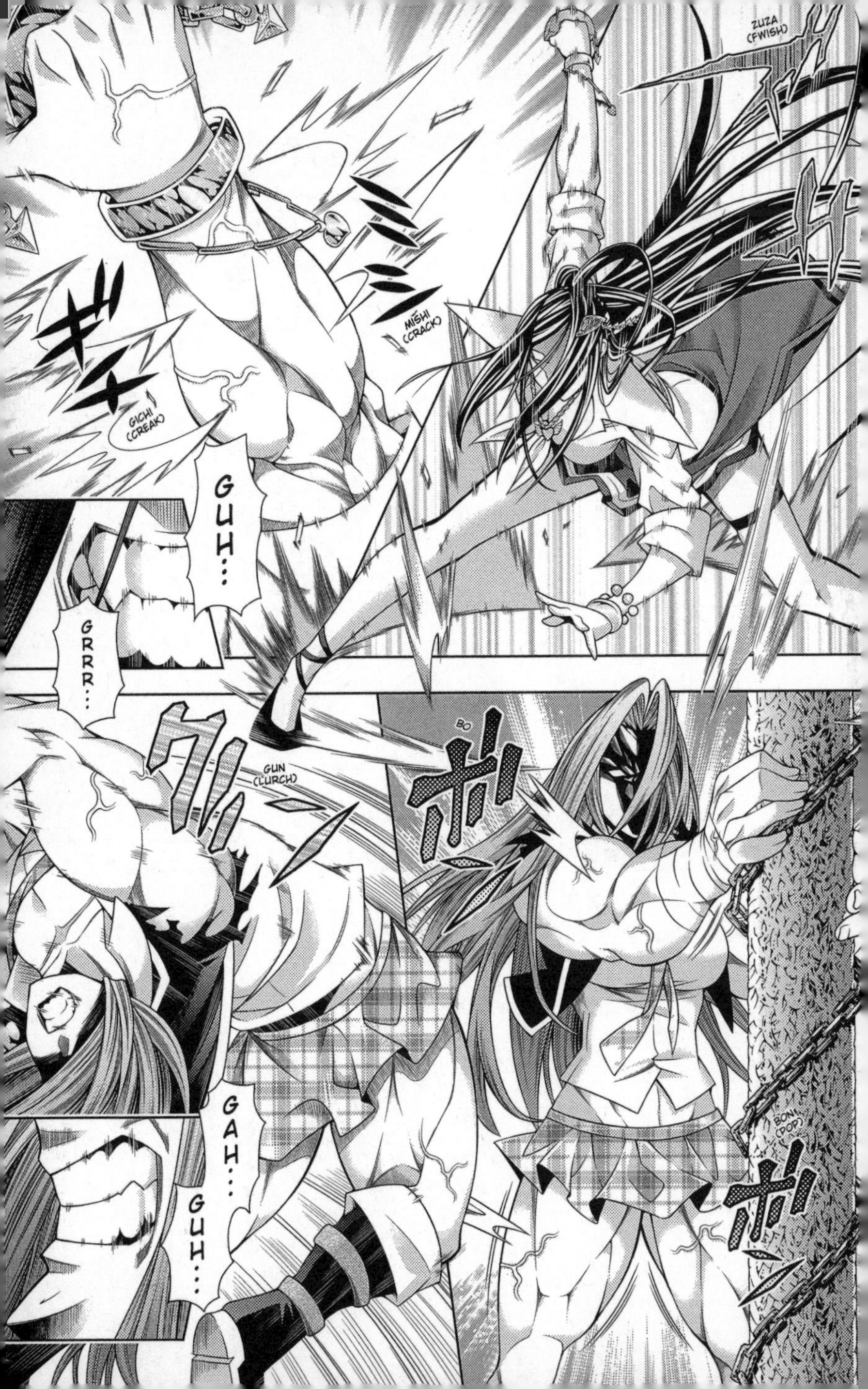
ZUZA
(FWISH)
MISHI
(CRACK)
GICHI
(CREAK)
GUH...
BO
GUN
(LURCH)
BON
(POP)
GRRR...
GAH...
GUH...

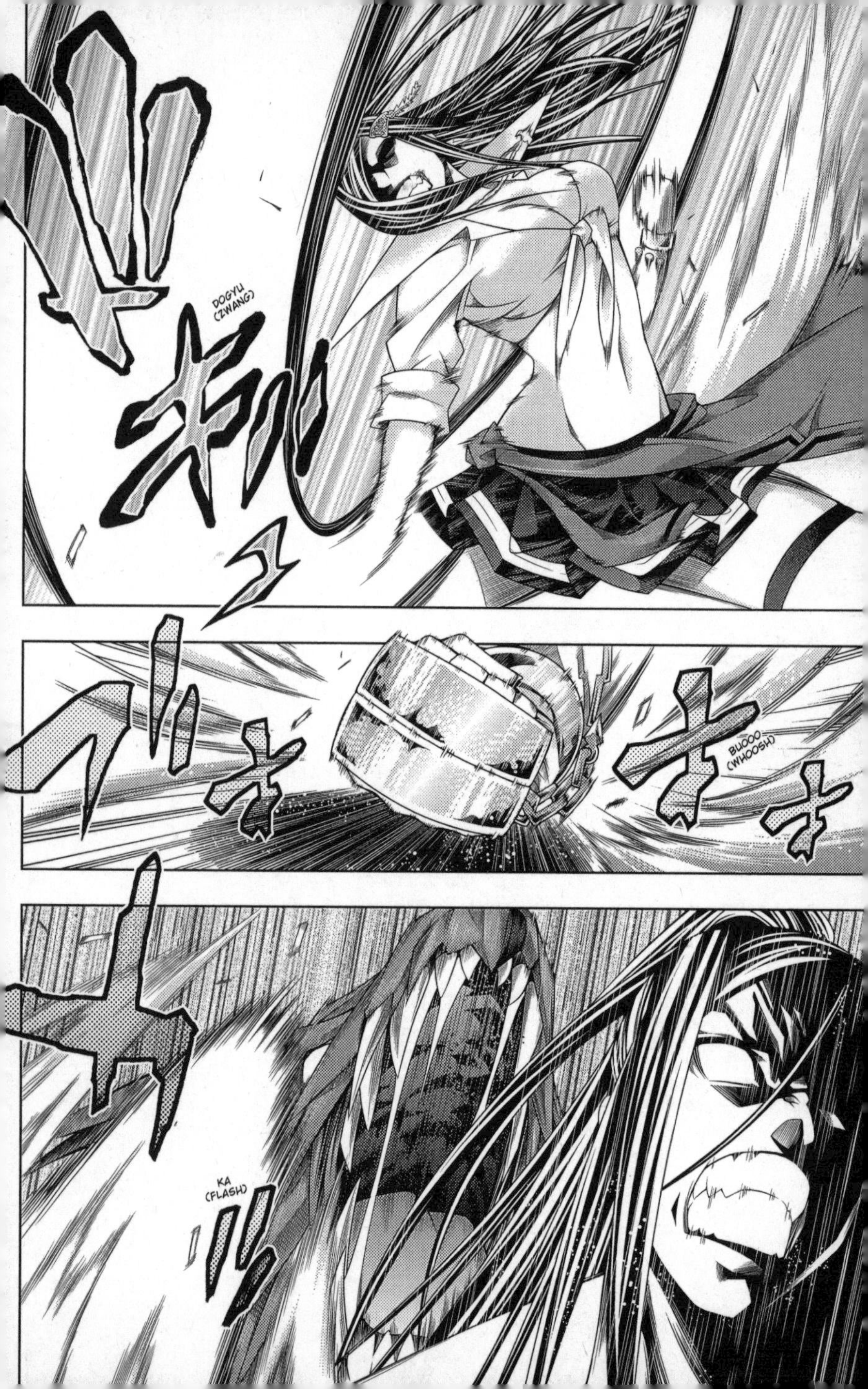
DOGYU (ZWANG)
BUOOO (WHOOSH)
KA (FLASH)

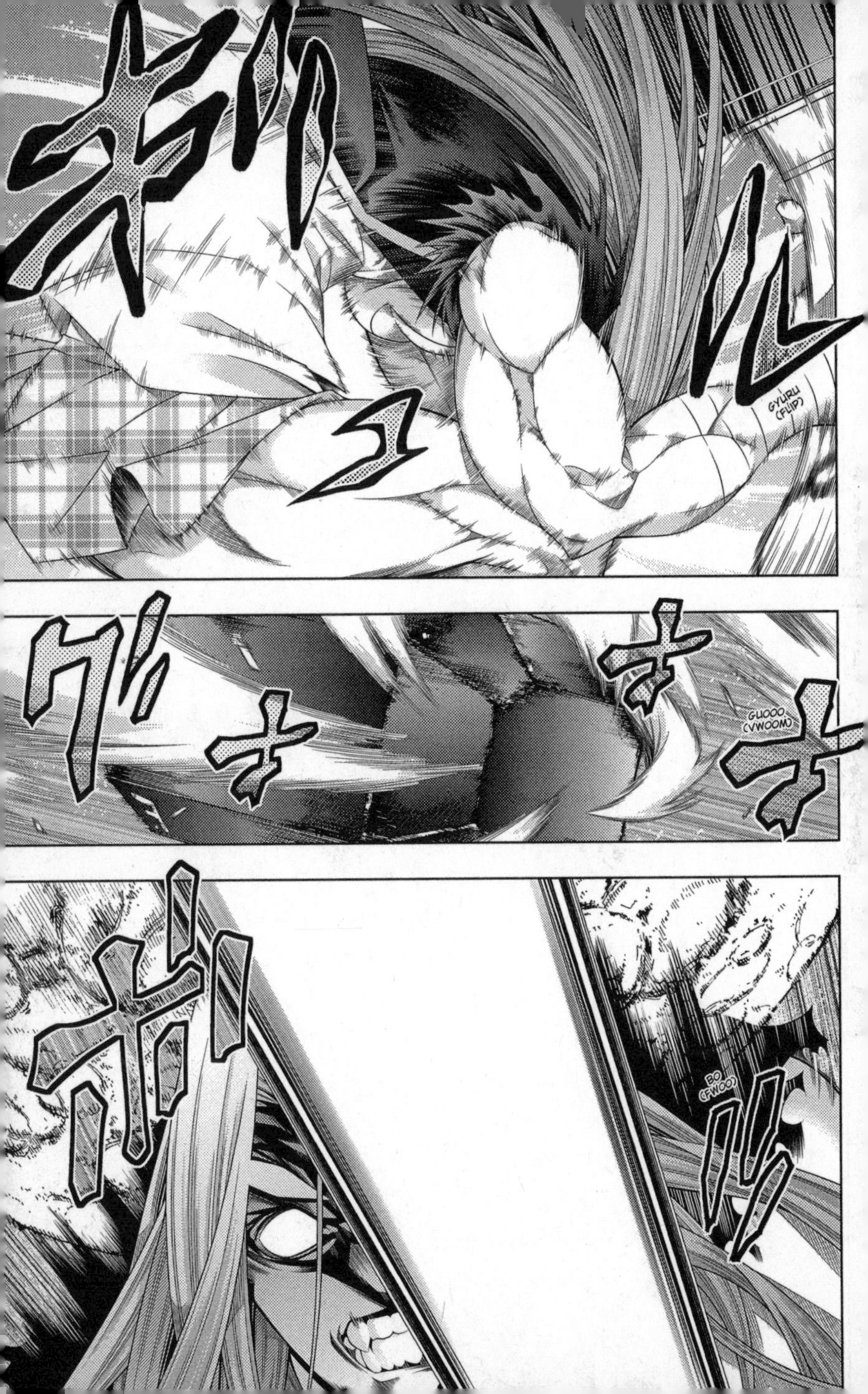
GYURU (FLIP)
GUOOO (VWOOM)
BO (FWOO)

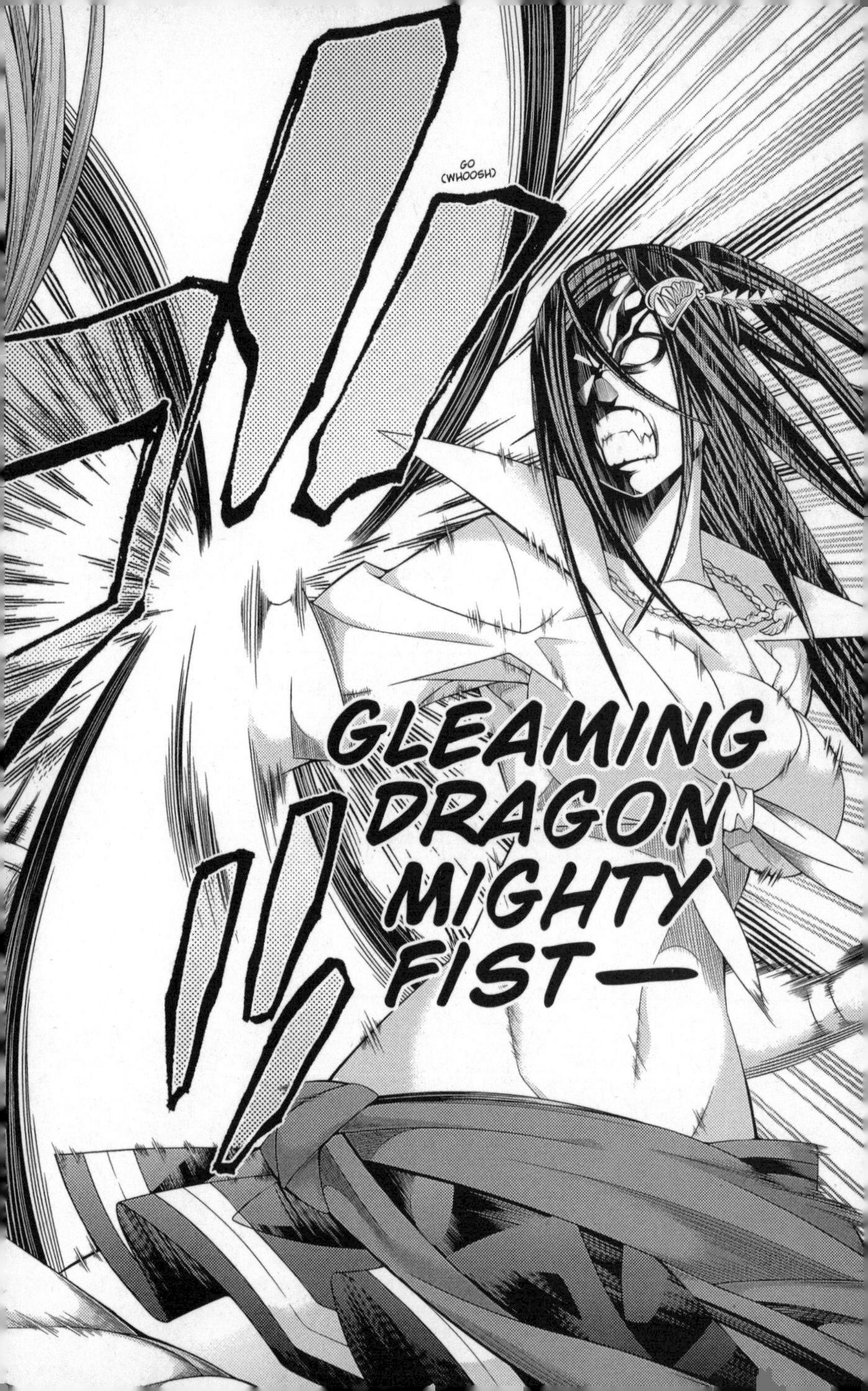
GO
(WHOOSH)
GLEAMING DRAGON MIGHTY FIST—

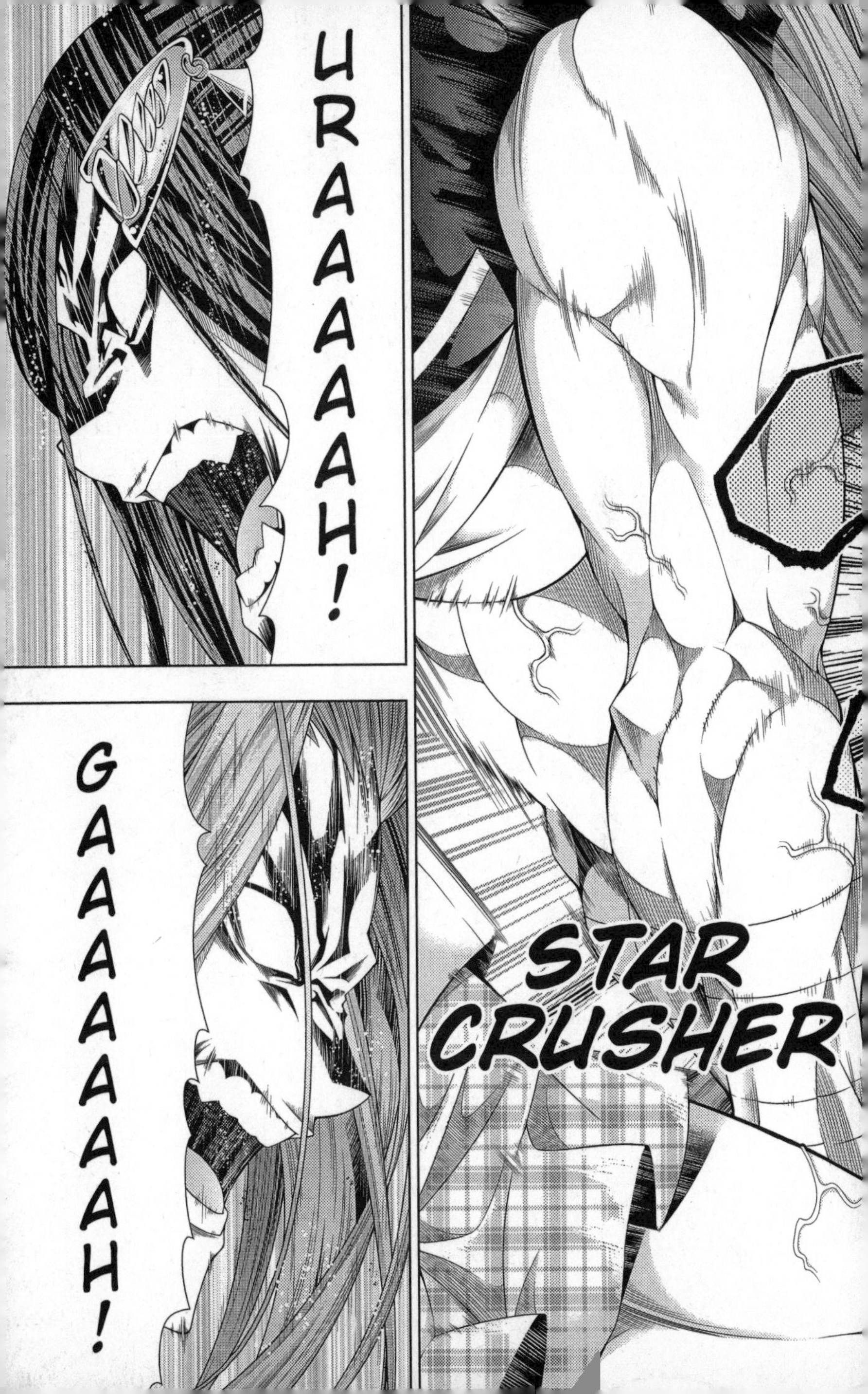
STAR CRUSHER
URAAAAAH!
GAAAAAAAH!

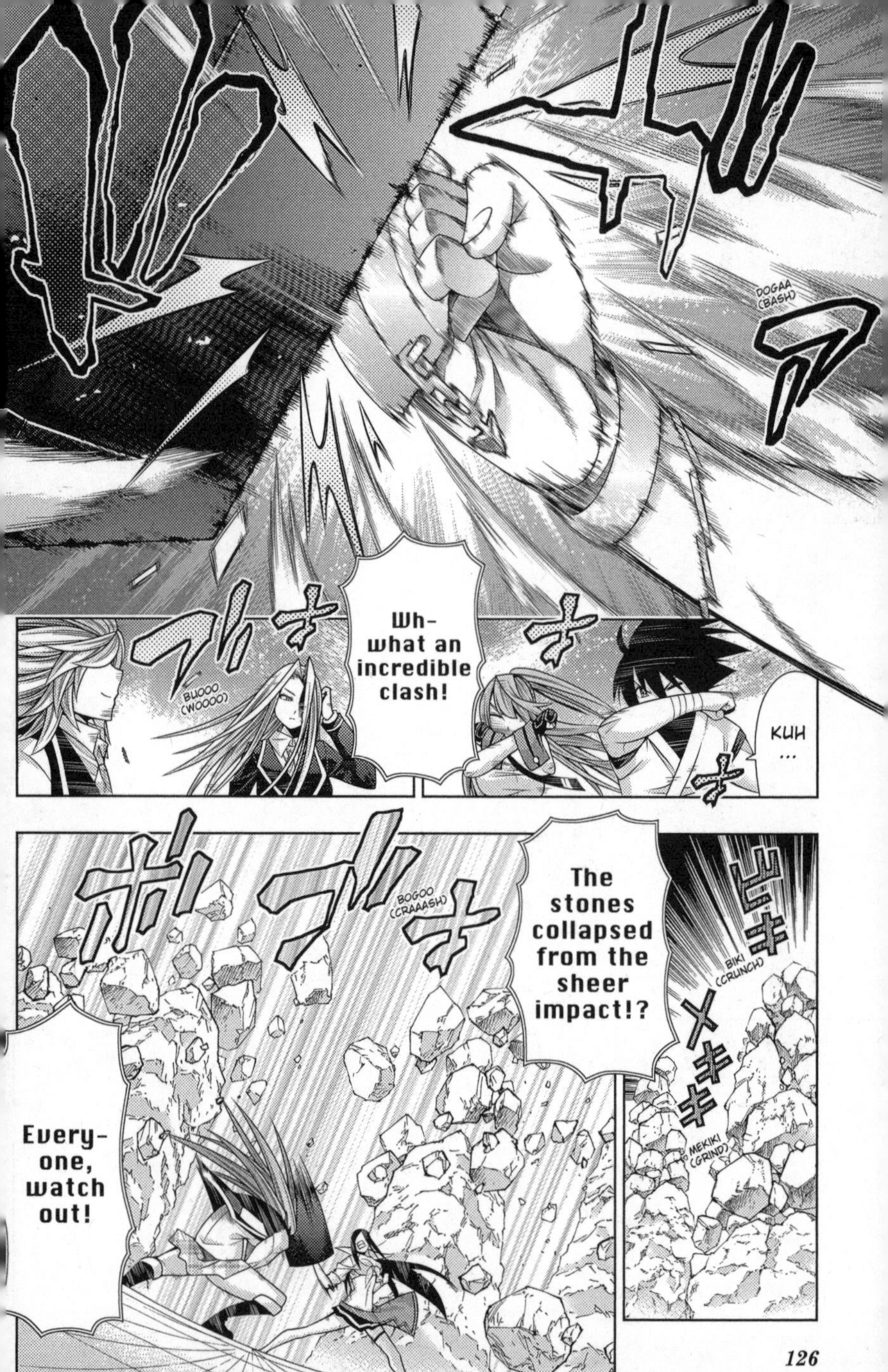
DOGAA (BASH)
KUH ...
Wh- what an incredible clash!
BUOOO (WOOOO)
BIKI (CRUNCH)
MEKIKI (GRIND)
The stones collapsed from the sheer impact!?
BOGOO (CRAAASH)
Every-one, watch out!

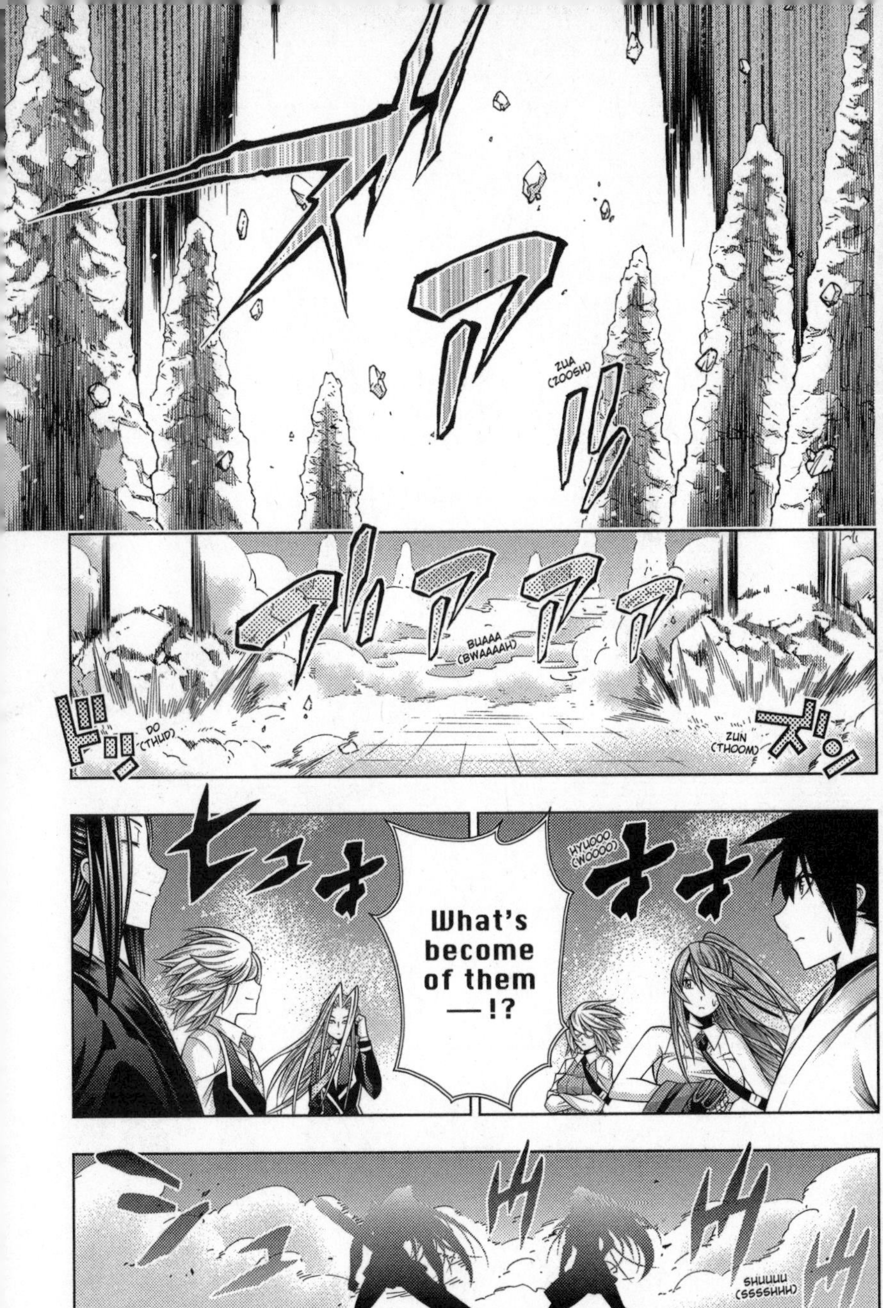
ZUA (ZOOSH)
ZUN (THOOM)
BUAAA (BWAAAAH)
DO (THUD)
HYUOOO (WOOOO)
What's become of them —!?
SHUUUU (SSSSHHH)

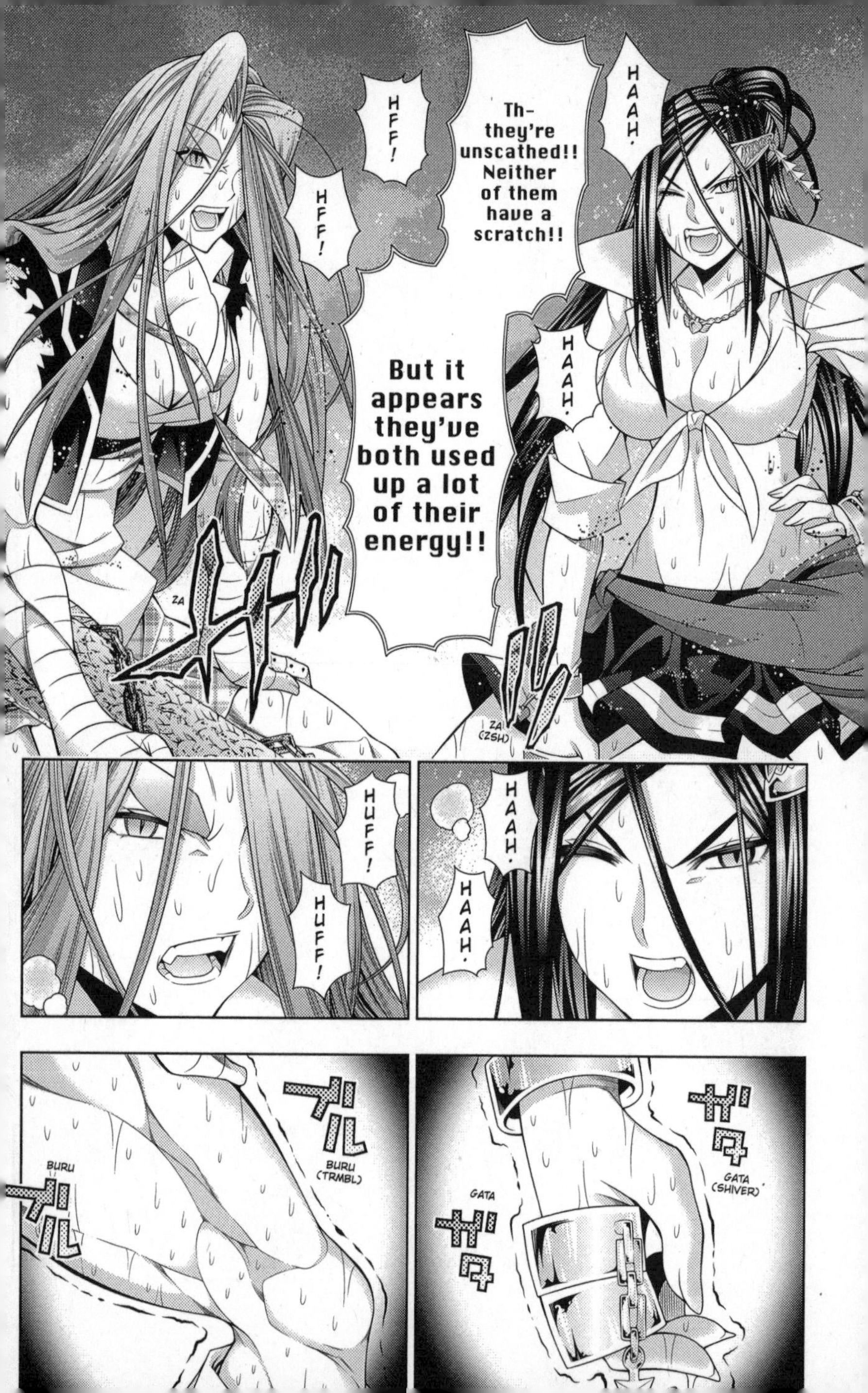
HAAH.
Th- they're unscathed!! Neither of them have a scratch!!
HFF!
HFF!
HAAH.
But it appears they've both used up a lot of their energy!!
ザッ
ZA (ZSH)
ザッ
ZA
HAAH.
HAAH.
HUFF!
HUFF!
ガタ
GATA (SHIVER)
ガタ
GATA
ブル
BURU (TRMBL)
ブル
BURU

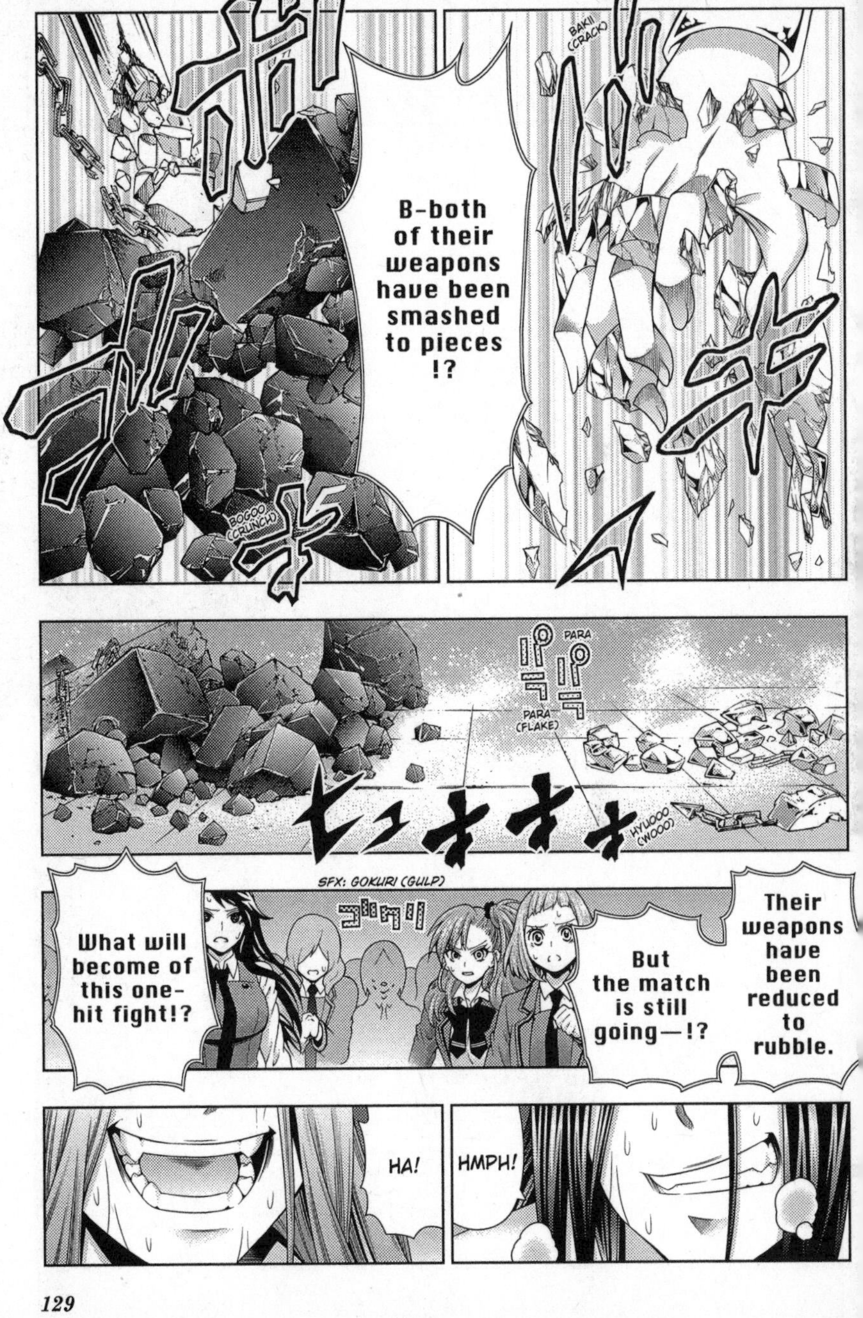
BAKII (CRACK)
B-both of their weapons have been smashed to pieces !?
BOGOO (CRUNCH)
PARA
PARA (FLAKE)
HYUOOO (WOOO)
Their weapons have been reduced to rubble.
But the match is still going—!?
SFX: GOKURI (GULP)
What will become of this one-hit fight!?
HMPH!
HA!

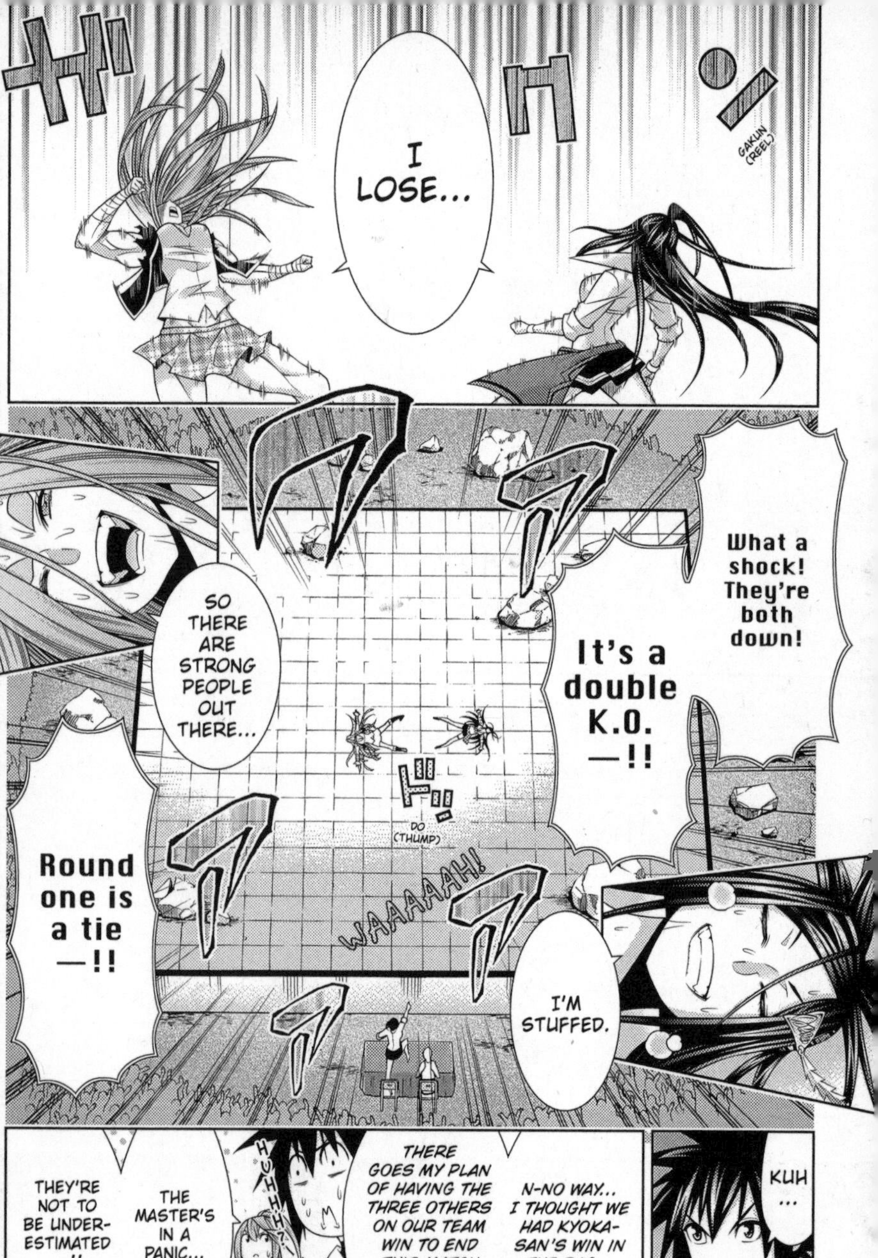
GAKUN (REEL)
I LOSE...
What a shock! They're both down!
It's a double K.O. —!!
I'M STUFFED.
SO THERE ARE STRONG PEOPLE OUT THERE...
DO (THUMP)
WAAAAAH!
Round one is a tie —!!
KUH ...
N-NO WAY... I THOUGHT WE HAD KYOKA-SAN'S WIN IN THE BAG...
THERE GOES MY PLAN OF HAVING THE THREE OTHERS ON OUR TEAM WIN TO END THIS MATCH BEFORE MY TURN!!
HUHHHH?!
THE MASTER'S IN A PANIC...
THEY'RE NOT TO BE UNDER-ESTIMATED ...!!

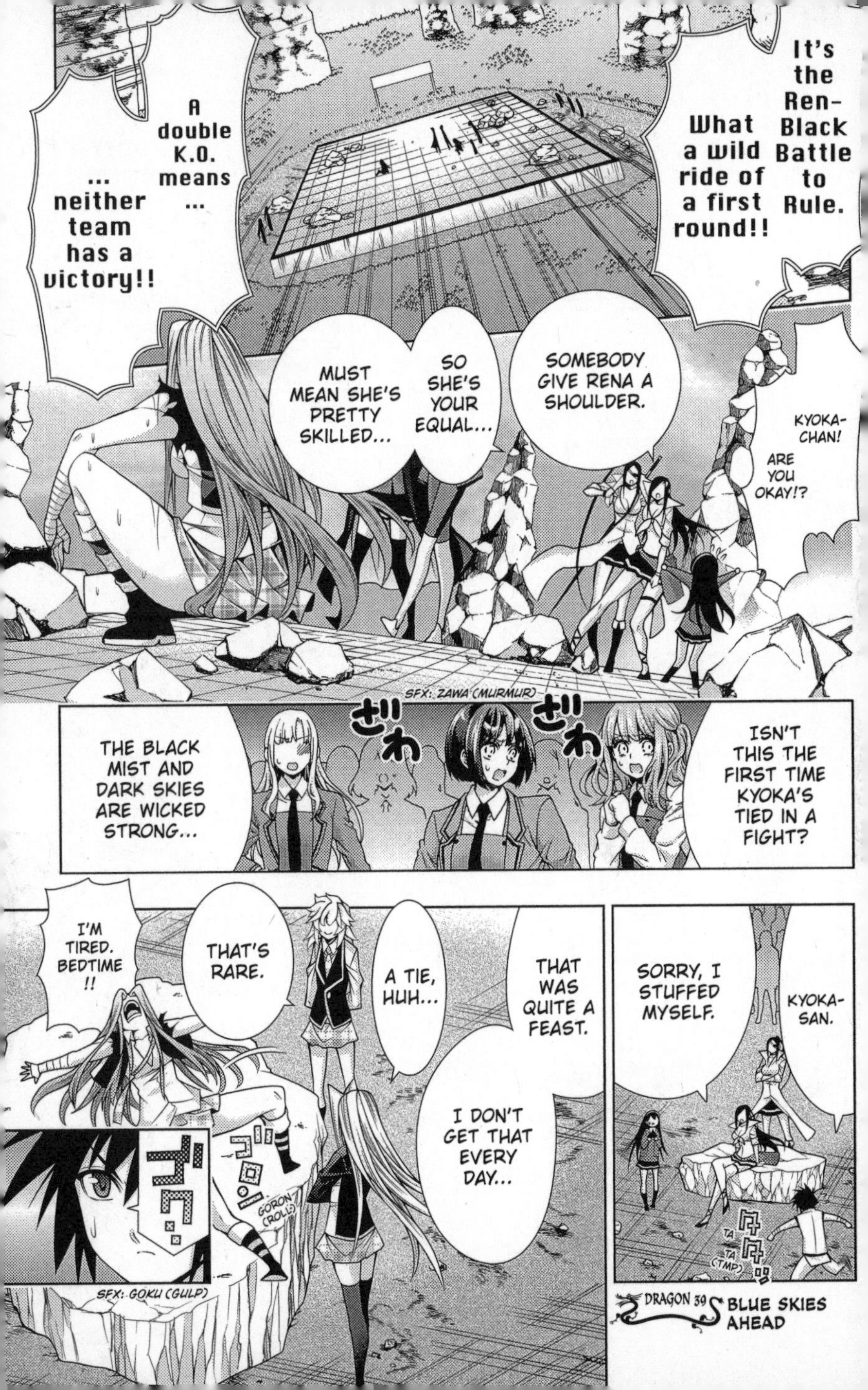
It's the Ren-Black Battle to Rule.
What a wild ride of a first round!!
A double K.O. means ...
... neither team has a victory!!
KYOKA-CHAN!
ARE YOU OKAY!?
SOMEBODY GIVE RENA A SHOULDER.
SO SHE'S YOUR EQUAL...
MUST MEAN SHE'S PRETTY SKILLED...
SFX: ZAWA (MURMUR)
ISN'T THIS THE FIRST TIME KYOKA'S TIED IN A FIGHT?
ざわ
ざわ
THE BLACK MIST AND DARK SKIES ARE WICKED STRONG...
KYOKA-SAN.
SORRY, I STUFFED MYSELF.
TA TA (TMP)
DRAGON 39 BLUE SKIES AHEAD
THAT WAS QUITE A FEAST.
I DON'T GET THAT EVERY DAY...
A TIE, HUH...
THAT'S RARE.
I'M TIRED. BEDTIME !!
GORON (ROLL)
SFX: GOKU (GULP)

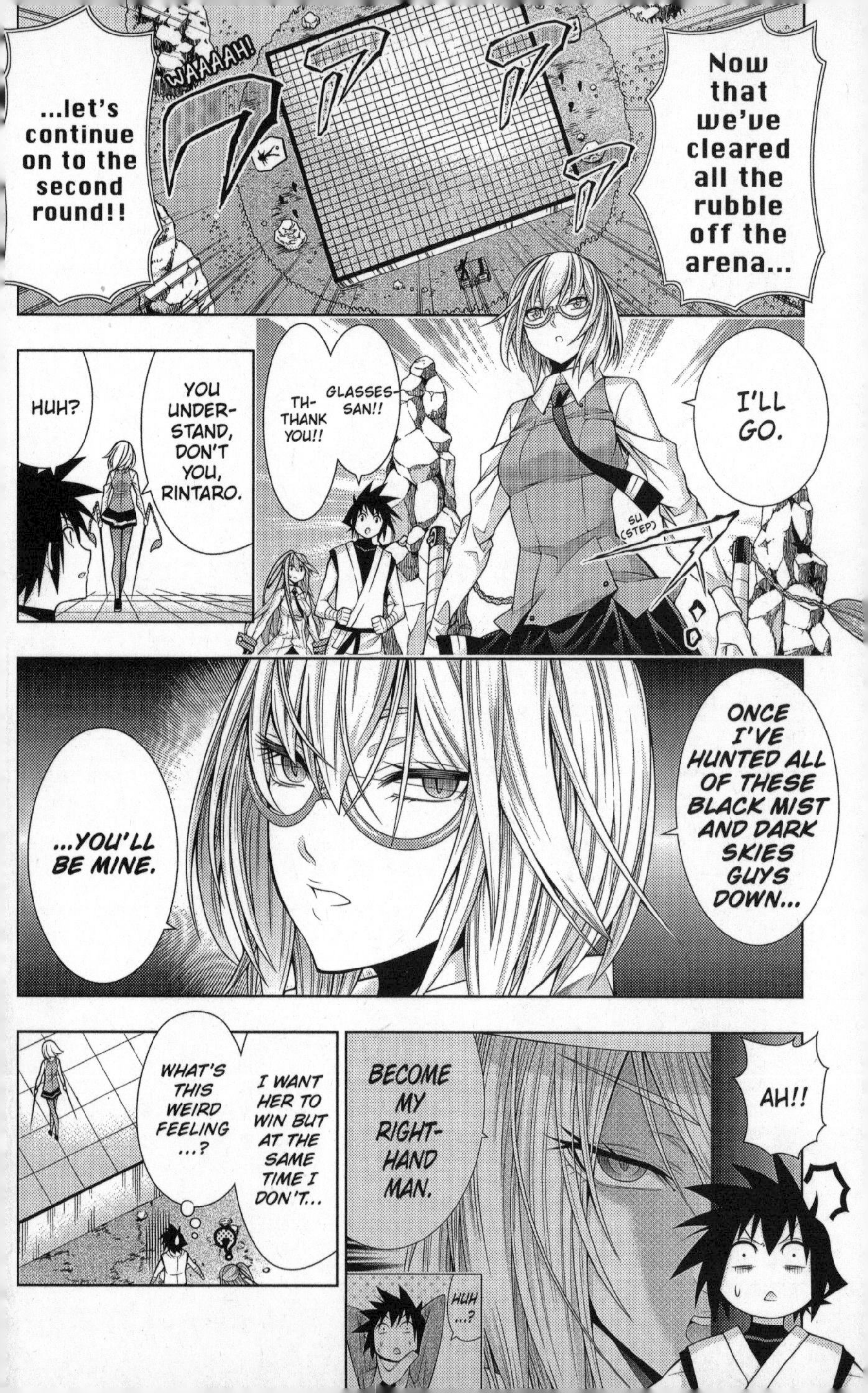
Now that we've cleared all the rubble off the arena...
WAAAAH!
...let's continue on to the second round!!
I'LL GO.
SU (STEP)
GLASSES-SAN!!
TH-THANK YOU!!
YOU UNDERSTAND, DON'T YOU, RINTARO.
HUH?
ONCE I'VE HUNTED ALL OF THESE BLACK MIST AND DARK SKIES GUYS DOWN...
...YOU'LL BE MINE.
AH!!
BECOME MY RIGHT-HAND MAN.
HUH...?
I WANT HER TO WIN BUT AT THE SAME TIME I DON'T...
WHAT'S THIS WEIRD FEELING...?

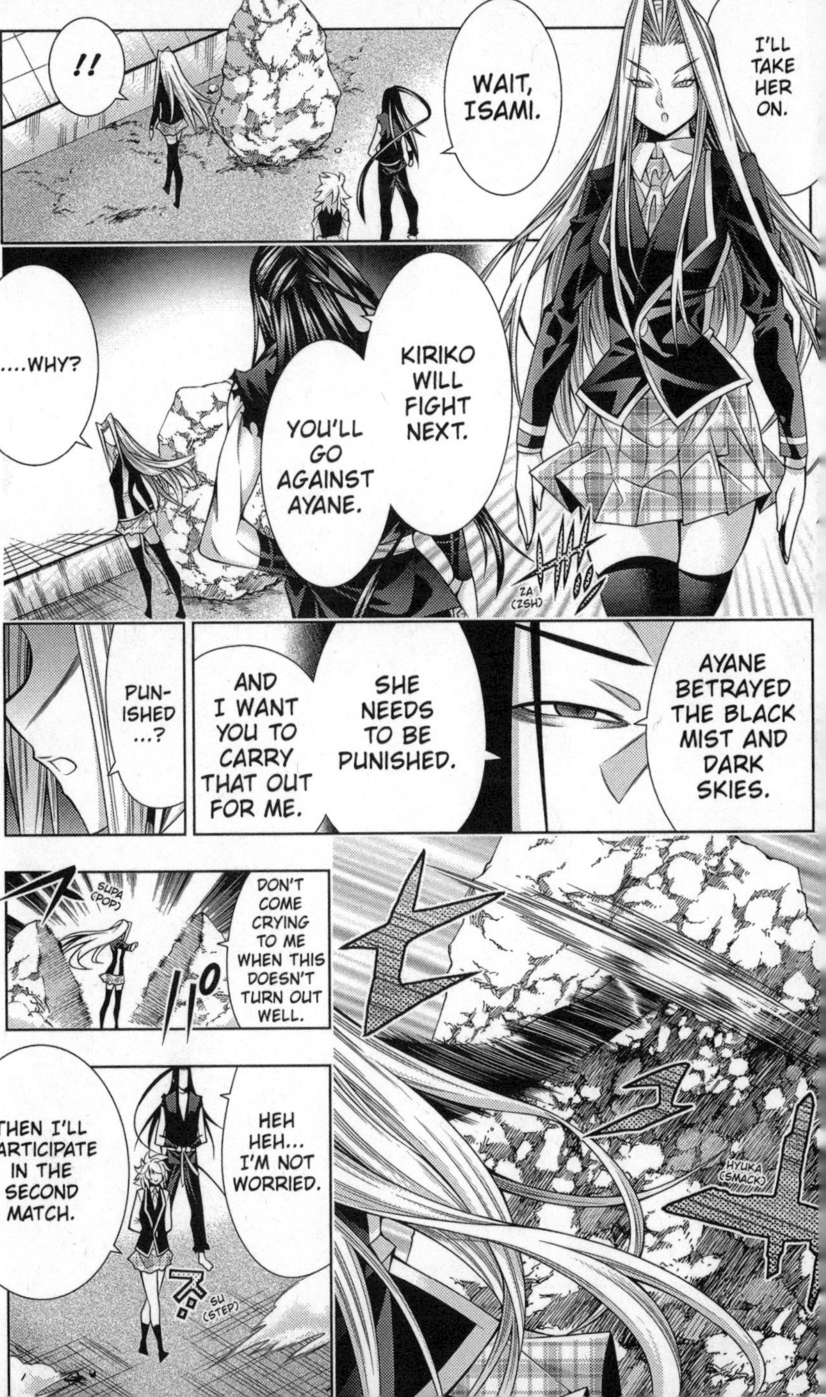
I'LL TAKE HER ON.
ZA (ZSH)
WAIT, ISAMI.
!!
KIRIKO WILL FIGHT NEXT.
YOU'LL GO AGAINST AYANE.
......WHY?
AYANE BETRAYED THE BLACK MIST AND DARK SKIES.
SHE NEEDS TO BE PUNISHED.
AND I WANT YOU TO CARRY THAT OUT FOR ME.
PUN-ISHED ...?
HYUKA (SMACK)
DON'T COME CRYING TO ME WHEN THIS DOESN'T TURN OUT WELL.
SUPA (POP)
HEH HEH... I'M NOT WORRIED.
THEN I'LL PARTICIPATE IN THE SECOND MATCH.
SU (STEP)

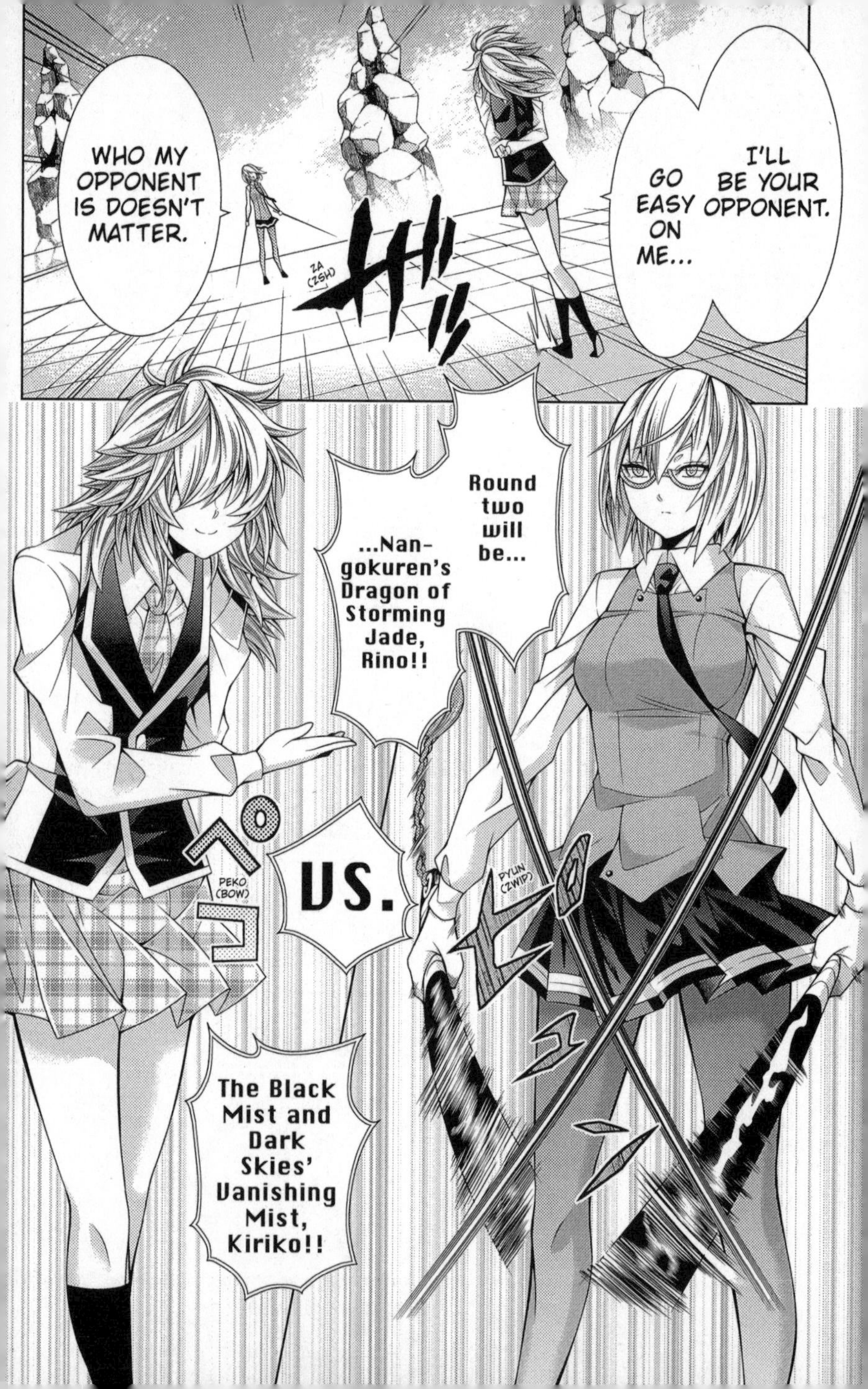
I'LL BE YOUR OPPONENT.
GO EASY ON ME...
ZA (ZSH)
WHO MY OPPONENT IS DOESN'T MATTER.
Round two will be...
...Nan-gokuren's Dragon of Storming Jade, Rino!!
PYUN (ZWIP)
VS.
PEKO (BOW)
The Black Mist and Dark Skies' Vanishing Mist, Kiriko!!

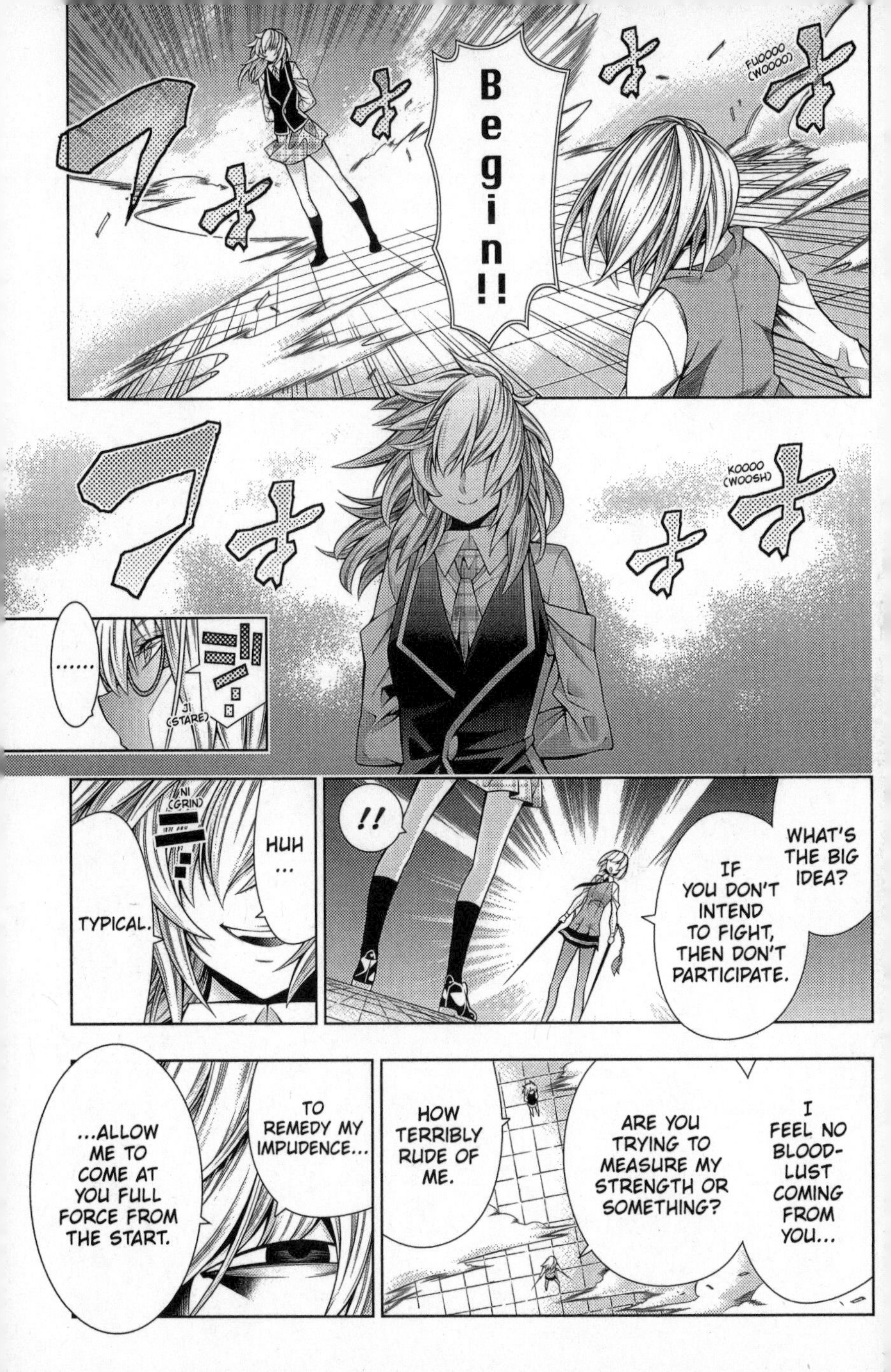
FUOOOO (WOOOO)
Begin!!
KOOOO (WOOSH)
......
JI (STARE)
WHAT'S THE BIG IDEA?
IF YOU DON'T INTEND TO FIGHT, THEN DON'T PARTICIPATE.
!!
NI (GRIN)
HUH ...
TYPICAL.
I FEEL NO BLOOD-LUST COMING FROM YOU...
ARE YOU TRYING TO MEASURE MY STRENGTH OR SOMETHING?
HOW TERRIBLY RUDE OF ME.
TO REMEDY MY IMPUDENCE...
...ALLOW ME TO COME AT YOU FULL FORCE FROM THE START.

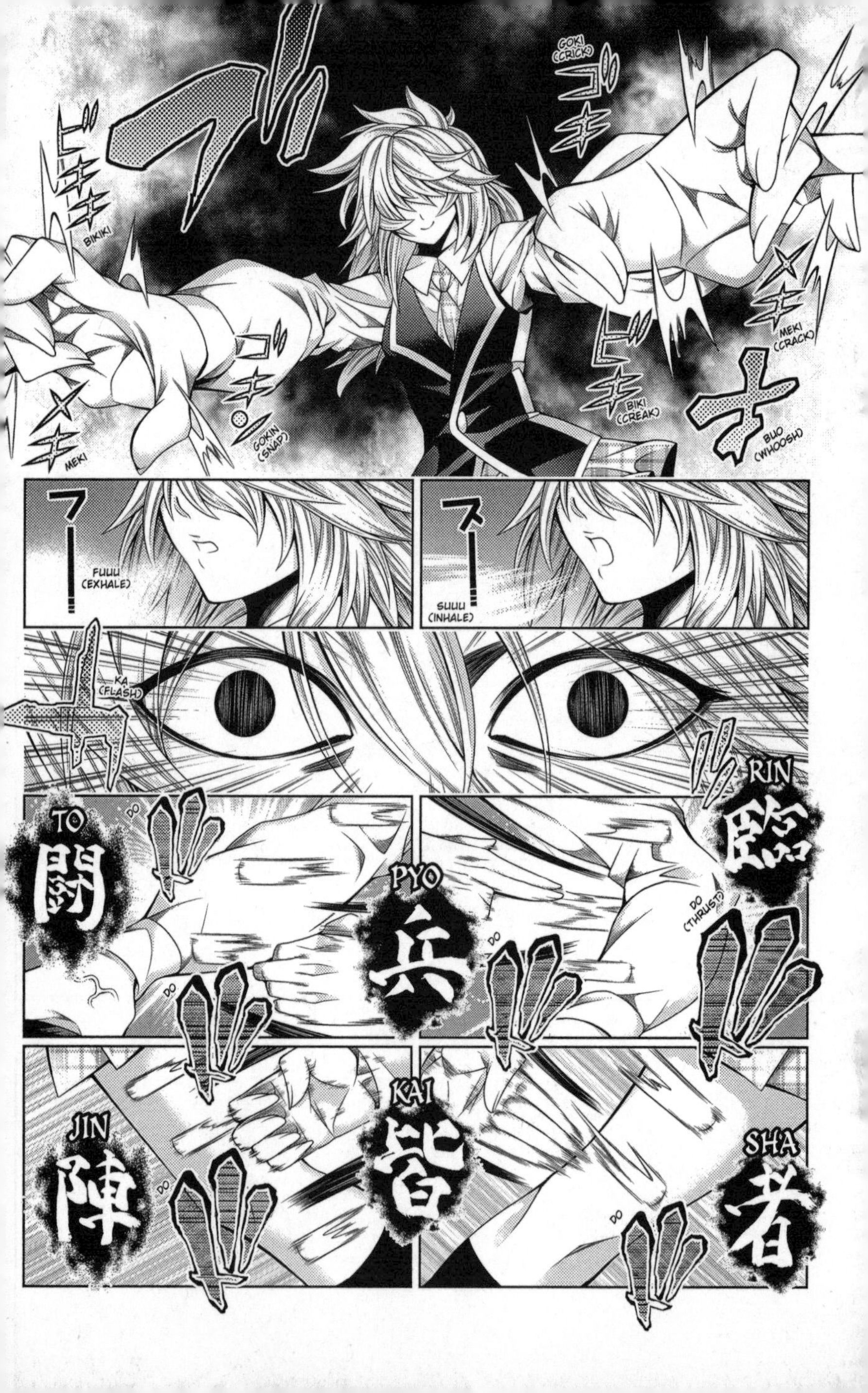
GOKI (CRICK)
MEKI (CRACK)
BIKI (CREAK)
BUO (WHOOSH)
GOKIN (SNAP)
BIKIKI
MEKI
SUUU (INHALE)
FUUU (EXHALE)
KA (FLASH)
RIN
臨
DO (THRUST)
DO
PYO
兵
TO
闘
DO
DO
SHA
者
DO
KAI
皆
JIN
陣
DO

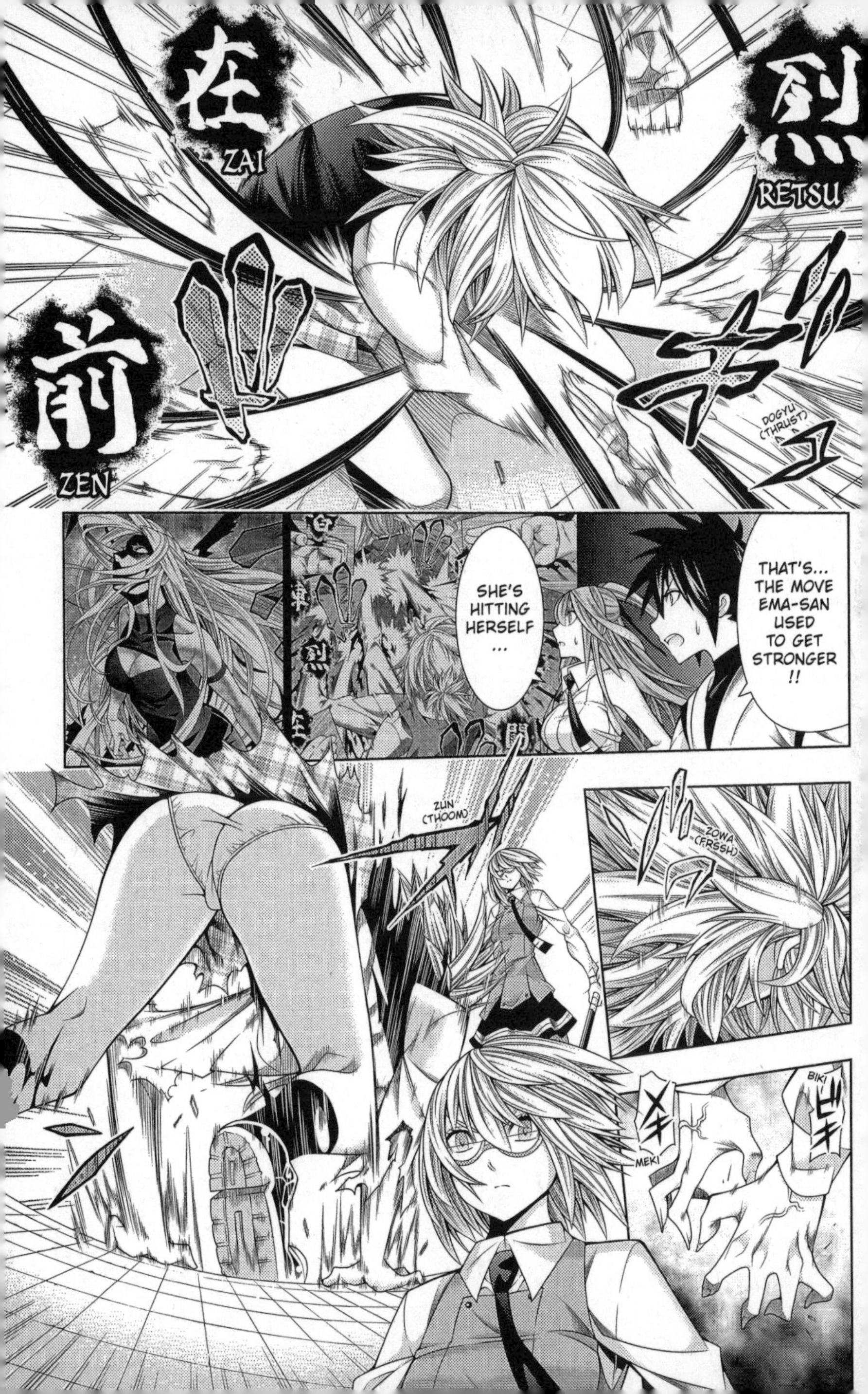

烈
RETSU
在
ZAI
DOGYU (THRUST)
前
ZEN
THAT'S... THE MOVE EMA-SAN USED TO GET STRONGER!!
SHE'S HITTING HERSELF...
ZOWA (FRSSH)
ZUN (THOOM)
BIKI
MEKI

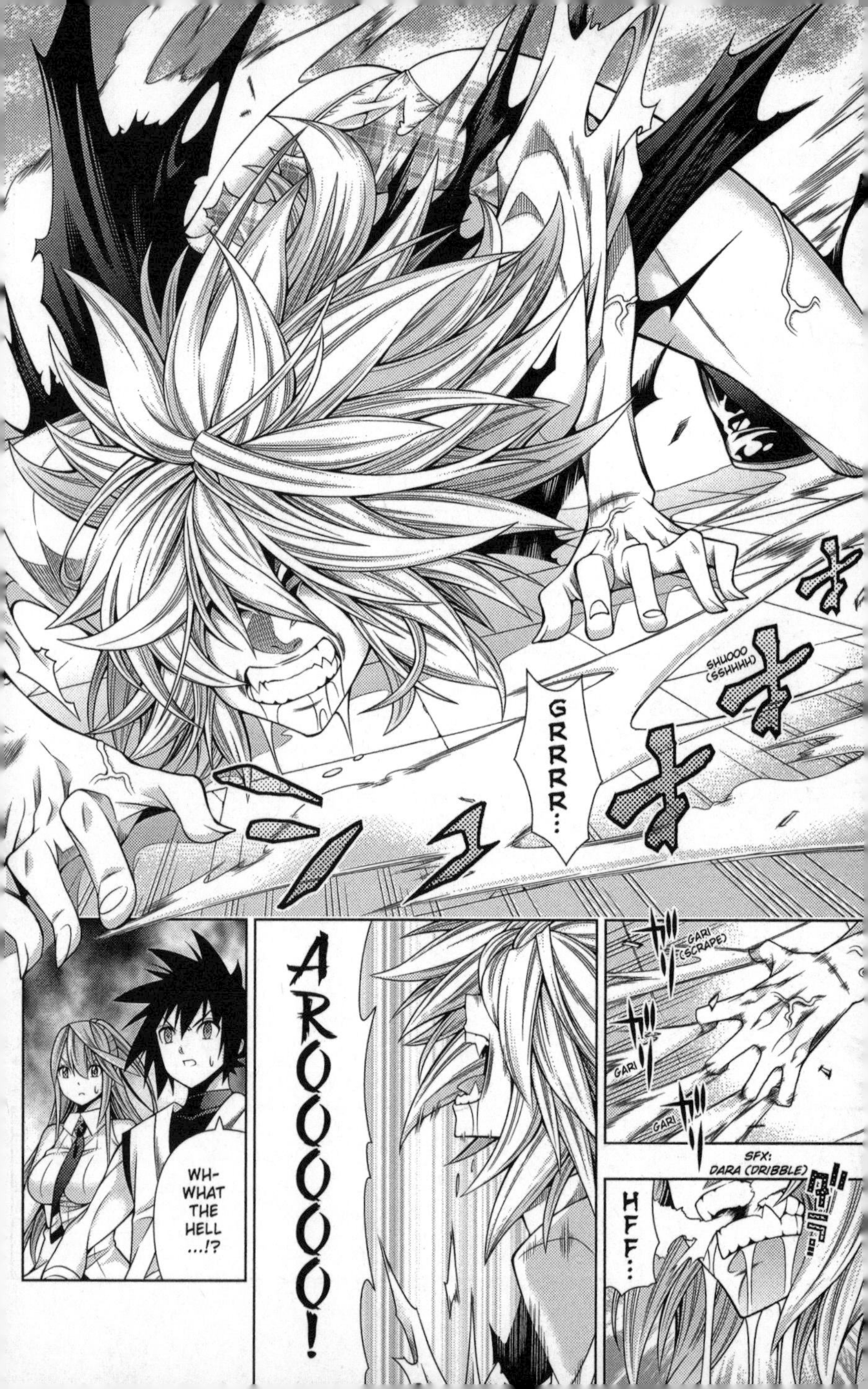
SHUOOO (SSHHHH)
GRRRR...
GARI (SCRAPE)
GARI
GARI
SFX: DARA (DRIBBLE)
HFF...
AROOOOO!
WH-WHAT THE HELL ...!?

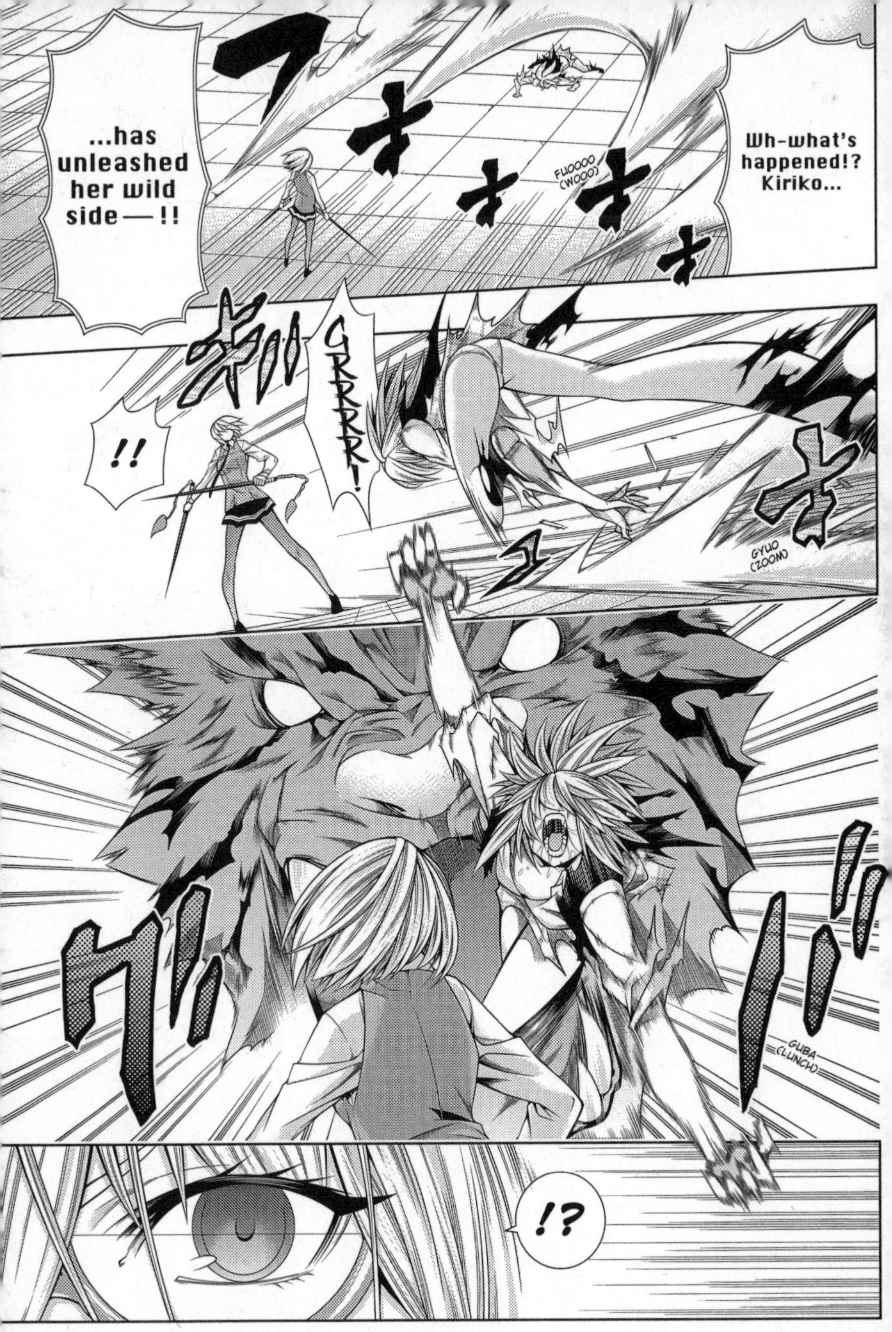
Wh-what's happened!? Kiriko...
FUOOOO (WOOO)
...has unleashed her wild side—!!
GYUO (ZOOM)
GRRRRR!
!!
GUBA (CLUNCH)
!?

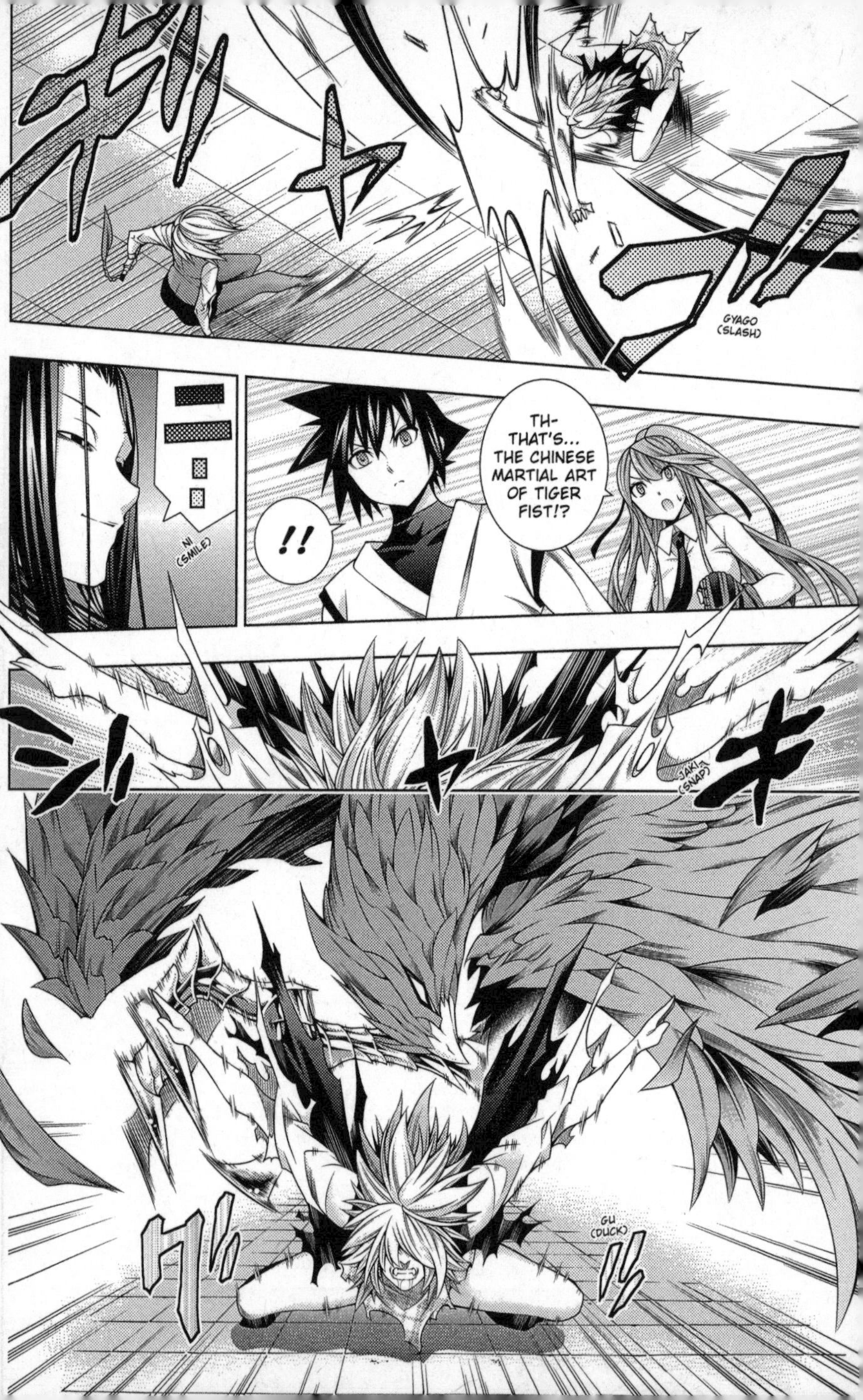
GYAGO (SLASH)
TH- THAT'S... THE CHINESE MARTIAL ART OF TIGER FIST!?
!!
NI (SMILE)
JAKI (SNAP)
GU (DUCK)

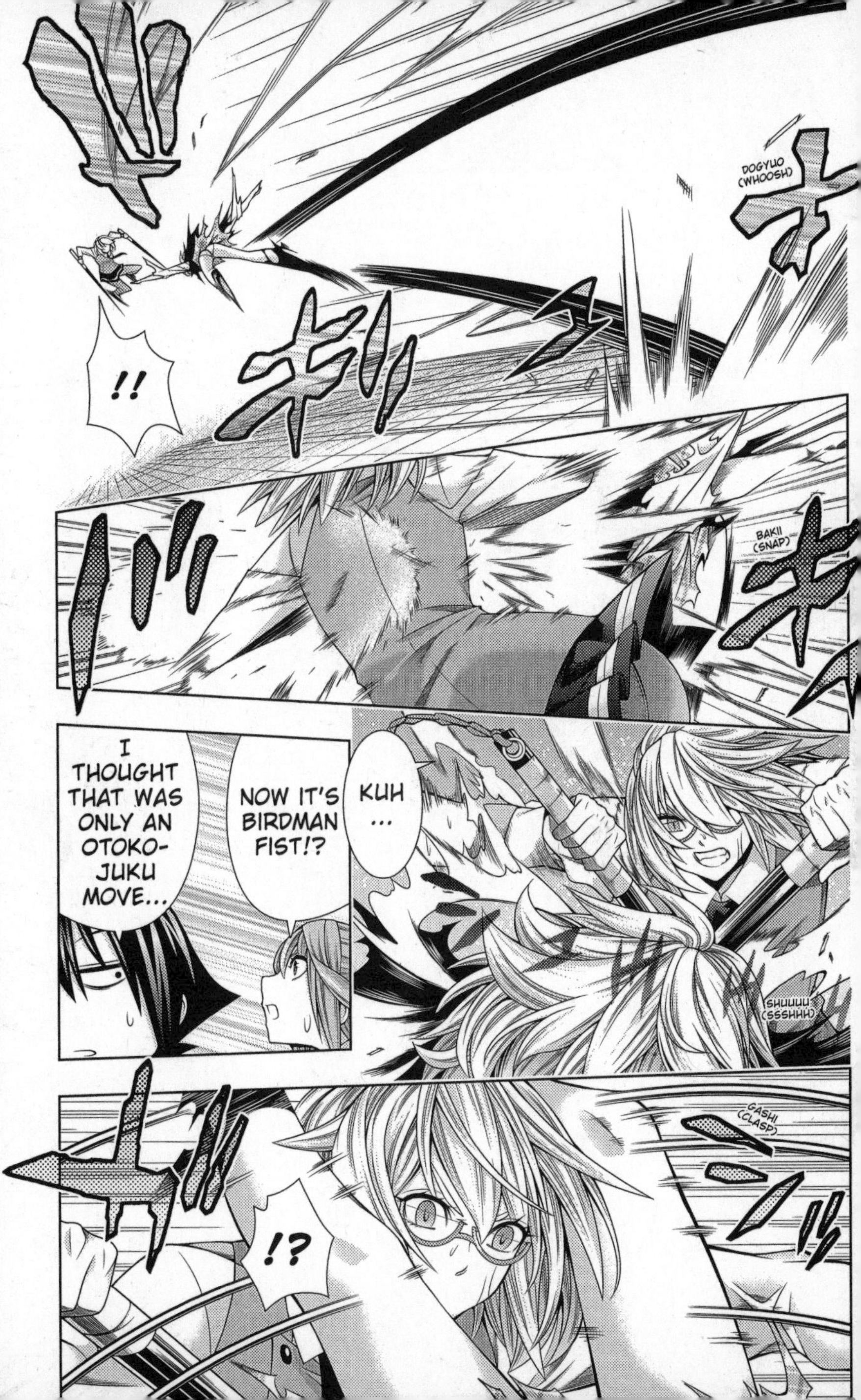

DOGYUO (WHOOSH)
!!
BAKII (SNAP)
KUH ...
SHUUUU (SSSHHH)
NOW IT'S BIRDMAN FIST!?
I THOUGHT THAT WAS ONLY AN OTOKO-JUKU MOVE...
GASHI (CLASP)
!?

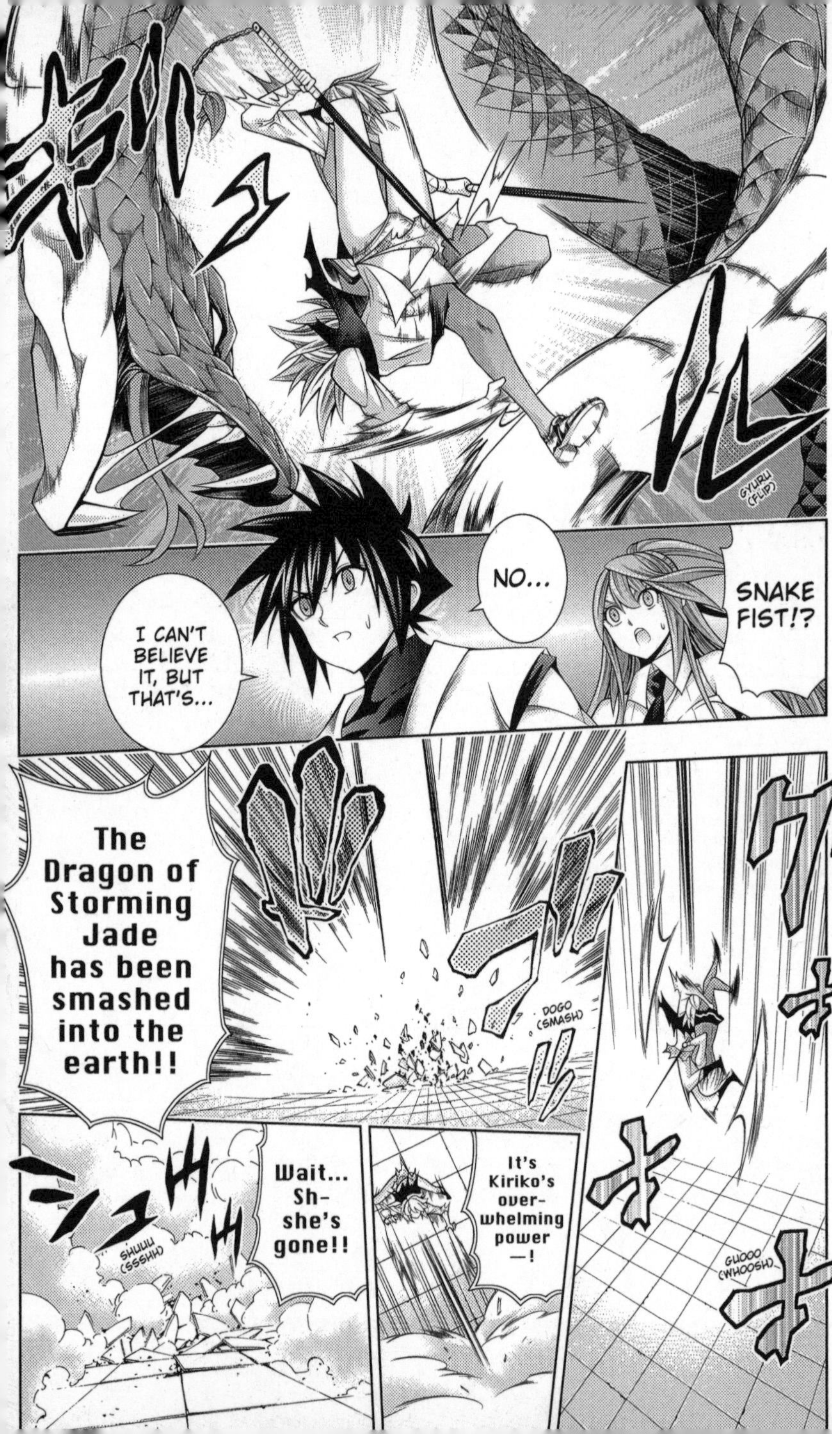
GYURU (FLIP)
SNAKE FIST!?
NO...
I CAN'T BELIEVE IT, BUT THAT'S...
GUOOO (WHOOSH)
DOGO (SMASH)
The Dragon of Storming Jade has been smashed into the earth!!
It's Kiriko's over-whelming power —!
Wait... Sh-she's gone!!
SHUUU (SSSHH)

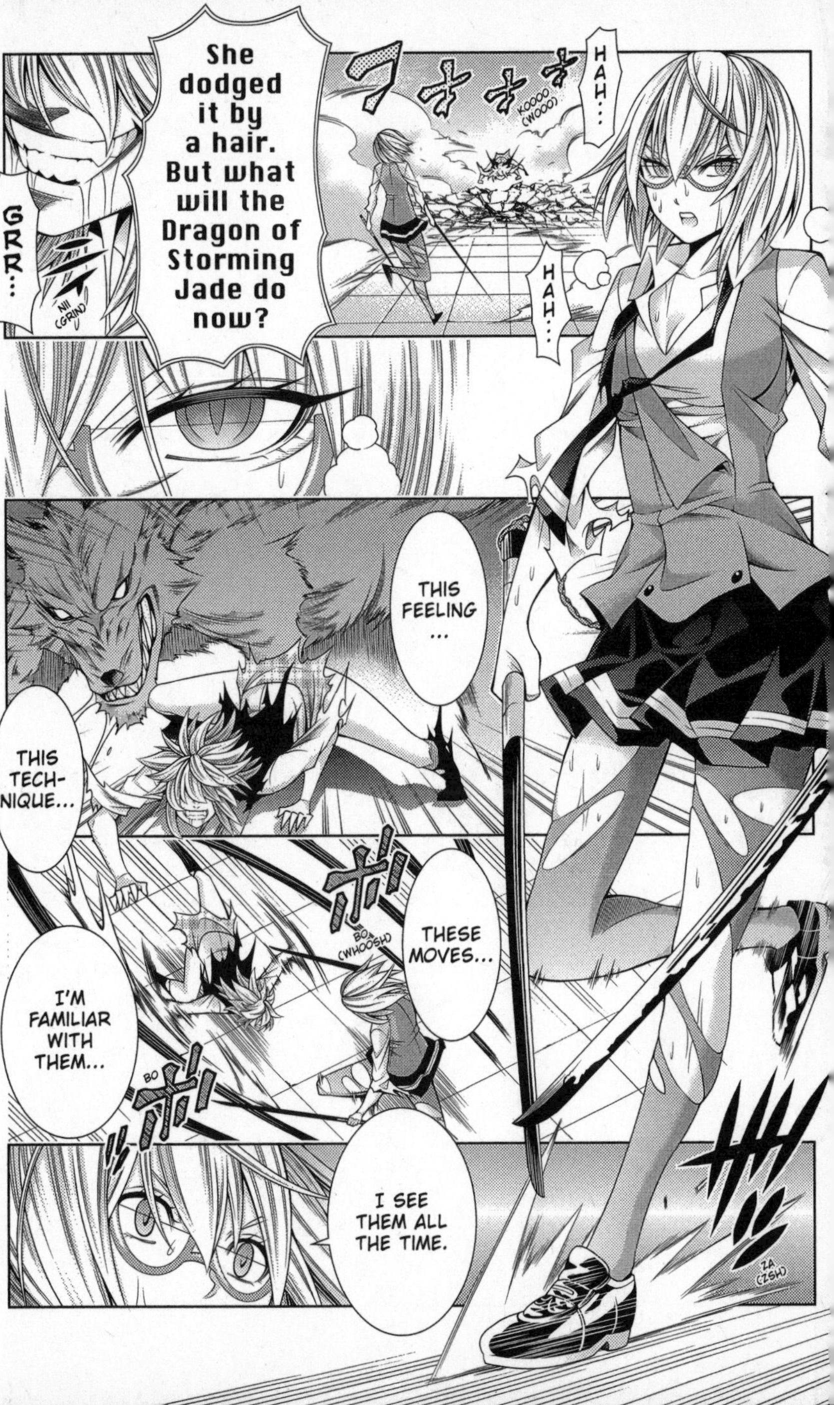
HAH...
HAH...
KOOOO (WOOO)
She dodged it by a hair. But what will the Dragon of Storming Jade do now?
GRR...
NII (GRIND)
THIS FEELING...
THIS TECH-NIQUE...
THESE MOVES...
BO (WHOOSH)
I'M FAMILIAR WITH THEM...
BO
I SEE THEM ALL THE TIME.
ZA (ZSH)

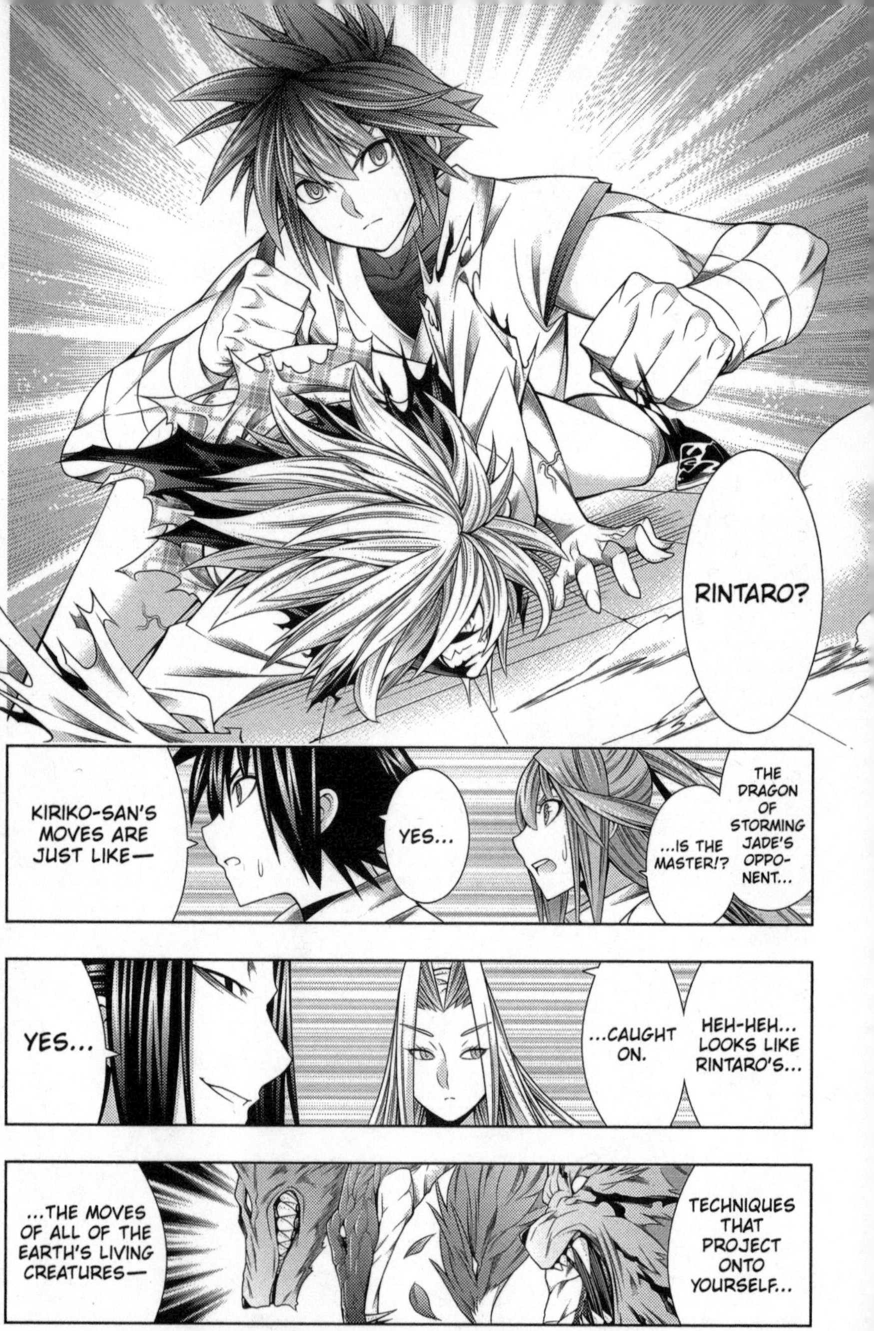
RINTARO?
THE DRAGON OF STORMING JADE'S OPPONENT...
...IS THE MASTER!?
YES...
KIRIKO-SAN'S MOVES ARE JUST LIKE—
HEH-HEH... LOOKS LIKE RINTARO'S...
...CAUGHT ON.
YES...
TECHNIQUES THAT PROJECT ONTO YOURSELF...
...THE MOVES OF ALL OF THE EARTH'S LIVING CREATURES—

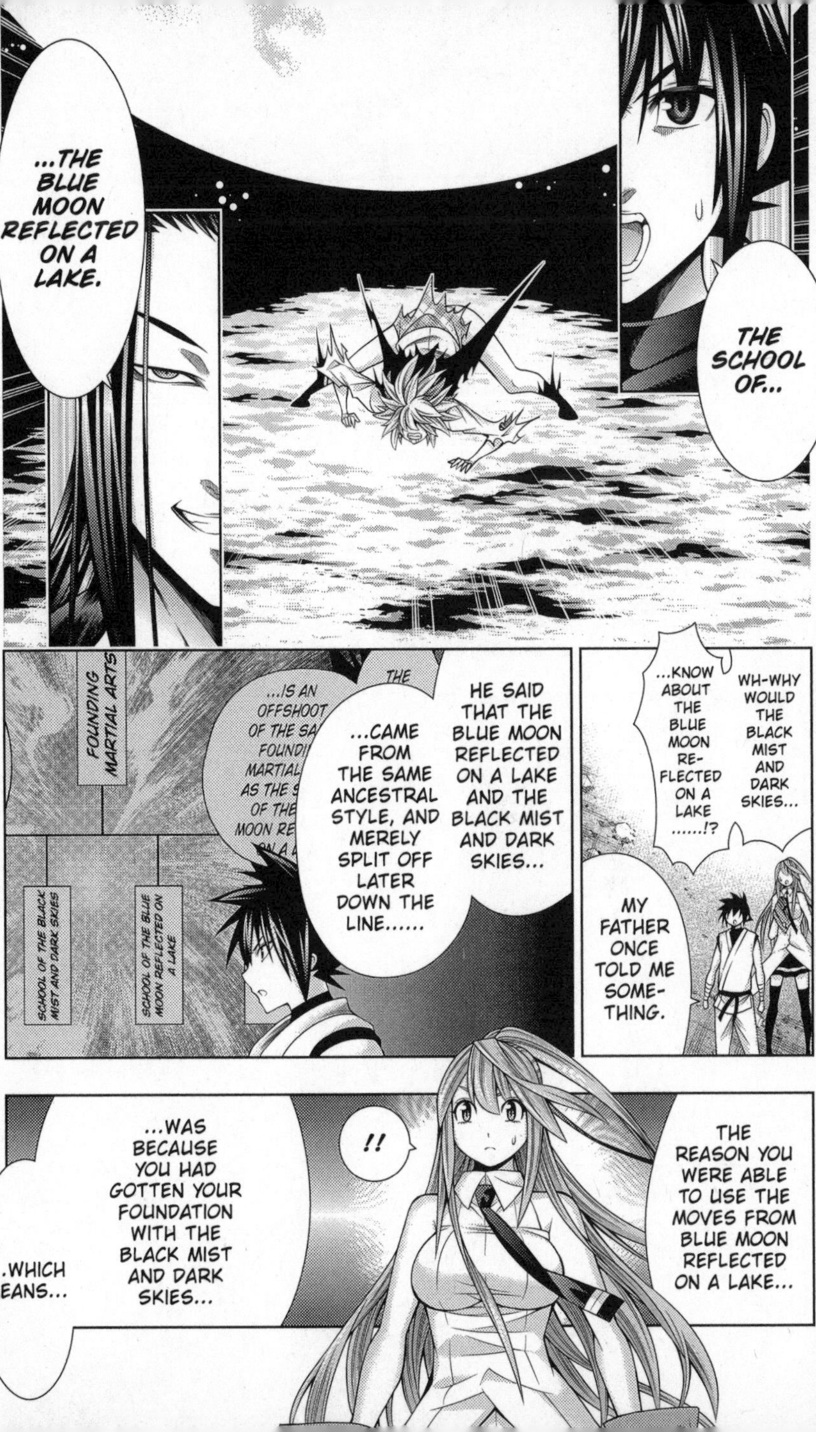
THE SCHOOL OF...
...THE BLUE MOON REFLECTED ON A LAKE.
WH-WHY WOULD THE BLACK MIST AND DARK SKIES...
...KNOW ABOUT THE BLUE MOON RE-FLECTED ON A LAKE ......!?
MY FATHER ONCE TOLD ME SOME-THING.
HE SAID THAT THE BLUE MOON REFLECTED ON A LAKE AND THE BLACK MIST AND DARK SKIES...
...CAME FROM THE SAME ANCESTRAL STYLE, AND MERELY SPLIT OFF LATER DOWN THE LINE......
...IS AN OFFSHOOT
FOUNDING MARTIAL ARTS
SCHOOL OF THE BLUE MOON REFLECTED ON A LAKE
SCHOOL OF THE BLACK MIST AND DARK SKIES
THE REASON YOU WERE ABLE TO USE THE MOVES FROM BLUE MOON REFLECTED ON A LAKE...
!!
...WAS BECAUSE YOU HAD GOTTEN YOUR FOUNDATION WITH THE BLACK MIST AND DARK SKIES...
...WHICH MEANS...

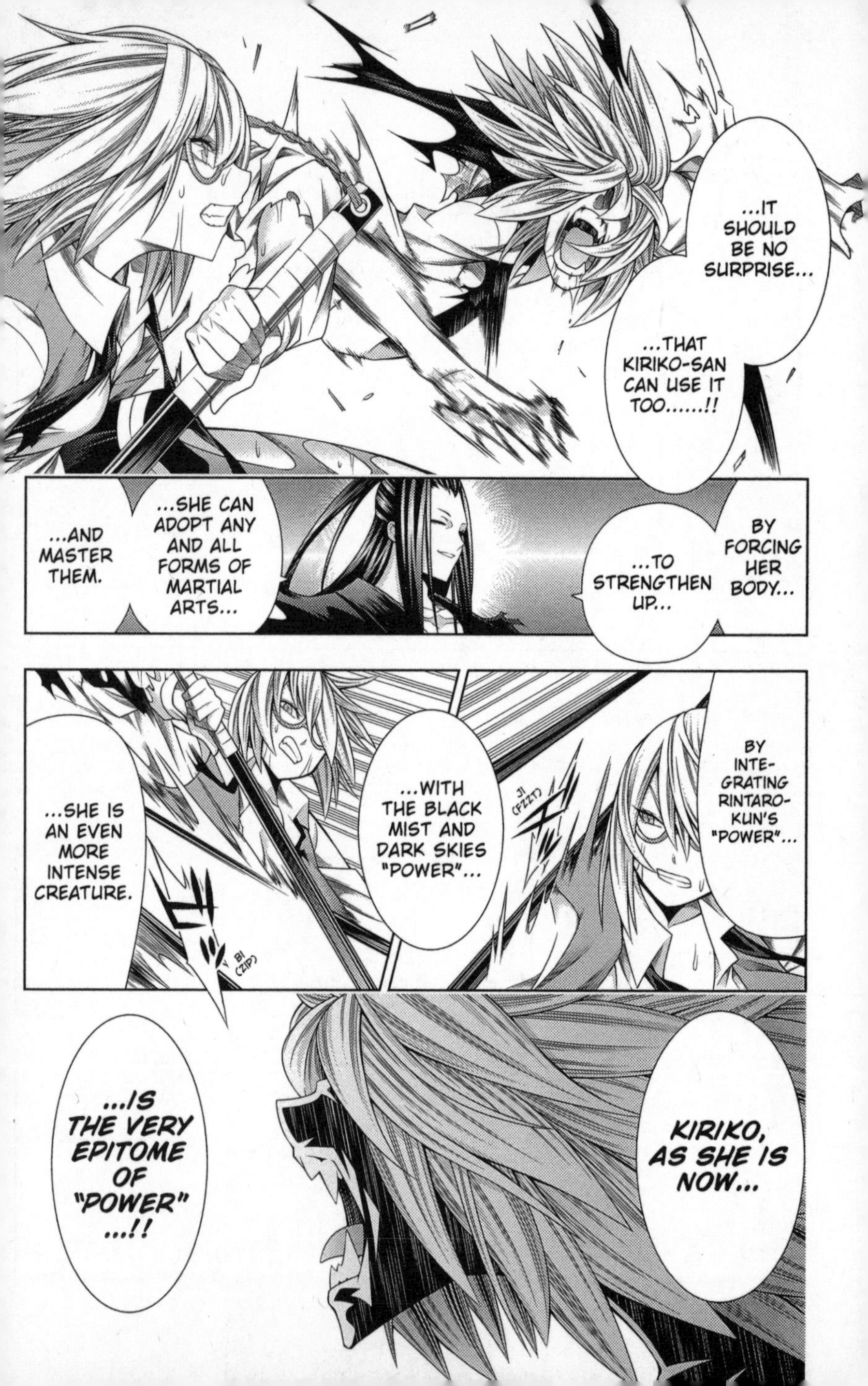
...IT SHOULD BE NO SURPRISE...
...THAT KIRIKO-SAN CAN USE IT TOO......!!
BY FORCING HER BODY...
...TO STRENGTHEN UP...
...SHE CAN ADOPT ANY AND ALL FORMS OF MARTIAL ARTS...
...AND MASTER THEM.
BY INTE-GRATING RINTARO-KUN'S "POWER"...
JI (FZZT)
...WITH THE BLACK MIST AND DARK SKIES "POWER"...
...SHE IS AN EVEN MORE INTENSE CREATURE.
BI (ZIP)
KIRIKO, AS SHE IS NOW...
...IS THE VERY EPITOME OF "POWER" ...!!

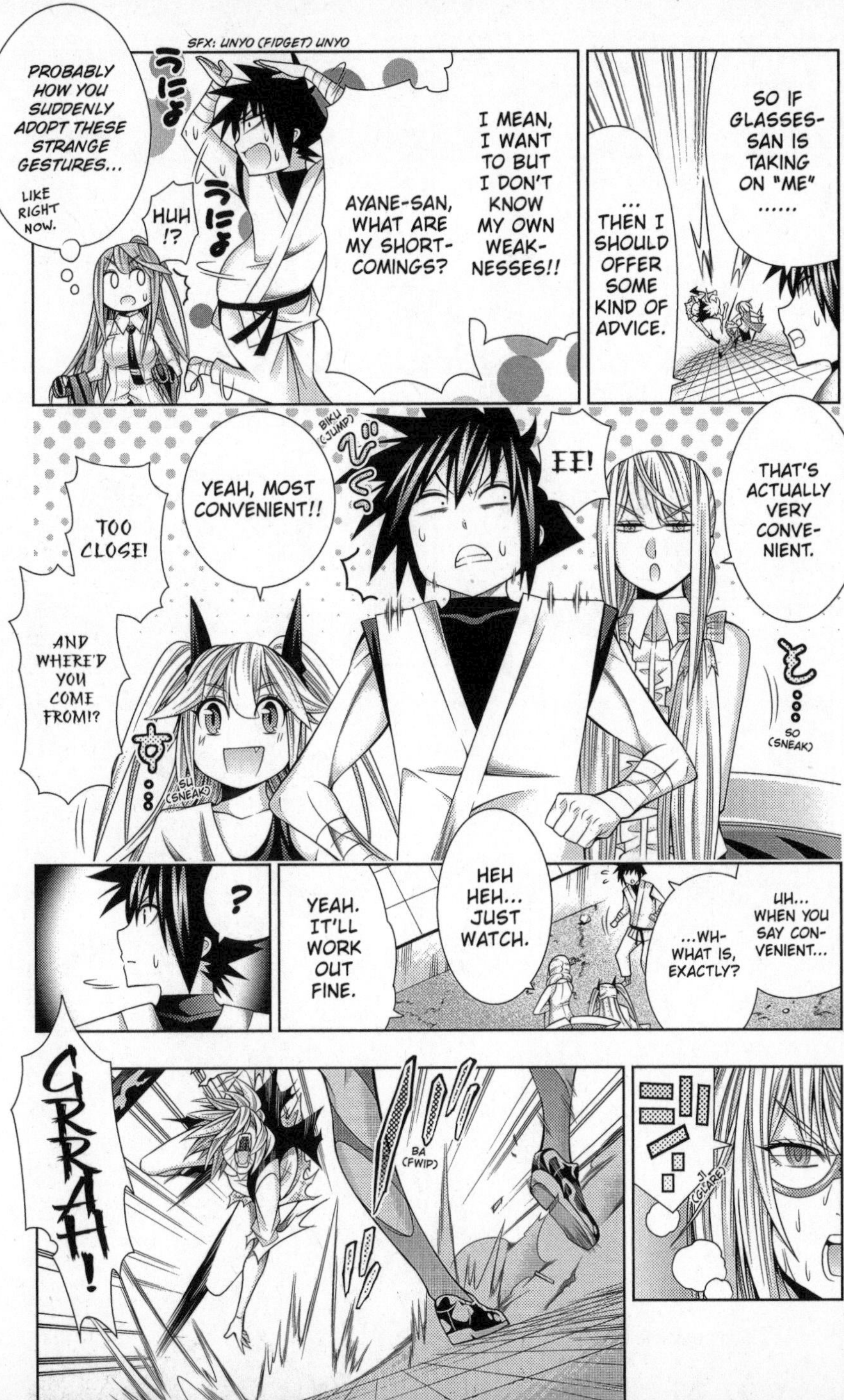
SO IF GLASSES-SAN IS TAKING ON "ME"......
... THEN I SHOULD OFFER SOME KIND OF ADVICE.
SFX: UNYO (FIDGET) UNYO
うにょ
うにょ
I MEAN, I WANT TO BUT I DON'T KNOW MY OWN WEAK-NESSES!!
AYANE-SAN, WHAT ARE MY SHORT-COMINGS?
HUH!?
PROBABLY HOW YOU SUDDENLY ADOPT THESE STRANGE GESTURES...
LIKE RIGHT NOW.
THAT'S ACTUALLY VERY CONVE-NIENT.
SO (SNEAK)
EE!
BIKU (JUMP)
YEAH, MOST CONVENIENT!!
SU (SNEAK)
TOO CLOSE!
AND WHERE'D YOU COME FROM!?
UH... WHEN YOU SAY CON-VENIENT...
...WH-WHAT IS, EXACTLY?
HEH HEH... JUST WATCH.
YEAH. IT'LL WORK OUT FINE.
?
JI (GLARE)
BA (FWIP)
GRRAH!

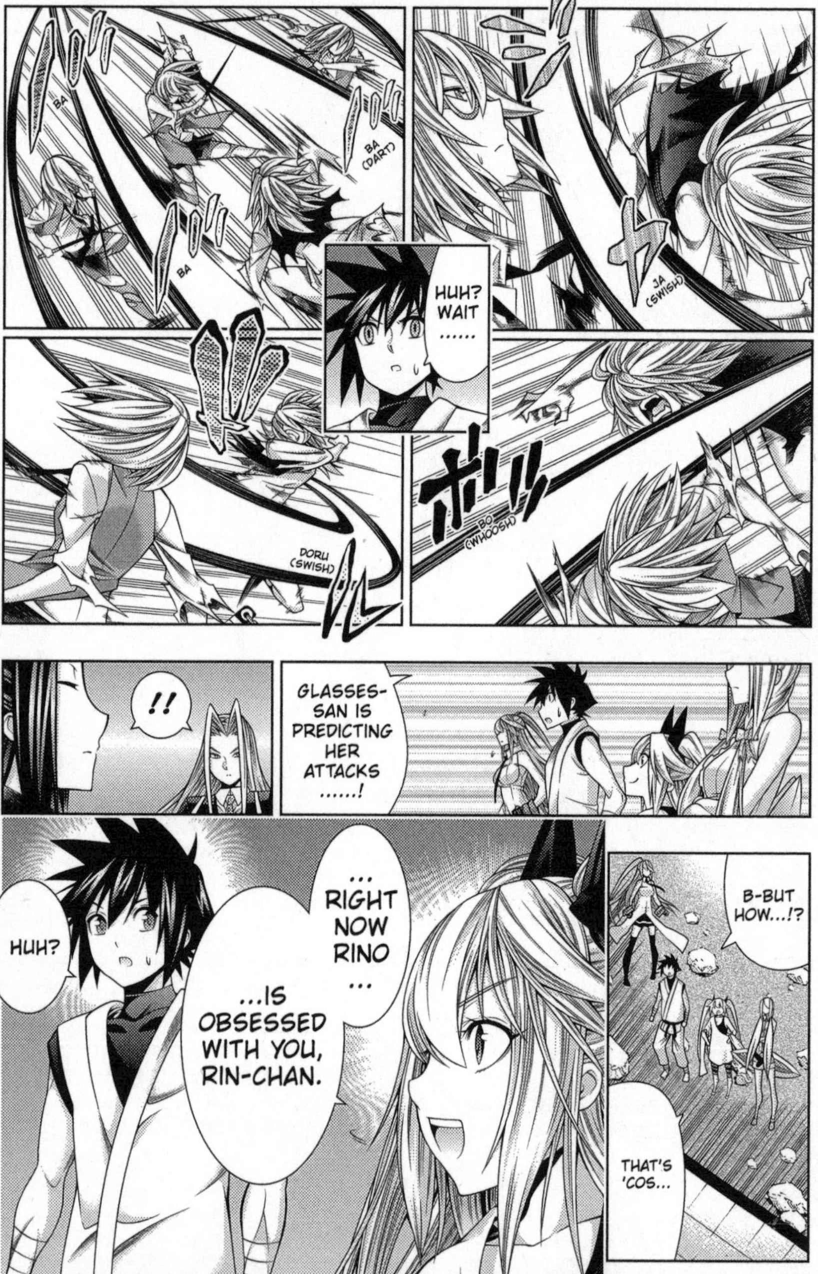
JA (SWISH)
BA (DART)
BA
BA
HUH? WAIT ......
BO (WHOOSH)
DORU (SWISH)
GLASSES-SAN IS PREDICTING HER ATTACKS ......!
!!
B-BUT HOW...!?
THAT'S 'COS...
... RIGHT NOW RINO ...
...IS OBSESSED WITH YOU, RIN-CHAN.
HUH?

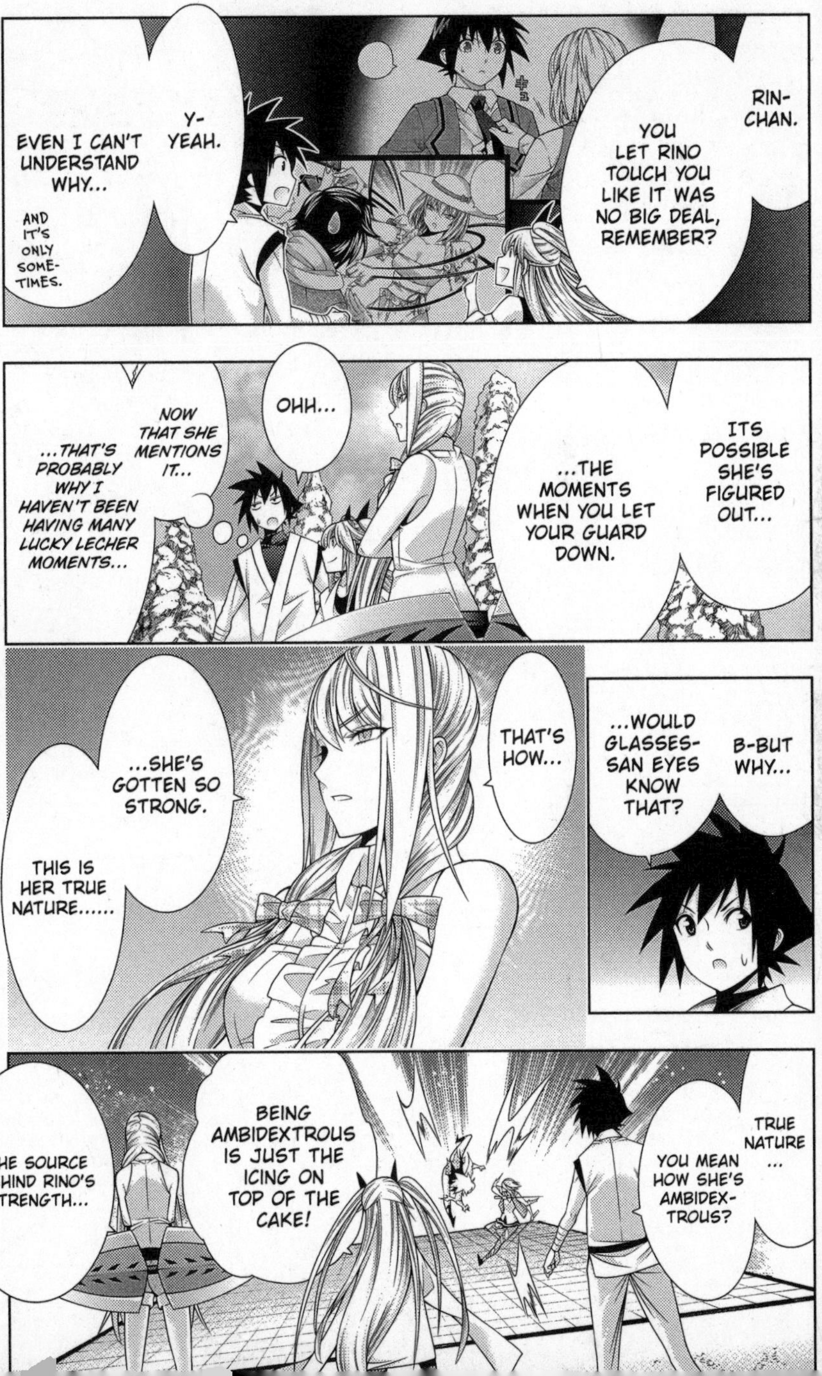
RIN-CHAN.
YOU LET RINO TOUCH YOU LIKE IT WAS NO BIG DEAL, REMEMBER?
Y-YEAH.
EVEN I CAN'T UNDERSTAND WHY...
AND IT'S ONLY SOME-TIMES.
ITS POSSIBLE SHE'S FIGURED OUT...
...THE MOMENTS WHEN YOU LET YOUR GUARD DOWN.
OHH...
NOW THAT SHE MENTIONS IT...
...THAT'S PROBABLY WHY I HAVEN'T BEEN HAVING MANY LUCKY LECHER MOMENTS...
B-BUT WHY...
...WOULD GLASSES-SAN EYES KNOW THAT?
THAT'S HOW...
...SHE'S GOTTEN SO STRONG.
THIS IS HER TRUE NATURE......
TRUE NATURE...
YOU MEAN HOW SHE'S AMBIDEX-TROUS?
BEING AMBIDEXTROUS IS JUST THE ICING ON TOP OF THE CAKE!
THE SOURCE BEHIND RINO'S STRENGTH...

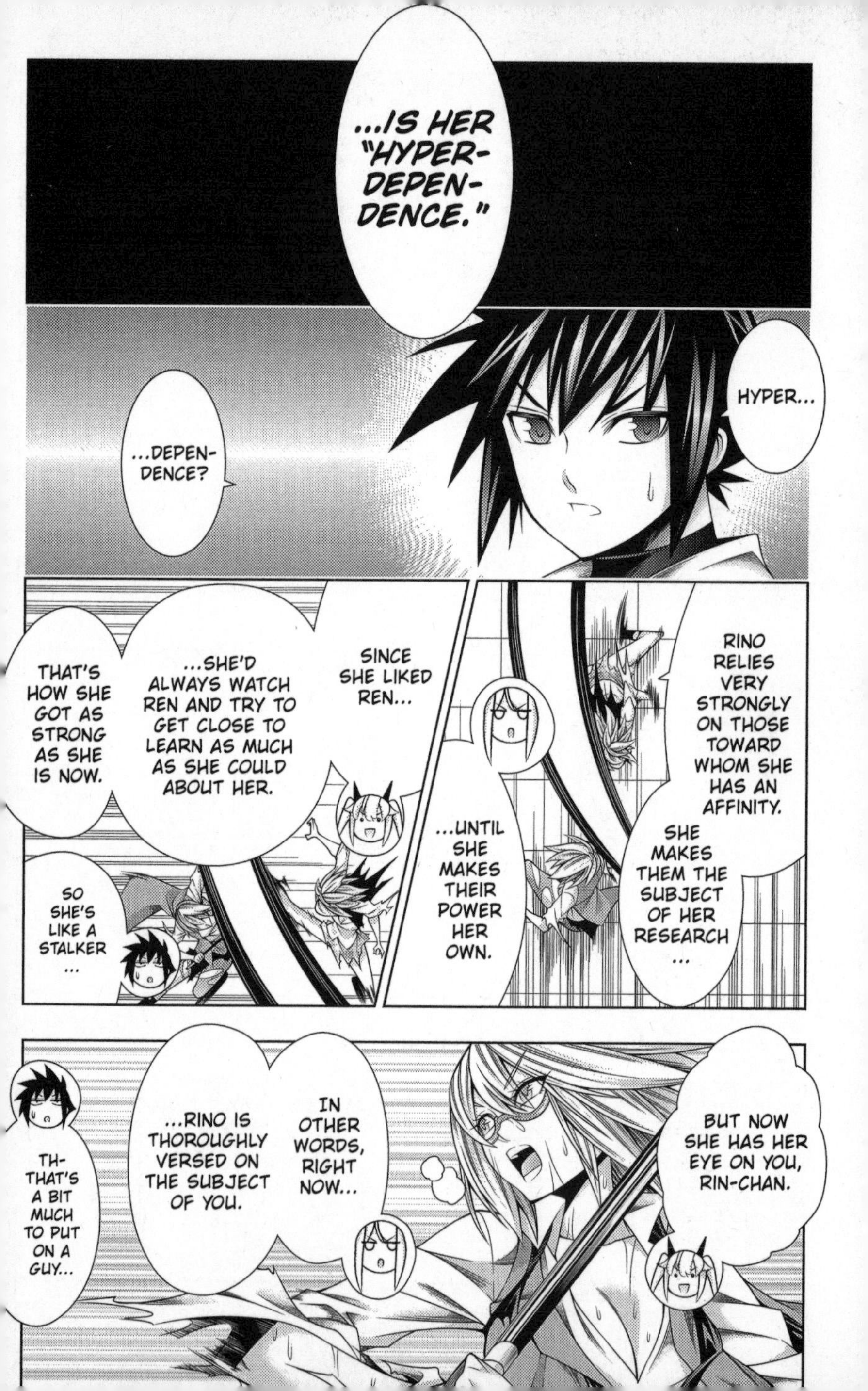
...IS HER "HYPER-DEPENDENCE."
HYPER...
...DEPENDENCE?
RINO RELIES VERY STRONGLY ON THOSE TOWARD WHOM SHE HAS AN AFFINITY.
SHE MAKES THEM THE SUBJECT OF HER RESEARCH...
...UNTIL SHE MAKES THEIR POWER HER OWN.
SINCE SHE LIKED REN...
...SHE'D ALWAYS WATCH REN AND TRY TO GET CLOSE TO LEARN AS MUCH AS SHE COULD ABOUT HER.
THAT'S HOW SHE GOT AS STRONG AS SHE IS NOW.
SO SHE'S LIKE A STALKER...
BUT NOW SHE HAS HER EYE ON YOU, RIN-CHAN.
IN OTHER WORDS, RIGHT NOW...
...RINO IS THOROUGHLY VERSED ON THE SUBJECT OF YOU.
TH-THAT'S A BIT MUCH TO PUT ON A GUY...

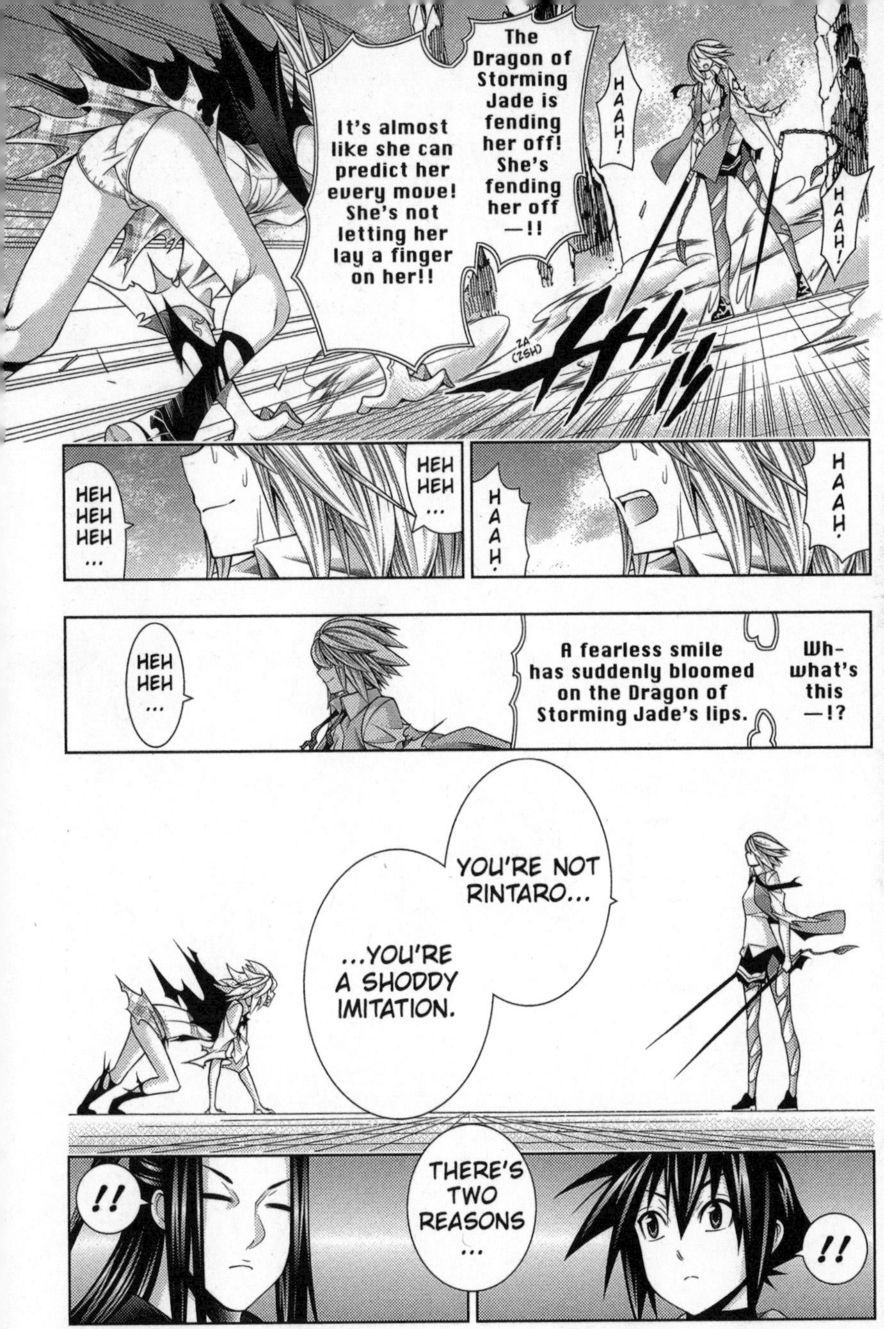

HAAAH!
HAAAH!
The Dragon of Storming Jade is fending her off! She's fending her off —!!
It's almost like she can predict her every move! She's not letting her lay a finger on her!!
ZA (ZSH)
HAAAH!
HAAAH!
HEH HEH ...
HEH HEH HEH ...
Wh-what's this —!?
A fearless smile has suddenly bloomed on the Dragon of Storming Jade's lips.
HEH HEH ...
YOU'RE NOT RINTARO...
...YOU'RE A SHODDY IMITATION.
!!
THERE'S TWO REASONS ...
!!

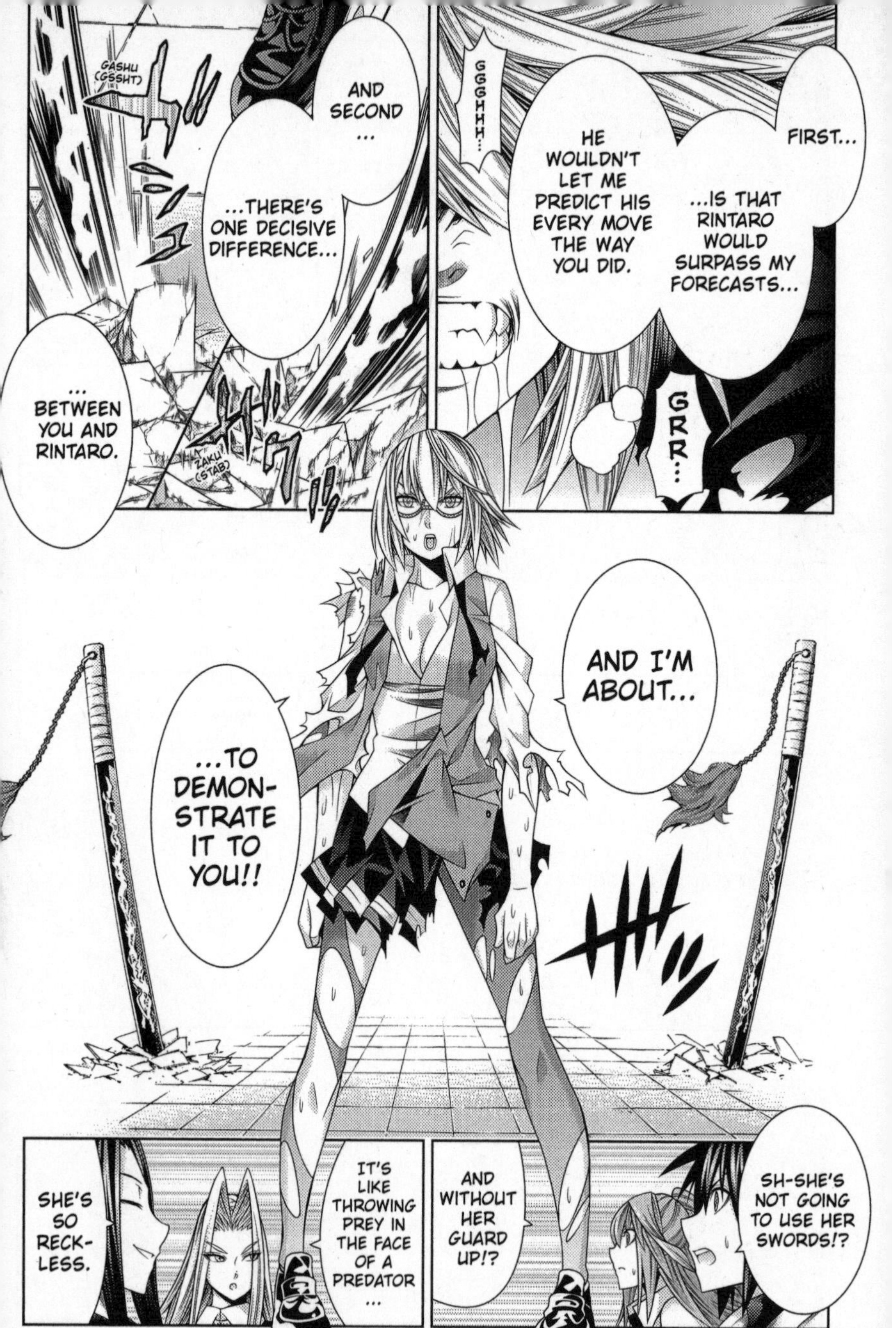
GGGHHH...
FIRST...
...IS THAT RINTARO WOULD SURPASS MY FORECASTS...
HE WOULDN'T LET ME PREDICT HIS EVERY MOVE THE WAY YOU DID.
GRR...
GASHU (GSSHT)
AND SECOND...
...THERE'S ONE DECISIVE DIFFERENCE...
...BETWEEN YOU AND RINTARO.
ZAKU (STAB)
AND I'M ABOUT...
...TO DEMON-STRATE IT TO YOU!!
SH-SHE'S NOT GOING TO USE HER SWORDS!?
AND WITHOUT HER GUARD UP!?
IT'S LIKE THROWING PREY IN THE FACE OF A PREDATOR...
SHE'S SO RECK-LESS.

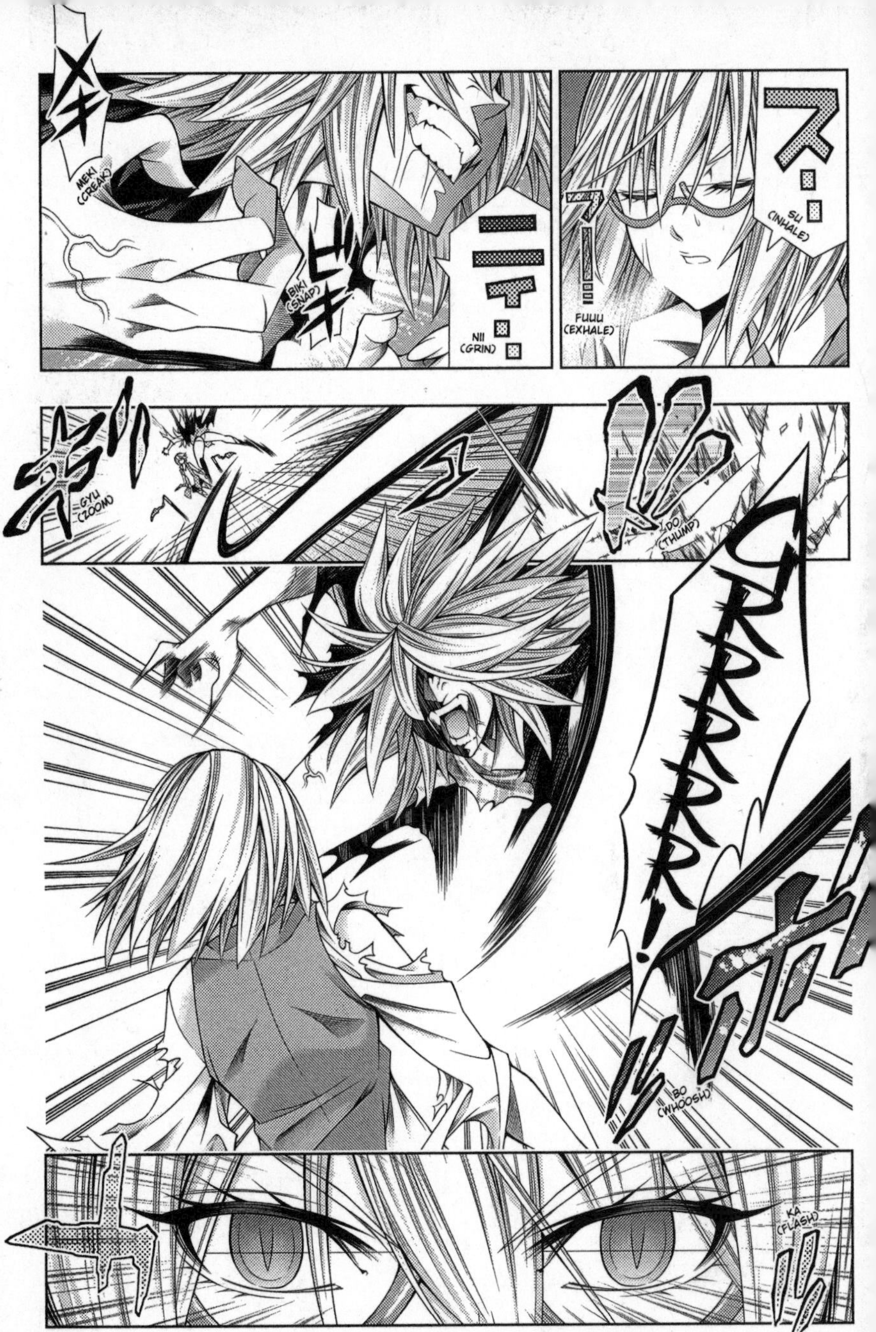
SU (INHALE)
FUUU (EXHALE)
NII (GRIN)
BIKI (SNAP)
MEKI (CREAK)
DO (THUMP)
GYU (ZOOM)
GRRRRRRR!
BO (WHOOSH)
KA (FLASH)

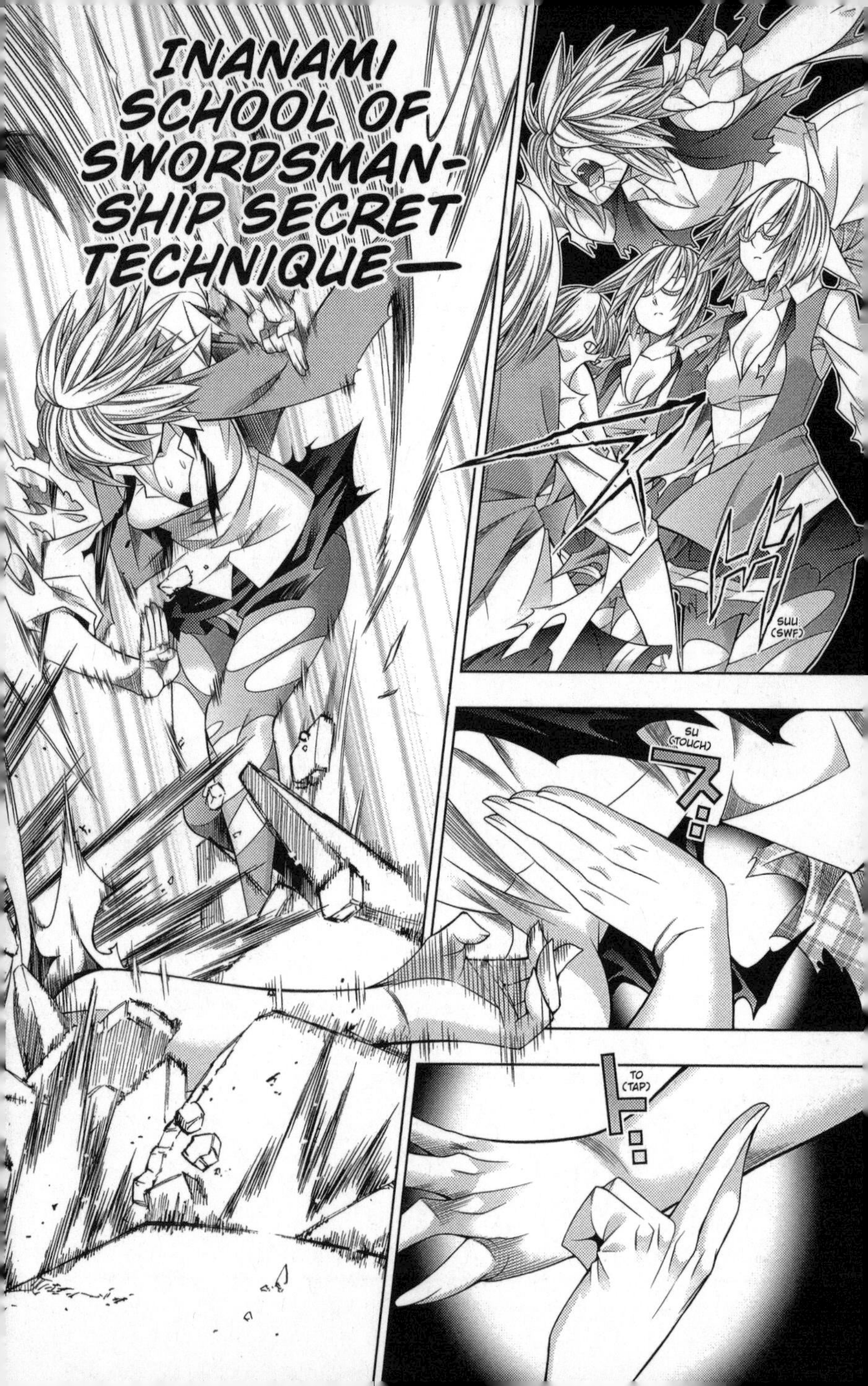
SUU (SWF)
SU (TOUCH)
TO (TAP)
INANAMI SCHOOL OF SWORDSMAN-SHIP SECRET TECHNIQUE—

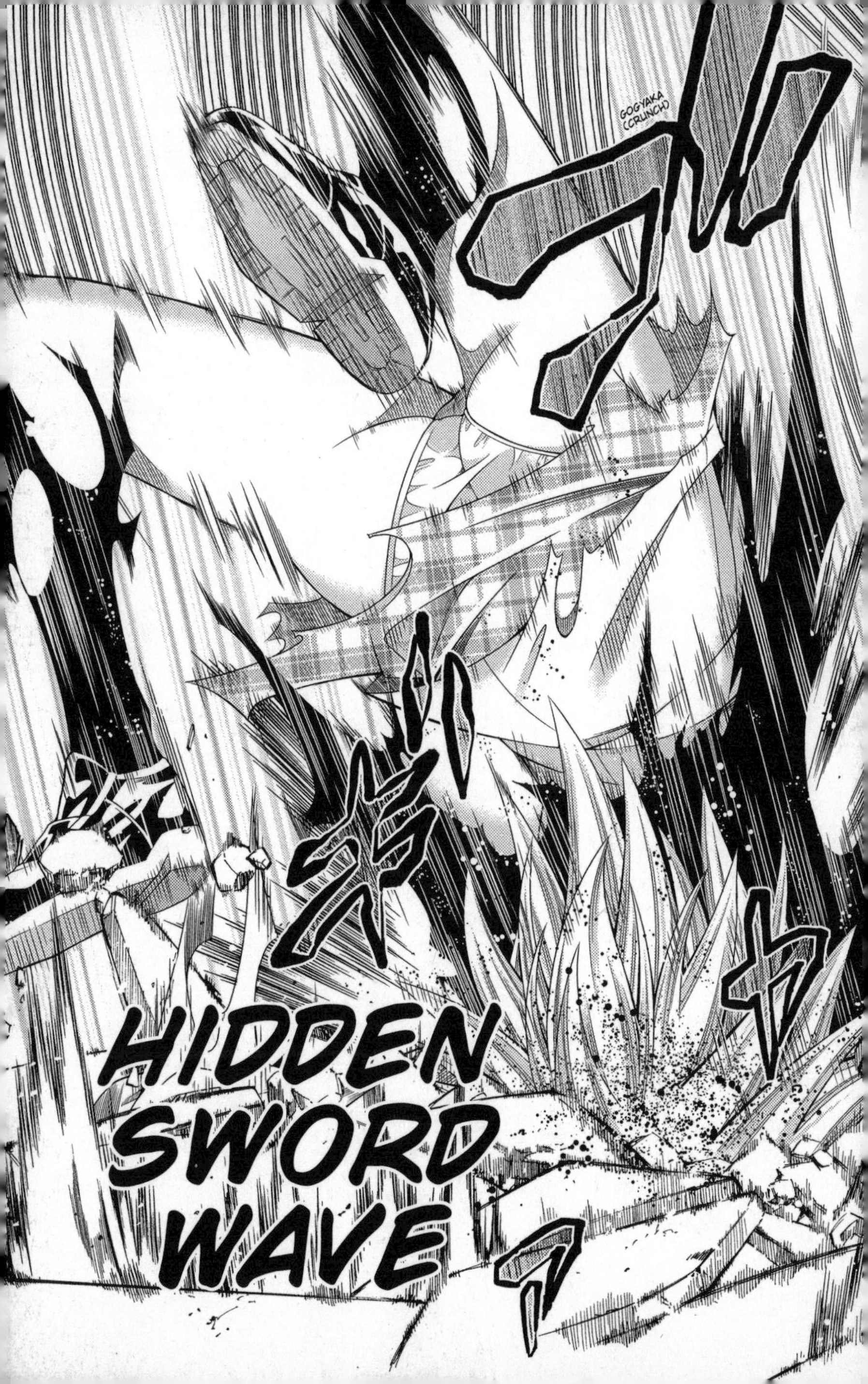
GOGYAKA
(CRUNCH)
HIDDEN SWORD WAVE

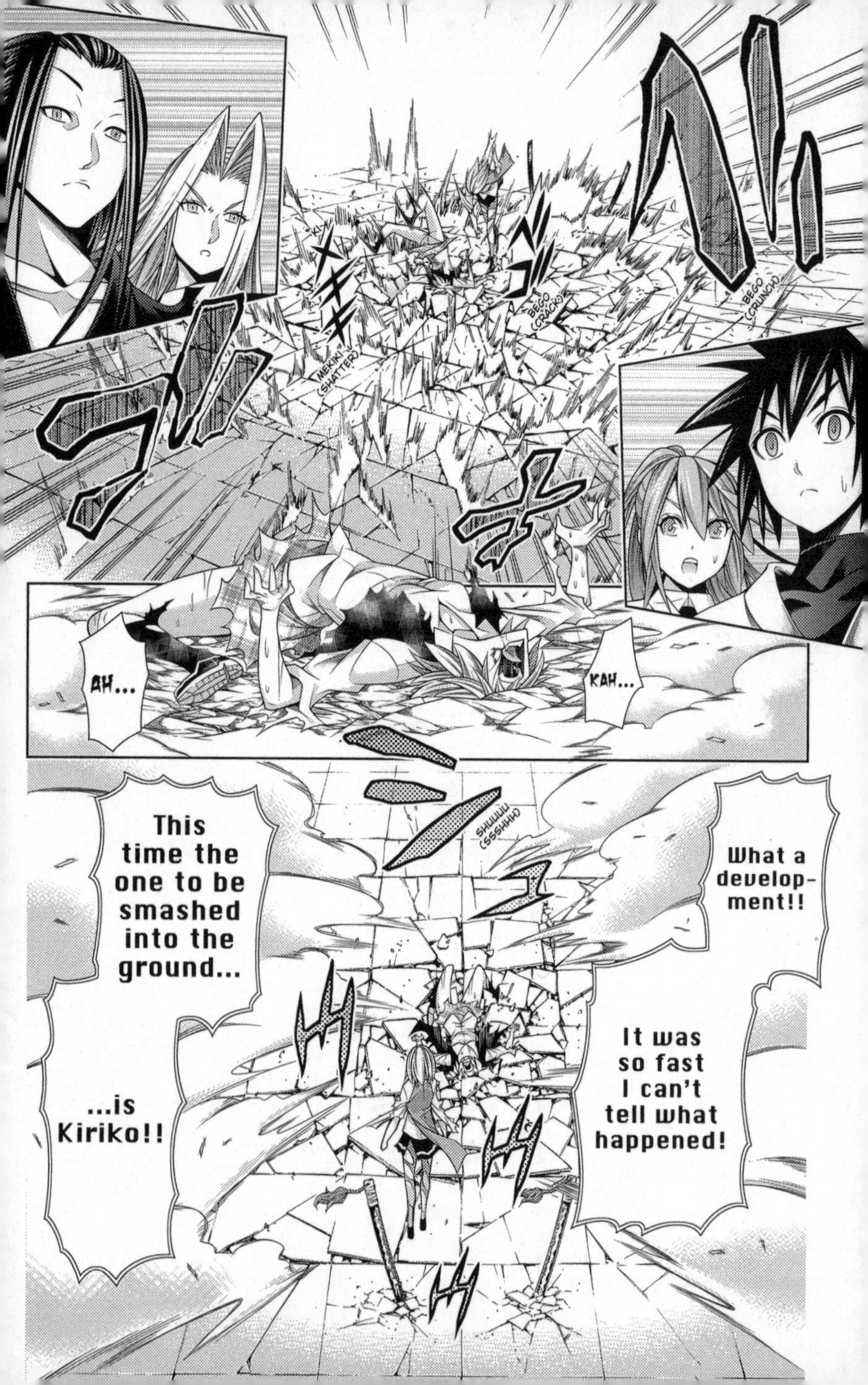
BEGO (CRUNCH)
BEGO (CRACK)
MEKIKI (SHATTER)
KAH...
AH...
What a development!!
It was so fast I can't tell what happened!
SHUUUU (SSSHHH)
This time the one to be smashed into the ground...
...is Kiriko!!

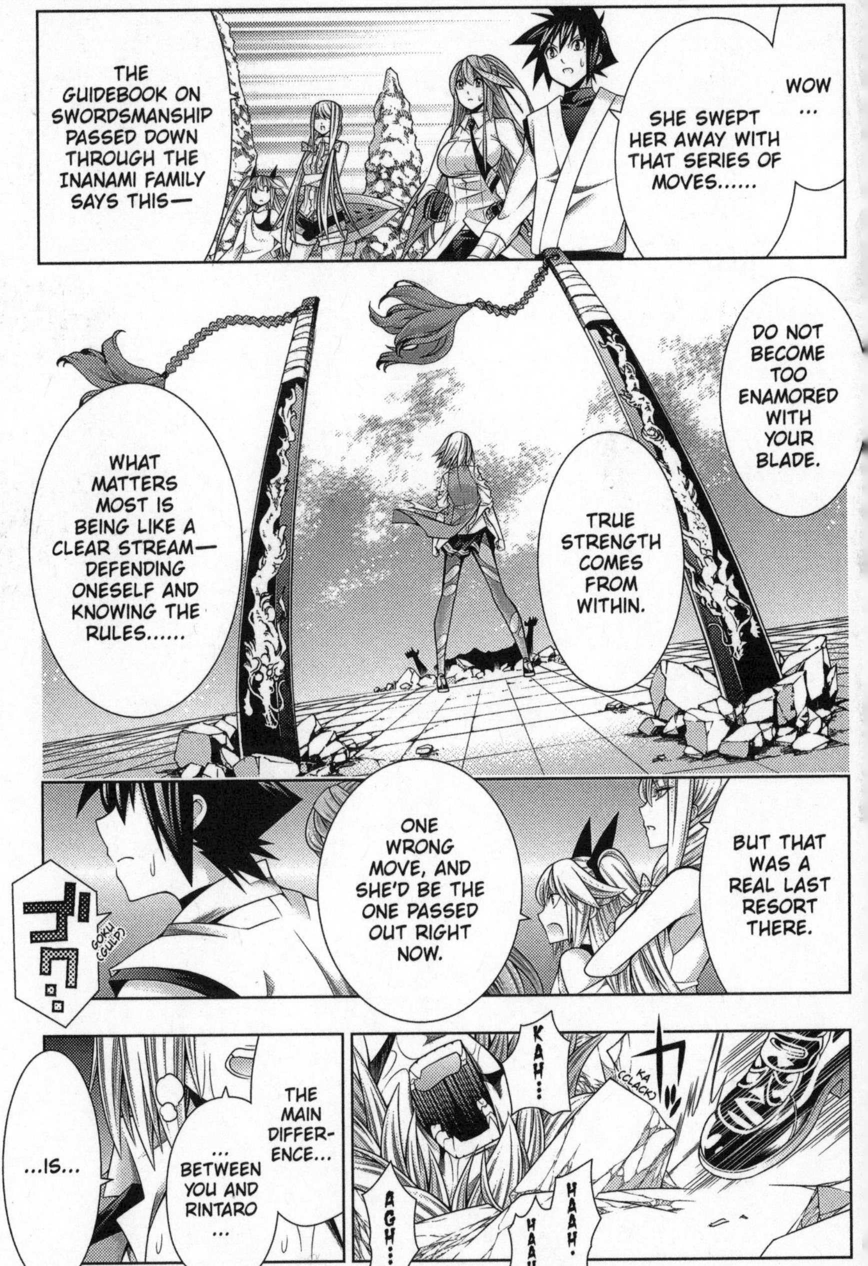
WOW...
SHE SWEPT HER AWAY WITH THAT SERIES OF MOVES......
THE GUIDEBOOK ON SWORDSMANSHIP PASSED DOWN THROUGH THE INANAMI FAMILY SAYS THIS—
DO NOT BECOME TOO ENAMORED WITH YOUR BLADE.
TRUE STRENGTH COMES FROM WITHIN.
WHAT MATTERS MOST IS BEING LIKE A CLEAR STREAM—DEFENDING ONESELF AND KNOWING THE RULES......
BUT THAT WAS A REAL LAST RESORT THERE.
ONE WRONG MOVE, AND SHE'D BE THE ONE PASSED OUT RIGHT NOW.
GOKU (GULP)
KA (CLACK)
KAH...
HAAH...
HAAH.
AGH...
THE MAIN DIFFER-ENCE...
...BETWEEN YOU AND RINTARO...
...IS...

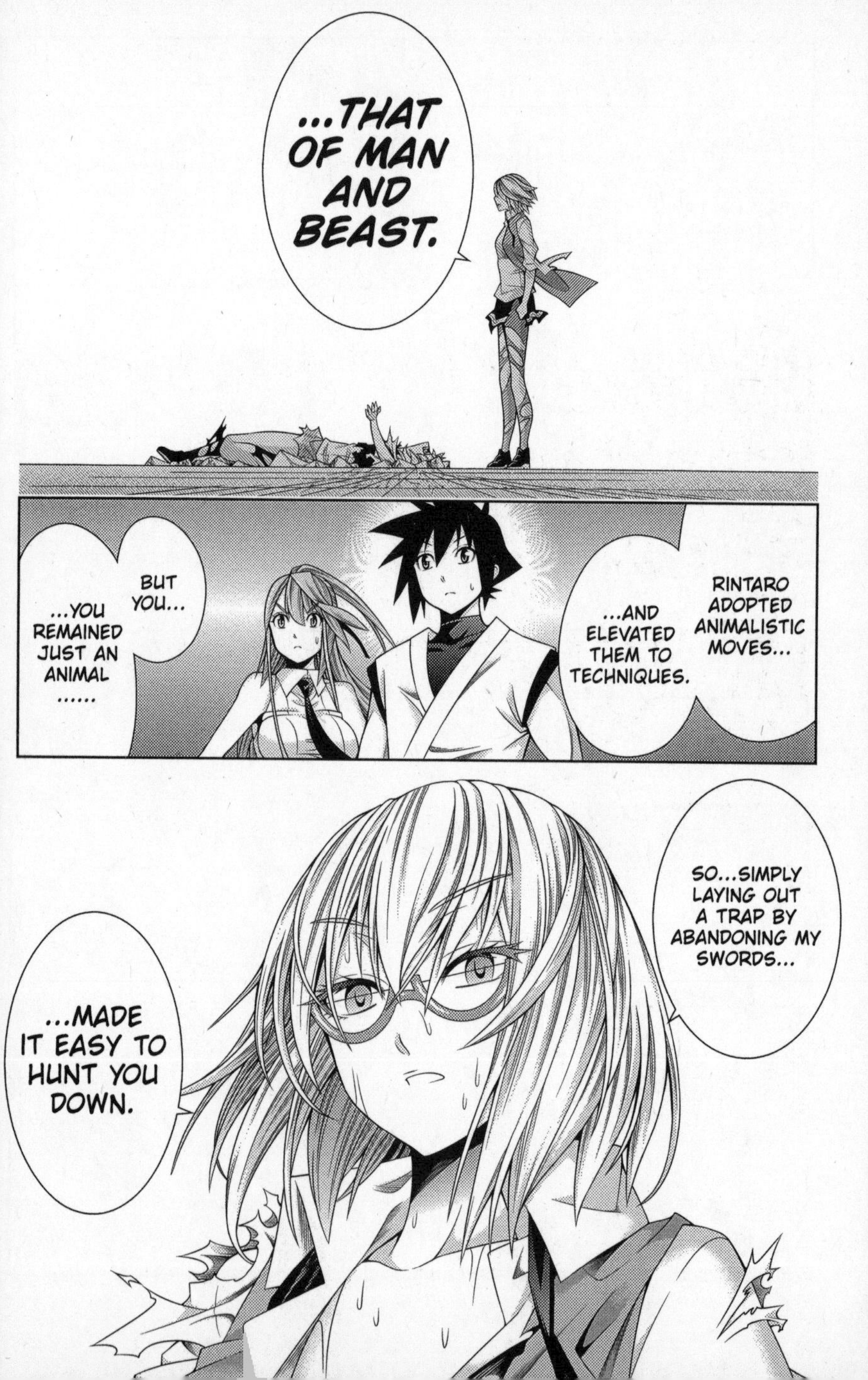
...THAT OF MAN AND BEAST.
RINTARO ADOPTED ANIMALISTIC MOVES...
...AND ELEVATED THEM TO TECHNIQUES.
BUT YOU...
...YOU REMAINED JUST AN ANIMAL ......
SO...SIMPLY LAYING OUT A TRAP BY ABANDONING MY SWORDS...
...MADE IT EASY TO HUNT YOU DOWN.

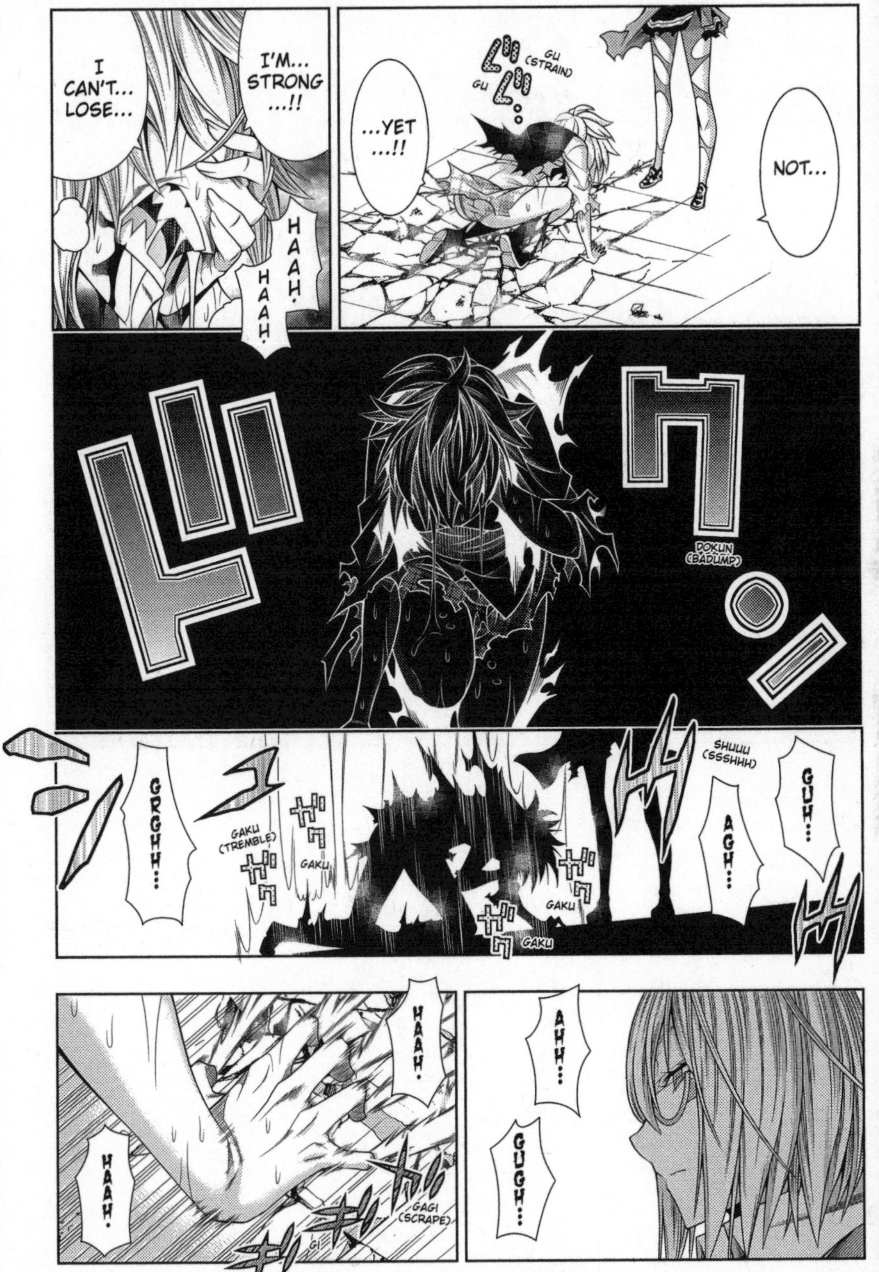
NOT...
GU (STRAIN)
GU
...YET ...!!
I'M... STRONG ...!!
I CAN'T... LOSE...
HAAAH.
HAAAH.
DOKUN (BADUMP)
GUH...
AGH...
SHUUU (SSSHHH)
GAKU
GAKU
GAKU
GAKU (TREMBLE)
GRGHH...
AHH...
GUGH...
HAAAH.
GAGI (SCRAPE)
GI
HAAAH.

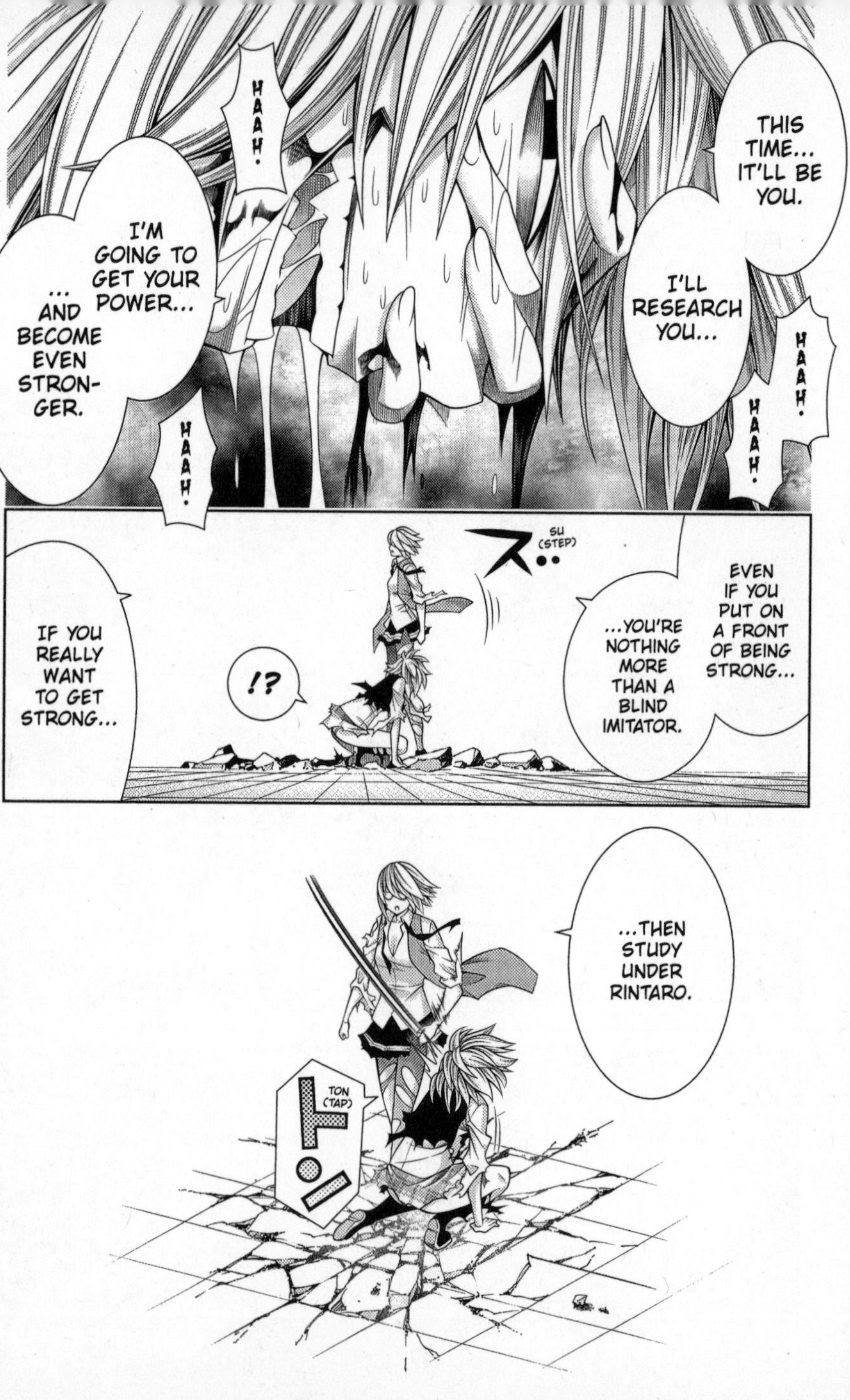
THIS TIME... IT'LL BE YOU.
I'LL RESEARCH YOU...
HAAAH.
HAAAH.
HAAAH.
I'M GOING TO GET YOUR POWER...
...AND BECOME EVEN STRONGER.
HAAAH.
EVEN IF YOU PUT ON A FRONT OF BEING STRONG...
...YOU'RE NOTHING MORE THAN A BLIND IMITATOR.
SU (STEP)
!?
IF YOU REALLY WANT TO GET STRONG...
...THEN STUDY UNDER RINTARO.
TON (TAP)

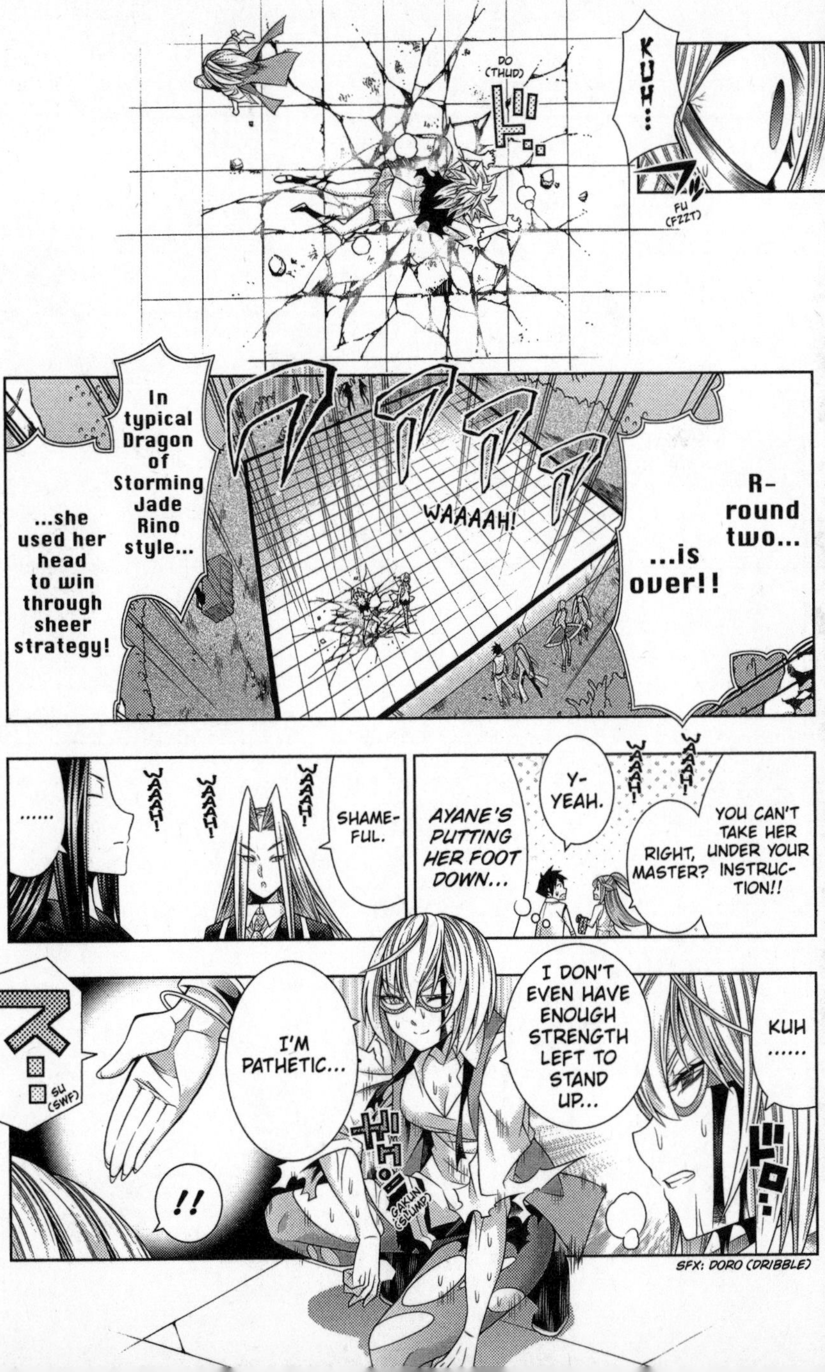
KUH…
FU (FZZT)
DO (THUD)
R-round two…
…is over!!
WAAAAH!
In typical Dragon of Storming Jade Rino style…
…she used her head to win through sheer strategy!
WAAAH!
WAAAH!
YOU CAN'T TAKE HER UNDER YOUR INSTRUCTION!!
RIGHT, MASTER?
Y-YEAH.
AYANE'S PUTTING HER FOOT DOWN…
WAAAH!
SHAME-FUL.
WAAAH!
WAAAH!
……
KUH……
I DON'T EVEN HAVE ENOUGH STRENGTH LEFT TO STAND UP…
GAKUN (SLUMP)
I'M PATHETIC…
!!
SU (SWF)
SFX: DORO (DRIBBLE)

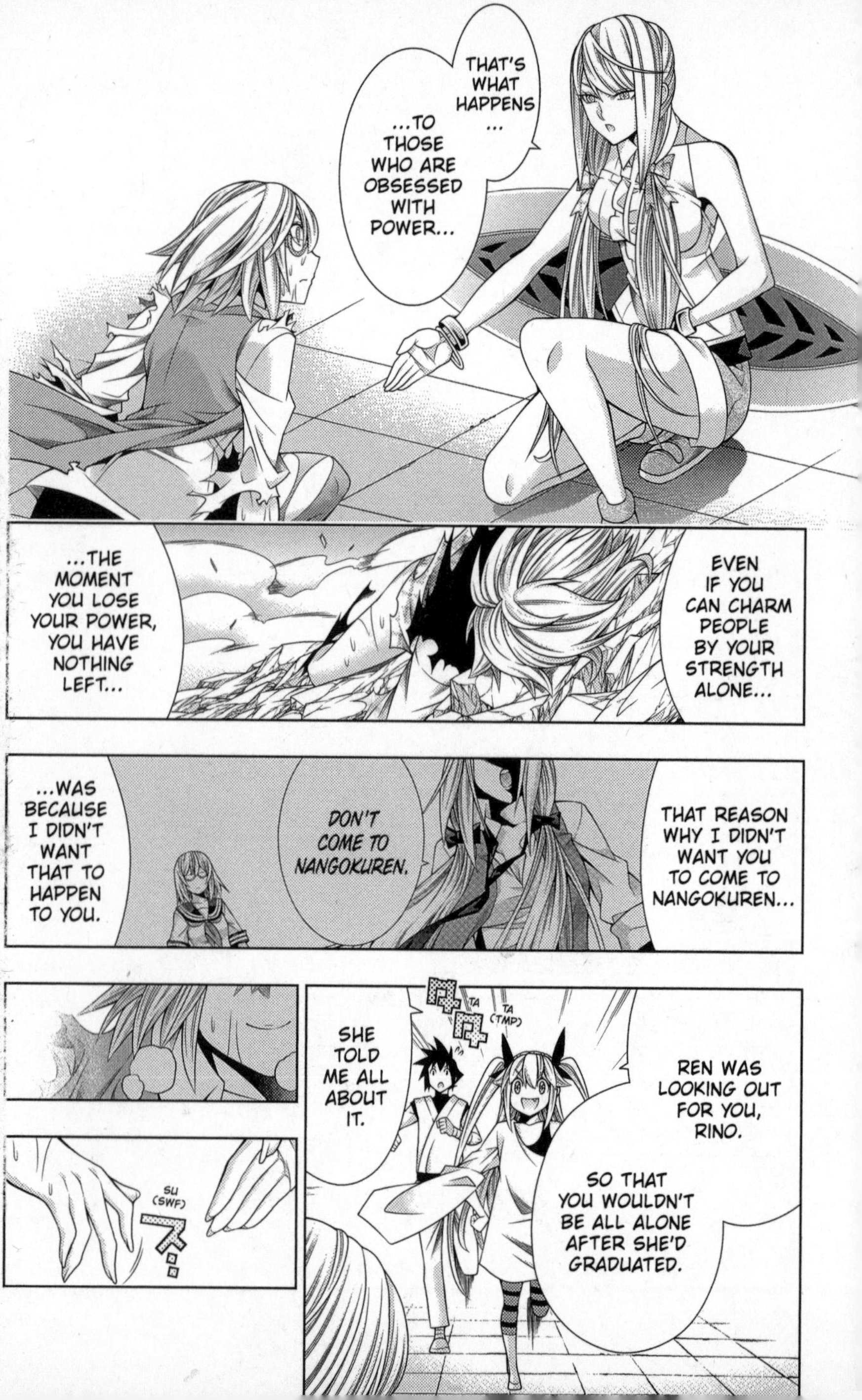
THAT'S WHAT HAPPENS...
...TO THOSE WHO ARE OBSESSED WITH POWER...
EVEN IF YOU CAN CHARM PEOPLE BY YOUR STRENGTH ALONE...
...THE MOMENT YOU LOSE YOUR POWER, YOU HAVE NOTHING LEFT...
THAT REASON WHY I DIDN'T WANT YOU TO COME TO NANGOKUREN...
DON'T COME TO NANGOKUREN.
...WAS BECAUSE I DIDN'T WANT THAT TO HAPPEN TO YOU.
TA TA (TMP)
REN WAS LOOKING OUT FOR YOU, RINO.
SHE TOLD ME ALL ABOUT IT.
SO THAT YOU WOULDN'T BE ALL ALONE AFTER SHE'D GRADUATED.
SU (SWF)

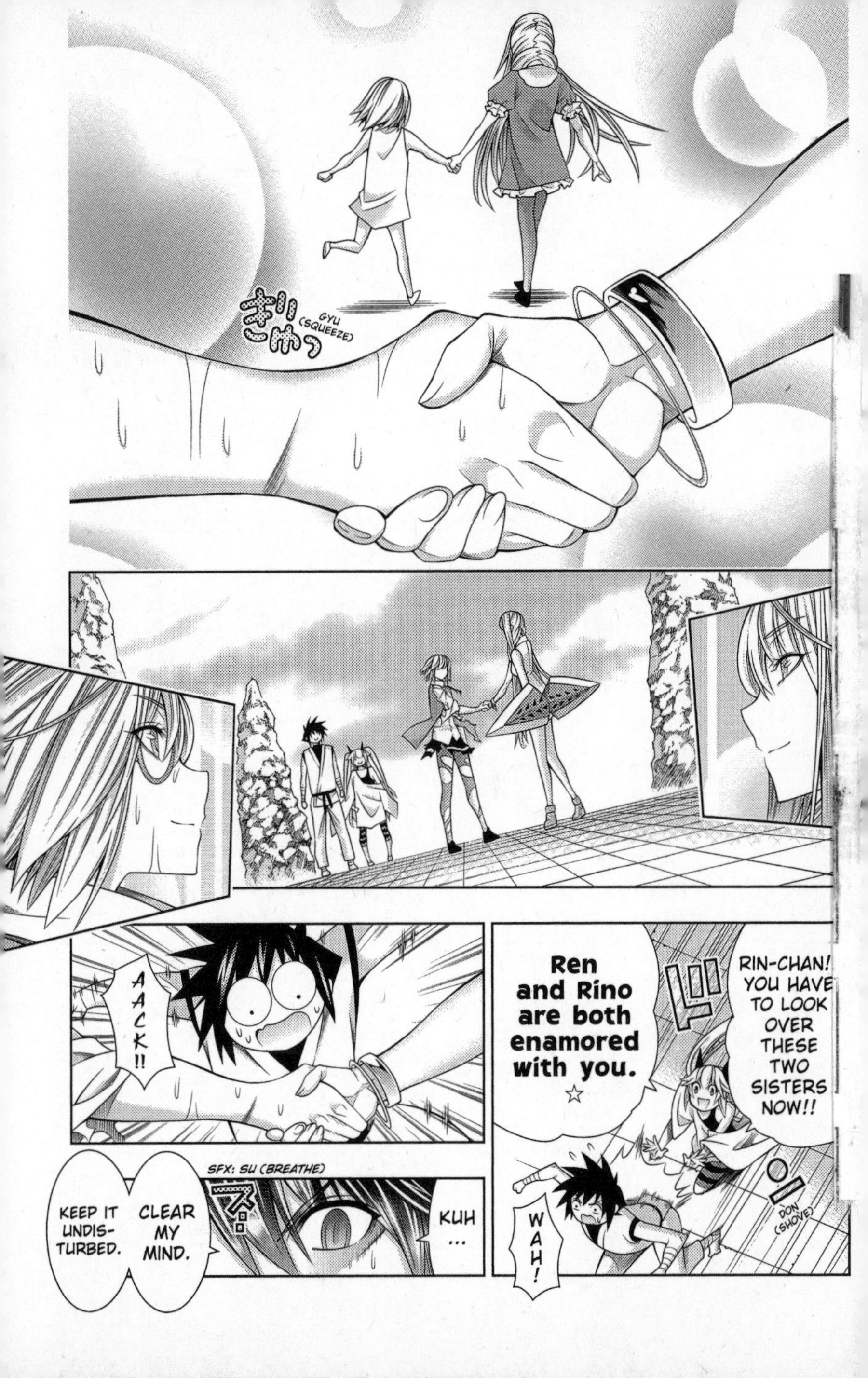
GYU (SQUEEZE)
RIN-CHAN! YOU HAVE TO LOOK OVER THESE TWO SISTERS NOW!!
Ren and Rino are both enamored with you. ☆
DON (SHOVE)
WAH!
AACK!!
KUH...
SFX: SU (BREATHE)
CLEAR MY MIND.
KEEP IT UNDIS-TURBED.

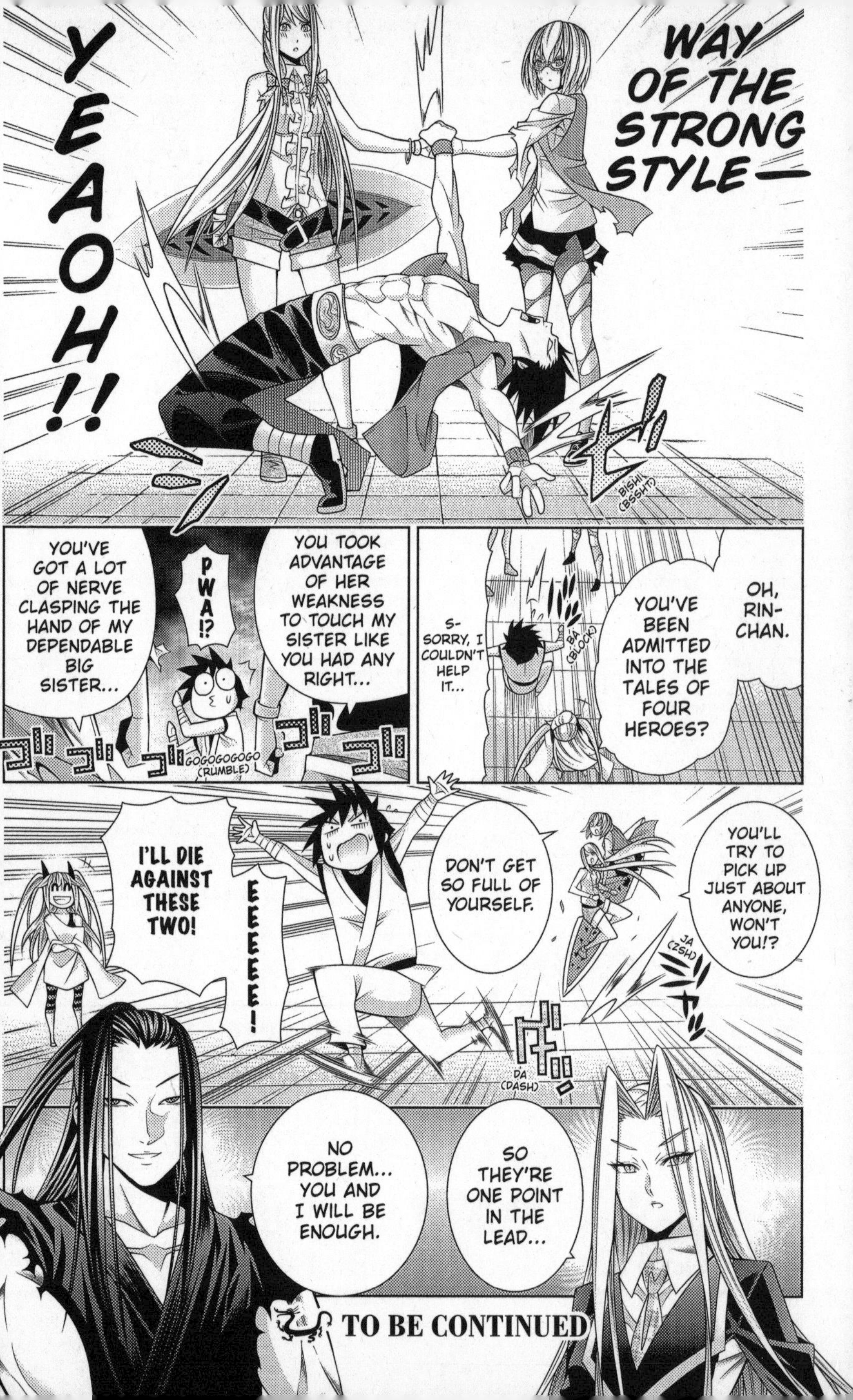
WAY OF THE STRONG STYLE—
YEAOH!!
BISHI (BSSHT)
OH, RIN-CHAN.
YOU'VE BEEN ADMITTED INTO THE TALES OF FOUR HEROES?
BA (BLOCK)
S-SORRY, I COULDN'T HELP IT...
YOU TOOK ADVANTAGE OF HER WEAKNESS TO TOUCH MY SISTER LIKE YOU HAD ANY RIGHT...
PWA!?
YOU'VE GOT A LOT OF NERVE CLASPING THE HAND OF MY DEPENDABLE BIG SISTER...
GOGOGOGOGO (RUMBLE)
YOU'LL TRY TO PICK UP JUST ABOUT ANYONE, WON'T YOU!?
JA (ZSH)
DON'T GET SO FULL OF YOURSELF.
EEEEEE!
I'LL DIE AGAINST THESE TWO!
DA (DASH)
SO THEY'RE ONE POINT IN THE LEAD...
NO PROBLEM... YOU AND I WILL BE ENOUGH.
TO BE CONTINUED

EPISODES FROM THE DATE WITH RINO

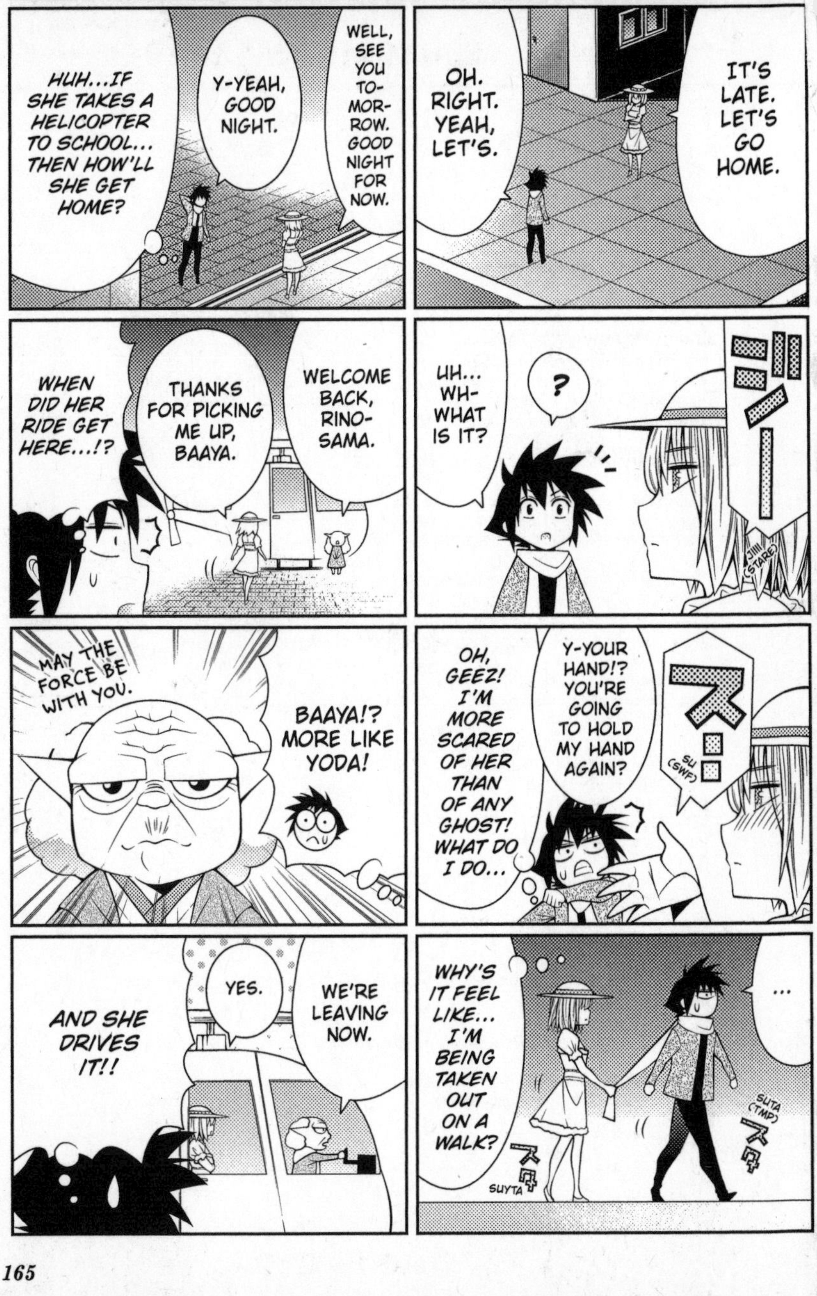
IT'S LATE. LET'S GO HOME.
OH. RIGHT. YEAH, LET'S.
WELL, SEE YOU TO-MOR-ROW. GOOD NIGHT FOR NOW.
Y-YEAH, GOOD NIGHT.
HUH...IF SHE TAKES A HELICOPTER TO SCHOOL... THEN HOW'LL SHE GET HOME?
JIII (STARE)
?
UH... WH-WHAT IS IT?
WELCOME BACK, RINO-SAMA.
THANKS FOR PICKING ME UP, BAAYA.
WHEN DID HER RIDE GET HERE...!?
SU (SWF)
Y-YOUR HAND!? YOU'RE GOING TO HOLD MY HAND AGAIN?
OH, GEEZ! I'M MORE SCARED OF HER THAN OF ANY GHOST! WHAT DO I DO...
BAAYA!? MORE LIKE YODA!
MAY THE FORCE BE WITH YOU.
...
SUTA (TMP)
WHY'S IT FEEL LIKE... I'M BEING TAKEN OUT ON A WALK?
SUYTA
WE'RE LEAVING NOW.
YES.
AND SHE DRIVES IT!!

DRAGONS RIOTING ❽

TSUYOSHI WATANABE

Translation: Christine Dashiell

Lettering: Anthony Quintessenza

DRAGONS RIOTING Volume 8
© TSUYOSHI WATANABE 2016
First published in Japan in 2016 by KADOKAWA CORPORATION, Tokyo.
English translation rights arranged with KADOKAWA CORPORATION, Tokyo, through TUTTLE-MORI AGENCY, INC., Tokyo.

English translation © 2017 by Yen Press, LLC

Yen Press
1290 Avenue of the Americas
New York, NY 10104

Visit us at yenpress.com
facebook.com/yenpress
twitter.com/yenpress
yenpress.tumblr.com
instagram.com/yenpress

First Yen Press Edition: September 2017

Yen Press is an imprint of Yen Press, LLC.
The Yen Press name and logo are trademarks of Yen Press, LLC.

Library of Congress Control Number: 2015952605

ISBNs: 978-0-316-47091-9 (paperback)
       978-0-315-47094-0 (ebook)

10 9 8 7 6 5 4 3 2 1

BVG

Printed in the United States of America